LANDSCAPES OF VOLUNTARISM

New spaces of health, welfare and governance

Edited by Christine Milligan and David Conradson

First published in Great Britain in June 2006 by

The Policy Press
University of Bristol
Fourth Floor
Beacon House
Queen's Road
Bristol BS8 1QU
UK

Tel +44 (0)117 331 4054
Fax +44 (0)117 331 4093
e-mail tpp-info@bristol.ac.uk
www.policypress.org.uk

British Library Cataloguing in Publication Data
A catalogue record for this book is available from the British Library.

Library of Congress Cataloging-in-Publication Data
A catalog record for this book has been requested.

ISBN-10 1 86134 632 8 hardcover
ISBN-13 978 1 86134 632 2

Cover design by Qube Design Associates, Bristol.
Front cover: photograph supplied by kind permission of Getty Images.
Printed and bound in Great Britain by MPG Books, Bodmin.

Contents

List of tables, figures, maps and plates   v

Notes on contributors   vii

Foreword: Beyond the shadow state?   xii
Jennifer Wolch

one   Contemporary landscapes of welfare: the 'voluntary turn'?   1
Christine Milligan and David Conradson

two   A 'new institutional fix'? The 'community turn' and the changing   15
role of the voluntary sector
Rob Macmillan and Alan Townsend

three   Renewal or relocation? Social welfare, voluntarism and the city   33
Christine Milligan and Nicholas R. Fyfe

four   Voluntarism and new forms of governance in rural communities   53
Bill Edwards and Michael Woods

five   New times, new relationships: mental health, primary care and   73
public health in New Zealand
Pauline Barnett and J. Ross Barnett

six   Informal and voluntary care in Canada: caught in the Act?   91
Mark W. Skinner and Mark W. Rosenberg

seven   Competition, adaptation and resistance: (re)forming health   115
organisations in New Zealand's third sector
Susan Owen and Robin Kearns

eight   The difference of voluntarism: the place of voluntary sector care   135
homes for older Jewish people in the United Kingdom
Oliver Valins

nine   Values, practices and strategic divestment: Christian social service   153
organisations in New Zealand
David Conradson

ten   Faith-based organisations and welfare provision in Northern Ireland   173
and North America: whose agenda?
Derek Bacon

eleven   Government restructuring and settlement agencies in Vancouver: 191
bringing advocacy back in
Gillian Creese

twelve   Developing voluntary community spaces and Ethnicity in   209
Sydney, Australia
Walter F. Lalich

thirteen The voluntary spaces of charity shops: workplaces or   231
          domestic spaces?
          Liz Parsons
fourteen The changing landscape of voluntary sector counselling in Scotland   247
          Liz Bondi
fifteen   Volunteering, geography and welfare: a multilevel investigation of   267
          geographical variations in voluntary action
          John Mohan, Liz Twigg, Kelvyn Jones and Steve Barnard
sixteen   Reflections on landscapes of voluntarism   285
          David Conradson and Christine Milligan

Index   295

List of tables, figures, maps and plates

Tables

2.1	The new spatial ladder of English governance	18
2.2	Some contextual features behind the 'community turn'	24
2.3	From the KWNS to the SWPR	27
4.1	Partnership characteristics at different territorial scales in rural Mid-Wales (Powys and Ceredigion)	59
6.1	'Home care received' and 'need for help with home care-related tasks' in Canada by gender, age and income	99
6.2	Formal and informal volunteering in Canada by gender, age and income	101
6.3	'Home care received' and 'need for help with home care-related tasks' in Ontario by gender, age and income	103
8.1	Preferences for formal and informal care among older people in the UK and older Jews living in London and the South East ($n = 486$)	142
9.1	Mission statements of the case study organisations	158
9.2	Organisational social service portfolios in 2004	162
9.3	Overall financial performance (1999-2003)	164
9.4	Rationalisation of service provision portfolios (1999-2004)	165
12.1	Australian population born in non-English speaking countries, by regions (1954-2001)	212
12.2	Religion in Australia: changes in denominational affiliation (1947-2001) (%)	213
12.3	Development of ethnic communal places: respondents by type and periods of development, Sydney, 1950-2000 (units)	217
12.4	Ethnic communal places: estimated total investment, by type and periods, Sydney, 1950-2000 (%, A$'000, 2000=100)	223
14.1	Voluntary sector counselling agencies in 2001	255
14.2	Types of counselling agency in urban and rural Scotland in 2001	259
15.1	Individual and contextual covariates	272
15.2	Volunteering across the regions: results from the 1987 and 1992 General Household Survey	274
15.3	Variance (standard error), credible interval and percentage of total unexplained variance in the multilevel model of volunteering at the individual, household and primary sampling unit (PSU) level for the null model	274
15.4	Results of fully adjusted multilevel logistic model of volunteering	276

15.5   Variance (standard error), credible interval and percentage of total   278
        unexplained variance in the multilevel model of volunteering at the
        individual, household and primary sampling unit (PSU) level for the
        fully adjusted model

Figures

6.1   Framework for exploring the dynamics of informal and voluntary care   95
6.2   Types of 'need for help' in Ontario   104
6.3   Receipt of home care within population that 'needs help' in Ontario   104

Maps

12.1   Locations of ethnic communal places: Cluster Bonnyrigg (2000)   222
14.1   Counselling agencies in Scotland (2001)   257
14.2   Population density versus counselling services in Scotland (2001)   258

Plates

12.1   Christina Lounge   220
12.2   Club Marconi   220

Notes on contributors

Derek Bacon is an independent voluntary sector researcher. From 1996 to 2003 he was Visiting Fellow and Research Student at the Centre for Voluntary Action Studies at the University of Ulster in Northern Ireland. His research focuses on the voluntary action work of churches in Northern Ireland and their contribution to social capital. His work has been published in *Splendid and Disappointing* (CVAS, 1998) and *Communities, Churches and Social Capital in Northern Ireland* (CVAS, 2003). He has presented papers at numerous national and international conferences and in 2001 was awarded the Campbell Adamson Prize for the best conference paper at the NCVO Annual Conference in London.

Steve Barnard is a research associate in the Geography Department at the University of Portsmouth, UK. His research work centres around numerical analysis of geographical variations in health-related matters, including multilevel modelling and synthetic estimation techniques.

J. Ross Barnett is Associate Professor in the Department of Geography, University of Canterbury, Christchurch, New Zealand. His teaching and research interests include health services restructuring and inequalities in health, particularly with respect to smoking, melanoma and diabetes.

Pauline Barnett is Associate Professor in Health Policy and Management in the Department of Public Health and General Practice, Christchurch School of Medicine and Health Sciences, University of Otago, New Zealand. Her research interests lie in public sector restructuring, particularly in mental health and primary care, and she teaches in the area of health systems, health policy and health management.

Liz Bondi is Professor of Social Geography and Co-director of Counselling Studies at the University of Edinburgh, UK. Informed by her long-standing involvement in feminist geography, her current research focuses on counselling and psychotherapy as socio-spatial practices, and on emotional geographies. Founding editor of the journal *Gender, Place and Culture*, she has published chapters in several edited collections, and numerous refereed journals. She is co-author of *Subjectivities, Knowledges and Feminist Geographies* (Rowman and Littlefield, 2002), and co-editor (with Joyce Davidson and Mick Smith) of *Emotional Geographies* (Ashgate, 2005).

David Conradson is Lecturer in Human Geography at Southampton University, UK. His research interests include the neoliberalisation of welfare provision, faith-based voluntary agencies and organisational spacings of subjectivity. His publications in these areas include work on community drop-in centres, contractual funding regimes and therapeutic landscapes.

Gillian Creese is Professor of Sociology at the University of British Columbia, Canada. She has published widely in the fields of Canadian immigration and settlement issues, and racialised and gender inequality within trade union organisations. She is the author of *Contracting Masculinity: Gender, Class, and Race in a White-Collar Union, 1944-1994* (Oxford University Press, 1999). Her current research examines the experiences of immigrants from countries in Sub-Saharan Africa. She is working on a book typescript entitled *African/Canadian Border Crossings: Migration, Exclusion and Belonging*.

Bill Edwards is Senior Lecturer at the University of Wales, Aberystwyth, UK. His research interests and publications focus on civil society, community leadership, citizen participation and power relations in rural small towns and the wider countryside. He has been involved in a wide range of projects for various funding bodies, local authorities and public agencies on these themes. He is currently Co-Director of the Wales Rural Observatory jointly run by Cardiff and Aberystwyth Universities, and funded by the Welsh Assembly Government.

Nicholas R. Fyfe is Reader in Human Geography at the University of Dundee, UK. His main areas of research are contemporary geographies of voluntarism and the geographies of crime and criminal justice. He is the author of *Protecting Intimidated Witnesses* (Ashgate, 2001), editor of *Images of the Street: Planning, Identity and Control in Public Space* (Routledge, 1998) and co-editor with Judith Kenny of *The Urban Geography Reader* (Routledge, 2005).

Kelvyn Jones is Professor of Quantitative Human Geography at the School of Geographical Sciences, University of Bristol, UK. His principal research interests include the geographies of mortality and the application of multilevel models to complexly structured social science research problems.

Robin Kearns is Associate Professor in the School of Geography and Environmental Science at the University of Auckland, New Zealand. He has published numerous refereed articles and book chapters as well as two books: *Putting Health into Place: Landscape, Identity and Well-being* (Syracuse University Press, 1998) and *Culture/Place/Health* (Routledge, 2001) (with Wilbert Gesler). His research centres on relationships between health and place and the social relations of research.

Walter F. Lalich is an associate of the Croatian Studies Centre, Division of Humanities, Macquarie University, Sydney, Australia. He was educated at the Universities of Zagreb and Western Australia. For his PhD at the University of

Technology, Sydney, he researched and analysed the development of communal places by ethnic collectivities in Sydney. He is currently converting his thesis into a book. His research interests are in diverse settlement issues, ethnic communal space, immigrants in urban environment, ethnic collective action, institutional sustainability and return migration.

Rob Macmillan is a Research Fellow at the Centre for Regional Economic and Social Research at Sheffield Hallam University, UK. His research interests cover the changing roles of the voluntary and community sector in both service delivery and community development, and particularly the contested position of voluntary and community sector infrastructure. His doctoral thesis at the University of Durham explored the dynamics of community-based voluntary action in relation to disadvantage in rural areas. His current research focuses on government strategies for reshaping the voluntary and community sector in the UK, including infrastructure, public service delivery and civil renewal.

John Mohan is Professor of Social Policy at the University of Southampton, UK. His research includes projects on the geography of health and healthcare, on social capital, and on volunteering and voluntary organisations. Recent and forthcoming publications include *Planning, Markets and Hospitals* (Routledge, 2002) and *Medicine and Mutual Aid* (with Martin Gorsky and Tim Willis: Manchester University Press, 2006).

Christine Milligan is Senior Lecturer and Associate Dean in the Faculty of Art and Social Sciences at Lancaster University, UK. She has published widely in refereed journals and edited collections and has authored a book on *Geographies of Care: Space, Place and the Voluntary Sector* (2001) and co-edited another on *Celtic Geographies* (2002). She has been involved in a wide range of research projects funded by various agencies including research councils and the public and voluntary sectors. Her current research interests focus on voluntary activism, mental health and care transitions and older people.

Susan Owen is a Senior Tutor in the School of Geography and Environmental Science at the University of Auckland, New Zealand. She teaches in the areas of environmental management and health geography. Her doctoral thesis explores the influence of a contract culture on the place of health organisations in New Zealand's third sector.

Liz Parsons is Lecturer in Marketing at Keele University, UK. Her current research interests include the application of marketing principles to the non-profit and voluntary sectors. She is also interested in issues surrounding culture and consumption, particularly in relation to buying and selling second-hand and antique goods.

Mark W. Rosenberg is Professor of Human Geography at Queen's University, Kingston, Canada. He is the Chairperson of the International Geographical Union Commission on Health and the Environment, Editor-in-Chief of the *Canadian Journal on Aging* and a North American Editor of *Environment and Planning C: Government and Policy*. His research interests focus on the aging of Canada's population and the implications for public policy, aging among the Canadian aboriginal population, access to healthcare services and global change, health and the environment.

Mark W. Skinner currently holds a Social Sciences and Humanities Research Council of Canada (SSHRC) Postdoctoral Fellowship at the University of Guelph, Canada. Specialising in Health Geography, Mark's research explores the relationships among public service restructuring, the changing nature of voluntarism and the provision of health and social care in the community. Featuring empirical cases from different jurisdictions undergoing welfare state reform, his recent work addresses the distinctive challenges facing voluntary organisations, volunteers and informal caregivers in rural and small town settings. Mark's work appears in such journals as *Environment and Planning C: Government and Policy*, *Geoforum* and *Health & Place*.

Alan Townsend is Emeritus Professor of Regional Regeneration and Development Studies, University of Durham, UK and Chair of Regeneration, Wear Valley District Council. After previous experience of regional development working from government offices, Alan was asked to help through joining a county voluntary body. He more recently became Chair of his mining village Community Partnership, and then a local Councillor and Council Committee Chair. All these roles combined in projects of the Single Regeneration Budget and Neighbourhood Renewal Fund for his area, allowing him to compare, and to study interactions between, the bodies in tripartite 'partnerships'. Much of his recent work is available at www.odpm.gov.uk, searching on 'cscr'.

Liz Twigg is Principal Lecturer in Geography, University of Portsmouth, UK. Her research interests focus on the analysis of large and complex health datasets, synthetic estimation techniques, health inequalities and contextual effects on health. These research areas have been explored using the examples of common mental disorders, health-related behaviours (that is, smoking and drinking) and the impact of social capital on health.

Oliver Valins is Senior Policy Analyst for the Strategic Social Policy Group at the Ministry of Social Development, New Zealand. The research for his chapter was undertaken while he was a Research Fellow for the Institute for Jewish Policy Research, a London-based think-tank that provides strategic planning advice to Jewish communities. He is the author of *Facing the Future: The Provision* *of Long-term Care Facilities for Older Jewish People in the United Kingdom* (Institute for Jewish Policy Research, 2002).

Michael Woods is Reader in Human Geography at the University of Wales, Aberystwyth, UK. His research interests focus on rural politics and governance including recent projects on power, participation and rural community governance in England and Wales, and on the role and future of town and community councils in Wales. He is author of *Rural Geography* (Sage Publications, 2005), *Contesting Rurality* (Ashgate, 2005) and co-author of *An Introduction to Political Geography* (Routledge, 2004).

Foreword: Beyond the shadow state?

Over the past two decades, the role of the non-profit, voluntary sector in the world of Western capitalist countries has been thrown into high relief. The sector has grown remarkably, expanding its activities and geographic reach. Moreover, as nation-state autonomy has eroded under the onslaught of globalisation, neoliberal policies towards welfare provision have gained momentum. Pressures to restructure the welfare state and to incorporate civil society organisations, such as foundations and non-profit institutions, into the state apparatus, have intensified. Under the guise of 'third way' approaches to domestic social policy that have taken firm root in many countries, voluntary sector organisations are now central actors in welfare state governance. They are also critical vehicles for service delivery and for citizenship action.

Traditional social science research on non-profit organisations has grown in volume and sophistication. This scholarship has emphasised the internal organisation behaviour of non-profits, relations between boards, staff and volunteers, and the challenges that the sector faces given a changing mix of funding opportunities. Non-profit research has also become far more international in scope, with a growing number of non-profit sector studies being conducted in Eastern Europe as well as the developing world.

But geographers have been leaders in the vanguard of critical scholarship on state–voluntary relations and their dynamics, and in particular have emphasised the role of the geographic context of voluntary action. Geographic research has highlighted the interdependence of the voluntary sector and government at various spatial scales, the uneven spatial patterns of non-profit sector resources, place-specificities of voluntary sector activities and activism, links between voluntarism and personal subjectivity, and the increasingly contradictory role that non-profit organisations play in politics and governance.

Nonetheless, the project of articulating a geography of voluntarism has only just begun. For that reason, this book represents an important and most welcome contribution. *Landscapes of voluntarism* showcases the richness of recent geographic work in the United Kingdom, Canada, Australia, New Zealand and the United States. It brings together some of the discipline's most insightful scholars to consider the changing dynamics of the welfare state and its implications for non-profit groups. Chapters focus on crucial subsectors such as health, mental health, social welfare and immigration assistance. In addition, there are considerations of the experience of the faith-based voluntary sector, newly valorised by many governments, as well as the particular place of commercial enterprise within the sector, which has exploded as non-profit organisations attempt to increase and/or stabilise their funding base through entrepreneurial activities. Also explored here are questions of who volunteers, where and why, and how such participation shapes individual subjectivity.

Despite the diversity of locales, topics and methodological approaches of these contributions, a number of central themes emerge powerfully from the book. One is that contemporary political-economic shifts have posed fundamental challenges to the state's social provisioning ability. Restructuring has catalysed the pursuit of a voluntary sector 'fix' that protects state legitimacy yet maintains flexibility and control. Such changes are thus generating new forms of governmentality that require additional research and exploration.

Second, under pressures of welfare state restructuring, many non-profit groups are being radically transformed. Professionalisation and managerial rationality have gone hand-in-hand with acceptance of state contracts and partnership agreements, on which more and more of the sector relies. With their demands for fiscal accountability, standards of practice and performance requirements, contracts and partnerships shape voluntary sector goals, service delivery practices and internal staffing and organisation.

Third, evolving state–voluntary sector relations tend to mute advocacy and activism. This has spurred the formation of topical coalitions, focused on particular issues that can pursue a change agenda without risk to individual organisations reliant on state contracts and budgets. This raises the questions of whether such coalitions are more or less effective in achieving goals for social change than individual organisations acting separately, and if coalitions promote or hinder interorganisational service delivery coordination and network formation.

Lastly, devolution of state responsibilities has created a complex, fragmented landscape of voluntarism. Often, the voluntary sector itself becomes polarised in the process. Established institutions can expand through state supports, such as contracts, grants and fees-for-service. Smaller or newer organisations are less able to flourish in a fluid, highly competitive environment, and may be lost in the mix. In such a climate, voluntary organisations of many types may find themselves less able to actively resist the state's policies and programme initiatives.

Landscapes of voluntarism also underscores the importance of incorporating non-profit sector institutions and actors within larger conceptual frameworks within human geography, and the social and policy sciences more generally. For example, urban geography has historically ignored the voluntary sector, and even approaches that directly explore issues of local governance, such as urban regime theory, typically ignore the voluntary sector as a key political actor. Similarly, geographies of concentrated poverty, social exclusion and polarisation focus on the welfare state and its changing scale relations, but not its myriad and diffuse non-profit partners. And areas within geography such as citizenship studies should be informed about how voluntary organisations shape opportunities for active citizenship, co-opting conflict and protest, channelling resistance, or providing venues for social movement mobilisation.

This volume also shows what we have yet to adequately discern about the voluntary sector itself. Why do people in particular places volunteer? Clearly sociodemographic characteristics matter but much remains unexplained: the fabric of volunteering opportunities, moral economies of different kinds of neighbourhoods and communities, time-space budgets of local households that hinder or facilitate voluntary effort. What is the role of hybrids such as for-profit spin-offs ranging from fancy museum shops and upscale non-profit catalogue 'stores' with professional staff to down-market thrift shops run by local volunteers feeling charitable, seeking work experience or just needing something to do? Do market and voluntary cultures clash, and if so, to what effect? How widespread, and in what types of sectors, are non-profit coalitions for advocacy springing up, designed to give organisations voice but shield them from state retribution? Have such coalitions been successful in producing policy or programme change?

Perhaps most vital of all, we know relatively little about what is happening outside the health/welfare sector. Most work on the voluntary sector – by geographers and others – has targeted health, mental health, community housing and a range of social services, all of which have been pillars of the post-Second World War welfare state in most developed countries. The arts and religion are also topics of considerable past research, but these activities have mostly remained beyond state purview. This may be changing, however, as the faith-based sector enters the social service delivery arena, and the implications of emergent state–faith-based sector relations are vital to unravel. Moreover, other branches of the state appear to be devolving rapidly, spawning non-profits in their wake, and many non-profits have emerged recently within an already fragmented, devolved governance landscape as unmet needs for service provision have become increasingly stark.

Education, land-use and the environment are examples here. Witness the proliferation of non-profits delivering educational services, establishing schools, pressuring the educational establishment, or lobbying for educational standards and testing. Or consider the emergence of non-profit land conservancies acquiring property for parks and wilderness preserves, mounting habitat or river restoration projects, and pressing for urban growth policies to combat sprawl. And more and more often, environmental non-profit groups are 'stakeholders' who sit at the table with state agencies to hammer out strategies for environmental regulation, as a means to improve decisions and avoid costly litigation later on. Even basic urban services such as recreation are now so threadbare that in some localities municipal governments are spawning non-profits to take responsibility for developing recreation facilities and managing related process of neighbourhood park management and governance. These dynamics call out for a spatial approach to analysis that will both enrich non-profit sector studies but also deepen a range of geographic theories, conceptual models and empirical research.

Landscapes of voluntarism reveals that the voluntary sector as 'shadow state' is more firmly entrenched than ever. Contributors show that we may be moving beyond the traditional arenas of 'shadow state' action, into entirely new spheres of public life and service provision. In turn, this is apt to intensify the penetration of non-profit sector actors and activities into everyday private life and to affect a range of livelihoods. Despite increasing financial accountability requirements tied to state funding, voluntary organisations remain largely beyond the purview of democratic accountability just as their historic role in promoting citizen engagement in civil society is transformed under mounting pressures to professionalise and adopt formalised decision making tied to public contracts. In the end, *Landscapes of voluntarism* will make readers think hard and ask new questions about the deepening instrumentality of non-profit organisations within emerging state formations, a polarising and geographically uneven landscape of voluntary sector resources and the social capital and networks they represent, and both the promises and problems of the voluntary sector approach to the pursuit of progressive social and environmental change.

Jennifer Wolch
Professor of Geography, University of Southern California

ONE

Contemporary landscapes of welfare: the 'voluntary turn'?

Christine Milligan and David Conradson

Introduction

Over the past two decades or so, governments in Australia, Canada, New Zealand, the UK and other Western states have sought to roll back state involvement in welfare provision. The aim has been to foster a radically pluralised social economy, with non-state actors centrally involved in the delivery of social and welfare services. As Salamon et al (1999) noted, voluntary organisations have formed a key element of this vision of pluralised welfare. The growing attention given to voluntarism, they argued, reflects the severe and ongoing fiscal pressures associated with public provision in Western states; intense doubts about the capability of national governments to deal with these matters effectively in isolation; and a breakdown in the neoliberal consensus that welfare problems can be dealt with by an encouragement of the private market. This constellation of concerns has, in part, led to the development of a 'third way' (Giddens, 1998), a central tenet of which is the belief that while both state and market have a legitimate role to play in the provision of social welfare, community and voluntary organisations are also critical players. Etzioni (2001) points out that a further core element of the 'third way' has been a desire to engage citizens in the development of responsible communities. Individuals socialised into a communitarian society, he maintains, have a moral obligation to that society and, hence, are likely to be more reasonable and productive than isolated individuals. Within this framework, voluntary organisations are seen to have an important role. Not only might they bridge the gap between state and market, but through their close connection to citizens and local communities, they also have the potential to act as sites for the development of active citizenship.

So it is not just welfare reform that has increased political interest in the voluntary sector. Concern over the erosion of citizenship and a perceived need to encourage the development of social capital has further underscored the potential of voluntarism as a mechanism through which to promote a local sense of civic responsibility and engagement (Brown, 1997; Putnam, 2000). In designating 2001 as the International Year of Volunteering, for example, the United Nations

(UN) highlighted an international interest in the fostering of civic engagement through volunteering (Morris, 1999). The extent to which neoliberal states have sought to actively engage with this 'third way' approach has led some commentators to conclude that a new consensus is beginning to emerge, one in which the voluntary sector is viewed as an attractive intermediate organisational form in relation to the somewhat tired state–market dichotomy. The promotion of the voluntary sector has been about fostering a sphere where politics can be democratised, active citizenship strengthened and more pluralist welfare formations realised (Brown et al, 2000). These developments have led commentators such as Kendall (2003) to note that, '[n]ot since the late nineteenth century, when voluntary action was integral to contemporary concepts of citizenship, and the associated infrastructure of charities and mutuals were the cause of considerable national pride, have organisations occupying the space between the market and the state commanded so much attention' (p 1).

Defining volunteering and the voluntary sector

In the brief discussion thus far, it is clear that the recent reawakening of interest in voluntarism in recent times has spawned a range of new terms to describe the voluntary sector. Each of these terms has gained currency in different quarters. The academic and policy literature is littered with references to non-governmental organisations (NGOs), non-profits, organised civil society, the social economy and the third sector, to give but a few examples. Yet as Kendall (2003) notes, this has been an essentially elite-led process – principally by academics and policy makers working in particular national contexts – that is not necessarily reflected on the ground. Neither can these terms be assumed to have equal relevance across all settings. In the UK, for example, the voluntary and community sector are still the most common collective nouns used to describe these organisations. The terminology differs in other countries, however, and given the international focus of this volume, it is important that individual chapters are able to reflect the discourses prevalent within their own national contexts. With this in mind, each chapter employs the terms commonly used by the academic, policy and practitioner communities to which it refers.

In addition to variation in the terminology used to describe organised voluntary activity, numerous commentators have highlighted the difficulties of attempting to define the sector (for example, Hedley and Smith, 1992; Giner and Sarasa, 1996; Anheier and Salamon, 1999). This is compounded by the diversity of roles and activities undertaken by voluntary organisations, encompassing lobbying and activism; mutual support and advocacy; leisure and cultural pursuits; as well as direct welfare service provision. In many instances organisations are involved in more than one of these activities, highlighting the complex nature of the sector. To add to the confusion, Anheier (2005) points out that in reality the boundary between public, voluntary and private sector provision is sometimes blurred and fluid as organisations 'migrate' from one sector to another or contain both profit and non-profit centres within them. For example, hospitals may change from public to voluntary status and vice versa, while services initially developed and provided by voluntary organisations can, over time, become the remit of state welfare. More recently, as the state has sought to retrench health and social welfare provision, many of the services it no longer provides – particularly those at the preventative end of the welfare spectrum – have been taken up by the voluntary and private sectors.

At one level of definition, the voluntary sector can be viewed as comprising organisations that are formal, non-profit distributing, constitutionally independent of the state and self-governing. While such organisations may employ paid staff and receive funding from the state their remit is to act for public rather than shareholder benefit (Taylor, 1992; Kendall, 2003). One further defining feature is their engagement with volunteers, whether in their day-to-day operation, on their management boards, or in both contexts.

The act of volunteering also requires some clarification. At its broadest level, it refers to the activity of individuals who give of their time to help others, without compulsion and for no monetary pay. However, when such activity occurs within the structure of a voluntary organisation, it is often referred to as *formal* volunteering (Anheier, 2005). This is distinct from *informal* volunteering, where an individual performs similar unpaid work, but outside the boundaries of any formal organisation (for example, shopping for neighbours, caring for a friend or family member or giving unpaid help at school functions). Further confusion can arise when an individual volunteers informally, outside the structure of a formal voluntary organisation, but within the formal structure of a statutory or private sector organisation (for example, as a school governor, or a parish or community councillor).

The problematic of attempting to define voluntarism and the voluntary sector lead Kendall and Knapp (1995) to conclude that, at best, it can be seen to resemble something of a 'loose and baggy monster'.

Geographical research on voluntarism

The debates around active citizenship, governance and neocommunitarianism that have underpinned the burgeoning interest in voluntarism also raise important questions about the relationship between voluntary activity and place. That is, how and why does voluntary activity develop in different ways in different places? To what extent do the different social, historical and political contexts within which voluntarism is located shape its development? While the contribution of geographers to these debates has been somewhat limited to date, existing work does offer some interesting insights into the significance of place as context. Hence, in this section we give a brief overview of some of those studies that have, in various ways, contributed towards a geographical understanding of voluntarism.

Perhaps the earliest contribution of geographers to voluntary sector debates came from those working in North America. The work of researchers such as Wolpert (1976, 1977), Wolch and Geiger (1983, 1986) and Wolpert and Reiner (1984, 1985), for example, first drew attention to the geographical dimensions of voluntarism. In particular their work revealed a spatial pattern of activity characterised by 'voluntary sector rich' and 'voluntary sector poor' parts of the city. That is, they were able to demonstrate that active volunteering was primarily the remit of more affluent communities whose employers were also important philanthropic donors. Economic restructuring, together with the flight of social capital, was argued to result not only in a reduced tax base for the support of public sector welfare services, but also a strategic withdrawal of the voluntary sector from neighbourhoods. This would leave a residual population with increased welfare needs, but at the same time a significantly reduced public and voluntary sector infrastructure with which to meet those needs.

The pattern of voluntarism identified in these early North American studies was broadly supported by the 1992 General Household Survey on Volunteering in the UK (Goddard, 1992). A localised study undertaken by Macdonald (1996), however, revealed that contrary to the 'middle-class' volunteer profile identified by this earlier research there was, at least in the North East of England, evidence of a growth in voluntary participation among unemployed people living in economically depressed localities. More recently, in an intrametropolitan comparison of the relationship between the geography of poverty and the voluntary sector in Southern California, Joassart-Marcelli and Wolch (2003) concluded that while the number of anti-poverty voluntary organisations and their levels of expenditure was greater in poorer cities, it was nevertheless still insufficient to ensure equal service for the poorest persons in these cities in comparison to those living in wealthier cities. What is, perhaps, most crucial about these studies is that they reveal that in seeking to understand who volunteers, where and why, it is important to take into account not only place and scale, but also the socio-cultural context within which voluntarism occurs. These are issues that contributors to this volume begin to unpick in more detail.

Adopting a broadly political geographic approach, Jennifer Wolch's (1990) book on voluntary sector transition and the politics of place has perhaps been the most influential geographical work in this field to date. Drawing on a comparison of voluntary sector activity in the US and the UK, Wolch sought to unravel the complex dilemmas faced by voluntary organisations in Western capitalist countries as they attempted to negotiate 'the new terrain between state and voluntary sector' (Wolch, 1990, p xvii). She argued that organisations that have been unable to resist the pressure to augment their resources with public funding, have often found themselves struggling to maintain autonomy in the face of increased state control. Despite the significance of Wolch's work, it is interesting to note that geographers only truly began to engage with ideas around the shadow state relatively recently. Indeed, with one or two notable exceptions, geographical work on voluntarism during the early 1990s was extremely limited. Hasson and Ley's (1994) cross-cultural comparison was perhaps one of the few early studies that engaged with the issues of voluntarism, partnership and governance which are now are the heart of 'third way' politics. In a study of neighbourhood organisations in Jerusalem and Vancouver, they demonstrated how renewed interest in civil society stimulated a revival of urban politics with an apparent decentring of power and a growth of partnership working, 'manifest in the emergence of new, hybridised forms of politics that are emerging in actual locations where the state and civil society overlap' (Milligan and Fyfe, 2004, p 76). While they do not explicitly engage with the concept of the 'shadow state', it is clear that an interest in state–voluntary sector relationships underpins their work.

With the elevation of the voluntary sector in various national policy agendas in the later half of the 1990s, a small but disparate body of geographical work began to emerge that sought to re-examine the relationship between voluntarism, place and the social and political context. Geographers from the US, Canada and the UK (for example, Brown, 1997; Milligan, 2001; Mitchell, 2001; Milligan and Fyfe, 2004) all sought to engage more or less explicitly with the concept of the shadow state. In various ways their work demonstrates how voluntary organisations, faced with such pressures, can find themselves on the horns of a dilemma. Should they accept state funding in the knowledge that while this will enable them to expand support to those individuals that are the basis of their raison d'être, it also brings with it an increase in state control? Or should they stand firm, maintaining their independence, but knowing that this is likely to place constraints on their ability to deliver and expand their services? Those opting for the first of these routes are seen to form part of what Wolch (1990) referred to as the 'shadow state'– a term that has now become firmly embedded in the lexicon of geographers working in the fields of governance and voluntarism.

With an eye to contemporary policy agendas, geographers have also sought to examine the relationship between place, voluntarism and active citizenship. Here, work has examined how the drive to professionalise within the sector may, contrary to political imperatives to promote active citizenship through voluntarism, be instrumental in promoting more passive forms of citizenship (Fyfe and Milligan, 2003a, 2003b; Milligan and Fyfe, 2005). As illustrated in a special issue of *Antipode* (Bondi and Laurie, 2005), geographers have also begun to engage with voluntarism from the perspective of neocommunitarianism (Fyfe, 2005). And there is also geographical research that engages with debates around voluntarism, governance and the social economy (see, for example, Kearns, 1992; Amin et al, 1999; Elwood, 2004; Jones, 2004).

While work on governance has pointed to the emergence of a new localism, commentators such as Gorsky et al (1999), Bryson et al, (2002) and Mohan (2003) have argued for the value of a historical geographic approach as a means of illustrating how the localism of voluntary welfare development led to considerable variation in provision, access and utilisation over time. Thus Gorsky and Mohan (2001) conclude that local prosperity and the popular appeal of certain healthcare institutions have been of more significance in explaining variations in the geography of voluntary action than need.

Debate around who volunteers, where and why, has also raised important questions around the gendered nature of volunteering and the role of women in voluntary activity. Soteri's (2001) work on women's organisations in London, England, for example, revealed the numerical dominance of female volunteers in agencies dealing with Black and Minority Ethnic (BME) issues, sexual and domestic violence, health and employment. In the field of social care, Milligan (2001) points to a pattern of voluntary labour that was predominantly female – a factor attributable to the traditional gendered nature of the caring role. Little (1997) examines the gendered nature of voluntarism further, maintaining that women's voluntary labour in rural communities in the UK has been crucial to their ongoing function following state withdrawal from basic service provision. Exploring the nature and circumstances of women's voluntary work in rural communities, she asserted that the extent to which voluntary activity dominates the lives of rural women is a specific feature of rural life that is intrinsically linked to smallness, self-sufficiency, willingness to help and preservation of traditional forms of community. Contributing to the rural community through voluntary labour is viewed by rural women as the price to pay for ensuring the survival of the particular lifestyle they value – as such, it is seen as a unique feature of rural identity that cannot occur in urban areas.

These claims for an urban–rural differentiation in gendered voluntary activity are reiterated in Teather's (1994) work on women's voluntary organisations in Australia. Traditional women's voluntary organisations in New South Wales are seen to shape their mission around a concept of rurality that is sharply delineated from that of metropolitan lifestyles and value systems. Traditional organisations refrain from challenging the deeply conservative attitudes to gender relations seen as integral to the social identity of rural communities, while newer, non-traditional rural women's organisations seek to challenge the male hegemony that typifies rural Australian communities. Thus, Teather notes that 'women's organisations in rural areas both institutionalise and deploy particular rural visions of life in pursuit of different social and political agendas' (1994, p 31). While these studies begin to tease out some of the issues around gender and voluntarism, the relationship between place, gender and voluntary activity is still relatively under-researched. Little is known, for example, about how gender acts to shape the changing social and political spaces of voluntarism in urban areas. Nevertheless, this work begins to raise some interesting questions around gender, active citizenship and space that warrant further exploration.

The geographical studies referred to above are spread across different continents, but they are all tied by the thread of state welfare reform, the concomitant expansion of the voluntary sector as a welfare provider, and the implications for service users located in particular places. Although they address a wide range of approaches and issues, they all, in their various ways, point to:

- the emergence of new political spaces in which the state and civil society are becoming hybridised, and within which voluntary organisations have become increasingly central to the implementation of policy and delivery of health and welfare services;
- the ways in which voluntary action can influence the nature of social, health and welfare services in particular places;
- the importance of understanding the social, historical and political context within which landscapes of voluntarism emerge.

These issues form the central focus of the book. Our concern is to bring together a body of contemporary geographical work that explores landscapes of voluntarism, governance and community action. We consider the extent to which place and spatiality are integral to understanding the development of welfare voluntarism.

Introducing the chapters

Voluntary action commonly develops in response to localised need and interests that change over time and space, hence the geographies of voluntarism are often uneven. These unfolding landscapes warrant consideration in terms of how and where voluntary actors are engaged in the planning and provision of welfare services, and what this might mean in terms of the delivery of local and national health and social welfare. They also invite an examination of those new configurations of governance that are developing between actors from the statutory, market and voluntary sectors, and the implications of these alliances for local democracy. The organisational spaces of individual voluntary organisations are also of interest, as environments collectively fashioned by staff and volunteers with a view towards assisting particular groups of users. These lines of enquiry are all important elements of a geographical perspective on voluntarism.

To address these issues, the book brings together a collection of new and innovative work by researchers working in Australia, Canada, New Zealand, the US and the UK. These are all states where issues of voluntarism and participation have become increasingly important for the development and delivery of social welfare policy. With a foreword from one of the foremost geographers working in this field, the volume draws together a significant body of work from scholars working on issues of voluntarism and its links to governance, health, care, faith, ethnicity, counselling, advocacy and professionalisation. Some of the themes that underpin the various chapters are not discrete. While all address the relationship between space, place and voluntarism, and aspects of professionalisation and governance are common threads that run through many of the chapters, some highlight the links between two or more of our key themes. Oliver Valins' chapter on voluntary Jewish care homes, for example, addresses the links between place, care and faith-based voluntarism, while Gillian Creese draws together issues of both ethnicity and advocacy, and Liz Bondi's chapter highlights the impact of professionalisation on voluntary counselling services. For this reason, we have chosen not to organise the book into formal sections, although there are clear links between some chapters and dominant themes running through them. We discuss this structure in the remainder of this chapter.

In differing, but interrelated ways, the first three chapters in the book explore issues of *governance, welfare and community*. Rob Macmillan and Alan Townsend, in Chapter Two, begin by drawing on four development strategies that they discern at the heart of New Labour's approach to the intensification of the 'community turn' in public policy in the UK. In doing so, they reflect on the new localism, emphasising community-based approaches to regeneration and social exclusion policies. These new policy developments, together with an increased emphasis on the voluntary sector in public service delivery, are seen to be representative of a 'new institutional fix' to the problem of welfare reform. However, Macmillan and Townsend point out that such developments are not without problems. Their chapter is thus concerned to draw out how the 'community turn' involves specific constructions of space, scale and temporality that have important consequences for the shape and structure of the emerging welfare state. Following this, in Chapter Three Christine Milligan and Nicholas R. Fyfe draw on theoretical debates around state–voluntary in[ter]dependence to consider how the voluntary sector in Scotland is responding to the political drive to reposition its role in the planning and delivery of social welfare and how this is manifest at local level. While continuing the theme of governance and partnership in urban regeneration and social exclusion addressed by Macmillan and Townsend, this discussion draws on a detailed case study of Glasgow to examine the effects of changing regeneration and social inclusion policies on the development of the voluntary sector over time. In doing so, the authors illustrate that while the new localism and governance arrangements can create a 'dynamic mosaic of opportunities for voluntary organisations to develop services in spatially defined communities' (p 41), they can also facilitate complex patterns of voluntary sector inclusion and exclusion that act to reinforce existing patterns of unevenness. The theme of voluntarism, partnership working and new forms of governance is continued by Bill Edwards and Michael Woods, whose chapter (Chapter Four) addresses voluntary sector engagement in rural communities. More specifically they demonstrate how the presence of low-level government (seen here as town, parish and community councils) in rural districts acts to change the dynamics of voluntary and community sector engagement in community governance. Theoretically, Edwards and Woods engage with ideas around the 'shadow state', noting that the relationship between low-level government and voluntary organisations differs significantly from that inherent in the 'shadow state' thesis. At this level of government–voluntary sector interaction, they maintain there is greater indication of interdependency, with little evidence of low-level councils' ability to exert control over the shape or actions of the voluntary and community sector. Drawing on case material from England and Wales to illustrate their arguments, they conclude that the variable experience of governance in rural districts indicates that it is strongly influenced by scale and spatial context.

The second broad theme in the book addresses the *intersection of health, care and voluntarism*. In Chapter Five, Pauline Barnett and J. Ross Barnett shift the focus away from the UK to consider how the restructuring of the welfare state in New Zealand has impacted on the relationship between the state and voluntary sector in the planning and delivery of healthcare. Following a brief historical overview, their chapter considers some of the key issues and tensions faced by the New Zealand voluntary sector over the past two decades and the wider impact of health sector changes. More specifically, they draw on the experiences of three key health sector groupings – community mental health, primary healthcare and public health – to consider the changing relationship between the state and health voluntary organisations in the light of New Zealand's retreat from neoliberalism in the late 1990s. Despite high levels of state control, the authors illustrate how the shift to a more decentralised district health board structure has accentuated regional differences in relationships between health voluntary organisations and government.

Continuing the theme of health and care, Mark Skinner's and Mark Rosenberg's chapter (Chapter Six) focuses on the Canadian context. Drawing on survey data from the Canadian Population Health Survey, they offer insights into the geography of informal and voluntary healthcare in the home and community. By interrogating this large-scale dataset, the authors demonstrate some of the spatial disparities in levels of informal care volunteering that exist at provincial level. Pointing to variations in the cultural and historical contexts that exist between the provinces, they suggest that these contexts significantly influence how civil society relations develop. Skinner and Rosenberg maintain that such findings highlight the need for a more nuanced understanding of the geography of informal voluntary care at local level. Shifting back to the New Zealand context in Chapter Seven, Susan Owen and Robin Kearns then argue that to understand how and where an organisation is located within the voluntary sector it is necessary to examine both structural influences and individual agency. To illustrate this, they present a detailed discussion of the effects of healthcare restructuring on the New Zealand voluntary sector during the 1980s and 1990s. Underpinned by the notion of governmentality, this chapter examines how the neoliberalising policies of this period gave rise to a shift in the relationship between government and the voluntary sector – one characterised by a new managerialism. Drawing on debates around competition and the rise of the contract culture, they illustrate how the voluntary sector has responded to these changes through processes of organisational adaptation and resistance.

The final chapter in this section dealing with health, care and voluntarism also addresses a third theme in the book, that of *faith-based voluntarism*. In this chapter, Oliver Valins considers the place of voluntary sector care homes for older Jewish people in the UK. Importantly, he discusses the role of volunteers within these care homes and considers questions about the 'added value' of faith-based voluntarism in the residential care sector, from the perspective of those using the services and their families. He maintains that the active involvement of local communities and volunteers in these voluntary care homes creates a greater sense of home, safety and belonging for residents and families than is possible in private care homes. Shifting to faith-based voluntary welfare services in New Zealand, in Chapter Nine David Conradson then addresses the presence of Christian voluntary organisations in social welfare provision. Drawing on case studies from the city of Christchurch, he discusses the welfare philosophies and service practices of these agencies and examines their responses to the challenges posed by neoliberal and third way welfare reform. Processes of strategic divestment are highlighted, as organisations struggle to preserve fidelity to their core visions while remaining financially sustainable. At a wider policy level, in Chapter Ten Derek Bacon then provides a comparative account of the role of faith-based organisations in the US, the UK and Northern Ireland. In his review, Bacon seeks to understand the agendas that underpin these developments in faith-based voluntary activity. In doing so, he draws out the distinction between faith-based and faith-related organisations and points to the way in which government faith-based policy initiatives in the US are raising concerns that signal not only a further retrenchment of state welfare, but also an attempt by the incumbent government to forge a closer alliance with the religious right. While government in the UK has sought to court faith communities, he notes that these organisations often exercise a more critical relation to neoliberal policy; certainly they cannot simply be viewed as a blank canvas for the scripting of government imperatives. While active in addressing issues of poverty and deprivation, their services also place significant emphasis on the transmission of culture and values. Finally, in considering voluntary provision in Northern Ireland, Bacon notes that while religious bodies have played a central role in the province, they are located within a stark religious divide where few would actively view themselves as conscious actors within the voluntary sector.

The fourth broad theme in the book concerns the *production of voluntary sector organisational spaces*. This is addressed by four authors in differing ways and at different scales. The first two contributions examine it with reference to the connections between migration, ethnicity and voluntarism at the city scale. Focusing on a period of welfare restructuring in Canada in the 1990s, in Chapter Eleven Gillian Creese focuses on how voluntary settlement agencies in Vancouver negotiated this critical period of restructuring and as a consequence became more closely drawn into the parameters of the 'shadow state'. She maintains that this restructuring became manifest in an uneven geography of access and voluntary welfare support for new migrants to the city. The resultant marginalisation led to a rise in political activism, with advocacy providing a key mechanism for both resisting the challenges of neoliberal policies and reconnecting settlement workers to community needs. In Chapter Twelve Walter F. Lalich then addresses the ways in which voluntary activity among migrant communities has acted to reshape the urban landscape in the Australian context. Focusing on the city of Sydney, he illustrates how these communities sought to adapt to their new environment by reshaping parts of the urban landscape through a collective voluntary action designed to meet their diverse social and cultural needs. These voluntary collective acts are seen to enhance social empowerment, fostering social capital among immigrant communities and thus enabling a further expansion of communal life. As a result of these diverse voluntary acts, Lalich maintains that immigrants both create and sustain new social opportunities, while at the same time reworking the urban social fabric.

Moving from a city-wide to an institutional focus, in Chapter Thirteen Liz Parsons then examines the highly localised spaces of the charity retail sector in the UK to consider some of the ways in which government policy is impacting on volunteering. Underpinned by notions of active citizenship, Parsons highlights the growing tension between the drive towards the corporatisation and professionalisation of charity shops and their dependence on a local volunteer labour force for whom informality and the social benefits of these spaces are key to their willingness to continue volunteering. Drawing on debates around traditional volunteers versus government-led initiatives aimed at promoting volunteering, the author explores some of the ways in which interpretations of volunteering are open to contestation. Continuing the theme of professionalisation, in Chapter Fourteen Liz Bondi then offers an evolutionary account of the growth and shift in the place of counselling within the voluntary sector over the past two decades in Scotland, highlighting variations in the geographies of differing counselling provision. Regarding the impact of the increasing drive towards professionalisation, Bondi notes how this has effected a narrowing of the definition of counselling, resulting in some organisations repositioning their services under a banner of advice and mutual support.

The penultimate chapter shifts away from the production of voluntary spaces to consider how we might develop a robust methodology for examining the relationship between the propensity to volunteer and the kinds of places in which people live. Drawing on statistical data from two General Household Surveys in the UK, in Chapter Fifteen John Mohan, Liz Twigg, Kelvyn Jones and Steve Barnard adopt a multilevel modelling approach to explore the relationship between individual and area characteristics. In doing so, they conclude that contrary to the findings of other researchers (for example, Williams, 2003), *regional* variations in volunteering are largely a function of composition. Hence, they are drawn to conclude, that if 'geography matters' in volunteering, it is at the subregional scale. Although Mohan et al's chapter is specifically linked to volunteering rather than the voluntary organisations, it does raise tantalising questions about the importance of scale.

Finally, it is worth stating in this introductory chapter that while the book covers a wide range of issues related to the changing landscapes of voluntarism in health, welfare and governance, it does not aspire to cover all those spatial issues that pertain to voluntarism. Rather, we have chosen to focus exclusively on developments in advanced capitalist welfare states where the voluntary sector has increasingly been viewed as a panacea for the problems of escalating demand on an overburdened welfare state. While we acknowledge the hugely important contribution of international NGOs to health and welfare (particularly in the developing world), their role as sites of resistance in oppressive regimes and the significant contribution of NGOs in addressing environmental issues that affect us both locally and globally, we make no attempt to address these themes in this volume. These issues, we believe, would warrant separate volumes in themselves.

References

Amin, A., Cameron, A. and Hudson R. (1999) 'Welfare as Work? The Potential of the UK Social Economy', *Environment and Planning A*, vol 31, no 11, pp 2033-51.

Anheier, H. (2005) *Nonprofit Organizations: Theory, Management, Policy*, London: Routledge.

Anheier, H.K. and Salamon, L.M. (1999) 'Volunteering in Cross-national Perspective: Initial Comparisons', *Law and Contemporary Problems*, vol 62, no 4, pp 43-66.

Bondi, L. and Laurie, N. (eds) (2005) 'Working the Spaces of Neoliberalism: Activism, Professionalisation and Incorporation', Special Issue of *Antipode*, vol 37, no 3, pp 393-631.

Brown, M. (1997) *RePlacing Citizenship: AIDS Activism and Radical Democracy*, London: Guilford Press.

Brown, K., Kenny, S., Turner, B. and Prince, J. (2000) *Rhetorics of Welfare: Uncertainty, Choice and Voluntary Associations*, London: Macmillan Press.

Bryson, J.R., McGuiness, M. and Ford, R.G. (2002) 'Chasing a "Loose and Baggy Monster": Almshouses and the Geography of Charity', *Area*, vol 34, no 1, pp 48-58.

Elwood, S. (2004) 'Partnerships and Participation: Reconfiguring Urban Governance in Different State Contexts', *Urban Geography*, vol 25, no 8, pp 755-70.

Etzioni, A. (2001) 'The Third Way is a Triumph', *New Statesman*, 25-27 June.

Fyfe, N. (2005) 'Making Space for "Neocommunitarianism"? The Third Sector, State and Civil Society in the UK', *Antipode*, vol 37, no 3, pp 536-57.

Fyfe, N. and Milligan, C. (2003a) 'Out of the Shadows: Exploring Contemporary Georgraphics of the Welfare Voluntary State', *Progress in Human Geography*, vol 27, no 4, pp 397-413.

Fyfe, N. and Milligan, C. (2003b) 'Space, Citizenship and Voluntarism: Critical Reflections on the Voluntary Welfare Sector in Glasgow', *Environment and Planning A*, vol 35, pp 2069-86.

Giddens, A. (1998) *The Third Way: The Renewal of Social Democracy*, London: Polity Press.

Giner, S. and Sarasa, S. (1996) 'Civic Altruism and Social Policy', *International Sociology*, vol 11, no 2, pp 139-60.

Goddard, E. (1992) 'Voluntary Work', *General Household Survey No 23, Supplement A*, London: HMSO.

Gorsky, M. and Mohan, J. (2001) 'London's Voluntary Hospitals in the Interwar Period: Growth, Transformation or Crisis?', *Nonprofit and Voluntary Sector Quarterly*, vol 30, no 2, pp 247-75.

Gorsky, M., Mohan, J. and Powell, M. (1999) 'British Voluntary Hospitals, 1871-1938: The Geography of Provision and Utilization', *Journal of Historical Geography*, vol 25, no 4, pp 463-82.

Hasson, S. and Ley, D. (1994) *Neighbourhood Organizations and the Welfare State*, Toronto: University of Toronto Press.

Hedley, R. and Smith, J.D. (1992) *Volunteering and Society: Principles and Practice*, London: Bedford Square Press.

Joassart-Marcelli, P. and Wolch, J. (2003) 'The Intrametropolitan Geography of Poverty and the Nonprofit Sector in Southern California', *Nonprofit and Voluntary Sector Quarterly*, vol 32, no 1, pp 70-97.

Jones, M. (2004) 'Social Justice and the Region: Grassroots Regional Movements and the "English Question"', *Space and Polity*, vol 8, no 2, pp 157-89.

Kearns, A. (1992) 'Active Citizenship and Urban Governance', *Transactions of the Institute of British Geographers*, vol 17, pp 20-34.

Kendall, J. (2003) *The Voluntary Sector*, London: Routledge.

Kendall, J. and Knapp, M. (1995) 'A Loose and Baggy Monster: Boundaries, Definitions and Typologies', in J.D. Smith, C. Rochester and R. Hedley (eds) *An Introduction to the Voluntary Sector*, London: Routledge, pp 66-95.

Little, J. (1997) 'Constructions of Rural Women's Voluntary Work', *Gender, Place and Culture*, vol 4, no 2, pp 197-209.

Macdonald, R. (1996) 'Labours of Love: Voluntary Working in a Depressed Local Economy', *Journal of Social Policy*, vol 25, pp 19-38.

Milligan, C. (2001) *Geographies of Care: Space, Place and the Voluntary Sector*, Aldershot: Ashgate.

Milligan, C. and Fyfe, N. (2004) 'Putting the Voluntary Sector in its Place: Geographical Perspectives on Voluntary Activity and Social Welfare in Glasgow', *Journal of Social Policy*, vol 33, no 1, pp 73-93.

Milligan, C. and Fyfe, N. (2005) 'Preserving Space for Volunteers: Exploring the Links Between Voluntary Welfare Organizations, Volunteering and Citizenship', *Journal of Urban Studies*, vol 42, no 3, pp 413-34.

Mohan, J. (2003) 'Voluntarism, Municipalism and Welfare: The Geography of Hospital Utilization in England in 1938', *Transactions of the Institute of British Geographers*, vol 28, no 1, pp 56-74.

Morris, D. (1999) 'Volunteering and Employment Status', *Industrial Law Journal*, vol 28, no 3, pp 249-68.

Putnam, R. (2000) *Bowling Alone: The Collapse and Revival of American Community*, New York, NY: Simon and Schuster.

Salamon, L., Anheier, H. and List, R. (1999) *Global Civil Society: Dimensions of the Nonprofit Sector (Inaugural Edition)*, Baltimore, MD: Johns Hopkins Center for Civil Society Studies.

Soteri, A. (2001) *A Profile Report on Women's Organisations in London's Voluntary and Community Sector*, London: Centre for Institutional Studies, University of East London.

Taylor, M. (1992) 'The Changing Role of the Non-profit sector in Britain: Moving Towards the Market', in B. Gidron, R. Kramer and S. Salamon (eds) *Government and Third Sector*, San Francisco, CA: Jossey Bass Publications, pp 147-75.

Teather, E. (1994) 'Contesting Rurality: Country Women's Social and Political Networks', in S. Whatmore, T. Marsden and P. Lowe (eds) *Gender and Rurality*, London: David Fulton Publishers, pp 31-49.

Williams, C. (2003) 'Developing Community Involvement: Contrasting Local and Regional Participatory Cultures in Britain and their Implications for Policy', *Regional Studies*, vol 37, pp 531-41.

Wolch, J.R. (1990) *The Shadow State: Government and Voluntary Sector in Transition*, New York, NY: The Foundation Centre.

Wolch, J.R. and Geiger, R. (1983) 'The Distribution of Urban Voluntary Resources: An Exploratory Analysis', *Environment and Planning A*, vol 15, pp 1067-82.

Wolch, J.R. and Geiger, R. (1986) 'Urban Restructuring and the Not-for-Profit Sector', *Economic Geography*, vol 62, pp 3-18.

Wolpert, J. (1976) 'Opening Closed Spaces', *Annals of the Association of American Geographers*, vol 66, no 1, pp 1-13.

Wolpert, J. (1977) 'Social Income and the Voluntary Sector', *Papers of the Regional Science Association*, vol 39, pp 217-29.

Wolpert, J. and Reiner, T. (1984) 'Service Provision in the Not-for-Profit Sector: A Comparative Study', *Economic Geography*, vol 60, pp 28-37.

Wolpert, J. and Reiner, T. (1985) 'The Not-for-Profit Sector in Stable and Growing Regions', *Urban Affairs Quarterly*, vol 20, pp 487-510.

TWO

A 'new institutional fix'? The 'community turn' and the changing role of the voluntary sector

Rob Macmillan and Alan Townsend

Introduction

Why has the voluntary and community sector become increasingly fashionable in social policies over recent years? This chapter explores how policies for regenerating deprived areas and tackling different aspects of social exclusion in the UK have taken what we describe as a 'community turn' which embraces an enhanced role for the voluntary and community sector (Imrie and Raco, 2003; Taylor, 2003).

The basis of our argument is that the voluntary and community sector appears to serve as a putative solution to a number of governing dilemmas. It offers governments the prospect of addressing, and being seen to address, intractable problems through welfare services provided beyond the state, which are thought to involve lower costs while being effective and innovative.

In turn we discuss three major tools of the 'community turn' at local level – governance, partnership and capacity building – to explore how relationships between local government and voluntary organisations are being reshaped. We argue that the emergence of an enhanced role for the sector can fruitfully be seen as part of an attempted 'institutional fix' (Peck and Tickell, 1994) in a broader project to restructure the postwar welfare state in an era of fiscal constraint.

The chapter concludes by considering the broader geographical consequences of the 'community turn' for voluntarism and for the changing 'postnational' welfare state. We suggest that the 'community turn' involves specific constructions of space, scale and temporality, which not only have important consequences for the shape and structure of the emerging welfare state, but also for the construction of a differentiated voluntary and community sector.

The 'community turn' in public policy

Before being heckled and given a slow hand-clap by the Women's Institute triennial conference in June 2000, the UK Prime Minister Tony Blair neatly summarised the importance of 'community' and 'community renewal' to the New Labour 'project' of responding to a rapidly changing society:

> At the heart of my beliefs is the idea of community. I don't just mean the local villages, towns and cities in which we live. I mean that our fulfilment as individuals lies in a decent society of others. My argument to you today is that *the renewal of community is the answer to the challenges of a changing world*…. (Blair, 2000; emphasis added)

New Labour's social and economic approach has been characterised as a 'third way' beyond both the old statist notions of traditional labourist social democracy, and the market-centred neoliberalism of the new right (Giddens, 1998, 2000). It is arguably within this distinction that the notion of 'community' has regained its salience. Although the concept of the 'third way' is the source of much debate (Hay, 1999; Finlayson, 2003; Hale et al, 2004), it remains an important narrative of what the current government claims to be about. The significance here is the extent to which the 'third way' acts as an ideological context which might privilege activity beyond the state in civil society, and in particular voluntary and community action. The Prime Minister made a more explicit ideological connection between the third way and the voluntary and community sector in a speech to the National Council for Voluntary Organisations (NCVO) in January 1999 (Blair, 1999):

> In the second half of the century we learnt that government cannot achieve its aims without the energy and commitment of others – voluntary organisations, business, and, crucially, the wider public. That is why the Third Sector is such an important part of the Third Way…. And history shows that the most successful societies are those that harness the energies of voluntary action, giving due recognition to the third sector of voluntary and community organisations.

But the community turn has not just been a politician's or speechwriter's rhetorical flourish. In the first place some of these ideas resonate quite strongly with academic and theoretical debates around communitarianism (Etzioni, 1997), the significance of civil society (Deakin, 2001) and most recently 'social capital' (Putnam, 1993, 2000). Secondly, since 1997 the government has sought to develop a deeper and clearer relationship with the sector in practice, so much so that one recent commentator has suggested that the sector is now being brought into the mainstream of the policy-making process (Kendall, 2003, pp 44-65). This can be seen in many policy developments, but perhaps stands out in four main initiatives:

- the unprecedented launch in November 1998 of the national compact on relations between government and the voluntary and community sector (Home Office, 1998): a set of principles and undertakings that provide a framework for relations between government and the range of organisations in the sector.

Increasingly local compacts are being published and developed throughout the country, although implementation remains patchy (Craig et al, 2005);

- the Cabinet Office Strategy Unit review of charitable law published in September 2002 (Cabinet Office, 2002), being taken forward as new legislation;
- the Treasury review into the role of the voluntary sector in the delivery of public services, also published in September 2002 (HM Treasury, 2002), involving additional resources from the Comprehensive Spending Review for 2003-06; and
- the expansion and relaunch of the Active Community Unit in the Home Office, the primary department with responsibility for the sector, and the associated development of 'civil renewal' as a potential key theme for the government's agenda in the next few years (Blunkett, 2001, 2003).

As part of the emerging 'civil renewal' agenda, former Home Secretary David Blunkett recently stressed the significance of the voluntary and community sector to the government's aspirations and overall programme:

> Departments ... need to reach out to the many voluntary organisations and community groups who are much closer to the problems which government is seeking to address, and *to involve them as strategic partners, valuing their expertise and knowledge and recognising their ability to devise new and different ways to solve difficult problems.* Government needs to be prepared to resource them to do this and develop their capacity to make the contribution of which they are more than capable, providing they have the right kind of support. (Blunkett, 2003, p 26; emphasis added)

Within this short quotation a clear steer is being given by the government on the importance of the sector (its ability to play a part in delivering objectives and the sector being closer to key issues and problems), the reasons why the sector is valued (for its expertise, knowledge and innovative capacity) and some of the problems which need to be addressed in order to fulfil this role (issues of capacity). Perhaps not surprisingly, there is little mention of the potential for more cost-effective or lower-cost provision of services. However, the repeated mention of this array of positive features of the voluntary and community sector is partly why we consider that the sector forms part of a wider 'institutional fix' for the state.

Governance, partnership and capacity building: the tools of the community turn

In this section we look more specifically at what we call the 'tools' of the 'community turn': governance, partnership and capacity building. One key to the 'community turn' is that central government found from experience that its spending on regeneration activity proved wasted if the local community were not thoroughly involved. Local community activists involved in such decision making may be working with larger voluntary organisations, local government and, less frequently, the private sector. They can thus be seen as a cornerstone of sets of *governance* relations extending in two directions, horizontally among other bodies of the area – which may be integrated together in a Local Strategic Partnership (LSP) – and vertically, in a chain of 'multilevel governance' which extends to Whitehall and beyond. Both dimensions are important.

Vertical devolution began to emerge from 1994 when John Major's Conservative government established integrated Government Offices in each region of England with a view to producing *regional* strategies associated with European Structural Funds (Evans and Harding, 1997; John and Whitehead, 1997). 'Regeneration' can be considered at a regional level, implemented principally through local authority districts, but is mainly defined through central government departments using detailed area-based statistics to identify individual neighbourhoods or wards for priority and funding. Add in the phenomenon of the European Union establishing 'priority *wards*' in areas receiving Structural Funds and it appears that in relation to agendas around regeneration and social exclusion, a *new spatial ladder of English governance* has been developed, as detailed in Table 2.1 below.

Given the complexity of relationships within and between the rungs of this ladder, it is appropriate to consider whether, beyond the rhetoric, power has been passed from central government to local communities. There would certainly

Table 2.1: The new spatial ladder of English governance

Primary scale	Actors/entities
Local	**Parish and Town Councils** (elected)
Local	**Neighbourhoods**, often used synonymously in government policy and statistics with **electoral wards**, and containing one or more residents' associations or community partnerships
Local	**Taskforce** and other bespoke action areas often defined as groups of wards for specific initiatives, such as industrial recovery, education, sport or children
District	**Local authorities** (elected), with other statutory agencies, private sector and voluntary and community sector representation bodies in an accredited **Local Strategic Partnership**
Subregional	**Subregional partnerships** (superimposed in some cases on an elected county council where they exist)
Regional	**Regional Development Agencies**, **Regional Assemblies** (of local authorities and regional institutions) and **Government Regional Offices**
National	**Central government departments and Parliament**
European Union	**Regional and Structural Funds**

seem to be a genuine element of devolution in the requirement for consultation of local people and community groups through community appraisals and other participatory mechanisms before schemes can go ahead. But in reality it is often the local authority regeneration department that has the best knowledge and networking position to deploy schemes, especially when several of the government's national regeneration programmes have been instigated within rather compressed timeframes without much time for consultation. However, we can itemise the main elements of the reorganised state as follows:

- The *projection of rights and responsibilities* onto individual partnerships represents the basis of a new contract for civil society; no longer is the national welfare state seen as competent to deal with most eventualities. Local people are now expected to work together and shoulder the responsibility for the condition, health or future development of their area; 'neighbourhood' and 'community' have been invoked as part of an attempt to shift the onus for addressing deeper social inequalities.
- The *localisation of policy failure* today stands in marked contrast to the past parliamentary demand for some central compensating mechanism which characterised the old 'top-down' regional policy. As an example, it was the Regional Development Agency and its appointed consultants who were getting all the bitter flak from local people over the closure of a local cement works as the main employer in the Pennine valley of Weardale in 2003 – not the national Department of Trade and Industry.
- The *centralisation of accounting for success*, with the threat of reduced funding and the possible imposition of government managers in failing authorities, schools or hospitals, is reflected in a renewed aim to implement national 'floor targets'.

The key mechanism through which these developments are enacted is the notion of *partnership*, implying an attempt to 'join up' the efforts to engage in physical, social and economic regeneration all over the country. Much has been written about the supposed benefits of 'partnership' working as a set of governance arrangements embracing joint collaboration between different stakeholders: government and other bodies in the community, voluntary and private sectors. Often, in practice, however, it may be viewed more instrumentally. For example, Osborne and Ross (2001, p 82) suggest that 'Partnership has fast become the "buzz word" to sprinkle liberally through any funding application in order to improve its chances of success'. There can be little doubt about the prevalence of partnership activity in the UK, often brought into being by the requirements and financial inducements of different grant regimes. The Government Office for the North East recently estimated that it is involved in about 160 partnerships, and it is common to report 40 or 50 in individual local authority districts. Beyond this, we can see that partnership has run with the grain of policy (Wilson and Charlton, 1997), because New Labour have generally stressed the issues that *require* cross-cutting joined-up governance – health and crime for example –

and these topics tend to draw in groups which are otherwise lacking from many local authority activities, for example, women, black and minority ethnic (BME) groups and young people.

Some of the origins of partnership working lie in the government's Modernisation Agenda for local government, involving an explicit rejection of the role of local authorities if they failed to modernise, matched by a new theoretical recognition of the world beyond the state. Thus:

> The days of the all-purpose authority that planned and delivered everything are gone…. It is in partnership with others – public agencies, private companies, community groups and voluntary organisations – that local government's future lies. Local authorities will still deliver some services but their distinctive leadership role will be to weave and knit together the contribution of the various local stakeholders. (Blair, 1998, p 13)

Prior to this, local authorities and the private and voluntary sectors had rarely joined together other than in temporary alliances in order to compete for the government's successive 'Challenge' Funds for regeneration and development. More recently the voluntary sector has increasingly been expected to play a more central part in these partnerships. It was the 2000 Local Government Act that required local authorities to prepare comprehensive Community Strategies working in partnership with the private, voluntary and community sectors in LSPs, a body of 20-80 people in each district. We suggest here that the national requirement for LSPs, which derived from a full review of deprivation and social exclusion, was an attempt to integrate the policy structure inherited to date; one of the aims of these partnerships is, for example, to *reduce complexity* by merging and joining up existing partnerships within its district, *and* to act as the 'steward' in government for the attainment of minimum national standards of different national ministries ('floor targets') in individual areas.

In the event, some voluntary organisations have gained an enhanced role as members of LSPs, winning access to the more established ring of stakeholders from statutory bodies. Community representation normally amounts to about three or four people on each LSP, but there are examples where they are judged as unrepresentative or commonly felt left out of decision making in sectoral policy groups. On the other hand, it can be argued that their representation is almost as great, in terms of numbers, as that of elected councillors. In many places there is considerable rivalry between councillors and community representatives over roles and different forms of legitimacy. The new role for councillors in many strategic and other partnerships is a remarkable change compared with past practice. The lack of change through democratic accountability in elections has arguably been replaced with change through periodic convulsions in some of the largest city partnerships, involving resignations of senior board members and managers and their replacement through government intervention. In this sense ultimate accountability flows through to central government.

At the time of writing, progress on LSPs regarding the 'mainstreaming' and coordination of stakeholders' work varies considerably between areas, with few LSPs having developed their strategies to detailed area and neighbourhood levels. The roles played by the voluntary and community sector are still somewhat embryonic. A major question, however, is whether under the Labour government the voluntary sector can be seen as more of a genuine partner (Taylor, 2001), involved not just in subcontracted work but in shaping priorities and formulating projects from inception. This can be an issue of variable *capacity*, which is uneven both spatially and in terms of institutional scales. This results partly from partnership fatigue and 'initiativitis'. There are too many partnerships, and too many initiatives, but not enough partners. Variable capacity is also a question of clout and credibility, as well as legitimacy, about those who have the time or resources to sit on various partnerships. The agents of partnership governance tend to wear many 'hats' and these are often at several different organisational and strategic scales.

There is, however, practical infrastructure support for the voluntary and community sectors in the shape of a range of 'Local Development Agencies' including Councils for Voluntary Service (CVSs) and Rural Community Councils, which provide *capacity building* support and services to local groups, and promote and support volunteering. In addition, the government provided national funds through regional offices in the Community Empowerment Fund, a three-year programme (2001/02-2004/05) designed to be used in the 88 most deprived local authority areas in England which qualify for the 'Neighbourhood Renewal Fund' (NRF) to facilitate an equal voice for the community sector in LSPs.

In general it is useful to appreciate that it is *development* and *project* expenditure that has so far been delegated to autonomous funding regimes. These are the subject of bids and accounting claims from the partnership bodies, in which the role of local authorities has been contained relative to the voluntary and community sectors. Much of the field of local project development requires *matched funding arrangements*, under which two or more sources of funds are required, meaning that the scheme must be seen as a priority by more than one (possibly isolated) body. A common criticism in national comment is that the lead partners for submissions require signatures from all kinds of unelected bodies, and have to go round and collect them in the last week before the government deadline. Some of these self-same bodies remain sleeping partners thereafter. In one case in a major city in the North East, one of the present authors was contracted to interview named partners of an early regeneration scheme. Such had been the changes and delays in securing funds that these partners had forgotten they were partners at all. In many cases, the private sector disappears from a partnership when pressures of time relative to the apparent gains exert themselves. Local authorities often remain as 'lead' bodies, but are partly dependent on a network of 'managing agents', such as the staff of subregional voluntary organisations, for the development and delivery of regeneration projects.

Rather than work getting lost in the general budget and overall performance of, say, a traditional local authority department with tenured staff, the use of a voluntary body which bids for the use of these shorter-term project funds is expected to produce results to a deadline from staff who can be identified and judged from the work. With the possible addition of a 'charitable ethos' embracing particular values, they might do a more reliable job in delivering a contracted-out service than the parent department itself. The strict methodologies for project applications, the regular auditing of expenditure and the evaluation of schemes might augur well for increasing the impact of schemes on the ground. However, it remains important to realise that the pressures of financial survival are very serious for autonomous bodies (Russell et al, 1995; Alcock et al, 1999); they need their own skills and training in modern procedures, computing, accounting and cash flow. Their unpaid governing bodies have to pay first attention to the probity and accounts of the organisation. Thus, their agendas tend to be dominated by housekeeping items, rather than assessments of the impact of their work. The governance of this area has been partly transferred to a group of committed, hard-working, unpaid and (mainly) non-elected individuals, prone to overwork (Taylor, 2001) at a time when people's giving of time to be councillors is in decline.

A 'new institutional fix'? Interpreting the community turn

We have described some features of the 'community turn' in practice. Here we aim to explain why the 'community turn' might be seen as part of an 'institutional fix'. In an important argument Peck and Tickell (1994) suggested that neoliberalism and other developing ideologies represented various attempts by governing elites to respond to an ongoing 'after Fordist' crisis.

The essence of their argument was that the postwar economic and social settlement, with its 'Fordist' emphasis on mass production and mass consumption, underpinned by Keynesian demand management and a comprehensive welfare state, was gradually unravelling. Contrary to prevailing arguments, they suggested that a stable form of 'post-Fordism', involving more flexible production systems, labour processes and welfare arrangements, would not automatically arise. Instead, the period 'after Fordism' was marked by continuing economic and social instability, with no enduring solution. Instead they note a relentless search for a 'new institutional fix' – a coordinated array of mechanisms designed to stabilise a changing economy and society.

Here, we borrow this concept and use it in a slightly more concrete way. The concept allows us to identify the way a particular policy direction – the 'community turn' – and a particular social and economic sector – the voluntary and community sector – is being used as a putative solution to a variety of policy dilemmas and constraints facing governments. In short, the voluntary and community sector helps government elites 'solve' (for the time being at least) a number of different problems. However, it is neither a settled nor uncontested solution. An 'institutional fix' continually evolves through contest, negotiation and deliberation.

To make sense of the 'community turn', it is necessary to look back over the dramatic shifts in the political economy since the 1970s. These shifts have tended to privilege governmental strategies which impose limits on the scope of progressive social policies, as well as strategies which can be distinguished from the spiralling costs and inefficiencies said to be characteristic of the public sector. It is amidst this complicated context that an enhanced role for the voluntary and community sector arises.

Throughout the 1990s policy makers have placed an increasing emphasis in relation to welfare issues on different policies of 'structural adjustment' (Pierson, 1998). This new focus, which seeks to align policies with what are seen to be the necessities of an increasingly global economic system, has replaced earlier concerns with the emergence of a crisis (in the 1970s) and how it came to be contained or managed (in the 1980s). The 'fiscal crisis' associated with the 1970s led to arguments around an 'overloaded' or ungovernable state in which increasing public expenditure threatened to crowd out private investment and consumption (O'Connor, 1973; Gough, 1979; Offe, 1984). Subsequent debate has mainly focused on the different responses of states and political elites to this 'crisis' (Pierson, 1994; Esping-Andersen, 1996). In the UK, as in some other states, neoliberal based governments in the 1980s and early 1990s sought to retrench and reshape the welfare state, involving efforts to introduce competitive market disciplines into public services, through privatisation, marketisation and new forms of managerialism. In those areas where the state has become increasingly subject to international economic pressures, social policies, in particular around social assistance and labour market policy, have similarly become more focused on supporting and enhancing competitiveness. In areas less sensitive to economic competitiveness states have sought to contain costs by improving efficiency and productivity, using privatisation and quasi-markets to introduce 'market disciplines' into the state (Pierson, 1998).

The overall social, political and economic context behind the rise of the 'community turn' can be summarised as the complex outcome of four developmental trajectories, as indicated in Table 2.2 and described below.

Watson and Hay (2003) argue that key figures in the development of 'New' Labour appropriated a *necessitarian* 'logic of no alternative' in their interpretation of the economic, political and social implications of globalisation. The adoption of a strong version of globalisation, with its requirement for a counter-inflationary macroeconomic orientation, economic competitiveness and a less actively interventionist state, implied that exogenous economic imperatives severely circumscribed the potential for a progressive and expansionary economic and social programme. The discursive construction of globalisation appears to have become more significant than the rather patchier evidence that makes up the

Table 2.2: Some contextual features behind the 'community turn'

Government political strategy	Government–citizen relationships
'Necessitarianism' (Watson and Hay, 2003) In this perspective globalisation creates exogenous imperatives for state policies which can only be breached with considerable cost. In particular, states must reshape policies in order to pursue and safeguard their own 'competitiveness'. This cannot be threatened by the expansive social welfare programmes associated with social democracy, and implies continuing constraints on state expenditures.	**'Disentitlementarianism'** (Peck, 1998) The basis on which citizens receive welfare support is being changed so that a passive 'something for nothing' approach is being gradually replaced by an active 'something for something' approach. This involves a redefinition of responsibility for welfare and in some areas makes entitlement conditional on particular forms of activity. In order to benefit from welfare services, recipients are increasingly expected to contribute and participate in certain ways.
'Managerialism' (Clarke and Newman, 1997) Faced with particular constraints – from above (global imperatives) and from below (electoral demands for low taxation) – states pursue performance-oriented strategies that seek to ensure 'more for less' from public services. This can be seen in the continuing use of output- and target-based regimes of accountability associated with the 'New Public Management', emphasising value for money, efficiency and effectiveness.	**'Communitarianism'** (Driver and Martell, 1997) In this view citizens are part of a whole inclusive community, and as well as having rights, owe certain reciprocal obligations to that community. The state's role is to enforce the acknowledgement and performance of these duties. Alongside this notion of 'rights and responsibilities', there is a greater emphasis on *participation* in the community – be that through labour markets or through community-based activity.

'reality' of globalisation in the first place. As Watson and Hay argue (2003, p 295) 'In this way, the contingent logic of social and economic reform with which New Labour has come to be associated is rendered necessary by the appeal to globalisation as an exogenous economic constraint'. However, importantly, they go on to suggest that the adoption of this logic was designed to meet domestic political ends *in advance* of the 1997 General Election. New Labour's electoral strategy was informed primarily by 'preference accommodation' rather than 'preference shaping' (Hay, 1999, ch 2) in which the primary task was not to upset the voters of 'middle England', which was not to be burdened with the higher taxes and heavier public spending associated with 'old' Labour and previous Labour governments.

This informed the pledges made by New Labour prior to the 1997 Election to maintain direct taxation rates at existing levels throughout the subsequent Parliament, and to maintain the existing Conservative government's spending plans for the first two years. Achieving this has meant that the New Labour government has continued, and adapted, the neoliberal emphasis on improving the efficiency of public services under the guise of the 'New Public Management' (Hood, 1991). Arguably this has involved the intensification of the *managerialism* of the state (Clarke and Newman, 1997; Newman, 2001), using specific techniques of performance management, audit, accountability, targets and an emphasis on outputs, outcomes and 'value for money', which has continued to be the defining characteristic of New Labour's approach to public policy and public services. Underpinned by public choice perspectives in political economy, this approach aims to increase the impact of public services while constraining the costs. By seeking to provide 'more for less', it must therefore be seen as a tool for dealing with essential services without increasing the burden of taxation and, as such, part of the ongoing politics of public expenditure constraint.

Several commentators have characterised the neoliberal political economy of welfare, including that followed for the most part by the New Labour government, as one of welfare retrenchment (Hay, 1998). The reality is perhaps a little more complex, and certainly contested among commentators (see Annesley, 2001). At stake here is the interpretation of such developments as the increasing focus on employment-centred social policy, backed by a stronger emphasis on conditionality and sanctions. This reorientation of the basis of citizenship has been termed by Peck, in the context of the US, as a particular form of the politics of *disentitlementarianism* (Peck, 1998). In some versions of this politics, problems of poverty and deprivation are reformulated into problems of 'welfare' and the behaviour of welfare recipients. If 'welfare' (now a term of abuse) is the real problem, then welfare needs 'reform'. Debates in the US have resonated quite strongly in the UK, where New Labour's 'new contract' for welfare requires the fashioning of a new welfare relationship between citizens and the state (DSS, 1998). 'Workfare' conditionality, involving a rebalancing of 'rights and responsibilities', and encapsulated in the government's New Deal employment programmes, operates under the new reciprocity principles of 'something for something' and 'hand-ups' rather than 'something for nothing' and 'handouts'.

New Labour's continued emphasis on 'rights and responsibilities' forms part of its adoption of a form of *communitarianism* as one of the guiding threads of 'third way' political philosophy (Driver and Martell, 1997; Heron, 2001). However, this agenda appears to run in two directions. On the one hand, rhetorically at least as we have seen, government ministers have made great play of themes of reviving community spirit, and have shown a great deal of interest in notions of community capacity, capability and social capital (PIU, 2001; Civil Renewal Unit, 2004). However, on the other hand, Driver and Martell (1997) and Heron (2001) argue that from a range of possible communitarian*isms*, New Labour has adopted and used a particularly regressive and conservative form, associated mainly with Etzioni (1997), in which the state takes on a strong proactive role in enforcing the acknowledgement and performance of obligations and duties which all citizens owe to the community as a whole (Hale, 2004). This can be seen in a number of policy areas, such as labour market policy, criminal justice and 'anti-social behaviour', and over education policy and the treatment of truancy. The guiding emphasis appears to be the need for the state to regulate and condition behaviour in order to strengthen the 'community'.

This quartet of trajectories – necessitarianism, managerialism, disentitlementarianism and communitarianism – which lie at the heart of the government's approach, has led to the intensification of a 'community turn' in public policy. In this, politicians, policy makers and think-tanks, both rhetorically and in policy formulation, have become increasingly interested in 'community-based' approaches across a wide range of policy areas (Imrie and Raco, 2003; Nash and Christie, 2003; Taylor, 2003). The task appears to involve seeking to construct strategies and policies somehow embedded in the idea of 'community', despite the conceptual difficulties accompanying the term. The argument here is that this approach is primarily designed to achieve 'third way' objectives for social and economic policy in an era characterised by continuing cost constraints. New Labour's mildly progressive aspirations, pursued by a range of 'quietly redistributive' measures (Lister, 1998, 2001), are tempered by the need to maintain its fiscal credibility with financial markets, the media and its electoral coalition dominated by the swing voters of 'middle England'. As a result New Labour has become increasingly interested in fashioning 'costless solutions to social problems' (Mohan, 2000; Mohan and Mohan, 2002). The 'community turn', reflected in the interest in concepts such as community capacity and social capital, in a new localism which emphasises community-based approaches to regeneration and tackling social exclusion, and in new policy developments such as the compact, LSPs and support for the role of the voluntary sector in public services delivery, is fundamentally part of this relentless search for more effective, costless solutions, 'beyond-the-state'. As such, it is appropriate to think of this 'turn' as part of an 'institutional fix', designed to achieve social and economic ends in a period marked by the unravelling and reshaping of the guideposts of the relatively comprehensive (social democratic) welfare settlement. In this new approach, an emphasis on redistribution, tackling inequality and a less meagre social security benefits system are rendered politically 'off-limits'. Instead, New Labour offers enhanced opportunities for 'participation' – in the labour market, in local decision making and in community activity and volunteering.

Arguably Jessop provides the most sophisticated account of the new political economy of the welfare state (1994, 1999, 2002). He maintains that part of the process of unravelling the Fordist regime of accumulation that characterised the 'Golden Age' postwar years is a complex reorientation of the state. Rather than a simple withdrawal or retrenchment, capitalist states are undergoing a complex 'hollowing out', involving a dispersal of powers and responsibilities upwards (to supranational bodies), downwards (to devolved regional, local and neighbourhood levels, as indicated in Table 2.1 above) and outwards (to a range of non-state actors and institutions). He posits a gradually emerging, but contingent and contested shift, from what he calls the 'Keynesian Welfare National State' (or 'KWNS'), exemplified in the postwar 'Golden Age' of Fordism, to a possible

'Schumpeterian Workfare Postnational Regime' (or 'SWPR') (Jessop, 1999, 2002). This is shown in Table 2.3 below.

The 'community turn' has some significance when seen in the light of the latter two dimensions of Jessop's quartet, that is, in relation to changes from 'national to postnational' scales and from 'state to regime' as preferred mode of governance. The national scale is no longer the primary locus of economic and social policy and political power, where both sub- and supranational scales are increasingly important. In this view, the apparent focus on local activity is part of a complex 'rescaling' of political, social and economic life. Additionally the shift from 'state' to 'regime' signals that non-state actors have increasingly become important elements in governance. Our relatively concrete description of governance and partnerships, involving new roles for the voluntary and community sector, becomes the notion of 'heterarchy' in Jessop's more abstract terms (Jessop, 2000). This is noted as a potential response to both market and state failure and implies 'horizontal self-organisation among mutually interdependent actors' (Jessop, 2000, p 15). It stresses the role of dialogue, negotiation and attempts to build locked-in interdependencies and solidarity across organisational and sectoral boundaries. In this view the state retains significant powers to steer different systems 'from a distance', by influencing not only the scales of economic and social activity, but also the context in which other actors at different scales operate, including here the voluntary and community sector.

Jessop suggests that a range of ideal-typical 'SWPR' variants may be envisaged, including neocommunitarian strategies, which:

> ... emphasise the contribution of the 'third sector' and/or the 'social economy' (both located between market and state) to economic development and social cohesion and the role of grassroots (or bottom up) economic and social mobilisation in developing economic strategies. They also emphasise the link between economic and community development, notably in empowering citizens and community groups; the contribution that greater self-sufficiency can make to reinserting marginalised local economies into the wider economy; and the role of decentralised partnerships that embrace not only the state and business but also diverse community organisations and other local stakeholders. (Jessop, 2000, p 179)

Table 2.3: From the KWNS to the SWPR

	Economic policy	Social policy	Scale	Mode of governance
from the 'KWNS'	Keynesian	Welfare	National	State
to the 'SWPR'	Schumpeterian	Workfare	Postnational	Regime

It is arguable, then, that the 'community turn' represents a core element of a neocommunitarian strategy. Two important aspects need to be drawn out here. First, the encouragement and expansion of the voluntary and community sector is best seen as part of a broader project to restructure the postwar welfare state in an era of fiscal constraint. The voluntary and community sector is attractive because it is thought to involve relatively inexpensive ways to supplement, complement and potentially replace, restructured welfare services. It offers the prospect of doing more with less money in fiscally constrained times. But given that a restructured welfare state involves different aims and objectives (that is, from 'passive' assistance to 'active' support), the voluntary and community sector also offers the prospect of doing things differently, more effectively and more responsively in a reoriented welfare state. Second, the 'community turn' and its concrete manifestation in the deployment of the voluntary and community sector also offers two less remarked on advantages for government elites: the possibility of politically being seen to address particularly intractable problems, such as deprivation and exclusion, but also the prospect of devolving responsibility to the voluntary sector for the success or otherwise of new policy approaches and initiatives. The voluntary and community sector thus becomes a potential 'dumping ground', both for difficult issues and for policy responsibility (Seibel, 1989).

A new landscape of voluntarism?

By way of conclusion, it is worth considering the broader geographical consequences of the 'community turn' for voluntarism and for the changing welfare state. As we have seen, the institutional fix is having significant consequences at a local level, as new initiatives and agendas reshape existing relationships between local government and the voluntary and community sector. These relationships involve the negotiation of various interdependencies between statutory authorities and voluntary organisations. For example, local authorities provide resources, including leadership and financial resources, whereas voluntary organisations and community groups provide the possibility of bringing additional resources into a local area (for example, funding from charitable and other sources), and generating additional resources within a local area (for example, volunteering, community capacity and social capital). They can also add an additional sense of legitimacy to newly emerging strategies, in terms of the extent to which they can be seen as 'close' or responsive to grassroots concerns. But faced with their own dependencies, capacity constraints and financial insecurities, voluntary organisations and community groups are not necessarily unwilling participants in the 'community turn'.

However, the variety, turbulence and complexity of overlapping partnerships, responsibilities and area-based programmes mean that the impact of the 'community turn' both varies across space and changes rapidly. With the current vogue for locally organised and area-based initiatives, intense spatial targeting with time-limited project and programme funding, further layers of complexity are being added to an already diverse voluntary and community sector. New projects and organisations are developed, new institutional structures for participation are created and new forms of competition between voluntary and community sector agencies develop as funding regimes emerge and change. The result is that a much more differentiated voluntary and community sector, in spatial, temporal and organisational terms, is being created and promoted at the margins of the welfare state. In effect the voluntary and community sector is being encouraged and promoted, through new funding regimes and programmes, to do some things, with some groups, at some scales, in some places, over defined periods of time. And since policy priorities and programmes appear to change with some frequency, discontinuities through time tend to arise for the provision of services by the voluntary and community sector, and in terms of the stability of those organisations and groups providing services.

The 'community turn' thus involves specific constructions of space, scale and temporality, which have important consequences for the shape and structure of the emerging welfare state. The voluntary and community sector is evidently becoming a significant component of a social programme which seeks to *target* social problems faced by certain groups and in certain areas more closely, not through direct social assistance, but through advice, guidance and specific project activities. However, while some of these issues are addressed in the following chapters, it is not yet clear whether the wider research and policy community has really appreciated or charted the spatial, temporal and organisational differentiation of the voluntary and community sector associated with the 'community turn'.

References

Alcock, P., Harrow, J., Macmillan, R., Vincent, J. and Pearson, S. (1999) *Making Funding Work: Funding Regimes and Local Voluntary Organisations*, York: York Publishing Services.

Annesley, C. (2001) 'New Labour and Welfare', in S. Ludlam and M.J. Smith (eds) *New Labour in Government*, Basingstoke: Macmillan, pp 202-18.

Blair, T. (1998) *Leading the Way: A New Vision for Local Government*, London: IPPR.

Blair, T. (1999) 'Third Sector, Third Way', Speech to the National Council for Voluntary Organisations annual conference, London, 21 January.

Blair, T. (2000) Speech to the Women's Institute's Triennial General Meeting, 7 June.

Blunkett, D. (2001) *Politics and Progress: Renewing Democracy and Civil Society*, London: Demos/Politicos.

Blunkett, D. (2003) 'Civil Renewal: A New Agenda', The CSV Edith Kahn Memorial Lecture, 11 June, London: Home Office.

Cabinet Office (2002) *Private Action, Public Benefit: A Review of Charities and the Wider Not-for-Profit Sector*, London: Strategy Unit Report, Cabinet Office, September.

Civil Renewal Unit (2004) *Firm Foundations: The Government's Framework for Community Capacity Building*, London: Civil Renewal Unit, Home Office, December.

Clarke, J. and Newman, J. (1997) *The Managerial State: Power, Politics and Ideology in the Remaking of Social Welfare*, London: Sage Publications.

Craig, G., Taylor, M., Carlton, N., Garbutt, R., Kimberlee, R., Lepine, E. and Syed, A. (2005) 'The Paradox of Compacts: Monitoring the Impact of Compacts', Online Research report 02/05 (www.homeoffice.gov.uk/rds/pdfs05/rdsolr0205.pdf, accessed 15 March 2006), London: Home Office.

Deakin, N. (2001) *In Search of Civil Society*, Basingstoke: Palgrave.

DSS (Department of Social Security) (1998) *A New Contract for Welfare: New Ambitions for Our Country*, Cm 3805, London: The Stationery Office.

Driver, S. and Martell, L. (1997) 'New Labour's communitarianisms', *Critical Social Policy*, vol 17, no 3, pp 27–46.

Esping-Andersen, G. (ed) (1996) *Welfare States in Transition*, London: Sage Publications.

Etzioni, A. (1997) *The New Golden Rule*, London: Profile Books.

Evans R. and Harding, A. (1997) 'Regionalisation, Regional Institutions and Economic Development', *Policy & Politics*, vol 25, no 1, pp 19–30.

Finlayson, A. (2003) *Making Sense of New Labour*, London: Lawrence and Wishart.

Giddens, A. (1998) *The Third Way: The Renewal of Social Democracy*, Cambridge: Polity Press.

Giddens, A. (2000) *The Third Way and its Critics*, Cambridge: Polity Press.

Gough, I. (1979) *The Political Economy of the Welfare State*, London: Macmillan.

Hale, S. (2004) 'The Communitarian "Philosophy" of New Labour', in S. Hale, W. Leggett and L. Martell (eds) *The Third Way and Beyond: Criticisms, Futures, Alternatives*, Manchester: Manchester University Press, pp 87–107.

Hale, S., Leggett, W. and Martell, L. (eds) (2004) *The Third Way and Beyond: Criticisms, Futures, Alternatives*, Manchester: Manchester University Press.

Hay, C. (1998) 'Globalisation, Welfare Retrenchment and the "Logic of No Alternative": Why Second-Best Won't Do', *Journal of Social Policy*, vol 27, no 4, pp 525–32.

Hay, C. (1999) *The Political Economy of New Labour: Labouring Under False Pretences?*, Manchester: Manchester University Press.

Heron, E. (2001) 'Etzioni's Spirit of Communitarianism: Community Values and Welfare Realities in Blair's Britain', in R. Sykes, C. Bochel and N. Ellison (eds) *Social Policy Review 13: Developments and Debates 2000-2001*, Bristol: The Policy Press, pp 63–87.

HM Treasury (2002) *The Role of the Voluntary and Community Sector in Service Delivery: A Cross Cutting Review*, London: HM Treasury.

Home Office (1998) *Compact: Getting Right Together. Compact on Relations between Government and the Voluntary Sector in England*, Cm 4100, London: Home Office, November.

Hood, C. (1991) 'A Public Management for all Seasons?', *Public Administration*, vol 69, no 1, pp 3-19.

Imrie, R. and Raco, M. (eds) (2003) *Urban Renaissance? New Labour, Community and Urban Policy*, Bristol: The Policy Press.

Jessop, B. (1994) 'From the Keynesian Welfare to the Schumpeterian Workfare State', in R. Burrows and B. Loader (eds) *Towards a Post-Fordist Welfare State?*, London: Routledge, pp 13-37.

Jessop, B. (1999) 'The Changing Governance of Welfare: Recent Trends in its Primary Functions, Scale, and Modes of Coordination', *Social Policy and Administration*, vol 33, no 4, pp 348-59.

Jessop, B. (2000) 'Governance Failure', in G. Stoker (ed) *The New Politics of British Local Governance*, Basingstoke: Macmillan, pp 11-32.

Jessop, B. (2002) *The Future of the Capitalist State*, Cambridge: Polity Press.

John, P. and Whitehead, A. (1997) 'The Renaissance of English Regionalism in the 1990s', *Policy & Politics*, vol 25, no 1, pp 7-17.

Kendall, J. (2003) *The Voluntary Sector: Comparative Perspectives in the UK*, London: Routledge.

Lister, R. (1998) 'Fighting Social Exclusion ... With One Hand Tied Behind Our Back', *New Economy*, vol 5, no 1, pp 14-18.

Lister, R. (2001) 'Doing Good by Stealth: The Politics of Poverty and Inequality Under New Labour', *New Economy*, vol 8, no 2, pp 65-70.

Mohan, J. (2000) 'New Labour, New Localism', *Renewal*, vol 8, no 4, pp 56-62.

Mohan, J. and Mohan, G. (2002) 'Placing Social Capital', *Progress in Human Geography*, vol 26, no 2, pp 191-210.

Nash, V. with Christie, I. (2003) *Making Sense of Community*, London: IPPR.

Newman, J. (2001) *Modernising Governance: New Labour, Policy and Society*, London: Sage Publications.

O'Connor, J. (1973) *The Fiscal Crisis of the State*, New York, NY: St Martins Press.

Offe, C. (1984) *Contradictions of the Welfare State*, London: Hutchinson.

Osborne, S.P. and Ross, K. (2001) 'Regeneration: The Role and Impact of Local Development Agencies', in M. Harris and C. Rochester (eds) *Voluntary Organisations and Social Policy in Britain*, Basingstoke: Palgrave, pp 81-93.

Peck, J (1998) '*Workfare*: A Geopolitical Etymology', *Environment and Planning D: Society and Space*, vol 16, no 2, pp 133-61.

Peck, J. and Tickell, A. (1994) 'Searching For A New Institutional Fix: The After-Fordist Crisis and the Global-Local Disorder', in A. Amin (ed) *Post-Fordism: A Reader*, Oxford: Blackwell, pp 280-315.

Pierson, C. (1998) *Beyond the Welfare State: The New Political Economy of Welfare* (2nd edn), Cambridge: Polity Press.

Pierson, P. (1994) *Dismantling the Welfare State?*, Cambridge: Cambridge University Press.

PIU (Performance and Innovation Unit) (2002) *Social Capital: A Discussion Paper*, London: Cabinet Office, April.

Putnam, R.D. (1993) *Making Democracy Work: Civic Traditions in Modern Italy*, Princeton, NJ: Princeton University Press.

Putnam, R.D. (2000) *Bowling Alone: The Collapse and Revival of American Community*, New York, NY: Simon and Schuster.

Russell, L., Scott, D. and Wilding, P. (1995) *Mixed Fortunes: The Funding of the Voluntary Sector*, Manchester: Department of Social Policy and Social Work, University of Manchester.

Seibel, W. (1989) 'The Function of Mellow Weakness: Nonprofit Organisations as Problem Solvers in Germany', in E. James (ed) *The Nonprofit Sector in Comparative Perspective*, New York, NY: Oxford University Press, pp 177-92.

Taylor, M. (2001) 'Partnership: Insiders and Outsiders', in M. Harris and C. Rochester (eds) *Voluntary Organisations and Social Policy in Britain*, Basingstoke: Palgrave, pp 94-107.

Taylor, M. (2003) *Public Policy in the Community*, Basingstoke: Palgrave.

Watson, M. and Hay, C. (2003) 'The Discourse of Globalisation and the Logic of No Alternative: Rendering the Contingent Necessary in the Political Economy of New Labour', *Policy & Politics*, vol 31, no 3, pp 289-305.

Wilson A. and Charlton K. (1997) *Making Partnerships Work*, York: York Publishing Services.

THREE

Renewal or relocation? Social welfare, voluntarism and the city

Christine Milligan and Nicholas R. Fyfe

Voluntarism in the contemporary UK policy landscape

Since its election to power in 1997, the UK Labour government has played a significant role in raising the profile of the voluntary sector within national policy discourse. As Wrigglesworth and Kendall observe, 'From being a shadow enclave at the periphery of the mental map of policy makers and shapers the [voluntary] sector has increasingly occupied centre stage in their minds' (2000, p 1). Addressing an audience of voluntary organisation representatives in 2004, Labour's Chancellor of the Exchequer, Gordon Brown, declared that since the 1990s there has been 'a quiet revolution in how voluntary action and charitable work serves the community' (www.ncvo-vol.org.uk). This 'quiet revolution' has its roots in the policies of the Conservative governments in the 1980s and 1990s. Articulating arguments advanced by many on the political right, the Conservatives championed the third sector as an antidote to an unresponsive, bureaucratic welfare state that stifled choice and community initiative. As a result, voluntary organisations have come to play increasingly important roles in areas such as local community development, health and social services, 'often in contractual relationships [with government] through which they received substantial sums of money' (Plowden, 2003, p 416).

The momentum behind developing the role and responsibilities of the third sector in UK society has significantly increased from the late 1990s as part of Labour's programme of welfare reforms (Powell, 1999; Clarke et al, 2000). The ideological and political foundations of this interest lie with the interplay between neoliberalism and neocommunitarianism that has characterised the development of Labour policy. Keen to distance itself from both the 'Old' Labour Left (pro-state, anti-market) and the Thatcherite Right (pro-market and anti-state); 'New' Labour has embraced the political philosophy of the 'third way' (Giddens, 1998). While this contains a neoliberal emphasis on the need to engage with the new 'realities' of globalisation and embrace the market, choice and competition, it also adopts a neocommunitarian stance by stressing the strategic importance of civil society for social cohesion and economic vitality. This neocommunitarian emphasis on civil society has been crucial not only to providing Labour with the type of 'post-Thatcherite edge it wants' (Driver and Martell, 1997, p 36) but also to promoting the role of the third sector within Labour policy discourse. For Labour, the third sector represents the 'organised vanguard' of civil society. 'Civil society', Gordon Brown declared, 'finds its greatest embodiment in the strength of voluntary organisations – a genuine third sector established not for self or for profit but for mutual aid and, most often, to provide help and support for those in need' (Brown, 2004, p 4).

The 'third way' also sees the voluntary sector as integral to the reform of basic public services such as education, health and welfare provision. New Labour has focused on a multilevel partnership approach to service provision. Field (1997) maintained that this represented not just a 'downsizing' of state responsibility but the recreation of a civil society based on partnership between the state, organisations and individuals. Partnership with civil society is thus seen as the means through which a raft of societal and political ills can be combated (Hodgson, 2004). One outcome of this development has been the emergence of a wide range of partnerships comprising state agencies and civil society groups.

The pre-election publication *Building the Future Together: Labour's Policies for Partnership between the Government and the Voluntary Sector* (Labour Party, 1997) gave an early indication of New Labour's commitment to the voluntary sector. This explained that in rejecting the old and arid split between 'public' and 'private' Labour recognised the richness and diversity of independent organisations and their potential (Labour Party, 1997). This commitment to the third sector has now been translated into a range of partnerships and policy initiatives. At a strategic level, the Labour government has introduced voluntary sector 'compacts' setting out commitments by the governments and the voluntary sector in each of the UK's four jurisdictions (England, Wales, Scotland and Northern Ireland) to improve multiagency working. The government has also examined the potential for increasing the role voluntary organisations play in public service delivery (HM Treasury, 2002) and explored the scope for modernising the infrastructure for regulating the third sector (Cabinet Office, 2002). More specific policy initiatives include the Active Communities Initiative, designed to increase the role of volunteering in community life, the New Deal for Communities, focused on involving community organisations in the regeneration of deprived neighbourhoods, and 'futurebuilders', an investment fund to strengthen the service delivery role of voluntary organisations in the areas of health and social care, crime and social cohesion, in education and for children and young people (HM Treasury, 2002, p 32).

In 'mainstreaming' the voluntary sector into public policy, however, it is clear that the government's repositioning of the sector has two distinct but overlapping aims. Firstly, the government wants voluntary organisations to play a more prominent role in the delivery of public services. After years of privatisation under successive Conservative governments, voluntary organisations are recognised as having vital resources to tackle local problems of social exclusion that are now 'outside the reach of state bureaucracy and beyond the interests of the private sector' (Morison, 2000, p 105). The second aim reflects Labour's neocommunitarian inspired 'philosophical enthusiasm for the third sector as an integral part of civil society' (Kendall, 2000, p 542) or, as one government minister put it, voluntary organisations are crucial to the 'reinvigoration of civic life' (Boateng, 2002, p 3). From this perspective, government clearly views voluntary organisations as key sites for promoting social cohesion via the development of citizenship and social capital. Voluntary organisations are seen as providing environments in which individuals can demonstrate their responsibilities as citizens as well as places that provide opportunities for empowerment by involving individuals in the delivery of services, providing 'opportunities for social participation, for democratic involvement at the local level, and thus for active citizenship' (Turner, 2001, p 200). Labour has also embraced the arguments of Putnam and others, that the third sector is a key site for the production and reproduction of social capital, those norms and networks that can improve economic efficiency and social cohesion (Putnam, 1993). As Gordon Brown (2004) confidently declared, 'We know from the theory and evidence on what is called social capital, that societies with strong voluntary sectors and civic society institutions have lower crime, greater social cohesion and better performing economies than those without'.

Standing at the crossroads?

Such laudatory discourse around the potential of the 'third way' cannot be accepted uncritically. Over a decade ago, Wolch (1990) cautioned that voluntary organisations are less accountable to the public than traditional state organisations because they are located outside formal democratic controls. While acknowledging the heterogeneity of the voluntary sector, she argued that increasing numbers of voluntary organisations were becoming intimately linked to the state, either directly or indirectly, through their reliance on state support, regulatory control and/or administrative oversight. Pointing to the emergence of what she referred to as a 'shadow state' apparatus (1990, p xvi), Wolch maintained that such a development signified not only 'profound dangers' associated with the ways in which cutbacks in voluntary activity may be associated with the erosion of basic entitlements, but also that the voluntary sector may become the vehicle for an increasing statisation of social life. With social welfare delivery increasingly channelled through non-state actors, any such development also raises critical questions about the spatially uneven structure of the voluntary sector and the potential impact on those dependent on social welfare services.

The dialectic of state–voluntary sector in[ter]dependence in social welfare has also been the subject of more recent debate. The shift from welfare rights to individual responsibility under a period of conservatism in the 1980s served to disrupt a prevailing pattern of voluntary sector development and provision backed by state grants and charitable support. Charged with increasing welfare responsibilities but reduced budgets (or budgets constrained by state oversight), one response has been a shift towards a new more commercial mode of operation, resulting in a widespread change in how voluntary organisations operate. In the US, for example, Salamon (1999) argued that cutbacks in state funding and the resultant fiscal squeeze faced by voluntary welfare providers led to an increase in fees and charging as a means of replacing lost revenues and a concomitant incursion of the for-profit sector into traditional areas of voluntary action. In the UK, the reduction in grant aid in favour of alternative funding mechanisms such as ring-fenced funding, competitive tendering and 'best value' meant that many voluntary welfare organisations found themselves subject to increasing administrative oversight and accountability from their state funders. In the drive to professionalise their services to meet these new demands some organisations have sought to change and rationalise their working practices and mode of operation, resulting in a distancing of their administrative centres from the communities they were set up to serve (Milligan and Fyfe, 2005).

As a consequence of these actions, voluntary organisations have found themselves subjected to criticisms about their motives for change and for taking on these new welfare roles. Questions have been raised about the extent to which their original mission statement and core values continue to underpin their organisation and its activities or whether organisations have become more concerned with justifying their own existence and protecting their employees (Milligan, 2001). Censure over claims of an over-professionalisation and bureaucratisation of the sector have, thus, resulted in a crisis of legitimacy stemming from how the public *thinks* voluntary organisations should behave (based on traditional notions of altruism and philanthropy) and the reality of how voluntary organisations need to respond to political and economic change in order to survive (Wolch, 1999). Moreover, Salamon (1999) points out that where social programmes fail to successfully alleviate the social and welfare problems of deprived communities, voluntary organisations charged with administering these programmes have found themselves caught in the crossfire between government and its critics.

How voluntary organisations should respond to this crisis in legitimacy has been the subject of much debate. On the one hand, commentators such as Salamon (1999) argue that there can be no return to a mythical 'golden age' of voluntary sector independence, nor can the voluntary sector successfully survive the drift towards marketisation. Rather, he calls for a 'renewal' of the voluntary sector that involves a shift away from traditional voluntary ideals of altruism and duty towards notions of empowerment, self-realisation, self-help and even self-interest. The voluntary sector should therefore rethink its role and operations, to reach a new consensus about its relationship with the statutory and private sectors and the community, one that jettisons the drive to maintain independence in favour of partnership working towards solving social and welfare problems. Under this scenario, arm's-length philanthropy must reconcile with citizen involvement and active engagement in seeking to solve societal problems and in making decisions over what causes are most worthy of support. On the other hand, Wolch (1999) argues that rather than trying to hold the centre of civil society through embracing partnership models of working, the voluntary sector should actively decentre – relocate to the margins – away from 'dominant institutions, powerful groups and privileged places' (p 25) in an attempt to create a new, more inclusive social contract. It is only by decentring, she maintains, that we can 'challenge the entrenched myths about sectoral independence and philanthropic values and enable voluntary organisations to address the profound problems that confront many societies today' (1999, p 26).

The views of Salamon and Wolch represent two polarised responses to the crisis of legitimacy within the voluntary sector. Neither are problem free. On the one hand, Deakin (1995) warns us of the 'perils of partnership' for voluntary organisations where partnership working is formed and performed on an uneven playing field. On the other, as Brown's (1997) work on AIDS activism in Vancouver clearly demonstrates, by opting to remain on the margins in order to act as 'spaces of resistance', voluntary organisations are likely to find themselves unable to offer the level and amount of welfare services that they could have done had they embraced a mode of partnership working. Decentring to the margins, then, can prove detrimental to the very groups these voluntary organisations set out to support. Other observers of the UK voluntary sector argue that, in reality, what we are seeing is a *bifurcation* of the welfare voluntary sector into 'grassroots' organisations at one end of the spectrum and much larger 'corporatist' welfare organisations on the other (Knight, 1993; Dahrendorf, 2003). Indeed, Knight argued more than a decade ago that 'not only is a divorce happening, but it is highly desirable' in that it would leave decentred, 'grassroots' organisations free to pursue ideals, change and reform (1993, p 297). Medium-sized or large organisations, he maintained, would be more supply-driven because their primary role is to deliver resources, yet as non-profit making organisations, they still fulfil 'a philanthropic or similar purpose in … that the "value-added" of the resources is transferred to the target group and increased in the process' (p 298). Given the significant role such organisations take in the planning and delivery of social welfare in the UK, they are more likely to be engaged in partnership working. The notion of a bifurcation of the voluntary sector thus infers that in reality, the voluntary sector response falls somewhere between the notions of renewal or decentring. Dahrendorf suggests that, in fact, the UK voluntary sector may be characterised as two sectors, 'one genuinely voluntary, happily remote from government … the other linked to government as well as business … subject to all sorts of controls and rules, and voluntary in name only' (preface to Kendall, 2003, p xiv).

How the voluntary sector is responding to the political drive to reposition its role in the planning and delivery of social welfare, and how this is manifest at local level, is explored in the remainder of this chapter. Drawing on case study material from the Scottish city of Glasgow, its concern is to critically examine two key issues. First, it examines the impact of changes in urban policy on voluntary sector development at local level. Second, it discusses how the voluntary sector is engaging with strategies of governance and partnership in contemporary Scotland and the extent to which this can be said to be contributing to a 'renewed' voluntary sector that offers real potential for holding the centre of civil society.

While acknowledging the diversity of the voluntary sector, it is, nevertheless, necessary to have a working definition. For the purposes of our work in Glasgow we thus adopted Taylor's (1992, p 171) definition of the voluntary sector as comprising:

> Self-governing associations of people who have joined together to take action for public benefit. They are not created by statute, or established for financial gain. They are founded on voluntary effort, but may employ paid staff and may have income from statutory sources. Some, by no means all, are charities. They address a wide range of issues through direct service, advocacy, self-help and mutual aid and campaigning.

This definition was adopted as it is closely aligned to that used by the Glasgow City Council (1997) and also accords with that used by Wolch (1990) in her analysis of the 'shadow state'.

Policy, partnership and the shift towards a new localism

Understanding the spatial development of voluntary welfare activity in Glasgow requires an appreciation of the recent history of urban policy making in Scotland. This has been dominated by the Urban Programme – a strategy that has relied on the geographical targeting of aid to a limited number of urban areas facing deprivation and social disadvantage (Taylor, 1988). Initially developed in the late 1960s, local authorities could sponsor projects originating within designated Areas of Priority Treatment (APTs) to bid in an annual competition for resources from central government. Successful initiatives were run by voluntary organisations and community groups within the APTs. Given the territorial extent of deprivation in Glasgow, many areas were eligible for Urban Aid – although not all chose to bid for these funds to support voluntary activity. As our own case material revealed, there was a significant interplay between the structural context provided by central state funding opportunities and the importance of human agency in the form of the bids put forward for Urban Aid by local council area coordinators in different parts of the city. As one local authority official explained, 'Drumchapel did very well out of the Urban Programme mainly because the Area Co-ordinator for the Drumchapel area was zealous in applying for Urban Aid while the then Area coordinator for Easterhouse wasn't'[1].

A review of the Urban Programme in the early 1990s noted that there was a need for greater coordination and integration of projects at local level. In particular, it was concluded that initiatives needed to be better combined with those of other public, private and voluntary sector agencies to address a wider strategic focus (Scottish Office, 1993). As a consequence, the Urban Programme was restructured in the mid-1990s to reflect this within newly designated Priority Partnership Areas (PPAs). The PPA concept encouraged the formation of city-wide partnerships between government and the private, voluntary and community sectors within a strategic framework for urban regeneration focused on specific geographical neighbourhoods. In restructuring the Urban Programme, the criteria for gaining PPA status changed from that of the former APTs. As a consequence, some areas lost out and voluntary organisations within these areas found themselves excluded from this source of income. Yet the changing eligibility criteria did not reflect any geographical change in *deprivation*, rather it was targeted at larger or more densely populated areas, as the coordinator of one voluntary organisation noted, 'the deprivation didn't go away, it didn't stop being a deprived area! But the criteria changed....And we lost that [PPA funding]' (Milligan, 2001, p 126).

In May 1998, the former Secretary of State for Scotland, Donald Dewar, announced a new phase of urban regeneration policy. The PPAs would evolve into new spatially targeted Social Inclusion Partnerships (SIPs), with some new SIPs set up as part of the government's broader social inclusion strategy. This development was viewed as reflecting a specifically Scottish theme as the Secretary of State maintained that, 'Scottish circumstances differ from England in that those suffering from exclusion in Scotland are disproportionately concentrated in specific communities' (Dewar, 1998, p 1). While SIPs build on established arrangements, a key twist has been their emphasis on addressing the perceived dynamics of exclusion and inclusion through a partnership approach based within the local communities. The Scottish Executive laid out clear guidelines about who the key players should be, with SIP boards made up of members drawn from the city council, the public and private sectors as well as representation from the local community and the voluntary sector. Glasgow gained SIP (or similar partnership) status for eight of the most deprived areas of the city. Each SIP was charged with tackling social exclusion within a geographically bounded area and ensuring that the community they represented played an active part both in the decision making of the partnership and in finding solutions for their particular area. In addition, Glasgow gained funding for three city-wide thematic SIPs (focusing on 'routes out of prostitution', young care leavers and GARA – Glasgow Anti-racist Alliance). So while the SIP development has largely retained the Urban Programme's commitment to spatially targeted policies, one innovative feature was the inclusion of some theme-based measures that cut across geographically defined areas of disadvantage and addressed processes of social exclusion within a city-wide context.

SIP developments added a further layer of complexity to the relationship between the voluntary sector and the local state that is of particular significance because it raises questions about how the development of voluntarism is bound up with new forms of governance in the city. In particular, it highlights the increasing importance of institutions that are not bound by traditional forms of accountability to local electorates. The individual SIP boards have an important degree of policy and fiscal discretion over the funding of voluntary sector projects in each SIP area that could be interpreted as a welcome development in terms of localism to social policy. Nevertheless, there are concerns about the more formal accountability of SIP boards to the wider community.

Within Glasgow, the SIP agenda operates within the framework of the Glasgow Alliance (established in 1998), a city-wide partnership whose members represent the key areas of city life, including the Scottish Executive, the City Council, the Greater Glasgow Health Board, Scottish Enterprise, Scottish Homes, Strathclyde Police, the Glasgow Council for the Voluntary Sector and Scottish Business in the Community. The Alliance assists the SIPs by providing a policy framework for action and conflict resolution, as well as facilitating shared learning and providing a range of support services. Its aim is to generate 'joined up thinking and action around key issues in the city' (Glasgow Alliance, 2002/03, p 2). The Alliance is an independent body – a factor viewed as crucial to its success in terms of depoliticising initiatives. Indeed, under the SIP arrangement, it would appear that the role of local government has been largely that of a 'strategic enabler' rather than a central player.

The recent developments in urban policy, outlined above, reflect a neoliberal fascination with 'third way' politics manifest in a discourse of partnership aimed at bringing together key stakeholders from government and the public, private, voluntary and community sectors, to work on key issues such as social exclusion, the alleviation of deprivation, community safety and the creation of healthy communities (DETR, 1998; Home Office, 2002). This strategy has resulted in the emergence of a 'new layer of institutional architecture' (Kendal, 2003, p 76) designed to encourage 'joined-up action' through partnership working with a wide range of agencies and organisations including the public, private, voluntary and community sectors (DETR, 1998, para 8.21). These partnerships often operate both in geographically defined spaces and beyond traditional democratic control (Chandler, 2000; Milligan and Fyfe, 2004). That is, local government has increasingly become one partner among many in partnership boards whose role encompasses the planning, development and delivery of services and strategies aimed at urban renewal and the alleviation of deprivation. As one Glasgow official noted:

> ... the culture of the old Urban Programme was that the council controlled the money, *they* decided where it went and where it went locally. That culture is *gone* now, because *they* don't make the decisions. Whether the Alliance likes a decision of not, SIP boards can make it as long as its within the rules. That's really quite, quite different to how the council would make its decisions.

Of course this must not be overstated given that the city council continues to play a key role in the funding of voluntary sector organisations. Nevertheless, in areas of most acute deprivation, the development of voluntarism is being significantly influenced by institutions that are largely funded centrally (that is, from Edinburgh), and following an agenda that has no formal democratic mandate. As one council official explained:'The decisions are taken locally over which we have no direct control. You could argue that a councillor is on the board [of each SIP] but the councillor can be outvoted and quite often is'. A key facet of this shift towards partnership working has therefore been the emergence of new localised spaces of governance, ones that operate in hybrid forms between the state and civil society (Brown, 1997).

Re-spatialising the voluntary welfare sector in Glasgow

The changing landscape of urban policy has had a considerable impact on how and where the local voluntary welfare sector develops. The Urban Programme, changes from APTs to PPAs, and the more recent SIP development have all had differing, but geographically defined, eligibility criteria attached to voluntary sector funding opportunities. While the skewing of funding is targeted at areas of greatest need, it also raises a number of problems. Each of these programmes has laid down layers of state funding potential for voluntary organisations in different parts of the city for limited periods of time. The net effect has been to create a dynamic mosaic of opportunities for voluntary organisations to develop services in spatially defined communities, but in doing so it can also create complex patterns of voluntary sector inclusion and exclusion. For example, the strong element of localism in the SIP programme meant that each SIP board was able to set its own strategic objectives. So while the Greater Pollock Partnership identified community capacity building and empowerment as one of its strategic aims and Greater Easterhouse identified 'image and communication', these themes were not common to all.

With SIPs setting their own priorities, some voluntary organisations found it difficult to establish a presence in some SIP areas. This has been a particular difficulty for organisations serving the needs of 'unpopular' client groups (for example, mental health and domestic violence). As the coordinator of a mental health organisation explained: 'the SIP thing is a particular problem because we cannot get mental health on the social inclusion agenda'. The inability to access such an important source of funding therefore had a significant impact on how specific subsectors have been able to develop across the city. The requirement that organisations should be physically located within a SIP area to be eligible for funding also acted to exclude those voluntary organisations set up to serve a city-wide agenda, as one commentator noted:

> In the social inclusion partnerships they [voluntary organisations] can see where the decision-making is because it's local. That creates quite serious difficulties for some of the big voluntary organisations

that cover the whole city that may not be active in any local area. This is a big difficulty, one that we haven't resolved yet.

Furthermore, because each SIP area has funding available for voluntary organisations to deliver services that contribute to the wider inclusion agenda, it contributed to what one local observer referred to as a 'feeding frenzy' for funding among non city-wide organisations as they targeted SIP areas as places for further service development.

The emerging pattern of inclusion and exclusion has been further exacerbated by those areas that did not receive funding through these territorially based funding programmes. As one voluntary sector respondent put it:

> These [SIP] areas have always had a heightened level of voluntary activity that has to a large extent been manufactured by the amount of resources that's available, but in other parts of Glasgow there is dearth of voluntary activity ... the social inclusion programme by its very nature creates another tier of indirect social exclusion.

Turok and Hopkins (1998) maintain that such areas can find themselves doubly penalised where the skewing of financial resources towards successful areas results in a progressive diversion of resources from losers, while the 'winner takes all' as a result of complex co-funding arrangements. As one city council respondent put it: 'not only do SIP monies concentrate in these areas, but it means that other agencies in the city think, "oh well, maybe we should concentrate on those SIP areas" – so they lever in more money to these areas whereas those outside felt ... more deprived than they were previously'. Given that SIPs overlapped extensively with previous territorial programmes, the net effect of this change in urban policy has been to reinforce existing patterns of unevenness in the development of voluntarism across the city.

While it can be argued that geographically targeted inclusion initiatives are specifically designed to alleviate problems in the most deprived areas of the city, the geography of need cannot always be packaged neatly into spatially bounded locales. Those who require social welfare support due to age or disability, for example, can be scattered widely across the city. Prudently addressed, the development of thematic SIPs had the potential to redress some of the exclusions noted above. Yet critical questions remain about how decisions were made in relation to the development of thematic SIPs, as one key official noted:

> When the whole social exclusion thing unfolded within the Scottish Parliament, everything was done at great speed, with a lot of pressure and trying to work with what we had ... in terms of people with disabilities, I think there's a good case for having a thematic SIP, but the fact is, that at the time nobody thought of it and the disability

organisations were not in the loop, because I don't think there's a disability SIP anywhere in Scotland.

For some subsectors, then, their inability to access the decision-making process at this critical juncture meant that they found themselves excluded from an important source of funding to develop services for the community of interest they were set up to serve.

As Hodgson (2004) argues, it is not enough to create a multiagency partnership and place it in a given area, thought also needs to be given to the historical experiences of that locale. In this case, early patterns of disparity in accessing resources in Glasgow had a knock-on effect on the longer-term development of local voluntary sector infrastructure and expertise in SIP areas. Commenting on the poor history of success in obtaining Urban Programme funding for the voluntary sector in the area, the chair of one SIP board noted: 'the infrastructure in our area is pitiful…. I feel strongly that we need the experience, expertise and the strength of existing voluntary organisations in other parts of the city to help us understand the system and give us more control…'. The lack of infrastructure and expertise in accessing resources resulted in a local demoralisation that acted to stifle the development of active citizenship within the area. This same respondent went on to note that:

> … the continual rejection of funding or withdrawal has to a certain extent brought people's heads down … if you are in a situation where there appears to be a negative bias towards your area to provide funding or maintain services and projects, then it is very difficult to think that you could actually bring that to the fore.

This limits the pool from which the local voluntary and community sector can draw in seeking to engage effectively in partnership working within these new spaces of governance. It also suggests that rather than stimulating the development of active citizenship, the succession of changes in geographically targeted urban policy initiatives may in fact act to hinder it.

Polarisation or privileged places?

In this final section, we draw on in-depth interview material with key actors from local, regional and national branches of voluntary organisations operating in the subsectors of community safety and black and minority ethnic (BME) groups, to illustrate how organisations have responded to the repositioning of the voluntary sector in the planning and delivery of social welfare in Glasgow.

Partnership working in some areas of social welfare activity is not new. Social services and community safety, for example, have a long history of public–voluntary sector partnership working in Glasgow. As a result, organisations operating in these subsectors have developed close working relationships with the state. As a consequence, they have a greater understanding of how to access and influence the policy process than newer sectors – for example, that which serves the needs of BME communities. As one respondent from the community safety sector commented, 'The way Glasgow does it, it's a very hands on approach, for example the development of the court social work service, we were here, actually tasked to look at that and write the plan for the council'. Being drawn into a closer working relationship with the state through public–voluntary partnerships can, however, have a significant impact on shaping the development and structure of an organisation.

To illustrate this, we draw on a case study of one nationwide voluntary organisation working in the field of community safety. Emerging in the mid-1980s, the origins of the organisation lie in volunteer grassroots developments at local level. With a remit that served both a local and nationwide agenda, local branches of the organisation were soon resourced through a mix of local authority and Scottish Office funding:

> … crime prevention panels were probably the most significant driver in the early stages, closely followed by the regional council (as was) and social work department. The Scottish Office at that point also took an interest, so various levels of resources became available to the organisation as things grew and developed, but in the first instance it was *completely* volunteer led.

As a consequence, 17 different branches of the organisation developed in an ad hoc way across Glasgow, resulting in disparities in what differing branches were able to deliver.

With a remit to support victims of crime, the organisation has a history of partnership working with a range of public sector bodies such as the police, the courts, the criminal justice department and social services. With community safety high on the agenda of both the city council and national government, it has also been closely involved with: local and national policy making; consultative bodies, such as crime prevention panels and community safety partnerships; and has developed strategic links with MSPs (Members of the Scottish Parliament) and officers of the national government. The development of these public–voluntary sector relationships has enabled the organisation to have an input into policy decision making and to expand their services widely across Scotland. However, as the Glasgow case material reveals, maintaining these relationships has also affected how the organisation has developed.

Firstly, organisational development is shifting away from bottom-up development of services based on grassroots initiatives towards a reactive response to the needs of their public sector partners. As one respondent noted:

> … we work very closely with social work and the police and I think it would be very wrong of us *not* to rise to the challenges they are

presenting ... we can provide a generic service, but we are also being asked to provide much more in-depth issue specific work ... and we have to be geared up to deal with that in a professional manner, because otherwise they are not going to make the referrals to us, they are going to go elsewhere.

Secondly, scrutiny by, and accountability to, their public sector funders together with the need to respond to the requirements of their public sector partners has led to increased levels of bureaucracy and professionalisation within the organisation. As a key individual within the organisation explained:

... they [the Scottish Executive] were saying 'what you've done up to now is great, but frankly in the current climate it's not politically acceptable, you need to be able to deliver services on a more consistent basis across the city'.

As a consequence, the organisation engaged in a process of restructuring resulting in a hierarchical and corporate structure with unified policy and decision making. While the harmonisation of service delivery and standards is designed to improve the quality of services delivered to service users, reorganisation has not been without its casualties. Restructuring has resulted in the loss of local autonomy and local identity, as the local community structure becomes a non-autonomous part of the bigger organisation. These developments have raised anxieties among local volunteers over the distancing of support and concerns that the organisation's flexibility and its ability to make decisions quickly – the traditional strengths of the voluntary sector – are being eroded.

The drive towards professionalisation and the need to deliver more complex services has also meant that the organisation has sought to recruit a new breed of 'specialist volunteers' who receive training to meet these complex needs. This has resulted in traditional volunteers becoming disaffected from the organisation as they feel 'pushed out' in favour of the new professional volunteer. As one member of the organisation explained, 'this increasingly management, performance culture – I'm a professional, I can live with that, and if you work for the government you'll feel like that too, but volunteers don't like it. There's an emerging issue for us that the things they're expected to do is kind of dehumanising the organisation'. This problem was widely recognised by respondents within our study. They noted that while it is clearly important to provide a good quality service, there is also a requirement to remain aware of the needs of local volunteers. One of the difficulties organisations face in the drive towards professionalisation is that it can have the effect of distancing the organisation from civil society, reducing the continuity of contact at local level. Both these aspects of voluntary participation, however, are seen as crucial to the continued and positive engagement of local volunteers with the organisation.

High levels of integration into partnership working and consultation with the state have also created a paradox for the organisation. Continuing to provide complex services makes them important partners in both planning and consultation processes. This, however, requires access to state funding which in turn creates tensions between their ability to campaign for change and knowledge of where their funding comes from. As one respondent commented:

> ... we have formal links with the Scottish Executive because their [X] Department is our primary funder. So there's an interesting tension. There's no doubt that high emphasis on the importance of that campaigning work has harmed our relationship with the Executive in relation to funding and resources. Despite all their promises about open consultation, and the voluntary sector compact, that's not the case and they have told me that off the record.

Campaigning, however, is seen as an activity that is fundamental to the organisation and its volunteers. Indeed, one respondent noted that volunteers *expect* organisations to get on their 'soapbox'. The organisation thus faces a crisis of legitimacy as it seeks to resolve the dilemma of maintaining high levels of integration with the state, in order to meet the rising expectations of both the public and their public sector partners, and meeting the expectations of volunteers without whom they would be unable to operate.

Similar dilemmas emerge at the local level as the new SIP arrangements further muddy the waters. As one respondent from the organisation put it:

> ... we work closely with the Social Inclusion Partnership Board but they can dictate as well, so if they are funding us, we are expected to come up with the goods in certain areas. It means we have to be very fluid in nature, we can't just say well this is the portion [of funding] we'll put in there, we have to look at the various conditions that we are asked to work in and go from there.

For this organisation, it has meant 'stepping outside' the comfortable working arrangements it has developed with the city council over the years to develop new working arrangements, with new partnership boards, each of which have differing sets of priorities. As one coordinator noted:

> ... each of the SIP boards have a different set of objectives, so when I come to do the application form, I've got to look up their aims and objectives because its all about social inclusion, helping people, empowerment etc. So you've got to get it just right for that particular group. I mean this year, for example, the North SIP Board are gonna' say, 'we want new projects, it's not for funding staff or buildings' ... so we have to come up with a new idea there.

While we draw specifically on one case study, here, to illustrate the impact of voluntary–public sector relationships, other national voluntary welfare organisations with branches in Glasgow expressed similar experiences. Rather than lying between the state and civil society, shifts in the relationship and working arrangements between large service-providing voluntary organisations, the public sector and different tiers of the state placed the politics of voluntary welfare development in Scotland in new locations – both beyond and inside traditional state-centred spaces.

Many smaller organisations faced differing experiences. This was particularly true of organisations working to support BME populations. Many of these organisations tend to be smaller, newer and with less experience of partnership working with the public sector and the state. There was evidence that both the local and national state was making a concerted effort to engage with these organisations on policy and planning issues. Organisations claimed, however, that the state often failed to recognise the problem of extensive consultation for small, locally based organisations, with limited resources. As one organisational leader commented:

> If we went to all the meetings that the Local Authority expects people to go to, 'cause they're liasing with the black community, you wouldn't get any work done! A number of years ago we were campaigning for people to actually *be* consulted. The problem is now you're consulted to death!

Organisations run completely by volunteers noted that their inability to engage with structures of the state arose from the state's failure to adapt its discussion mechanisms to meet the needs of volunteers. As a respondent from one such organisation noted, 'our impact on the council is somewhat limited … and the reason we can't do a lot more is because we haven't any paid staff that can work office hours. Because in the evening we'd all be there, but holding them at 10 o'clock, that's impossible'. In fact, we found only limited evidence that BME organisations were engaged in those partnerships and forums where strategic level decision making occurred. To compensate for their lack of experience and influence at the organisational level, many of these smaller organisations revealed that they had joined forces with other larger or umbrella organisations in order to campaign or influence policy. As the coordinator of one BME organisation commented:

> … at the organisational level we need support, we need guidance about how we can lobby about certain issues. But a lot of the time we work alongside Age Concern or other community based organisations because they seem to do more on campaigning and everything so we are just part of them … we don't have a voice on our own to input directly into the Scottish Executive so we would use these groups.

> Obviously it's not as effective as having a direct dialogue with them, but we are still a very small organisation so we cannot work on our own.

Others joined forums such as the GARA and the Scottish Refugee Councils as a means of developing wider links and influence in the policy-making process.

Interestingly, the dilemma of funding versus the ability to campaign was seen as less of an issue for many BME organisations. In part, this arose from the fact that the BME sector in Glasgow was far smaller than other voluntary welfare subsectors, hence the local and national states were keen to encourage their development. In part, a thematic SIP for the BME sector had been funded in Glasgow, thus organisations did not face the same exclusions or geographically targeted funding difficulties that other subsectors did. Finally, some small locally based organisations are interested only in improving the lives of the local community they were set up to serve. Such organisations are content to remain on the margins and hence have no interest in developing links that may enable them to influence a wider policy agenda.

Conclusion

In this chapter, we sought to examine how the UK voluntary sector is responding to the political drive to reposition its role in the planning and delivery of social welfare, and how this is manifest at local level. In examining these issues, we considered conceptual debates around the 'renewal' or 'decentring' of the voluntary sector. This debate has focused mainly on voluntary sector change within the US. Our case study, however, indicates that while the UK voluntary sector may be facing similar challenges, such a polarised debate is perhaps too simplistic and needs to take account of the diversity of the sector both in terms of organisational size and variation in the development of subsectors within the voluntary sector. For voluntary organisations that lack a national/regional presence or who are located in a relatively new subsector that has yet to develop strong working relationships with the state, the issue or decentring or renewal has not been an option. They are, de facto, located on the margins. We did however, find evidence of other organisations that had made a conscious choice to maintain independence by choosing to 'sit outside' partnership structures and seek alternative funding mechanisms. This enabled organisations to develop, lobby and take action for change based on their volunteer membership decision making. While this comes at a cost in terms of expansion of services to their target group, they have nevertheless begun to find ways of influencing the wider policy agenda by working with and through other larger organisations. Other large national voluntary organisations in 'established' subsectors have clearly shifted towards 'renewal', embracing partnership working with both the state and the private sector. Although such organisations are delivering increasingly more and more complex services they can also be seen to be increasingly taking on those characteristics of the 'shadow state'. This development also creates a dilemma for organisations where their ability to lobby and campaign for change is compromised by their dependence on state funding. The delivery of more and increasingly complex services also comes at a cost to volunteering. Such services require fewer, but highly trained, 'professional volunteers'. We have argued elsewhere that these developments are leaving limited 'space for volunteers' (Milligan and Fyfe, 2005), and indeed seem diametrically at odds with the current Labour government's agenda for promoting active citizenship and civil renewal through voluntary action.

This chapter also explored how changes in urban policy and the shift to local governance and partnership working is impacting on local voluntary sector development. These developments in urban policy are, of course, not confined to Glasgow (see Goodwin, 2004; Turok, 2004), but as our case study demonstrated, the changing landscape of urban policy has a considerable impact on how and where local voluntary welfare develops. While these policies are designed to target some of the most deprived areas of the city, they can also act to create complex patterns of voluntary sector inclusion and exclusion. The new SIP development and new institutional architecture set up to manage SIPs has not only acted to reinforce existing patterns of unevenness, but has proven particularly difficult for voluntary organisations serving the needs of 'unpopular' client groups.

In August 2003 the Scottish Executive announced the development of a new framework that will supersede the SIP initiative. SIPs will be integrated within Community Planning Partnerships (CPPs) in an effort to strengthen their contribution to 'closing the opportunity gap between disadvantaged communities and the rest of Scotland' (Scottish Executive, 2003, p 2). From 2005/06 funding will be allocated through a local authority-wide CPP with funding based largely (although not exclusively) on the 2004 Index of Deprivation. It will, however, continue to be geographically targeted, with thematic funding remaining only where a 'more effective and justifiable approach can be put forward' (Scottish Executive, 2003, p 12). The setting of local priorities will be brought to an end, focusing instead on five national priorities built around environment and community safety, work, health, education and engaging young people. Funding to organisations and projects in SIP areas that do not directly contribute to national priorities will be realigned. Hence it is expected that CPPs will move away from funding a wide range of individual and discrete projects towards a limited number of key priorities. How this will play out in practice is yet to be seen, but the changing basis on which the 'geography of need' will be assessed, together with a new emphasis on national priorities, infers that voluntary organisations providing services that do not directly address the five key priorities are, once again, likely to find their funding withdrawn. Rather like a kaleidoscope, then, the mosaic of voluntary welfare in the city will shift, as organisations respond to new national priorities and engage with a new layer of 'institutional architecture' as they seek to respond to this new policy agenda.

Note

[1] Drumchapel and Easterhouse are specific areas within the city of Glasgow.

Acknowledgement

The research on which this chapter is based was funded by the Economic and Social Research Council, Reference No R000223093.

References

Boateng, P. (2002) 'Foreword', in HM Treasury, *The Role of the Voluntary and Community Sector in Service Delivery: A Crosscutting Review*, London: HM Treasury, p 3.

Brown, G. (2004) Speech to the National Council for Voluntary Organisations' Annual Conference (www.ncvo-vol.org.uk).

Brown, M. (1997) *RePlacing Citizenship: AIDS Activism and Radical Democracy*, London: Guilford Press.

Cabinet Office (2002) *Private Action, Public Benefit: The Organisational and Institutional Landscape of the UK Wider Nonprofit Sector*, London: Cabinet Office.

Chandler, D. (2000) 'Active Citizens and the Therapeutic State: The Role of Democratic Participation in Local Government Reform', *Policy & Politics*, vol 29, no 1, pp 3-14.

Clarke, J., Gewirtz, S. and McLaughlin, E. (eds) (2000) *New Managerialism, New Welfare?*, London: Sage Publications.

Dahrendorf, R. (2003) 'Foreword', in J. Kendall, *The Voluntary Sector*, London: Routledge, pp xiii-xiv.

Deakin, N. (1995) 'The Perils of Partnership: The Voluntary Sector and the State 1945-1992', in J.D. Smith, C. Rochester and R. Hedley (eds) *An Introduction to the Voluntary Sector*, London: Routledge, pp 40-65.

DETR (Department of the Environment, Transport and the Regions) (1998) *Modern Local Government in Touch with the People*, London: DETR.

Dewar, D. (1998) 'Tackling Social Exclusion in Scotland', Inaugural Lecture to the Scottish Urban Regeneration Forum, 8 May, Wester Hailes, Edinburgh.

Driver, S. and Martell, L. (1997) 'New Labour's Communitarianisms', *Critical Social Policy*, vol 52, pp 27-46.

Field, F. (1997) 'Welfare: The Third Way', Speech at the Victoria and Albert Museum, 24 September.

Giddens, A. (1998) *The Third Way: The Renewal of Social Democracy*, London: Polity Press.

Giner, S. and Sarasa, S. (1996) 'Civic Altruism and Social Policy', *International Sociology*, vol 11, no 2, pp 139-60.

Glasgow Alliance (2002/03) *Brief Annual Report*, Glasgow: Glasgow Alliance.

Glasgow City Council (1997) *The Council and the Voluntary Sector: Working Together for the Good of the City*, Glasgow: Glasgow City Council Publications.

Goodwin, M. (2004) 'The Scaling of "Urban" Policy: Neighbourhood, City or Region?', in C. Johnstone and M. Whitehead (eds) *New Horizons in British Urban Policy: Perspectives on New Labour's Renaissance*, London: Ashgate, pp 173-84.

HM Treasury (2002) 'The Role of the Voluntary and Community Sector in Service Delivery: A Cross-cutting Review', London: HM Treasury (www.hm-treasury.gov.uk/media/890/03/CCRVolSec02.pdf).

Hodgson, L. (2004) 'Manufactured Civil Society: Counting the Cost', *Critical Social Policy*, vol 24, no 2, pp 139-64.

Home Office (2002) *Draft Guidance on Community Cohesion*, London: LGA Publications.

Kendall, J. (2000) 'The Mainstreaming of the Third Sector into Public Policy in England in the Late 1990s: Whys and Wherefores', *Policy & Politics*, vol 28, no 4, pp 541-62.

Kendall, J. (2003) *The Voluntary Sector*, London: Routledge.

Knight, B. (1993) *Voluntary Action* (2nd edn), London: CENTRIS.

Labour Party (1997) *Building the Future Together: Labour's Policies for Partnership between the Government and the Voluntary Sector*, London: Labour Party.

Milligan, C. (2001) *Geographies of Care: Space, Place and the Voluntary Sector*, Aldershot: Ashgate.

Milligan, C. and Fyfe, N. (2004) 'Putting the Voluntary Sector in its Place: Geographical Perspectives on Voluntary Activity and Social Welfare in Glasgow', *Journal of Social Policy*, vol 33, no 1, pp 73-93.

Milligan, C. and Fyfe, N. (2005) 'Preserving Space for Volunteers: Exploring the Links between Voluntary Welfare Organizations, Volunteering and Citizenship', *Journal of Urban Studies*, vol 42, no 3, pp 417-34.

Morison, J. (2000) 'The Government–Voluntary Sector Compacts: Governance, Governmentality, and Civil Society', *Journal of Law and Society*, vol 27, no 1, pp 98-132.

Plowden, W. (2003) 'The Compacts: Attempts to Regulate Relationships between the Government and the Voluntary Sector in England', *Nonprofit and Voluntary Sector Quarterley*, vol 32, no 3, pp 415-31.

Powell, M. (ed) (1999) *New Labour New Welfare State? The Third Way in British Social Policy*, Bristol: The Policy Press.

Putnam, R.D. (1993) *Making Democracy Work: Civil Traditions in Modern Italy*, Princeton, NJ: Princeton University Press.

Salamon, L.M (1999) 'The Non-profit Sector at the Crossroads: The Case of America', *Voluntas: International Journal of Voluntary and Nonprofit Organisations*, vol 10, no 1, pp 5-23.

Salamon, L.M, Anheier, H. and List, R. (1999) *Global Civil Society: Dimensions of the Nonprofit Sector (Inaugural Edition)*, Baltimore, MD: Johns Hopkins Center for Civil Society Studies.

Scottish Executive (2003) *Integrating Social Inclusion Partnerships and Community Planning Partnerships*, Edinburgh: Communities Scotland.

Scottish Office (1993) *Progress in Partnerships: A Consultation Paper on the Future of Urban Regeneration Policy in Scotland*, Edinburgh: Scottish Office.

Taylor, P. (1988) 'The Urban Programme in Scotland', *Local Economy*, vol 3, no 2, pp 205-18.

Taylor, M. (1992) 'The Changing Role of the Non-profit Sector in Britain: Moving Towards the Market', in B. Gidron, R. Kramer and L. Salamon (eds) *Government and Third Sector*, San Francisco, CA: Jossey Bass Publications, pp 147-75.

Turner, B.S. (2001) 'The Erosion of Citizenship', *British Journal of Sociology*, vol 52, no 2, pp 189-210.

Turok, I. (2004) 'Scottish Urban Policy: Continuity, Change and Uncertainty Post-Devolution', in C. Johnstone and M. Whitehead (eds) *New Horizons in British Urban Policy: Perspectives on New Labour's Renaissance*, London: Ashgate, pp 111-28.

Turok, I. and Hopkins, N. (1998) 'Competition and Area Selection in Scotland's New Urban Policy', *Journal of Urban Studies*, vol 35, no 11, pp 2021-61.

Wolch, J.R. (1990) *The Shadow State: Government and Voluntary Sector in Transition*, New York, NY: The Foundation Centre.

Wolch, J.R. (1999) 'Decentring America's Nonprofit Sector: Reflections on Salamon's Crises Analysis', *Voluntas: International Journal of Voluntary and Nonprofit Organisations*, vol 10, no 1, pp 25-35.

Wrigglesworth, R. and Kendall, J. (2000) *The Impact of the Third Sector in the UK: The Case of Social Housing*, Centre for Civil Society Working Paper 10, London: London School of Economics and Political Science.

FOUR

Voluntarism and new forms of governance in rural communities

Bill Edwards and Michael Woods

Introduction

It is now widely accepted that the way in which the UK is governed has undergone a significant transition since the 1980s, with a system of 'government', which emphasised the political monopoly of the state, giving way to a new system of 'governance', in which the process of governing is conducted through partnerships, networks and 'tangled hierarchies' of public, private and voluntary sector actors, agencies and institutions. Although defined by Stoker (1996) as 'the development of governing styles in which boundaries between and within the public and private sectors have become blurred' (p 2), the evidence since the 1980s is that governance arrangements have been as much about engaging the voluntary sector as about engaging the private sector. As Leach and Percy-Smith (2001) note in a more inclusive definition, the process of governing 'is no longer assumed to involve a single, homogeneous all-powerful government, but rather a shifting combination of public departments and agencies, quasi-public bodies, private and voluntary sector organizations, operating at different but interdependent levels' (p 22).

The transition towards a new system of governance has hence contributed to the reawakening of a latent tradition of voluntarism within UK political and civic culture. Philanthropy and voluntary action played important roles in establishing and developing public services and facilities during the late 19th and early 20th centuries, including schools, hospitals, social housing, libraries and cultural amenities, and so on (Hunt, 2004). During the 20th century, however, many of these activities were absorbed by the state, driven by two ideological imperatives that formed the basis of the 'welfare state': first, the principle of universal provision across the territory of the state, and second, that the delivery of public services should be accountable to elected representatives in either local or national government. While the voluntary sector never entirely withdrew from involvement with public services, its activities largely became confined to more peripheral functions, such as auxiliary support (for example, meals on wheels services), additional fundraising (for example, by hospital leagues of friends), and, increasingly, advocacy activities on behalf of marginalised groups (Brenton, 1985; Deakin, 1995).

The re-engagement of the voluntary sector from the 1980s onwards was initiated as part of a wider restructuring of the state under the Thatcher government. Informed by a New Right ideology of 'small government', the Thatcherite reforms sought to 'roll back' the activities of the state through privatisation, deregulation and the contracting out of services to private or voluntary sector agencies. Moreover, while the fostering of market-led private sector provision may have been the key ambition of such reforms, the increased activity of the voluntary sector also suited the moral agenda of Thatcherism, articulated in Margaret Thatcher's remarks to the Church of Scotland General Assembly in 1988 that the 'exercise of mercy and generosity' cannot be delegated to others but that each individual citizen has a duty of care (Kearns, 1992). In this moral vision, reliance on the state is bad, while voluntarism and active citizenship are good, wholesome and rewarding. Not dissimilar moral influences can be identified in the continuing support for voluntary sector engagement in governance under New Labour, whose 'third way' discourse is replete with references to 'values', 'responsibilities' and 'duties' (Fairclough, 2000), and whose approach to local governance is arguably informed by ideas of 'self-governing communities' and local citizenship drawn from civic republicanism (Barber, 1999; Williams, 2004). These themes are recognised in a range of government policies and are specifically noted in Blair's foreword included in the four national published voluntary sector compacts (Morison, 2000):

> The work of the voluntary and community organizations is central
> to the Government's mission to make this the Giving Age. They enable
> individuals to contribute to the development of their communities.
> By so doing, they promote citizenship, help to re-establish a sense of
> community and make a crucial contribution to the shared aim of a
> just and inclusive society. (Welsh Office, 1998, p 3)

In practice, however, the engagement of the voluntary sector in governance has developed in a piecemeal fashion, responding to different opportunities that have arisen in different contexts, at different times, at different scales. Some voluntary organisations picked up contracts or funding to provide local services as part of local government reforms in the 1980s, others were drawn into partnerships as 'non-state' actors or community representatives to meet requirements for funding for social and economic regeneration, yet others took advantage of deregulation to establish a presence in education, healthcare and childcare. Cuts to public spending, and the closure or rationalisation of public services or facilities, also created vacuums that have often been filled by voluntary action, particularly in deprived communities. Finally, the advent of the National Lottery funds stimulated a proactive voluntarism that is grant-driven and increasingly grant-dependent.

The shadow state and community governance

The development of these trends has changed the relationship of the voluntary sector to the state. Commentators in both the UK and the US have highlighted the growing interdependence of the state and the voluntary sector, as the state relies on voluntary sector organisations to deliver key welfare provision and as voluntary organisations rely on public funds for finance. Hence, Wolch (1989) suggested the existence of a 'shadow state' of voluntary sector organisations 'with collective service responsibilities previously shouldered by the public sector, administered outside traditional democratic politics, but controlled in both formal and informal ways by the state' (p 201). One manifestation of this control in Britain was the 'cross-cutting review of the voluntary sector' undertaken by the Treasury in 2002, which, in considering the role of the voluntary sector in governance, also promoted a 'modernisation' agenda for the voluntary sector (Osborne and McLaughlin, 2004).

However, Leach and Percy-Smith (2001) argued that the role of the voluntary sector in relation to the state has evolved 'from being, typically, on the receiving end of grants handed out by the statutory sectors, to contracting with the statutory sector to provide certain services, and, now, to being partners in community governance' (p 95). In other ways, they perceive voluntary and community organisations (VCOs) to have become proactive agents who are in some instances *sharing responsibility* for community governance with statutory institutions rather than simply acting as the delivery contractors (see also Osborne and McLaughlin, 2004). Although the Treasury's 'cross-cutting review' of the voluntary sector has been argued to herald a shift away from the paradigm of community governance and the co-governance of local services back towards a principle of co-production with VCOs acting as service agents (Osborne and McLaughlin, 2004), it can also be contended that VCOs are now so embedded in the governance structures of many local communities that to effect a retreat would be a complicated process.

The 'community governance paradigm' to which Osborne and McLaughlin refer is a model that was developed as part of the 'new localism' agenda of the New Labour government after 1997, and which sought the involvement of VCOs not only in service delivery but also 'in the design of the public policy space for public services' (Osborne and McLaughlin, 2004, p 574). This includes the engagement of VCOs in area regeneration and renewal and as such built on a longer trajectory of VCO enrolment in partnerships as representatives of local communities (see Colenutt and Cutten, 1994; Bailey et al, 1995; Atkinson and Cope, 1997; Miller, 1999; Raco and Flint, 2001). Under New Labour, the National Strategy for Neighbourhood Renewal, the New Deal for Communities and the Single Regeneration Budget have all positioned VCOs as leading players both within local action groups operating at the neighbourhood scale and on Local Strategic Partnerships constituted at local authority level (Taylor et al, 2002; Imrie and Raco, 2003; Whitehead, 2004). In particular, this approach is designed for, and associated with, urban neighbourhoods where no formal structure of local government existed at the community scale. In such contexts, community associations, residents' or tenants' groups and ethnic community organisations could all be perceived as legitimate representatives of community interests, helping to bridge the 'scalar gap' between the neighbourhood and the local authority (see also Whitehead, 2003, 2004, on attempts to develop a more formal 'democratic' alternative model in Walsall).

Yet, in large parts of England and Wales, formal local government institutions already exist at the community scale in the form of parish, town and community councils[1]. However, the involvement of local councils in service provision is limited, such that many councils spend much of their time and resources on areas of community life where their activities overlap with those of VCOs (Woods et al, 2003). In these areas, the engagement of VCOs in community governance has happened alongside formal institutions of government, not as a substitute for them, thus raising specific questions of legitimacy, competition and scale. At the same time, however, concerns have been expressed about the low level of contestation of parish, town and community council elections and about the demographic profile of councillors (Edwards and Woods, 2004). Accordingly, some government bodies, development agencies and local authorities have questioned the legitimacy of parish, town and community councils as representatives of the community and have instead promoted the establishment and engagement of alternative VCOs. Thus, while in some communities there are strong working partnerships between the local council and VCOs, in others the relationship can be fractious and even confrontational.

Definitions and focus of this chapter

In this chapter we explore the roles of VCOs in *working alongside* formal institutions of local government in community governance. First, we examine the enrolment of VCOs in partnerships at various scales from the community to the region, highlighting issues of the effectiveness of engagement by VCOs and scales of representation. Second, we discuss the interactions between parish, town and community councils and VCOs within communities. In so doing we examine how relations between councils and VCOs can be shaped by geographical context and the constitution of the local voluntary and community sector. The examples presented in these sections are drawn from a series of research projects undertaken since the mid-1990s, including work on partnership working in Mid-Wales and the Borders, for the Joseph Rowntree Foundation (Edwards et al, 2000), on participation in rural community governance in England and Wales, for the Economic and Social Research Council (Woods and Edwards, 2002), and on town and community councils in Wales, for the Welsh Assembly Government (Woods et al, 2003).

For the purposes of this chapter we define voluntarism as organised activity within society that involves 'self-governing associations of people who have joined together to take action for public benefit' (Taylor, 1992, p 171). Such 'voluntary and community organisations' (VCOs), moreover, are 'independent, do not distribute profits and are governed by non-paid volunteers' (Fyfe and Milligan, 2003a, p 398)[2]. Finally, in establishing the context for our investigation, we understand 'community governance' in broader terms than those implied in the usage by Osborne and McLaughlin (2004) referred to earlier. We define community governance – or more strictly at a local level, community *self-governance* – as activities that involve either the provision of public services within the community, or the representation of community interests to external agencies, as undertaken by actors who are positioned themselves as part of the community (see also Edwards and Woods, 2004).

Incorporating the voluntary and community sector through partnership working

Wolch (1989) observes that 'the shadow state may be seen as a corporatist strategy, designed to create "partnerships" with components of civil society' (p 201). Partnership working is a key strategy in the neoliberal restructuring of the state, acting as a mechanism through which state functions have been devolved to non-state actors and resources have been brought into the process of governing. Although the discourse of partnership working in the UK initially emphasised the engagement of private sector partners, partnerships have come increasingly to incorporate VCOs, creating a web of interconnections that constitutes Wolch's 'shadow state'. As we describe in this section, partnerships are now employed to engage VCOs in governance at a range of scales and in many different forms[3].

Voluntary sector compacts

The commitment of the state to working in partnership with the voluntary sector has been reaffirmed by the 'voluntary sector compacts' in England and Wales in 1998, and subsequently by many local authorities (Morison, 2000). These have sought to establish a new transparent partnership with the voluntary and community sector which encompassed shared values, recognition of a mutual strategic role for the government and voluntary sectors, acknowledgement of the representative role of the voluntary sector and its need for resources to maintain activities.

These developments signalled a repositioning of the voluntary and community sector as a partner in a new form of governance operating at both strategic and local scales. Taylor and Bassi (1998), Rose (2000) and Morison (2000) have emphasised the challenges posed by this attempt to incorporate associational groups active within civil society into a new set of relationships with government. Morison (2000) has interpreted this through the lens of governmentality (following Rose and Miller, 1992). While such papers contextualise and frame a critical reading of both compacts and partnership working, few queries as yet have been raised over what the consequences are for the voluntary and community sector in engaging with partnerships at different scales of operation or what the consequence of the requirement to mobilise community and voluntary groups might be at a local level where the geography of their presence varies quite considerably.

The nature of partnership working

Partnerships take many forms, and definitions vary, as does the relative emphasis on the integration of public, private and voluntary or community sectors. They also importantly are empowered to address different issues at different territorial scales – from partnerships built to meet policy needs across regional territories to far more local, themed ventures focused on a single community. The agendas and territorial impact of partnerships may therefore overlap producing a confusing complexity of initiatives shaping development in any given area, with the voluntary and community sector represented in different ways at different scales of operation. Such partnership activity is positioned as evidence of a shift from govern*ment* to govern*ance* (Jessop, 2000). It empowers the stakeholders with the capacity to govern through decision making and allocation powers comparable to those of elected representatives, yet without their ballot box accountability.

However, for partnerships to create the opportunity for a new coalition of actors to establish a formal and lasting governance role continuity or permanence is essential. Invariably the duration of partnership activity is fixed, defined by strategic intent, and hence the governing bloc and those stakeholders within it may have limited time to exercise a governance function. However, the current embeddedness of this mode of working means that when a partnership's life or funding comes to an end, another partnership is invariably spawned or emerges in parallel, but with the important caveat that it may not always follow exactly the same terms of reference.

While this process of incorporation in partnership activity creates more joined-up thinking and empowers those stakeholders who are included to play a key role in the new forms of strategic and delivery intervention, it raises key questions over how each sector might be represented at different scales of activity and how informed, accountable and representative that voice is in the deliberations that ensue. These matters are important if this new mode of working is seen to represent a consistent and durable mode of governance that empowers through incorporation and action rather than simply co-presence.

It is surprisingly difficult to identify precisely the full extent of partnership working in any area even though non-governmental, local authority and voluntary and community groups frequently make broad claims to be working in partnership with others. Table 4.1 indicates from work we have recently undertaken on rural regeneration partnerships operating across rural Wales and the Welsh Borderland, that in this set of partnerships there was considerable diversity of structure and practice (Edwards et al, 2000). The evidence on participation in partnership working in that study revealed the dominant presence of representatives of public

Table 4.1: Partnership characteristics at different territorial scales in rural Mid-Wales (Powys and Ceredigion)

Territorial scale of partnership activity	Number of partnerships	Date of initiation of partnership			Duration of partnership		Frequency of representation of partners from different sectors				Voluntary sector representatives on partnerships
		Prior to 1993	1994-96	1997-2000	Ongoing	Limited life	Q	LA	V	P	
Regional and above	62	8	27	27	34	28	56	40	23	34	Paid officials of overarching national VCOs
County	35	2	15	18	26	9	30	28	13	25	Officials of County Voluntary Associations Selected representatives of particular voluntary sector interests Officials of county-wide 'communities of interest'
Subcounty area/place	20	0	9	11	5	15	17	19	12	11	Representatives reflecting the local range of voluntary and community groups in particular places
Total	117	10	51	56	65	52	103	87	48	70	

Key: Q = quango; LA = local authority; P = private sector; V = voluntary/community sector.

Source: Edwards et al (2000)

or semi-public bodies and a growing, but not universal, incorporation of the voluntary/community sector. The sector only held key stakeholder roles in just over two fifths of the initiatives examined. It was also apparent that VCO representation in many of these partnerships operating at scales above the local is through officers drawn from overarching organisations, for example the Welsh Council for Voluntary Organisations or the Powys Association of Voluntary Organisations, rather than selected community groups. The advantage of a stakeholder presence at this level is that it does allow such bodies to operate strategically for the sector, but it is incumbent on these groups to reflect the views of the organisations they represent and to inform and be accountable to their constituencies. As Morison (2000) argues, their engagement bridges the divide between the political and civil with benefits for joint working at an institutional/organisational level, but it also raises important questions about empowerment, accountability and control. Only at the subcounty level does local voluntary and community engagement occur and these partnerships are often of fixed duration and constituted a minority of all partnerships in operation. This engagement of voluntary and community groups in local neighbourhood and rural community regeneration has a long history, but has only recently been legitimised in policy and practice (DETR/MAFF, 2000). However, recognition of the need to incorporate those active in local civil society is now firmly established, and their future influence will depend on the attitudes of local councils towards their incorporation (Edwards and Woods, 2004). In summary, the evidence indicates that the scale, context and territoriality of partnership working are critical to how the VCO sector is incorporated.

Inevitably VCOs at each of these levels of partnership activity vary in the professional and local knowledge they bring to the table. In national, regional and county level partnerships much of the VCO representation is by a professional cadre of officers well versed in the needs and competencies of organisations within their remit. At the subcounty and community level of VCO engagement, there is far greater variation and far less professional understanding of the working practices, strategic intent and priorities of those others engaged in the partnership. Here the volunteer or community representative is often challenged by the language, bureaucracy, short-termism and funding pragmatism of partnership working. It was also apparent in these studies that local areas vary in the numbers of voluntary groups active and willing to participate in partnership activities.

Cities, towns and larger villages all have a range of local voluntary associations and community groups covering a varied domain of activity, but other areas are less 'association rich'. The consequence is that inevitably the geography of participation through VCOs is uneven. Alongside this, the very nature of the housing market and the inevitable segregation of stock that has emerged have resulted in residential communities and neighbourhoods with very different financial, educational, professional resources, prior experiences and competencies to bring to bear on participation in voluntary and community associations. Inevitably, therefore, the opportunity for the voluntary and community sector to participate in the new form of governance that is emerging is scale and context dependent and this has in part contributed to the recognition by government that an alternative route through which local engagement may be mobilised is through a revitalised town, parish and community council sector. It is the key site through which community self-governance occurs and it is to this theme that the chapter now turns.

Voluntary sector engagement in rural community governance

In her analysis of the Los Angeles voluntary sector, Wolch (1989) notes that 'it is within urban communities that the impacts of shadow state formation are experienced on an everyday basis' (p 202). The community, she argues, is the context in which services are delivered by the voluntary sector operating under the sponsorship and direction of the state; and it is frequently organisations that are constituted at a community scale that take on responsibilities of service delivery in the shadow state. Implicit in this model is scalar 'devolution' of responsibility from state institutions that exist at a metropolitan or regional scale to groups organised at a more local territorial scale (see Geiger and Wolch, 1986; Wolch, 1989, 1990). As Fyfe and Milligan (2003a, 2003b; also Milligan and Fyfe, 2004) detail, this scalar redistribution is accompanied by a spatial fragmentation of service provision as the uneven spatial distribution of voluntary resources produces uneven geographies of voluntary sector engagement that are frequently at odds with the geography of welfare need.

However, it should be noted that most studies of the shadow state have been undertaken in metropolitan and urban contexts where the established institutions of the local state are constituted at a city-wide scale. In these situations, the devolution of responsibilities to voluntary groups can be elided with devolution to communities because there is no pre-existing tier of community governance as part of the state (or only bodies such as community boards with no service delivery function). Indeed, groups such as neighbourhood watch committees and housing associations have in many urban neighbourhoods formed a tier of community governance that is located within the shadow state.

Yet in the smaller towns, rural districts and many suburbs of England and Wales the engagement of VCOs in governance is performed alongside town, parish or community councils that form the lowest tier of the local government system. The presence of these local level councils changes the dynamics of voluntary and community sector engagement in community governance, in part because of the ambiguous position that the councils have traditionally held in transgressing the boundary between the state and civil society. In this section we argue that relations between local level councils and VCOs represent a web of mutual coexistence that both pre-dates the rise of neoliberalism and is embedded more in the networks of individual agency than in institutional strategy. In doing so, we draw on evidence from four pieces of empirical research: a survey of elections to town, parish and community councils in England and Wales between 1998 and 2000; surveys of local councillors and interviews with councillors and community group officers conducted in four case study areas of southern England (see Edwards and Woods, 2004); a survey of 475 town and community councils in Wales covering all aspects of their constitution and activities; and surveys of local councillors and focus groups of councillors conducted for 17 case studies in Wales (see Woods et al, 2003).

Town, parish and community councils and the voluntary and community sector

Institutionally, town, parish and community councils (collectively referred to as local level councils) are part of the state, established by statute, exercising statutory powers, funded by the tax payer and elected by common franchise. Culturally, however, town, parish and community councils often bear greater similarity to the voluntary and community sector than to the other tiers of local government. Many town, parish and community councillors are fiercely defensive of their non-professional status and their contribution as volunteers, and many of the activities undertaken by such councils, particularly in supporting social and cultural events, reflect the interests of VCOs more than the conventional functions of local government. Moreover, many town and parish councils have formally aligned themselves with the voluntary and community sector as members of rural community councils in England. Town and parish councils make up over half the membership of Cheshire Community Council, for example, and around two fifths of the members of the community councils for Northumberland and Suffolk.

This historic affinity between local level councils and the rural voluntary sector is reflected in patterns of mutual support and the blending together of resources. For example, the provision of grant aid to local clubs and associations is a major budget item for many councils. Around 85% of town and community councils in Wales made donations to local groups in 2001-02, injecting an estimated £1 million into the voluntary sector across Wales (Woods et al, 2003). The range of organisations supported varies significantly between councils, but commonly includes youth groups, sports clubs and teams, arts and drama societies and charities, as well as contributions towards local festivals and Christmas parties for pensioners. A number of larger voluntary sector organisations also benefited from grants from town and community councils in Wales, including the Samaritans, Citizens Advice Bureaux, Shelter Cymru, the Disability Alliance, Childline, Carers Outreach and Women's Aid, among others. Grants are made for both revenue and capital funding and are often a major source of income for smaller local VCOs.

Most donations by local level councils to VCOs are made under the provisions of section 137 of the 1972 Local Government Act, which permits councils to spend up to £5 per elector on 'any purpose, which in its opinion is of direct benefit to its area or to the inhabitants' (Local Government Act 1972, section 137).

Other support, however, is made under provisions in various legislation that permit councils to grant aid the maintenance of certain facilities by third parties, including cemeteries, entertainment premises, community halls, playing fields, swimming pools and village greens. Around half of the town and community councils in Wales, for example, grant aid the provision of village halls or community centres, usually by village hall associations or trusts. Arrangements of this type can be regarded as a form of contracting out of community governance functions to VCOs that has been operational for several decades.

As well as providing financial support to VCOs, many local level councils also have formal representation on the management boards of local VCOs. Over two thirds of town and community councils in Wales are represented on village hall or community centre committees; over a quarter are represented on festival committees, community association boards and playing field association committees; and one in five have representation on the management committees of the local Citizens Advice Bureau and youth groups.

These arrangements have created relations of dependency in so far that some community organisations only exist to carry out a grant-aided function on behalf of a council, while others could not survive without the funds that they receive from the council. There is, however, little evidence of 'the state' – in the shape of the local level council – 'controlling' either formally or informally the activities of these groups except in fairly specific cases. Moreover, the conditions under which such arrangements are forged differ from those inherent to the concept of the shadow state. Funding is usually provided not as part of a contracting-out of services, but as a form of community philanthropy, using locally raised funds to support 'deserving causes'.

Cross-sectoral activity of individual participants

The interconnection between town, parish and community councils and VCOs is provided not only by formal ties but also by individuals who are both councillors and active members of community groups. Most local level councils are not party political and over a third need to co-opt some of their members due to a shortage of candidates standing for election. In these circumstances, prominence in a local society or organisation can often lead to recruitment as a councillor, as two parish councillors in Dorset noted:

> 'Well I'm really involved right from a small age, because my parents were involved in village life; fundraising for the village school when we had it, village hall, Royal British Legion, everything ... and you're involved in the ... well, the system itself and dragged along, and it sort of started from there really.... Well it came around, you see [a former councillor] retired from the parish council, didn't want to stand for re-election, and they were one member short, and he said to

me they were looking for a new member, and "Would you be interested?".' (parish councillor, Dorset)

'I think there were elections in '91, or '92, I can't remember now; anyway … and I hadn't thought about it. I mean I'd been involved in organising things for the village hall and so on, but not on the council … erm, and someone up the road actually, who I'd got a lot of time for, said "You ought to stand for the parish council".' (parish councillor, Dorset)

Indeed, of 146 town and community councillors surveyed in 17 councils in Wales, around a quarter considered their involvement with the council to be an extension of their work with local community organisations, and over half identified their experience of voluntary community activity as one of their main contributions to the council. Moreover, councillors not only tend to continue their involvement with these groups after joining the council, but many become involved in additional activities subsequent to joining the council. For example, 139 town and parish councillors surveyed in four case study areas in England in 2002 collectively held 180 officer roles in other local organisations. On average, each councillor had been active in 2.3 other organisations prior to joining the council, and had become active in a further 1.6 organisations subsequently. Hence, many VCOs in rural and small town communities have de facto representation on town, parish and community councils, strengthening the informal ties between the two sectors. As such, the unidirectional influence of the state in directing voluntary sector activity envisaged in the shadow state thesis is made more complex at a community scale by the participation of individuals nurtured through voluntary and community groups in formal local government.

Partnerships between local level councils and VCOs

More recently, local level councils have begun to work more formally in partnership with the voluntary and community sector. The impetus for this development has been twofold. The promotion of partnership working as a requirement of funding from programmes administered by national or regional agencies, such as Rural Challenge in England and the Market Town Initiative in Wales during the 1990s (Jones and Little, 2000; Edwards et al, 2001, 2003), encouraged the enrolment of both councils and local VCOs into new project delivery partnerships. At the same time, some local level councils have identified partnership working with local VCOs as a means of circumventing restrictions on their own powers in securing resources for specific projects, for example in bids to the Community Fund. However, to date only a small minority of local level councils have entered into formal partnerships, and such arrangements remain far less significant as a conduit for voluntary and community sector engagement in community governance than the more established and often informal mechanisms described above.

Yet, despite the historical interplay of connections between local level councils and the voluntary and community sector, in many communities relations have become increasingly uneasy as councils and VCOs are seen as competing to represent community interests and lead community projects. The disproportionately male, middle-class and middle- or late-aged composition of most town, parish and community councils and the fiscal and social conservatism of many councils are perceived by critics both within the community and in external agencies as making councils less appropriate vehicles for community governance than VCOs:

> 'Community associations meet regularly, no one knows what the community council is doing, there is no publicity for its meetings. There is little engagement between the different organisations.' (community association member, Carmarthenshire)

> 'There is a view in some towns that organisations such as Chambers of Trade reflect at least part of the local community needs far better.' (community development worker, Powys)

This critique has also been promoted from within the voluntary sector, together with the argument that VCOs have a greater flexibility than local level councils when it comes to involvement in areas such as community regeneration:

> 'In terms of the community regeneration agenda we are keen, again, to see resources delegated to local community associations – where possible, and where local communities want it, to enable them to manage as much as possible local services and the regeneration of their own communities. And I mean, I am aware that there have been discussions about whether or not Community Councils are the vehicle for that. And I think our preferred vehicle would be community associations and the voluntary and charitable sector, because – well, I think firstly because it's – again, it's strengthening voluntary action; secondly, it enables those organisations, if they're charitable, to access resources that only they can access; and maybe secondly, by dint of being charitable you are not political, and maybe enables community associations to be more inclusive ... than a body which is run on party-political lines.' (policy officer, Wales Council for Voluntary Action)

The problem with this argument, however, is that it risks misrepresenting town, parish and community councils. As noted earlier, most local level councils are not party political and therefore are not politicised in the way implied in the quote above; indeed, it could be argued that the minority of councillors elected in party-political contests have a greater claim to a mandate of community representation than those co-opted on non-political councils. At the same time, many councillors are themselves critical of the increasing involvement of voluntary and community groups in activities that they regard as the concern of town, parish and community councils, arguing that VCOs by definition lack democratic accountability:

> 'The problem with those sorts of groups is that they are not democratic, in other words the public do not have the right to be able to vote them out. We are at the ballot box, every four years or five years, therefore if people don't like what we are saying, they just don't vote for us. With those neighbourhood forums and things like that, they are appointed and there is a danger that they are appointed because of political views.' (chair, National Association of Local Councils Wales)

Geographies of voluntary and community sector engagement

Tensions such as these have helped to produce a variable geography of voluntary and community sector engagement in community governance. There are communities in which the town, parish or community council enjoys a strong productive relationship with local VCOs, working in formal or de facto partnerships to blend resources to enhance the overall capacity to act of the community. Similarly in some communities the overlapping memberships of the council and local groups and the sharing of resources and tasks means that governance of community life is essentially blurred between the statutory and voluntary sectors. Yet in other communities the moribund nature of the local council permits VCOs to take the lead in community governance, while in yet others open conflict can exist.

This geography is shaped by factors of scale, setting and socioeconomic context. Councils for larger communities are more likely to have formal partnership arrangements with VCOs, are more likely to provide grant aid, and have a wider range of local organisations (and branches of national VCOs), with which to engage. In contrast, it is in smaller communities with relatively little recent change that the informal integration of councils and local voluntary groups through key individuals is likely to be strongest. Market towns, particularly those in regions designated as priorities for rural development, will be subjected to the strongest external pressure for VCO engagement in community governance. Market towns can, however, also be the most likely sites of conflict between local level councils and VCOs, particularly if they have experienced significant social recomposition in recent years. As such, the engagement of the voluntary and community sector in community governance cannot be generalised as a universally standard process, but must be understood as a complex set of dynamics that are heavily contingent on locality factors.

Conclusion

The engagement of the voluntary and community sector has become one of the key features of the transition to a new system of local governance in Britain. The promotion of such engagement is replete with the vocabulary of empowerment, diversity and active citizenship, yet the practice of VCO engagement presents a more complex picture than that suggested by the rhetoric. This complexity is in part a reflection of the diversity of the voluntary and community sector but is also produced by the conditions of VCO incorporation into governance structures, and the ways in which these build on existing relations between VCOs and local government institutions. In this chapter we have focused on two arenas of VCO engagement in governance. First, representatives of the voluntary and community sector have been enrolled into partnerships that contribute to strategic local governance or to the delivery of governance functions in areas such as rural regeneration. The involvement of voluntary and community sector representatives in partnerships is intended to draw in the resources of VCOs and to provide an alternative route for the representation of community interests to that provided by formal local government. Yet in practice, the actual contribution made by VCOs to partnerships can be compromised by their limited resources. Voluntary and community sector representatives sitting alongside partners from the public or private sectors who have injected finance or other material resources may feel that their input carries less weight, and may also be disadvantaged by unfamiliar language and working practices that are rooted in the public sector. Moreover, many VCOs employ a relatively small staff such that the participation of senior officers in partnership meetings represents a cost that is not shared by larger public sector partners. As such, while the engagement of VCOs in partnerships has been advocated by national voluntary sector representative associations because there are perceived to be opportunity gains, the actual benefit to individual VCOs of participation in partnerships can often be questioned, as can the difference made by VCO engagement to the process of governance in such instances. In this way, the engagement of the voluntary and community sector in partnerships with the state appears to reflect the asymmetrical relationship suggested in the thesis of the shadow state.

In the second arena, that of VCO engagement with town, parish and community councils, the benefits both to voluntary and community organisations and to community governance as a whole are more apparent, but actual practice is still variable. Significantly, in many of the communities where local level councils and VCOs work together most successfully, the form of engagement is one that pre-dates the contemporary mode of governance and is often founded on informal networks between individual leaders in the community. In contrast, it is often attempts to position VCOs as representatives of the local community, or to direct external resources through VCOs (both strategies that form part of contemporary local governance), that provokes tension and even conflict between councils and VCOs. Relations in this context can be close, and involve mutual dependencies, but they also differ from the model of the shadow state in a number of ways, reflecting less a neoliberal state strategy and more a complex heritage of historic associations and communal philanthropy.

These variable experiences of voluntary and community sector engagement in governance are strongly influenced by scale and spatial context. Firstly, the scale at which engagement takes place will affect the VCOs that are enrolled, the form of engagement and the resources that they are able to contribute. The participation of county or national voluntary sector bodies in strategic partnerships is a very different form of engagement to a community association receiving funds from a parish council to maintain a village hall. Secondly, scale also influences the capacity of VCOs to represent others. Voluntary and community sector partners in county or regional level partnerships may have means of consulting affiliated VCOs, but they primarily speak for their own organisation. Community groups at a local level similarly represent a particular section of the community. As such, attempts to engage the voluntary and community sector in governance that position VCOs as the representatives of a community can be misconstrued. Thirdly, models of voluntary and community sector engagement cannot be imposed without regard for the institutional histories of particular localities. The presence of a town, parish and community council and their record of activity, the established relations between local organisations and councils, and the place that local organisations occupy within the leadership structures of communities all have a bearing on the potential for VCO engagement in community governance to be successfully enhanced. It cannot be assumed that voluntary and community sector engagement in local governance will automatically lead to community empowerment, greater active citizenship and better governance; rather the geographical factors that influence examples of good and bad practice need to be more fully understood by researchers and more fully recognised in policy.

Notes

[1] The 8,285 parish and town councils in England and 737 town and community councils in Wales provide a fairly comprehensive coverage of rural areas, but are also found in suburban neighbourhoods, small- and medium-sized towns and former mining districts. Indeed, their territorial coverage is spreading, with around 100 new parish and town councils established in England since 1997, mostly in urban settings.

[2] We recognise, however, that this definition encompasses a wide range of groups, operating within different fields of activity, with differing degrees of formality and levels of resources and with different social and political objectives. Thus, our analysis includes both representative bodies for the voluntary sector that are professionally staffed, and community groups operating at a local scale that exist only through the voluntary participation of their members.

[3] These include the contracting out of specific services, the involvement of VCOs in local-scale partnerships engaged in regeneration or community development activity, and the participation of voluntary sector representatives on strategic partnerships. In addition to initiatives of UK state institutions, partnership working has also been promoted through the European Union Structural Funds and by the conditions of grants from the various funds established to distribute Lottery money in the 1990s.

References

Atkinson, R. and Cope, S. (1997) 'Community Participation and Urban Regeneration in Britain', in P. Hoggett (ed) *Contested Communities: Experiences, struggles, policies*, Bristol: The Policy Press, pp 201-21.

Bailey, N. with Baker, A. and MacDonald, K. (1995) *Partnership Agencies in British Urban Policy*, London: UCL Press.

Barber, B. (1999) 'Clansmen, Consumers and Citizens: Three Takes on Civil Society', in F. Fullwider (ed) *Civil Society, Democracy and Civic Renewal*, Oxford: Rowman and Littlefield, pp 9-30.

Brenton, M. (1985) *The Voluntary Sector in British Social Services*, London: Longman.

Colenutt, B. and Cutten, A. (1994) 'Community Empowerment in Vogue or Vain', *Local Economy*, vol 9, no 3, pp 236-50.

Deakin, N. (1995) 'The Perils of Partnership: The Voluntary Sector and the State, 1945-1992', in J. Davis-Smith, R. Rochester and R. Hedley (eds) *An Introduction to the Voluntary Sector*, London: Routledge, pp 40-65.

DETR/MAFF (2000) *Our Countryside: The Future – a Fair Deal for Rural England*, Cm 3016, London: The Stationery Office.

Edwards, B. and Woods, M. (2004) 'Mobilizing the Local: Community, Participation and Governance', in L. Holloway and M. Kneafsey (eds) *Geographies of Rural Cultures and Societies*, Aldershot: Ashgate, pp 173-96.

Edwards, B., Goodwin, M., Pemberton, S. and Woods, M. (2000) *Partnership Working in Rural Regeneration: Governance and Empowerment*, Bristol/York: The Policy Press/Joseph Rowntree Foundation.

Edwards, B., Goodwin, M., Pemberton, S. and Woods, M. (2001) 'Partnerships, Power and Scale in Rural Governance', *Environment and Planning C: Government and Policy*, vol 19, pp 289-310.

Edwards, B., Goodwin, M. and Woods, M. (2003) 'Citizenship, Community and Participation in Small Towns: a Case Study of Regeneration Partnerships', in R. Imrie and M. Raco (eds) *Urban Renaissance? New Labour, Community and Urban Policy*, Bristol: The Policy Press, pp 181-204.

Fairclough, N. (2000) *New Labour, New Language?*, London: Routledge.

Fyfe, N. and Milligan, C. (2003a) 'Out of the Shadows: Exploring Contemporary Geographies of the Welfare Voluntary State', *Progress in Human Geography*, vol 27, no 4, pp 397-413.

Fyfe, N. and Milligan, C. (2003b) 'Space, Citizenship and Voluntarism: Critical Reflections on the Voluntary Welfare Sector in Glasgow', *Environment and Planning A*, vol 35, pp 2069-86.

Geiger, R.K. and Wolch, J. (1986) 'A Shadow State? Voluntarism in Metropolitan Los Angeles', *Environment and Planning D: Society and Space*, vol 43, pp 351-66.

Hunt, T. (2004) *Building Jerusalem: The Rise and Fall of the Victorian City*, London: Weidenfeld and Nicolson.

Imrie, R. and Raco, M. (eds) (2003) *Urban Renaissance? New Labour, Community and Urban Policy*, Bristol: The Policy Press.

Jessop, B. (2000) 'Governance Failure', in G. Stoker (ed) *The New Politics of British Local Governance*, Basingstoke: Macmillan Press, pp 11-32.

Jones, O. and Little, J. (2000) 'Rural Challenge(s): Partnerships and New Rural Governance', *Journal of Rural Studies*, vol 16, no 2, pp 171-83.

Kearns, A. (1992) 'Active Citizenship and Urban Governance', *Transactions of the Institute of British Geographers*, vol 17, pp 20-34.

Leach, R. and Percy-Smith, J. (2001) *Local Governance in Britain*, London: Macmillan.

Miller, C. (1999) 'Partners in Regeneration: Constructing a Local Regime for Urban Management', *Policy & Politics*, vol 27, no 3, pp 343-58.

Milligan, C. and Fyfe, N. (2004) 'Putting the Voluntary Sector in its Place: Geographical Perspectives on Voluntarism and Social Welfare', *Journal of Social Policy*, vol 33, no 1, pp 73-93.

Morison, J. (2000) 'The Government–Voluntary Sector Compacts: Governance, Governmentality and Civil Society', *Journal of Law and Society*, vol 27, no 1, pp 98-132.

Osborne, S.P., and McLaughlin, K. (2004) 'The Cross-cutting Review of the Voluntary Sector: Where Next for Local Government – Voluntary Sector Relationships?', *Regional Studies*, vol 38, no 5, pp 573-82.

Raco, M. and Flint, J. (2001) 'Communities, Places and Institutional Relations: Assessing the Role of Area-based Community Representation in Local Governance', *Political Geography*, vol 20, no 5, pp 585-612.

Rose, N. (2000) 'Community, Citizenship and the Third Way', *American Behavioural Scientist*, vol 43, pp 1395-411.

Rose, N. and Miller, P. (1992) 'Political Power Beyond the State: Problematics of Government', *British Journal of Sociology*, vol 43, pp 173-205.

Stoker, G. (1996) 'Introduction: Normative Theories of Local Government and Democracy', in D.S. King and G. Stoker (eds) *Rethinking Local Democracy*, London: Macmillan, pp 1-27.

Taylor, M. (1992) 'The Changing Role of the Non-profit Sector in Britain: Moving Toward the Market', in B. Gidron (ed) *Government and Third Sector*, San Francisco, CA: Jossey-Bass Publications, pp 147-75.

Taylor, M. and Bassi, A. (1998) 'Unpacking the State: The Implications for the Third Sector of Changing Relationships between National and Local Government', *Voluntas*, vol 9, no 2, pp 113-36.

Taylor, M., Craig, G., Warburton, D., Parkes, T. and Wilkinson, M. (2002) *Willing Partners? Voluntary and Community Organisations in the Democratic Process*, Final research findings, Brighton: University of Brighton.

Welsh Office (1998) *Compact between the Government and the Voluntary Sector in Wales*, Cm 4107, Cardiff: HMSO.

Whitehead, M. (2003) 'Love thy Neighbourhood – Rethinking the Politics of Scale and Walsall's Struggle for Neighbourhood Democracy', *Environment and Planning A*, vol 35, pp 277-300.

Whitehead, M. (2004) 'The Urban Neighbourhood and the Moral Geographies of British Urban Policy', in C. Johnstone and M. Whitehead (eds) *New Horizons in British Urban Policy*, Aldershot: Ashgate, pp 59-74.

Williams, M. (2004) 'Discursive Democracy and New Labour: Five Ways in which Decision-makers Manage Citizen Agendas in Public Participation Initiatives', *Sociological Research Online*, vol 9, no 3 (www.socresonline.org.uk/9/3/williams.html).

Wolch, J. (1989) 'The Shadow State: Transformations in the Voluntary Sector', in J. Wolch and M. Dear (eds) *The Power of Geography: How Territory Shapes Social Life*, Boston, MD: Unwin Hyman, pp 197-221.

Wolch, J. (1990) *The Shadow State: Government and Voluntary Sector in Transition*, New York, NY: The Foundation Center.

Woods, M. and Edwards, W.J. (2002) *Participation, Power and Rural Community Governance in England and Wales*, Final report to ESRC Award No L215 25 2052, Aberystwyth: University of Wales, Aberystwyth.

Woods, M., Edwards, B., Anderson, J., Gardner, G. and Hughes, R. (2003) *The Role, Functions and Future Potential of Community and Town Councils in Wales*, Report to the Welsh Assembly Government, Cardiff: Welsh Assembly Government.

FIVE

New times, new relationships: mental health, primary care and public health in New Zealand

Pauline Barnett and J. Ross Barnett

Introduction

As in many Western countries, the role of voluntary agencies in healthcare provision in New Zealand has undergone significant change in recent years. At the macro-level, there have been clear shifts in the relationship between the state and the voluntary sector, with tensions evident between central and regional/ district levels of decision making as health funding has been devolved but central constraints maintained (Health Services Research Centre, 2003). At a more micro-level there has been discussion of the functioning of voluntary organisations and the nature of volunteering itself, and the way that increased accountability imposed through contracts has required more sophisticated governance arrangements (Nowland-Foreman, 1998). In this chapter we examine these developments in more detail. We begin by providing some historical context and then examine the broad experience of health non-governmental organisations (NGOs) under state restructuring from the mid-1980s to 2005. The term 'health NGO' is in current use in New Zealand by government, health funders and voluntary agencies themselves to describe independent, not-for-profit organisations participating in health and disability sector activity. Drawing on the experience of three key health sector groupings – community mental health, primary healthcare and public health agencies – we review how key issues such as contracting and accountability relationships, management and professionalism and good service practice have been addressed since the 1980s. In particular, we show that the introduction of the internal market in the 1990s led not only to the rapid growth of health NGOs, but also to the emergence of substantial regional differences in contracting relationships and public accountability. At the same time, however, the new decentralised contracting environment, while encouraging innovation, undermined good service practice by making it more difficult for health NGOs to cooperate with each other and represent their communities effectively. The chapter has a particular focus on the period since the late 1990s when a more constructive relationship between health NGOs and the state began to evolve.

Given the concentration of much research on larger voluntary organisations (Halfpenny and Reid, 2002), and the need for place- and sector-based interpretations of voluntarism (Fyfe and Milligan, 2003a, 2003b; Milligan and Fyfe, 2004), we conclude with a discussion of the implications of this experience at both macro- (governance and accountability) and micro- (NGO process and practice) levels.

Historical context

In the early days of organised government in New Zealand, the state resisted strongly any involvement in health and welfare provision, believing that this responsibility was better discharged by family and community assistance as the need arose (Thomson, 1998). Voluntarism in health services, therefore, has a long history. In the mid–19th century hospitals were established in the new colony by local subscription, with the state having minimal involvement, although from the late 19th century local authorities had a role in supporting both hospitals and charitable aid (Tennant, 1989).

Voluntarism was also present in the primary care sector, which was funded entirely from personal resources. From the late 19th century friendly societies (mutual aid cooperatives), lodges and local groups created informal insurance arrangements to protect members from the costs of doctors' fees (Hay, 1989). With increasing settlement in the early 20th century, gaps in services began to be filled by charitable organisations, some going on to be important national (Dow, 1995) and local (Allan, 1996) institutions.

In New Zealand the formation of the welfare state in the late 1930s saw a significant change in the role of voluntary agencies generally, with them largely taking a role secondary to state provision (Munford and Nash, 1994). In health, hospitals became centrally funded, run by local boards. Primary care was funded on a fee-for-service basis by the government. Between the 1950s and 1970s, voluntary agencies and groups increasingly received grants from the state to support their work in providing essential health services such as well-child services and the long-term care of older people. The security and adequacy of funding was assisted by agencies cultivating a close relationship with politicians as well as officials. At the macro-level, however, there was little accountability for performance or scrutiny of either process or outcomes. Funds were 'granted' and the expectation was that, at the micro-level, these would supplement charitable funds or 'in-kind' efforts of volunteers. Two decades of this 'ad hoc' approach, when examined by public sector reformers in the 1980s, were deemed to be contributing to a problematic fragmentation of services and lack of accountability (Laugesen and Salmond, 1994).

Health and disability NGOs in a restructured state

Health restructuring and NGOs

From 1984 the public sector in New Zealand experienced major restructuring along managerialist lines, with the objective of creating greater efficiency, more accountability and less involvement of government in work that could be done more effectively by private or community organisations (Suggate, 1995; Boston et al, 1996; Nowland-Foreman, 1997). Initially, there were few implications for the health voluntary sector, as health provision remained largely managed by central government; in addition, local hospitals and area health boards (AHBs) made little effort to engage more widely with health NGOs, preferring to allocate funds to their own services. From 1990 onwards, however, reforms instituted by the neoliberal National government had a major influence on health and disability NGOs, both through the market-style restructuring of health services and the realignment of responsibility for disability support services.

Market reforms had a significant impact on NGO participation in health and disability services. The changes proposed in 1991 and implemented in 1993 created a managed market for services, devolving most funding to four regional health authorities (RHAs) to purchase local services in a competitive environment. The RHAs, unlike their predecessor AHBs, had no services of their own and therefore were free to contract with any hospital, health or community provider that met their service specifications. This provided significant opportunities for NGOs to enter the 'health market' for the first time, with the number of health NGOs growing rapidly during the 1990s (Black, 2000; Owen, 2005). Their flexibility and closeness to the community were clearly attractive to the RHA purchasers, as were the relatively low prices that could be negotiated or imposed. The successor to the RHAs in 1998, the national Health Funding Authority, pursued a similar strategy but with less emphasis on competition and more on collaboration.

At the same time the government chose to reassign responsibility for the provision of disability support services (for older people, in mental health and for those with physical and sensory disabilities) away from social welfare to the health sector. By 1999, health and disability sector NGOs dominated all public funding to the voluntary sector, receiving NZ$366 million out of $676 million (54%) of the annual disbursement, mainly through expenditure by the Health Funding Authority (Ministry of Social Policy, 2001). Despite this level of funding, by the end of the 1990s there were areas of dissatisfaction on the part of the health and disability NGOs, and overall an increasing level of tension between the government and all voluntary organisations. This was exacerbated by the decision in 1998 to cease government support for, and engagement with, three important multisector coordinating and advocacy bodies, including the National Council of Christian Social Services and the National Federation of Voluntary Welfare Organisations. The government's position was therefore made explicit:

that it regarded a voluntary organisation as 'just another provider' and did not recognise the special contribution that such agencies made to the community.

A change in government in 1999 saw a Labour-led coalition move away from centralised funding of health services by creating 21 district health boards (DHBs) to manage local population-based budgets for health and disability services, with collaboration to be the primary method of planning and integrating services at the local level. The move was presented as a model that would facilitate NGO involvement in the health and disability sector and provide a greater local focus for services.

The changing environment for health NGOs

The paradox, then, was that by the end of the 1990s there had been an enormous growth in voluntary agency participation in the health sector, and yet health and disability NGOs, along with others, felt undervalued and unrecognised. The tensions between the National-led (conservative) government and all voluntary agencies had not gone unnoticed by the Labour opposition and prior to the 1999 election it promoted the concept of a 'compact', similar to that advocated by the Blair government in the UK, between the government and the voluntary sector.

Once it came to power in 1999 the new Labour government moved to develop this concept by establishing, in August 2000, a Joint Working Party with representatives from both government and voluntary organisations. Led by the Minister for Social Development, this 'special relationship' between the government and voluntary organisations was characterised as a 'written handshake', with the government signing, in December 2001, a 'Statement of Government Intentions' for an improved relationship between itself and the community sector.

The Ministry of Health and the health and disability sector NGOs developed a special 'health' version of the compact process: *The Framework for Relations between the Ministry of Health and NGOs in the Health and Disability Sector.* This *Framework*, again referred to as a 'written handshake', provided for six-monthly forums for health NGOs to discuss key issues with the Ministry of Health and other relevant agencies. The Health and Disability Sector NGO Working Group works on behalf of the forum, undertaking research and advocacy of issues of the day (Health and Disability Sector NGO Working Group, 2005a, 2005b). This initiative took place against the background of yet another health sector restructuring in 2000, as mentioned above, whereby 21 DHBs were established to fund local services, with an explicit mandate to encourage collaboration and integration of services.

Throughout the 1990s some recurrent issues thus emerged for health NGOs. The first was the nature of the relationship with the state and its agents, and the extent to which contracting and accountability arrangements compromised the traditions, ethos and potential community contribution of voluntary agencies. The second issue was the extent to which the demands of the contracting process and its requirements actually changed the character of agencies so that their management and service arrangements were actually little different from private and state sector organisations. Thirdly, the key elements of 'good practice' in health NGOs, such as collaboration, community engagement and the flexibility to innovate, were challenged.

Key NGO groupings: mental health, primary care and public health

In order to understand the impact of health sector change on NGOs we have identified three key groups of agencies that, because of their diversity, can play a particular part in understanding the developing relationship between the government and health-related NGOs. These are community mental health agencies, primary care services and public health NGOs. Our discussion of the experience of these agencies is based on a series of research projects conducted over the period 1995-2004. This work involved an analysis of regional variations in contracting relationships between state agencies and community mental health services (Newberry and Barnett, 2001; Barnett and Newberry, 2002), an investigation of regional differences in the growth of community involvement in the provision of hospital and primary care services (Barnett and Barnett, 2003, 2004), and a study of voluntary sector involvement in public health (Fear and Barnett, 2003). More recently the 'Health Reforms Project' has investigated changing patterns of contracting between the state and health NGOs as a result of moves away from the neoliberal market model of the 1990s (Barnett and Clayden, 2004).

In the case of the first group of health NGOs, community mental health services, there were a number of agencies already established in 1991 when market-led health reform was announced, but these operated in relatively limited spheres. Between 1992-95 there was quite rapid growth in the volume of community services overall (Ernst and Young, 1996), with a 13% decline in hospital beds and 22% increase in community places, with much of the 50% growth in staff numbers in the non-government sector. By 1999 community mental health agencies, for example, attracted nearly 30% of all public mental health expenditure (Ministry of Health, 2000).

Primary care services, the second group of health NGOs, have not traditionally been seen as part of the voluntary sector and, indeed, in New Zealand had been only partially government funded and largely delivered by the private sector (Barnett et al, 1998). However, during the 1990s, alternative forms of primary care services emerged, drawing on some government funds but managed through non-profit community structures. The first of these, which have been termed 'third sector' primary healthcare services (Crampton et al, 2001), were formed specifically to target low-income and other disadvantaged groups such as Maori and Pacific people and migrant populations. They were community governed, with representation from patient groups, and worked together in a consortium, Health Care Aotearoa. Another set of primary care organisations emerged in rural areas (rural primary care trusts), arising from threats to close small rural hospitals and the risk of losing the local doctor and other support services. These rural trusts, representing a resistance to health restructuring, were formed by local communities and governed and managed locally while holding contracts from the health funder (Barnett and Barnett, 2003). Rural trusts emerged particularly in the Southern RHA that faced the greatest fiscal deficit. By contrast, community-run trusts were a less favoured alternative in the Midland RHA, which preferred greater for-profit involvement in the provision of services. These agencies have a dual significance for this discussion. First, they introduced a voluntary dimension to primary care in New Zealand and, second, they provided models for the Labour government's Primary Health Care Strategy, which established primary health organisations that are required to have a component of community governance (King, 2001). The implementation of this policy, while not without its problems, has created a new set of community oriented primary healthcare organisations now covering most of the population (Barnett and Barnett, 2004).

Public health agencies, the third group of NGOs, are a disparate group of organisations, groups and coalitions with a commitment to improved health status and roles that include health promotion, disease prevention, advocacy and community engagement on health issues. During the early 1990s there was uncertainty as to how public health would be addressed in the market environment. The government's policy document was explicit that public health services were relevant to the government because they 'reduce publicly funded treatment costs' (Upton, 1991, p 107), but initial plans for a public health purchasing agency were abandoned. An independent body, the Public Health Commission, set up to advise the Minister on public health issues was disestablished in 1995 (Barnett and Malcolm, 1998). This removal of high level advocacy for public health called into question the government's commitment in this area and left a number of public health NGOs vulnerable to funding loss.

The experience of these three groups of agencies through the 1990s and beyond are instructive of the uncertain relationships between health NGOs and the state, and are explored below in relation to the key issues already identified: contract and accountability relationships, management and professionalism within NGOs and issues of good practice.

Issues for health and disability NGOs: 1990-2004

Contract and accountability relationships

Since the early 1990s the relationship between government and the NGOs has been maintained largely through the contracting process. Few health and disability NGO contracts have been directly with the Ministry of Health, but through its purchasing and funding agents, the four RHAs (1993-97), the single Health Funding Authority (1997-2000) and, since 2001, 21 DHBs. The government has had some contracts directly with NGOs, largely for policy advice or some national service provision, particularly in the areas of public health and health promotion/social marketing. The issues for NGOs have related to both the contracting processes and the contract terms and accountability provisions.

Inevitably the contract relationship has required increasing formality between health NGOs and government funding agencies (Wilson et al, 2001), with some transition required on the part of NGOs to understanding and accepting the differences between grant funding and contractual purchasing (Rivers Buchan Associates, 1995), including the recognition that the financial risk was clearly passed to the provider.

Research into community mental health agencies in the mid-1990s revealed that the four RHA purchasers had substantially different contracting styles and relationships. Newberry and Barnett (2001) identified five desirable criteria for effective contracting in community mental health, a sector with high uncertainty and variable client needs. According to the NGOs surveyed, these criteria – effective communication and consultation, timeliness, a coherent approach, appropriate use of power and fostering a mutualist culture – were only fulfilled by one of the four RHAs, with two other RHAs meeting only one criterion (Newberry and Barnett, 2001, p 139). Similarly, monitoring service performance was carried out variably across the four RHAs. As a member of staff at one agency commented: 'they are in the process of developing four different systems to measure the same thing' (Barnett and Newberry, 2002, p 197).

The experience of rural primary care trusts in contracting was equally uncertain. Despite most trust leadership having significant business experience, almost all the trusts reported the process of negotiating contracts with the RHAs as difficult and protracted (Barnett and Barnett, 2001, p 232). They found the negotiators inexperienced either in contracting or in health, the policy framework uncertain and staff turnover high. One trust reported dealing with 16 different RHA staffers, while another reported that it took four years to negotiate a suitable contract.

Both community mental health agencies and the rural trusts found that funding agencies tended to resist contracting for overall services and preferred to contract for individual service 'fragments', such as separating the contract for rehabilitation from the contract for accommodation. This approach is consistent with market theory but likely to undermine coordination of services and best use of resources. Relationships between health NGOs and their funding agencies improved during the late 1990s as a coalition government (1997-99) moved away from excessively commercial practices. An informal unpublished survey by the NGO–Ministry of Health Forum of NGO relationships with DHBs in 2003 demonstrated a further improvement in relationships: '[they are] always available and open to our perspective'; 'a good relationship with DHB staff at the grass roots'. However, there is still the view expressed that that DHBs do not understand the NGO sector, with interviewees commenting that the DHBs were 'not forthcoming with information, but expect us to be' and that there is 'no meaningful consultation with families and consumers'.

In the early 1990s, under a market framework, regional differences were reflected in the terms of contracts as well as the negotiating process. In relation to community mental health one RHA had reasonably broad, but ambiguous terms, one had flexible service specifications mutually agreed with NGOs, with two reported to have imposed highly prescriptive provisions (Newberry and Barnett, 2001, p 140). The ambiguous terms were reported as 'being used against us', while overly specific terms were considered too restrictive for community mental health. One RHA had explicit terms to protect itself from liability. This was found in other contracts, with Kelsey (1995) reporting on a contract between the Northern RHA and the Society for Intellectual Handicap, a major national NGO. The contract specified that: 'the RHA ... was immune from liability, could alter the contract at 8 weeks notice, could cancel the contract but require services to continue for six months, could insist on complex records and statistics and compliance with statutory requirements' (p 293).

In the community mental health area there was concern, even 'frustration' (Walmisley, 2003, p 232), that contract terms continued to be described in terms of inputs, with little opportunity to specify the desired outputs and outcomes (Health Services Research Centre, 2003, p 69). All respondents to a 1997 survey of agencies reported an absence of requirements to report on quality, with one person describing the performance monitoring as 'simple, cheap and ineffective' (Barnett and Newberry, 2002, p 200). This concern persisted even after the change of government in 1999 and the introduction of DHBs. In a case study of a large DHB, one agency reported: '... we haven't been held accountable and we want to be more accountable.... But we are accountable financially ... but actually what we are *doing* isn't looked at' (Barnett and Clayden, 2004, p 38). Another commented: 'The monitoring has been pretty slack' but acknowledged that 'the DHB has taken the bull by the horns and started to move on that' (Barnett and Clayden, 2004, p 39).

Besides the restrictive nature of some contract terms, there were issues for health NGOs regarding their freedom to speak out and to advocate for client groups or on public health issues. The early Society for Intellectual Handicap contract reported above included terms preventing criticism of the funding agency. This was characteristic of some funders and there were concerns about the extent to which this would prevent NGOs from undertaking some of their traditional advocacy roles. A survey of mental health agencies in the mid-1990s reported that few respondents felt prevented from engaging in advocacy work, although some acknowledged 'more vulnerability and a more circumspect approach' (Barnett and Newberry, 2002, p 201).

The extent to which the acceptance of government contracts inhibited advocacy roles continues to be debated. In general larger, well-established agencies encountered fewer problems than smaller ones. In the case of the Public Health Association of New Zealand, a small NGO, its annual grant from the Department of Health was not renewed in 1991 following the change to a more neoliberal government. This was widely interpreted as a rejection of the high profile advocacy role of the Association, which had challenged commercial interests (particularly the pharmaceutical companies) during the late 1980s. Despite this, the Public Health Association of New Zealand continued to publish strong statements on equity and the social determinants of health (PHANZ, 1992) and undertake research into the consequences of contracting on public health (PHANZ, 1992).

Advocacy, however, did become an integral part of contract provisions for some health NGOs during the later 1990s, especially where such advocacy reflected the government's interest and where NGOs were clearly seen to be doing the government's work. For example, from 1997 onwards a coalition of nutrition groups, the Agencies for Nutrition Action, received successive contracts to promote healthy eating and to undertake consultation processes on the issues on behalf of the government (Fear and Barnett, 2003). Nutrition advocacy, therefore, was seen as an acceptable cause and specifically funded by the state.

Although there is still some cynicism about the intentions of the government, the relationship between the state and health NGOs appears to have improved since 1999. For example, in a survey of health NGOs conducted in November 2003, 47.6% of respondents were in regular communication with their local DHB and over half (56.3%) felt that such communication was helpful. One third of the respondents also believed that their DHB members shared the government's commitment to a strong and respectful relationship with NGOs, as expressed in the Statement of Intent (Health and Disability Sector NGO Working Group, 2003). Nevertheless the issue of advocacy remains contentious. In October 2003 questions were asked in Parliament regarding the propriety of Ministry of Health contracts with anti-smoking groups that included clauses requiring the lobbying of Members of Parliament (MPs). A review of the contracts by independent auditors indicated that there were a small number of contracts (six in all) that contravened public service rules and the Code of Conduct. The purpose of the Code is to maintain the political neutrality of the public service, with the auditors considering that the provisions of the Code had been breached. It was proposed that in future government contracts were to exclude lobbying activity explicitly, to cease using the word 'advocacy' and to incorporate a precise statement of services being purchased. In addition, the Ministry of Health issued a 'guideline' that appeared to restrict the scope of activity on the part of agencies receiving contracts from the state. Strong representations by health NGOs have seen this guideline withdrawn, with a more considered approach taken by the Ministry (Matheson, 2005), and the recognition, for example, that a contract for services should not necessarily constrain an independent voluntary board in its advocacy role. There continues to be concern among health NGOs and the issue remains unresolved.

Management and professionalism in NGOs

The demands for increased flexibility and accountability through contracts had an immediate impact on health NGOs, most notably through increasingly sophisticated requirements for the management of employment relations and financial and other forms of organisational reporting.

In the case of community mental health services this was linked to both deregulation of the New Zealand labour market (1991 Employment Contracts Act) and increasing compliance requirements in areas such as health and safety, privacy and consumer protection regulation (Barnett and Newberry, 2002, p 196). While the managerialist contracting environment, with its focus on activity reporting, was seen by some health NGOs as 'close to heresy', and to have taken some time to adjust to, there is also the view that it actually forced agencies to improve management performance (Newberry and Barnett, 2001; Walmisley, 2003, p 231). Despite some problems, a majority of community mental health agencies reported in the mid-1990s that there were positive features for them including management improvements, better accountability and staff development. Similarly, local rural primary care trusts supported specific health sector labour deregulation that gave them greater flexibility in use of staff. Local employment contracts reflected this, including arrangements for multitasking of nurses and particularly the flexibility for nurses to work in both hospital and community settings as and when needed, and not on a rigid roster basis (Barnett and Barnett, 2003, p 65).

In agencies where there has been a strong tradition of volunteering, such as community mental health agencies, there has been a reported decline in service-related volunteers. Changes in information and accountability requirements in contracting required agencies to appoint paid and qualified staff in both administrative and service roles. Agencies that had always had a strong volunteer ethos reported feeling 'distanced' from clients, with others restricted in the scope of volunteer activities by the terms of the contract (Barnett and Newberry, 2002, p 202). While use of volunteers may have declined (except for in increasingly sophisticated governance roles) and the number of paid staff increased, there was continuing concern about the intensification of work, the need for staff to go the 'extra mile' and the continued downward pressure on resources (Barnett and Newberry, 2002, p 202).

Good practice

There are some aspects of health NGO history and philosophy that make them valuable to the community beyond any direct provision of contracted services. These include a collaborative approach, an engagement with the community and the flexibility to innovate and develop services in alternative ways.

The desire to work with other agencies, whether voluntary, state or for-profit, is a strongly held value among many health NGOs, and was undermined by the competitive environment of the health market. The community mental health services, where patient issues and the network of services are both complex, is particularly dependent on open communication and collaboration. A number of agencies felt that both practices were undermined during the 1990s. Of the four

RHAs, only one encouraged regular information sharing between community mental health agencies, sponsoring the functioning of a 'beneficent network' as opposed to the more 'coercive networks' developed by the three other RHAs (Newberry and Barnett, 2001, p 147).

Public health agencies also experienced the impact of competition on their desire to collaborate. The coalition of Agencies for Nutrition Action found that collaboration was difficult when resources were at stake. Fear and Barnett (2003) report that the coalition, despite intense efforts, failed to present a joint bid for funds with participants finding it difficult to balance the commitment to collaboration with the requirements of their own organisations, the successful bidder eventually deciding to 'go-it-alone'. The agencies, while strongly motivated by health promotion principles that valued intersectoral action, collaboration and open communication, did not anticipate the strain that a market environment would put on their relationships. It is possible that a stronger, more entrepreneurial, style of leadership might have been more effective but would have required some surrender of agency autonomy so that progress was not always dependent on the achievement of consensus (Fear and Barnett, 2003, p 12).

In primary care, the determination by the primary healthcare agencies and rural primary care trusts to develop more integrated and coordinated services has had a significant impact on the wider health arena. The successful experience of these organisations became the basis for the development of the Labour government's (1999) Primary Health Care Strategy (King, 2001), and its establishment of primary health organisations. The philosophy underpinning community-led multidisciplinary primary healthcare was first developed in New Zealand through the NGO experiments of the 1990s, and is expected to be a defining feature of the new primary health organisations as they mature.

There is evidence that, despite the contracting environment, some health NGOs continue to see themselves as contributing in a special way to the local community, reflecting the manner in which the community or consumers are engaged in the organisation. The nature of community involvement, however, appears to have changed. There is some evidence that volunteers have become redundant to many voluntary organisations, where they are increasingly being replaced by paid workers with specialist skills (Saville-Smith and Bray, 1994). International research suggests that the introduction of paid staff and the increased professionalisation of the voluntary sector leads to a subsequent fall in volunteer commitment and the marginalisation of volunteers (Russell and Scott, 1997). Although data on volunteering trends is poor, both local (Gardner, 2000; McNeil, 2002) and international (Putnam, 1995) evidence suggests a decline in the number of volunteers since 1999. Despite such indications of a decline in 'frontline' volunteering, there is increasing significance attached to community governance. The commitment of the leadership and the support gained in local communities for both primary healthcare organisations and local rural health trusts is an indication of a local engagement over and above the provision of services. Crampton (2004) argues that true primary healthcare, as promoted by the World

Health Organisation since the 1970s, can only be possible through a community development model that involves local governance and accountability structures, including local ownership and decision making. Similarly, rural health trusts have reported that, despite the burden of time and effort by the local community, the experience is an empowering one with control over local services and supportive links with other trusts (Barnett and Barnett, 2003).

It is evident that many health NGOs have been highly proactive in service innovation since 1990. Walmisley (2003, p 232) comments that some NGOs have tended in the past to be in awe of health funding agencies, but in fact such agencies are often waiting for providers to take initiatives in service development. There are examples of such NGO leadership in community mental health (Walmisley, 2003), with Barnett and Clayden (2004) reporting that a number of providers interviewed claimed to be strongly proactive, for example: 'Our job is to be innovative and provide solutions to the DHB.... My view is that we go to them and say, well, what do you need? We've got a lot of expertise, how can we help you *meet that need?*' (p 36 [emphasis in original]). Overall, the result has been a significant expansion in types of facilities and range of services, and particularly a response to unmet needs (for example, services to rural communities, and to the indigenous Maori population).

Similarly, in primary care, initiatives have been driven by NGOs in response to community needs. In the case of the rural trusts, the threat to local services led to protest action and local mobilisation. Outcomes have been improved access to a wider range of services (for example, local counselling services, respite care) and more sustainable services for the future (Barnett and Barnett, 2003). Health Care Aotearoa services provide examples of services targeted to special needs, including Maori (Hand, 1998) and Pacific (Tukuitonga, 1999) communities.

So, while there is no doubt that since 1990 there has been a responsiveness to local and special needs, it is clear that this has been led as much by health NGOs as the funders and funding policy.

Discussion

The changing relationship with the state

At the macro-level, health NGOs are now held at 'arm's length' from the central state, with funding and contracting responsibility devolved to DHBs. Devolution has removed the traditional opportunities for NGOs to lobby politicians directly and the prospect of 'pork-barrelling' is now remote. Health NGOs have to compete with fellow NGOs, as well as government and private agencies, for funds from a capped district budget for service delivery; the idealised outcome is that they form part of a coordinated approach to district and regional healthcare provision. In fact NGOs in, for example, the mental health area, have taken leadership roles in this venture and are seen as key participants. The tradition of a direct relationship with the state, however, has been partly retained through the formalised forum and the active role of the Health and Disability Sector NGO Working Group. The Working Group has significantly changed the perception of both government and officials on the importance of NGOs (King, 2005), ensuring collective access to high-level policy-makers and ministers and, through its research and advocacy, maintaining the NGOs' roles as community advocates with government.

The Health and Disability Sector NGO Working Group is also providing additional access to the 'corridors of power' for health NGOs by linking them with the DHBs' collective organisation, District Health Boards New Zealand. DHBs, with their majority of elected members, are seen by the government as the 'frontline' of engagement with the community on health matters. In their relationships with the state at both national and district level, health NGOs have been able to establish a specialised role that is consistent with the engagement goals of government. Therefore, while they are certainly doing the state's work, they have additional status and are no longer seen as 'just another provider'.

Maintaining a voluntary ethos

Besides their independence from government and their not-for-profit status, a critical dimension of NGOs is their community relevance and, as Fyfe and Milligan (2003b) have indicated, it is important to determine whether restructuring has enhanced or diminished this connection. As charitable funds have become more difficult to acquire, most health NGOs have accepted the need for state-funded contracts in order to survive, and the question remains whether the attendant increase in professionalism and managerialism undermines their essential character. There is no doubt that 'volunteering' has changed significantly in some health NGOs, with a decline in 'hands-on' volunteers and the emergence of a cadre of 'dominant status' volunteers (Lemon et al, 1972). These individuals are typically well-educated and often engage in providing governance and other specialist expertise. This professionalisation is consistent with the overall experience in New Zealand (Zwart and Perez, 1999) and elsewhere (Gaskin and Davis Smith, 1997; Goss, 1999). Even in organisations that do not accept government funds and that have large numbers of service volunteers (such as the Cancer Society of New Zealand), volunteer jobs have become more formalised, with job descriptions and more formal training requirements. In this respect New Zealand is no different from other Western countries, such as the UK (Billis and Harris, 1992; Russell and Scott, 1997), Australia (Liamputtong and Gardner, 2003) or the US (Smith, 1996), where similar trends have also occurred.

It has been suggested that increased managerialism and professionalism, and a decline in 'hands-on' volunteers, has undermined social connectedness and social capital within the community (Wilson et al, 2001; Fyfe and Milligan, 2003b). Crampton (2004), however, indicates that genuine community governance can play a strong role in promoting this, as illustrated by the experience of voluntary sector health providers (Neuwelt and Crampton, 2005).

Conclusion

This chapter has explored the changing environment of NGOs involved in the health and disability sector in New Zealand, examining how relations between government and NGOs have changed in the light of a retreat from neoliberalism since the late 1990s. We have highlighted these changes in three ways. First, we have traced the emergence of a representative health and disability NGO collective organisation, supported by the state and with access to high levels of government and the bureaucracy. Second, we have shown how three key groups of agencies have dealt with specific issues in different ways. Third, we have noted, where appropriate, how decentralisation resulted in variable regional responses, especially in service organisation and contracting. However, given that particular sets of voluntary organisations are also embedded in particular places (Milligan and Fyfe, 2004), we suggest that further research focus particularly on the interaction between organisational change and place and how the trends we have identified have played themselves out in different locational contexts. Building on Wolch's (1990) findings of the geographically uneven development of the voluntary sector, our findings suggest that more attention should be paid to regional differences in sectoral change and the implications of such differences for voluntary organisations themselves and the clients they serve. In New Zealand, at least, despite high levels of state control, the move to more decentralised DHBs has accentuated local differences in contracting relationships and levels of government involvement in health NGOs. In the light of such trends we suggest that future research pays more attention to contextual differences in the evolving government–voluntary sector relationship so as to provide more nuanced accounts of evolving patterns of welfare reform in the voluntary sector.

References

Allan, V. (1996) *Nurse Maude: The First Hundred Years*, Christchurch: The Nurse Maude Foundation.

Barnett, P. and Barnett, R. (2001) 'Community Ventures in Rural Health: The Establishment of Community Health Trusts in Southern New Zealand', *Australian Journal of Rural Health*, vol 9, pp 229-34.

Barnett, R. and Barnett, P. (2003) '"If You Sit On Your Butts You Will Get Nothing": Community Resistance to Hospital Closures in Southern New Zealand', *Health and Place*, vol 9, pp 59-71.

Barnett, R. and Barnett, P. (2004) 'Primary Health Care in New Zealand: Problems and Policy Approaches', *Social Policy Journal of New Zealand*, vol 21, pp 49-66.

Barnett, P. and Clayden, C. (2004) *Canterbury District Health Board: First Report. Health Reforms Evaluation Project*, Wellington: Health Services Research Centre, Victoria University.

Barnett, P. and Malcolm, L. (1998) 'To Integrate or De-integrate: Fitting Public Health into New Zealand's Reforming Health System', *European Journal of Public Health*, vol 8, pp 79–86.

Barnett, P. and Newberry, S. (2002) 'Reshaping Community Mental Health Services in a Restructured State: New Zealand 1984–97', *Public Management Review*, vol 4, no 2, pp 187–208.

Barnett, R., Barnett, P. and Kearns, R. (1998) 'Declining Professional Dominance? Trends in the Proletarianization of Primary Care in New Zealand', *Social Science and Medicine*, vol 46, no 2, pp 193–207.

Billis, D. and Harris, M. (1992) 'Taking the Straw of Change: UK Local Voluntary Agencies Enter the Post-Thatcher Period', *Non-profit and Voluntary Sector Quarterly*, vol 21, no 3, pp 221–5.

Black, J. (2000) 'The Development of the Voluntary Sector in Canterbury, New Zealand', Unpublished MA thesis, Christchurch: Department of Geography, University of Canterbury.

Boston, J., Martin, J., Walsh, P. and Pallott, J. (1996) *Public Management: The New Zealand Model*, Auckland: Oxford University Press.

Crampton, P. (2004) *The Exceptional Potential in each Primary Health Organisation: A Public Health Perspective*, Opinion piece on the relationship between public health and primary care for the National Health Committee, Wellington: National Health Committee.

Crampton, P., Dowell, A. and Woodward, A. (2001) 'Third Sector Primary Care for Vulnerable Populations', *Social Science and Medicine*, vol 153, no 11, pp 1491–502.

Dow, D. (1995) *Safeguarding the Public Health: A History of the New Zealand Department of Health*, Wellington: Victoria University Press.

Ernst and Young (1996) *1995 Stocktake of Mental Health Services*, Wellington: Ministry of Health.

Fear, H. and Barnett, P. (2003) 'Holding Fast: The Experience of Collaboration in a Competitive Environment', *Health Promotion International*, vol 18, no 1, pp 5–14.

Fyfe, N. and Milligan, C. (2003a) 'Space, Citizenship and Voluntarism: Critical Reflections on the Voluntary Sector in Glasgow', *Environment and Planning A*, vol 35, pp 2069–86.

Fyfe, N. and Milligan, C. (2003b) 'Out of the Shadows: Exploring Contemporary Geographies of Voluntarism', *Progress in Human Geography*, vol 27, no 4, pp 397–413.

Gardner, R. (2000) *The Value of Volunteering*, Christchurch: Canterbury Volunteer Centre.

Gaskin, K. and Davis Smith, J. (1997) *A New Civic Europe? A Study of the Extent and Role of Volunteering*, London: National Centre for Volunteering.

Goss, K.A. (1999) 'Volunteering and the Lost Civic Generation', *Voluntary and Non-profit Sector Quarterly*, vol 28, no 4, pp 378–415.

Halfpenny, P. and Reid, M. (2002) 'Research on the Voluntary Sector: An Overview', *Policy & Politics*, vol 30, no 4, pp 533-50.

Hand, D. (1998) 'Indigenous Health in New Zealand: "By Maori, For Maori"', *Australian Nursing Journal*, vol 5, no 10, pp 18-21.

Hay, I. (1989) *The Caring Commodity*, Auckland: Oxford University Press.

Health and Disability Sector NGO Working Group (2003) *Survey of NGO–DHB Relationships*, Wellington (www.moh.govt.nz).

Health and Disability Sector NGO Working Group (2005a) *Report on NGO Relationships with the Ministry of Health*, Wellington (www.moh.govt.nz).

Health and Disability Sector NGO Working Group (2005b) *Non-Government Organisations (NGOs) and the Primary Health Care Strategy*, Wellington (www.moh.govt.nz).

Health Services Research Centre (2003) *Interim Report on Health Reforms 2001 Research Project*, Wellington: Health Services Research Centre, Victoria University.

Kelsey, J. (1995) *The New Zealand Experiment: A World Model for Structural Adjustment*, Auckland: Auckland University Press/Bridget Williams Books.

King, A. (2001) *Primary Health Care Strategy*, Wellington: Ministry of Health.

King, A. (2005) Opening address to the 7th Health and Disability NGO Forum, 7 April, Christchurch (Speech Notes) (www.moh.govt.nz).

Laugesen, M. and Salmond, G. (1994) 'New Zealand Health Care: A Background', *Health Policy*, vol 29, pp 1-182.

Lemon, M., Palasi, B.J. and Jacobson, P.E. (1972) 'Dominant Statuses and Involvement in Formal Voluntary Associations', *Journal of Voluntary Action Research*, vol 1, no 2, pp 30-42.

Liamputtong, P. and Gardner, H. (eds) (2003) *Health, Social Change and Communities*, Sydney: Oxford University Press.

McNeil, J. (2002) *Decline in Volunteering a Threat to Civil Society*, Auckland: Maxim Institute.

Matheson, D. (2005) Address to the 7th Health and Disability NGO Forum, Christchurch, 7 April (Speech notes) (www.moh.govt.nz).

Milligan, C. and Fyfe, N. (2004) 'Putting the Voluntary Sector in its Place: Geographical Perspectives on Voluntary Activity and Social Welfare in Glasgow', *Journal of Social Policy*, vol 33, no 1, pp 73-93.

Ministry of Health (2000) *Health Expenditure Trends in New Zealand (1980-1999)*, Wellington: Ministry of Health.

Ministry of Social Policy (2001) *Communities and Government: Potential for Partnership: Whakato-pu-Whakaaro*, Wellington: Communications Unit, Ministry of Social Policy.

Munford, R. and Nash, M. (1994) *Social Work in Action*, Palmerston North: Dunmore Press.

Neuwelt, P. and Crampton, P. (2005) 'Community Participation in the Primary Health Care Sector in Aotearoa New Zealand', in P. Davis and K. Dew (eds) *Health and Health Care in Aotearoa New Zealand* (2nd edn), Auckland: Oxford University Press, pp 194-210.

Newberry, S. and Barnett, P. (2001) 'Negotiating the Network: The Contracting Experience of Community Mental Health Agencies in New Zealand', *Financial Accountability and Management*, vol 17, no 2, pp 133-52.

Nowland-Foreman, G. (1997) 'Can Voluntary Organisations Survive the Bear-hug of Government Funding under a Contracting Regime? – A View from Aotearoa-New Zealand', *Third Sector Review*, vol 3, no 1, pp 5-39.

Nowland-Foreman, G. (1998) 'Purchase of Service Contracting, Voluntary Organisations, and Civil Society. Dissecting the Goose that Lays the Golden Eggs?', *American Behavioral Scientist*, vol 42, no 1, pp 108-23.

Owen, S. (2005) 'Placing Health Organisations in New Zealand's Third Sector', Unpublished PhD thesis, Auckland: Department of Geography, University of Auckland.

PHANZ (Public Health Association of New Zealand) (1992) *Social, Cultural and Economic Determinants of Health: A Review of the Literature*, Wellington: PHANZ.

Putnam, R.D. (1995) 'Bowling Alone: America's Declining Social Capital', *Journal of Democracy*, vol 6, no 1, pp 65-78.

Rivers Buchan Associates (1995) *RHAs Don't Fund, They Purchase Services*, Wellington: New Zealand Federation of Voluntary Welfare Organisations.

Russell, L. and Scott, D. (1997) *Very Active Citizens? The Impacts of Contracts on Volunteers*, Manchester: Department of Social Policy and Social Work, University of Manchester.

Saville-Smith, K. and Bray, M. (1994) *Voluntary Welfare: A Preliminary Analysis of Government Funding to the Non-Profit Welfare Sector*, Wellington: New Zealand Institute for Social Research and Development Ltd.

Smith, S. (1996) 'Transforming Public Services: Contracting for Social and Health Services in the US', *Public Administration*, vol 74, Spring, pp 113-27.

Suggate, D. (1995) *An Overview of the Voluntary Sector*, Wellington: Department of Internal Affairs.

Tennant, M. (1989) *Paupers and Providers: Charitable Aid in New Zealand*, Wellington: Allen and Unwin and Historical Branch, Department of Internal Affairs.

Thomson, D. (1998) *A World without Welfare*, Auckland: Auckland University Press/ Bridget Williams Books.

Tukuitonga, C. (1999) *Primary Health Care for Pacific People in New Zealand*, Auckland: Pacific Health Centre, University of Auckland.

Upton, S. (1991) *Your Health and the Public Health*, Wellington: New Zealand Government.

Walmisley, G. (2003) 'Mental Health Services and Deinstitutionalisation: How Community Agencies can Deliver Effective Services for People with Disabilities', in R. Gauld (ed) *Continuity amid Chaos: Health Care Management and Delivery in New Zealand*, Dunedin: University of Otago Press, pp 229-40.

Wilson, C., Hendricks, A.K. and Smithies, R. (2001) 'Lady Bountiful and the "Virtual Volunteers": The Changing Face of Social Service Volunteering', *Social Policy Journal of New Zealand*, vol 17, pp 124-46.

Wolch, J.R. (1990) *The Shadow State: Government and the Voluntary Sector in Transition*, New York, NY: The Foundation Centre.

Zwart, R. and Perez, E. (1999) *Gift Work: Analysis of the 1996 Census Data on Unpaid Voluntary Work Done Outside the Household*, Wellington: Department of Internal Affairs.

SIX

Informal and voluntary care in Canada: caught in the Act?

Mark W. Skinner and Mark W. Rosenberg

Introduction

Contemporary Western societies are undergoing social, political and economic change as they come to terms with major shifts in the global economy. The adjustment process has been characterised in part by national policies promoting rapid and far-reaching restructuring of economies and societies (Pinch, 1997). Within this context, governments have sought to reconfigure their responsibilities with respect to the provision of public services (Cope and Gilbert, 2001). Although experiences vary considerably within and between nation states, the attendant reworking of central–local relations and public–private responsibilities has facilitated shifts in the nature of both local governance and the organisation and delivery of healthcare services (Lewis and Moran, 1998; Joseph and Knight, 1999). These transformations have had important implications for voluntary organisations, community groups and volunteers, particularly given the challenges these actors face in reconciling increasing demands for care in the home and community with processes of statutory retrenchment and the broader unevenness of healthcare provision (Kearns and Joseph, 1997; Milligan, 1998; Wiles, 2003a).

The healthcare sector provides a particularly important example of the dynamic and complex interlinkages between processes of restructuring, shifting forms of governance and voluntarism. In response to the fiscal crisis of the state, health restructuring during the 1980s and 1990s generally involved the application of deregulatory principles to particular services and institutions (Pinch, 1989; Barnett, 2000). This 'public service restructuring', as it is generally referred to in human geography and the social sciences, can be seen as an orchestrated set of policies, measures and institutional actions (for example, devolution, privatisation, rationalisation) used by governments to reduce their roles in the funding or delivery of healthcare services (Pinch, 1997). Implicit in this process has been the renegotiation of the roles and responsibilities of the state, civil society and marketplace (Moran, 1999). A common result has been increasing interdependence of the public, private and informal and voluntary sectors in the provision of healthcare services, especially at the local level (Milligan, 2000).

A central process in the changing nature of 'local governance' (Goodwin and Painter, 1996) has been a move away from state-led, hierarchical coordination of public services towards a greater emphasis on community-based providers. In the health sector, this local community has often been understood to include family, friends and neighbours, all of whom are now expected to play active and direct roles in the delivery of healthcare services (for example, Crampton et al, 2001). Indeed, key academic and public policy debates surrounding contemporary state–civil society relations in countries such as Canada, New Zealand and the UK highlight the potential of local non-state institutions and informal networks to mediate the impacts of public service restructuring processes in general and healthcare reforms in particular (for example, Wolch, 1990; Kearns and Joseph, 1997; Milligan, 2001). Within these debates, voluntarism is sometimes presented as a compromise between the state and civil society in an attempt to resolve the many health and social problems facing contemporary Western societies (Fyfe and Milligan, 2003).

In this context, 'voluntarism' typically refers to the use of voluntary organisations, community groups and volunteers to meet welfare needs (Pinch, 1997). It is clear that, in Canada and elsewhere, this approach also plays an important role in the provision of healthcare (Hall and Banting, 2000). Key studies highlight the blurring of state and civil society boundaries (for example, Wolch, 1990; Brown, 1997; Milligan, 2001), while also raising concerns about the impacts of public service restructuring and local governance on the viability of informal and voluntary providers (Wistow, 1995). Underlying this concern is recognition that the processes of change affecting voluntarism in many Western welfare states have, at times, quite different local manifestations (Fyfe and Milligan, 2003). The changing dynamics of voluntarism, therefore, provide the basis for understanding the roles, responsibilities and interrelationships of informal and voluntary sector providers as they relate to the provision of healthcare services.

In this chapter, we investigate the relationships among public service restructuring, the changing nature of local governance and the dynamics of voluntarism within the context of Canada's universal, comprehensive and public healthcare system. Noting that this system has undergone extensive restructuring since the mid-1980s, we consider in particular the ascendancy of the informal and voluntary sector in the provision of healthcare, and focus specifically on the case of home and community care. The term 'informal and voluntary sector' is used throughout the chapter in reference to those families, friends and neighbours who are involved in providing care on a volunteer basis, either *formally* through voluntary organisations and community groups that are not part of the state (that is, non-governmental) and are not market-driven (that is, non-profit), or *informally* as individuals. To illustrate the link between healthcare and voluntarism, we draw on data from Statistics Canada's National Population Health Survey (NPHS) and National Survey of Giving, Volunteering and Participating (NSGVP). The results from the analyses of these broad-scale population-based surveys represent user (demand) and provider (supply) perspectives respectively, and provide a cross-section of the dimensions of informal and voluntary care in Canada in the late 1990s. Ultimately, the findings provide a platform for reflecting on the link between voluntarism and healthcare, and a discussion of potential avenues for future research on the geography of informal and voluntary care.

The geography of informal and voluntary care

Recent work within health geography, and elsewhere in human geography, has highlighted the critical importance of understanding care in various settings and from various perspectives (see the 2003 special issues of *Environment and Planning A* and *Social and Cultural Geography*). The relations, practices and experiences of different types of care such as mental health services (for example, Kearns and Joseph, 2000; Parr and Philo, 2003), complementary and alternative medicine (for example, Williams, 2000; Wiles and Rosenberg, 2001; Andrews, 2002, 2003) and palliative care (for example, Brown, 2003) have been examined. A key area of study centres on the growing concern for the spatial dimensions of voluntarism as they relate to care in general, and healthcare in particular (Wolch, 1990; Brown, 1997; Milligan, 2001), and it is here that the research in this chapter is situated. Specifically, our approach to understanding the link between voluntarism and health contributes to the emerging literature by addressing the important distinction between formal and informal volunteering, with a focus on the provision of healthcare services in the home and community in Canada.

As noted above, within the informal and voluntary sector there is a marked divergence between care that is provided on a volunteer basis formally through voluntary organisations and community groups on the one hand (that is, *formal volunteering*), and care that is provided on a volunteer basis outside of organisations or groups on the other (that is, *informal volunteering*). While studies of voluntarism highlight the growing significance of both formal and informal volunteering in the provision of healthcare services, they also draw attention to the uneven levels of voluntary activity across space and within specific places as they relate to the political context of welfare state reforms (for example, the rise of the shadow state) (Milligan and Fyfe, 2004). Geographic research particularly emphasises the place-based differences in the nature and meaning of voluntary activity (for example, Wolch and Geiger, 1983; Wolpert and Reiner, 1984, 1985), and more recently, how changes in national welfare programmes affect the role of both formal and informal volunteers in the direct provision of care and in fostering access to services (for example, Milligan, 2001). The latter focus draws on theorisations of social capital (for example, Lochner et al, 2001) and citizenship (for example, Brown, 1997), which resonate with concern for understanding the complex webs of interaction that surround the ascendancy of informal and voluntary care in countries such as Canada.

Researching voluntarism in Canada

In Canada, public service restructuring has been facilitated primarily through the reworking of central–local relationships (that is, between the federal, provincial and municipal governments) and public–private responsibilities (that is, between public, private and voluntary sectors). In the health sector, government has worked to reduce its role in both the funding and delivery of services (Rosenberg and James, 1994). Strategies here have included the centralisation and rationalisation of services according to cost-efficiency and/or accessibility criteria, the devolution of responsibilities for direct delivery of services to the private and voluntary sectors, and the privatisation of services previously provided and/or funded by the state (Hanlon and Rosenberg, 1998; James, 1999; Cloutier-Fisher and Joseph, 2000; Hanlon, 2001). One outcome of such strategies has been an increasing interdependence of public, private and voluntary sector institutions in healthcare (for example, Rekart, 1993). As a result, the Canadian context is characterised by a growing reliance on voluntary organisations, community groups and volunteers to provide healthcare services at the local level both formally and informally. Underlying this transformation, however, is the highly debatable assumption that local informal and voluntary sector providers have the capacity and willingness to play active and direct roles in the provision of healthcare services (Hall and Reed, 2000).

While the implicit assumptions of government rationalisation, devolution and privatisation have generated heightened interest in the capacity of the informal and voluntary sector (Hall and Banting, 2000), empirical research on voluntary sector health providers remains relatively limited, particularly within human geography. Growing interest in linking voluntarism and health is, however, reflected in a recent inventory of 'voluntary health sector'-related research in Canada that lists 101 journal articles published between 1971 and 2001, of which approximately 90% were published since 1990 (Dorman, 2002). Studies focused variously on health policy, structural and functional aspects of provider organisations, and the experiences of volunteer providers and recipients of care in light of the increasing demand for informal and voluntary care associated with Canada's aging population, decreasing levels of government funding associated with restructuring, and shifts in the overall character of the volunteer base (for example, LaPerriere, 1998). More general research on voluntarism in Canada has focused on the number of voluntary organisations (primarily registered charities), their size, scope, finances and operations (for example, Day and Devlin, 1997; Hall and Macpherson, 1997), as well as the characteristics of formal and informal volunteers providing care (for example, Reed and Selbee, 2000, 2001a; Selbee and Reed, 2001). Studies based primarily on analyses of data available from Statistics Canada reveal that the proportion of people who volunteer formally is declining, while the proportion of people who volunteer informally is increasing (for example, see Hall et al, 1998, 2001). As part of the changing nature of volunteering in Canada, the relative proportions of women and seniors are also increasing, as is the overall intensity of voluntary activity. As Reed and Selbee (2001b) report, for example, a shrinking core of volunteers are providing the majority of services, with only 9% of Canadian adults accounting for 80% of total hours volunteered across the country in 2000. Overall, these trends emphasise the need to understand formal and informal volunteering as it relates to the issues surrounding the restructuring of the Canadian health sector.

The literature on restructuring, governance and voluntarism forms an important backdrop for understanding how the delivery of healthcare services and voluntarism intertwine in Canada. In particular, the informal and voluntary sector responds to the dynamics of changing governance and public sector restructuring. Key elements of this relationship are captured in a descriptive model for exploring the dynamics of informal and voluntary care (see Figure 6.1). The model provides a framework for conceptualising the various forces of change associated with restructuring, namely the repositioning of regulatory responsibility for public services between central and local levels of government on the one hand, and public and private spheres of interest on the other. It also highlights the changing

Figure 6.1: Framework for exploring the dynamics of informal and voluntary care

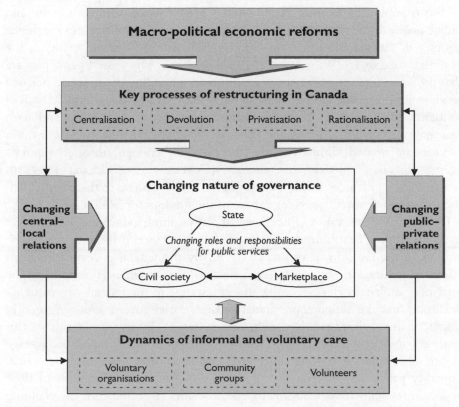

Source: Adapted from Skinner and Rosenberg (2002, p 38)

nature of governance, as direct responsibilities for public services shift from the state to civil society, the marketplace and ultimately the informal and voluntary sector. In essence, the interrelated processes of change among restructuring, governance and voluntarism are represented by the connections between the specific components of the model (that is, arrows) which signal the overall shifting responsibilities that place increasing pressure on voluntary organisations, community groups and volunteers. The contextual literature described above, and encapsulated in Figure 6.1, informs our approach to understanding informal and voluntary care – in Canada and elsewhere – by providing a specific framework for exploring the manifestation of issues that link voluntarism to the delivery of healthcare in general, and home and community care in particular. Further consideration, however, must first be given to the health policy context within which informal and voluntary care occurs.

Health and home care policy in Canada

To understand the delivery of healthcare (and home and community care) as it relates to voluntarism in a Canadian context, one needs to understand that there is no Canadian healthcare system per se, but 10 provincial and three territorial healthcare systems, each of which shares a common set of principles as enshrined in the federal 1984 Canada Health Act (CHA). Indeed, some academic and public policy debates argue that healthcare provided for the military and aboriginal peoples in Canada constitute two additional healthcare systems, bringing the potential total to 15 (Wilson and Rosenberg, 2002). The shared principles are that provinces and territories are responsible for providing medical and hospital services (the *comprehensive principle*), which cover all provincial and territorial residents (the *universality principle*) without any economic barriers and with reasonable geographical access (the *accessibility principle*), regardless of where those services are needed within Canada (the *portability principle*) through a public agency (the *public administration principle*) (Government of Canada, 1984). In return for the provinces' and territories' agreement to adhere to these principles, the federal government provides a share of the funding for healthcare.

By the early 1990s, various forces were at play resulting in increasing differences in the delivery of healthcare across the provinces and territories, and, it might be argued, in the breakdown of the CHA. Firstly, the federal government, in its efforts to reduce a growing national deficit, reduced its financial support to the provinces and territories. Secondly, and in response to the federal government's declining financial support, provincial and territorial governments engaged in restructuring their respective healthcare systems. Thirdly, as a result of this restructuring, the number of hospitals or hospital beds was reduced, the average length of stay times in hospitals decreased, and day surgery procedures increased. Fourthly, provincial governments changed the governance structures of their healthcare systems, making locally based authorities responsible for the planning and/or delivery of healthcare services. Depending on the ideology of the provincial or territorial governing party, this was accompanied by either increasing centralisation or decentralisation of funding responsibility. Fifthly, the first four trends led to a growing demand for care in the home and community, and this outstripped the ability of local health authorities to provide services. The result was a growing role for private organisations, voluntary sector agencies and informal providers in the delivery of home and community care. Finally, and somewhat ironically, because there was agreement among the federal, provincial and territorial governments that home and community care lay 'outside' of the mandate of the CHA, there has been substantial variation across Canada in terms of who is eligible for such services, what services are included, who is responsible and how much of care in the home and community is paid for through the provincial or territorial health insurance plans (see Health Canada, 1998). This has resulted in a growing call for a national 'home care' plan, either enshrined within the CHA or in the form of similar principles (for example, Romanow, 2002).

As a result of these wide-ranging changes in Canadian healthcare policy, the organisation and delivery of healthcare services – something already characterised by uneven development and spatial inequalities – has been shifting away from hospital- and institutional-based care towards care in the home or elsewhere in the community (Coyte and McKeever, 2001). In general, home and community care, hereafter referred to as 'home care', now occupies a pivotal position within the overall healthcare system in Canada, encompassing a continuum of publicly and privately funded health services and support for seniors, other adults living with continuing care needs and children with disabilities (Hollander, 2002). Home care services address a diverse range of health needs, including chronic conditions that require intensive care, palliative care and relief care for informal and voluntary caregivers (Stephenson and Sawyer, 2002). Although the configuration differs across the provincial and territorial health system in Canada (see Alexander, 2002), these services are divided generally into 'in-home services', which include homemaking services (for example, cleaning, laundry and shopping), personal support services (for example, bathing and toileting), professional support services (for example, nursing and rehabilitation therapies) and 'community support services' (such as meals-on-wheels, caregiver respite and transportation). These services are provided formally through a mix of public health institutions, and voluntary and private sector organisations, which is supplemented by a network of unpaid caregivers drawn from those family, friends and neighbours that comprise the informal and voluntary sector (Aronson and Neysmith, 1997). Across Canada, however, it has become clear that the informal and voluntary sector plays an increasingly active and direct role in the provision of home care services (that is, the rise of informal and voluntary care) (for example, Wiles, 2003a).

The ascendancy of informal and voluntary care in the home and community is an especially salient issue within Canadian healthcare policy and practice. Indeed, the changes in central–local relations and public–private responsibilities associated with public service restructuring, and articulated through public policy (for example, Ontario HSRC, 2000), are predicated on the assumption that public provision of healthcare services can be replaced effectively by informal and voluntary sectors at the local level (Evans and Shields, 2002). The shift away from institutional–based care is symptomatic of the interrelated processes of change associated with restructuring, governance and voluntarism, whereby the informal and voluntary sector bears an increasing share of responsibility for the delivery of public services in general and healthcare services in particular (see Figure 6.1).

In essence, informal and voluntary home care can be seen as a local manifestation of healthcare restructuring processes promoting a shift away from institutional–based care, and changes in the nature of governance that emphasise the ascendancy of informal and voluntary sectors in the provision of healthcare services. A cross-sectional analysis of home care in Canada illustrates that the issues surrounding the shift towards informal and voluntary care discussed above are becoming increasingly important for our understanding of the link between healthcare and voluntarism. To this end, the remainder of the chapter focuses on the case of publicly funded home care in Canada.

Illustrating trends in home care services and voluntarism

To shed light on the relationship between healthcare and voluntarism in Canada, we now turn to the empirical example of informal and voluntary home care, which we explore using results from the 1998-99 NPHS and the 1997 NSGVP. These broad-scale surveys provide comprehensive information on Canadian public health and voluntarism, respectively, and their integration provides the empirical basis for understanding the utilisation (demand) and provision (supply) of informal and voluntary home care at various scales in the late 1990s (that is, national, regional, provincial, metropolitan, urban and rural). All of the results that follow have a statistical significance of 95% or higher ($p<0.05$), based on Chi-Square tests of weighted estimates from the NPHS and NSGVP. Other technical details about the methodology employed in the analysis are reported in Skinner and Rosenberg (2002).

The major types of home care help needed by Canadians include acute medical or post-surgical care, rehabilitative care, palliative care, supportive care (for those with ongoing physical and personal needs related to a chronic health condition) and others such as mental health needs and caregiver relief (Keefe, 2002). As shown in Table 6.1, in 1998-99, approximately 2.7% of the total Canadian population reported receiving some type of formal home care service with some variation from province to province. Those receiving home care were most likely to receive nursing services, help with housework or personal care (Statistics Canada, 1998-1999a). The use of home care differed according to gender, age and income, and differences from province to province were marginal (see Table 6.1).

In contrast to the numbers of those who received care, approximately 11% of the total Canadian population indicated they needed some form of help with

Table 6.1: 'Home care received' and 'need for help with home care-related tasks' in Canada by gender, age and income

	Canada		Western Canada		Ontario		Quebec		Atlantic Canada	
	Home care received	Need for help	Home care received	Need for help	Home care received	Need for help	Home care received	Need for help	Home care received	Need for help
% of total population	2.7	11.1	2.4	10.9	3.1	11.3	2.2	10.3	2.7	13.3
% of male population	1.8	7.9	1.5	7.3	2.1	7.7	1.7[a]	8.0	1.9	10.9
% of female population	3.5	14.1	3.4	14.4	4.0	14.7	2.7	12.5	3.4	15.6
% of population under 65	1.0	6.8	0.9	6.9	1.2	7.0	0.8[a]	5.8	1.0	8.3
% of population over 65	11.5	37.5	10.7	35.2	13.1	37.4	9.9	38.5	11.6	43.0
% of population with AHI below $40,000	4.8	17.4	4.3	16.7	6.6	18.8	3.5	15.9	4.0	19.1
% of population with AHI above $40,000	1.0	6.5	1.0	6.7	1.1	7.0	[b]	5.3	1.1	6.3

Notes:

AHI = annual household income

[a] According to Statistics Canada (1998-1999b), the coefficient of variation for this estimate is between 16.6% and 33.3%: it has a high sampling variability and must be interpreted with caution.

[b] According to Statistics Canada (1998-1999b), the coefficient of variation for this estimate is greater than 33.3%: it is unacceptable for release.

Source: Statistics Canada (1998-1999a)

home care. Again there is some regional variation in the level of help required, and those who required help were most likely to indicate that they needed help with heavy household chores although tasks such as shopping, meal preparation, personal care and moving about the house were also mentioned (Statistics Canada, 1998-1999a). The need for home care-related tasks also varied with gender, age and income (see Table 6.1).

The gap between home care received and home care needed is a manifestation of the processes of restructuring in the Canadian healthcare system. There is no way of determining how much of the gap reflects a total absence of services, and how much it reflects the role of informal caregiving and the desire to relieve informal caregivers of these responsibilities. The data on home care received, home care needed and the gap between them, however, directs us to the role that volunteers play in providing home care formally and informally.

Voluntary activities in Canada are coordinated through various organisations, and span a wide range of interests that include: arts and culture; education and youth development; employment and economic agencies; environment and wildlife; foreign and international development; health; law and justice; multidomain agencies such as the Red Cross and YM/YWCA; religion; social services; society and public benefit; and sports and recreation (Hall et al, 1998). Several of the activities coordinated through health and social services organisations relate directly to the utilisation of home care services discussed above. Home care-related voluntary activities include providing care and support; preparing, delivering and serving food; driving; and undertaking household maintenance (Statistics Canada, 1997a).

For the purposes of measuring voluntarism in general, and for our purposes of examining the role that volunteers play in providing home care in particular, Statistics Canada defined 'volunteers' as those individuals aged 15 and over, who willingly perform a service without pay, through a group or organisation, and who volunteered at least once in the 12 months preceding the NSGVP (Statistics Canada, 1997a). Using this definition, approximately 31% of the total population in Canada was involved in some type of formal voluntary activity in 1997. Table 6.2 shows that, regionally, Western Canada had the most volunteers per capita (37.3%), as compared to Quebec, which had the least (22.1%).

Excluded from the Statistics Canada definition of 'volunteer' are those people who give their time as individuals, unconnected to formal group structures or activities. As indicated in Table 6.2, approximately 73% of the total population volunteers 'informally'. Similar to the interregional variations in formal volunteering, Western Canada had the most informal volunteers per capita (77.3%) and Quebec had the least (67.2%). Informal volunteers are involved in various types of activities including housework; yard work and maintenance; shopping and driving; support for the sick and elderly; support for recovery from short-term illness; visiting the elderly; babysitting; assistance with correspondence; teaching and coaching; and business and farm work (Statistics Canada, 1997a). The first five types of informal activities listed above also relate directly to the

Table 6.2: Formal and informal volunteering in Canada by gender, age and income

	Canada		Western Canada		Ontario		Quebec		Atlantic Canada	
	Formal volunteer	Informal volunteer	Formal volunteer	Informal volunteer	Formal volunteer	Informal volunteer	Formal volunteer	Informal volunteer	Formal volunteer	Informal volunteer
% of total population	31.4	73.1	37.3	77.3	32.0	73.2	22.1	67.2	35.7	76.0
% of male population	29.4	70.9	33.8	74.9	29.7	70.3	22.5	66.2	32.2	73.8
% of female population	33.3	75.3	40.8	79.7	34.2	75.9	21.7	68.2	39.1	78.2
% of population under 65	32.9	75.8	39.4	80.5	33.1	75.3	23.3	68.9	38.0	79.5
% of population over 65	22.8	57.8	25.5	59.2	25.6	60.8	15.2	52.1	22.7	56.3
% of population with AHI below $40,000	25.3	67.5	30.0	71.1	25.9	64.8	18.6	64.7	29.7	73.2
% of population with AHI above $40,000	37.1	73.5	43.8	82.8	36.2	78.9	26.8	70.7	45.0	80.5

Note:

AHI = annual household income

Source: Statistics Canada (1997b)

use of home care services. Within the broad trends of formal and informal volunteering gender, age, income and regional differences also appear (see Table 6.2).

Geographic variation in home care and voluntarism not only takes place among the provinces, but also exists *within* the provinces. We can use the province of Ontario as an example, for the trends in Ontario are similar to those nationally (see Tables 6.1 and 6.2). Our analysis focuses on 'metropolitan' Ontario, as represented by the Toronto Census Metropolitan Area (CMA); 'urban' Ontario, which includes those built-up areas outside of CMAs with a population concentration of 1,000 or more and a population density of 400 or more per km²; and 'rural' Ontario, which includes those remaining enumeration areas (Statistics Canada, 1997a, 1998-1999b).

In Ontario, approximately 3% of the total population received some type of formal home care service, and approximately 11% of the total population required some form of help with tasks relating to home care. While these percentages mirror the national averages, as shown in Table 6.3, what stands out within the provincial analysis is that metropolitan Ontario has the lowest relative use of home care and the lowest relative need for help. The within-province analysis also shows that when gender, age and income are taken into account the patterns of use and need become increasingly complex (see Table 6.3).

Also mirroring the national trends, the home care services used and the types of help needed are similar in Ontario. Figure 6.2 indicates that the general pattern of need for help is consistent within Ontario; however, there is a disparity between the types of home care services received and the types of help required. The disparities suggest that there are a number of types of help needed that were not met through formal home care service provision in 1998-99.

Indeed, a key consideration when exploring the utilisation and provision of home care services is: how many individuals are receiving informal care? Following Yantzi and Rosenberg (2001), this question can be resolved, in part, by using the percentage of respondents in the NPHS who identified a need for help with home care-related tasks who also received formal home care services. Figure 6.3 shows that in Ontario, only approximately 20% of the total population that required help received formal home care services. It can be inferred that individuals who identified a need for help but who did not receive formal home care services either relied on the informal sector to provide the assistance or care required, or did not receive any care at all. Within the province, rural Ontario had the smallest proportion of population who needed help and did not receive formal home care. This suggests that with respect to the utilisation of home care services in Ontario, both the informal and formal sectors are important components, and, in turn, this raises questions regarding the scope of formal and informal volunteering.

Voluntary activity in Ontario also replicates the national trends. Thirty-two per cent of the total provincial population were involved in formal volunteering and approximately 73% were involved in informal volunteering in 1997. Due to

Table 6.3: 'Home care received' and 'need for help with home care-related tasks' in Ontario by gender, age and income

	Ontario		Toronto CMA		Urban Ontario		Rural Ontario	
	Home care received	Need for help	Home care received	Need for help	Home care received	Need for help	Home care received	Need for help
% of total population	3.1	11.3	2.4	8.8	3.5	13.0	3.8[a]	12.5
% of male population	2.1	7.7	2.0	6.1	b	8.6	b	9.7
% of female population	4.0	14.7	2.9	11.5	b	17.0	b	15.2
% of population under 65	1.2	7.0	b	5.2	b	8.3	b	7.9
% of population over 65	13.1	37.4	b	34.9	b	38.9	b	38.2
% of population with AHI below $40,000	6.6	18.8	b	13.8	b	21.7	b	22.3
% of population with AHI above $40,000	1.1	7.0	b	6.4	b	7.5	b	7.1

Notes:

AHI = annual household income

[a] According to Statistics Canada (1998-1999b), the coefficient of variation for this estimate is between 16.6% and 33.3%: it has a high sampling variability and must be interpreted with caution.

[b] According to Statistics Canada (1998-1999b), the coefficient of variation for this estimate is greater than 33.3%: it is unacceptable for release.

Source: Statistics Canada (1998-1999a)

Figure 6.2: Types of 'need for help' in Ontario

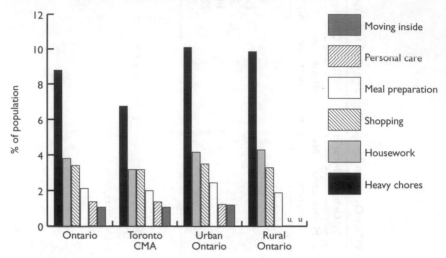

Note:
ᵘ According to Statistics Canada (1998-1999b), the coefficient of variation for this estimate is greater than 33.3%: it is unacceptable for release.
Source: Statistics Canada (1998-1999a)

Figure 6.3: Receipt of home care within population that 'needs help' in Ontario

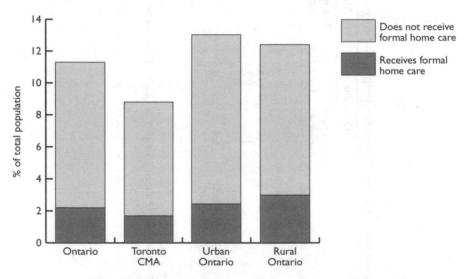

Source: Statistics Canada (1998-1999a)

the sample limitations of the NSGVP, however, comparisons between metropolitan, urban and rural Ontario can not be done.

The scope of the voluntary sector in Ontario can, however, be explored using the proportion of the population involved in different types of home care-related formal and informal voluntary activities. While people in Ontario were involved in a wide range of formal volunteer activities, according to the NSGVP, in 1997, approximately 4-7% of the provincial population were involved in some type of formal volunteering relating directly to the provision of home care in Ontario (namely, collecting, serving and delivering food; providing care and support; driving; and maintenance). With respect to informal volunteering, people from Ontario also participated in a wide range of activities, with approximately 25-40% of the provincial population involved in some type of informal volunteering relating directly or indirectly to the provision of home care. Activities here included shopping and driving; yard work and maintenance; housework; supporting the sick and elderly; and supporting recovery from short-term illness.

The NPHS and NSGVP results from Ontario and Canada suggest that with respect to the utilisation of home care services and the provision of informal and formal volunteer activities, both the informal and voluntary sectors are important components of the healthcare system. Even at the broad geographic scales utilised, the results also show how 'uneven' the distribution of home care services, and informal and formal volunteer activities are across Canada.

Linking home care and voluntarism

The Statistics Canada data provide insights into the utilisation and provision of informal and voluntary home care in Canada, and Ontario, as it appeared in the late 1990s. The cross-sectional data illustrate the key trends and variations in the use and type of formal and informal home care, and in the extent and type of formal and informal voluntary activity. Overall, the empirical evidence from our research suggests that the current state of informal and voluntary care reflects the changing nature of local governance and dynamics of voluntarism associated with public service restructuring conceptualised in Figure 6.1.

The results also point to the considerable empirical and conceptual challenges of researching the linkages between restructuring, governance and voluntarism as they relate to healthcare services. While national surveys such as the NPHS and NSGVP provide broad pictures of the trends and issues surrounding healthcare and voluntarism, they do not shed light on the richness of experiences of change, both positive and negative, at the level of communities and individual volunteers. These limitations prompt us to reflect on how we conceptualise and contextualise healthcare and voluntarism. With respect to the conceptual framework proposed above, our analysis reveals aspects of healthcare and voluntarism as they relate to broad trends of restructuring and governance; however, there is a clear need for more detailed research into the local dynamics of informal and voluntary care, and how these are manifested in the experiences of specific places. Such work would extend research already carried out on the geographies of informal and voluntary care (for example, Milligan, 2001; Conradson, 2003; Staeheli and Brown, 2003), including that undertaken in the Canadian context (for example, Joseph and Martin-Matthews, 1993; Cloutier-Fisher and Joseph, 2000; Williams, 2001, 2002; Wiles, 2003a, 2003b; Cloutier-Fisher and Skinner, 2006).

While there is much variation in the utilisation of home care and provision of home care-related voluntary activities between regions in Canada and within Ontario, there are no discernible spatial patterns. This result is indicative of the idiosyncratic nature of provincial home care policies that stems, in part, from the lack of national regulatory standards concerning home care (CHCA, 1998; Romanow, 2002). At the same time, it is also symptomatic of the interdependent nature of healthcare (and voluntary sector) policy decision making in Canada, which leads to diverse and disparate experiences within and between provincial and territorial jurisdictions. Nevertheless, taking the case of Ontario, the Canadian data demonstrate that the informal and voluntary sectors are major components of the local organisation and delivery of home care.

Interestingly, we observe significantly lower levels of informal and formal voluntary activity in general, and with respect to home care services in particular, between the province of Quebec and the rest of Canada. While there is limited empirical evidence for understanding the lower levels of voluntarism in the province of Quebec (for example, Reed and Selbee, 2001a), key debates within the Canadian (mostly Quebec francophone) literature suggest that the explanation lies in the historical development of state–civil society relations in French Canada (for a recent example see Vaillancourt et al, 2002). In contrast to English Canada, the history of Quebec's informal and voluntary sector is based more on a continental model of collective responsibility than on individual philanthropy embedded in English civil law (White, 2001). Consequently, the provincial government plays a much larger role in health and social services in Quebec than in other jurisdictions in Canada (Jenson and Phillips, 2000), thereby leading to increased levels of formal provision of care in the home and community, and likely reducing the demand or the need for the informal provision of home care.

Various types of formal and informal home care services, including nursing, housework, personal care and meal preparation, are used for managing acute illness and supporting individuals with long-term, complex care needs. More significantly, the evidence that less than one quarter of the national population who require help with home care-related tasks receive formal home care services means three quarters of the population who need help rely on the informal and voluntary sector to provide care, find other ways to cope, or forego any type of help at all. The other side of the home care/voluntarism coin reveals that various types of (formal and informal) volunteer activities, including housework, maintenance, support for the sick, elderly, support for short-term recovery, preparing and delivering food, shopping and driving, are related directly to the organisation and delivery of formal and informal home care.

The results of this analysis accentuate the suggestion that the development of informal and voluntary home care in Canada and Ontario reflects the changing nature of local governance associated with public service restructuring. Indeed, the development of informal and voluntary care is a harbinger of the broader reorientation of state–civil society relations, which are moving towards a greater mix of public, private and informal and voluntary sector roles and responsibilities with respect to public service provision. The far-reaching transformation of public service provisioning and governance resonates with concern for the restructuring of landscapes within which informal and voluntary care occurs. Such is the case in Canada, especially given the continuing promulgation of federal, provincial and territorial health policies that place care in the home and community beyond the legislative principles of the CHA, which leads us to question: how long will Canadian informal and voluntary care be caught outside of the Act?

Conclusion

Current discourse and debates surrounding restructuring, governance and voluntarism inform the exploration of informal and voluntary care presented in this chapter. Specifically, the integration of the concepts and findings from the literature provides a framework for understanding the dynamics of informal and voluntary care with respect to the broad social, political and institutional context within which it takes place. Ultimately, this research sheds light on how the interrelated processes of change associated with restructuring, governance and voluntarism play out through the organisation and delivery of healthcare services at the macro-scale.

The case of informal and voluntary home care in Canada described here sheds further light on the complex link between voluntarism and health. The analysis of broad-scale survey results at national, regional and subprovincial (metropolitan, urban and rural) levels provides an empirical basis for understanding the ascendancy of voluntary organisations, community groups and volunteers as major players in the local organisation and delivery of healthcare services. It also strengthens the contextual foundation for conceptualising the changing dynamics of informal and voluntary care as a local manifestation of responses to public service restructuring processes (including the attendant reworking of central–local relations and public–private interests) and changes in the nature of governance (including the shifting responsibilities for health and home care towards civil society).

The Canadian data, while limited in many ways, provides enough evidence to elucidate the geographical expression of healthcare and voluntarism, and to suggest that the relationship between the changing nature of governance, the dynamics of voluntarism and the provision of healthcare services should be pursued further at the local level. The trends reinforce the need for more detailed analyses that integrate healthcare and voluntarism data at meaningful geographical and administrative scales that reflect communities as places, not just as statistical units. These conclusions build on the relatively limited geographical literature surrounding restructuring, governance and voluntarism, and engage directly the need to consider in greater depth the importance of the informal and voluntary sector with respect to healthcare issues such as home and community care. It is here that the conceptual framework for exploring the development of informal and voluntary care illustrated in Figure 6.1 could prove useful in understanding voluntarism in 'emplaced' rather than abstract terms.

Although theoretical links between restructuring, governance and voluntarism as they relate to healthcare services are being developed in academic and public policy discourses, there is still a need to think about how to explore the scope of these relationships empirically. Indeed, if public service restructuring processes in general, and healthcare reforms in particular, continue to depend on the ascendancy of the informal and voluntary care in the home and community, why not begin to pursue appropriate information at this level? Regardless of the theories, methods and data employed, future research on voluntarism and health will require more attention to the place-specific particularities of local communities, thereby addressing poignant calls in the literature to shed light on the curious neglect of voluntarism as it relates to healthcare services.

Acknowledgements

The Social Sciences and Humanities Research Council of Canada (SSHRC) provided financial support for the first author through SSHRC Doctoral Fellowship Award No 752 2002 1597. Partial support for the first author was also received in the form of a Canadian Health Services Research Foundation (CHSRF)/Canadian Institute of Health Research (CIHR) Research Training Award. Financial support for some of the background research for this chapter is from the SSHRC funded project, *Geographies of Volunteerism*, Research Grant No 410 2004 2229. The views expressed, however, are solely those of the authors and in no way reflect the views of the SSHRC, CHSRF/CIHR or the Government of Canada.

References

Alexander, T. (2002) 'The History and Evolution of Long-term Care in Canada', in M. Stephenson and E. Sawyer (eds) *Continuing the Care: The Issues and Challenges for Long-Term Care*, Ottawa: CHA Press, pp 1-56.

Andrews, G.J. (2002) 'Private Complementary Medicine and Older People: Service Use and User Empowerment', *Ageing and Society*, vol 22, pp 343-68.

Andrews, G.J. (2003) 'Placing the Consumption of Private Complementary Medicine: Everyday Geographies of Older People's Use', *Health and Place*, vol 9, pp 337-49.

Aronson, J. and Neysmith, S.M. (1997) 'The Retreat of the State and Long-term Care Provision: Implications for Frail Elderly People, Unpaid Family Carers and Paid Home Care Workers', *Studies in Political Economy*, vol 53, pp 37-66.

Barnett, J.R. (2000) 'Rationalising Hospital Services: Reflections on Hospital Restructuring and its Impacts in New Zealand', *New Zealand Geographer*, vol 56, no 1, pp 5-21.

Brown, M.P. (1997) *Replacing Citizenship: AIDS Activism and Radical Democracy*, New York, NY: The Guilford Press.

Brown, M. (2003) 'Hospice and the Spatial Paradoxes of Terminal Care', *Environment and Planning A*, vol 35, pp 833-51.

CHCA (Canadian Home Care Association) (1998) *Portraits of Canada: An Overview of Public Home Care Programs*, Prepared for Health Canada by the CHCA and l'Association des CLSC et des CHSLD du Québec (available at www.cdnhomecare.on.ca).

Cloutier-Fisher, D. and Joseph, A.E. (2000) 'Long-term Care Restructuring in Rural Ontario: Retrieving Community Service User and Provider Narratives', *Social Science and Medicine*, vol 50, pp 1037-45.

Cloutier-Fisher, D. and Skinner, M.W. (2006) 'Levelling the Playing Field? Exploring the Implications of Managed Competition for Voluntary Sector Providers of Long-term Care in Small Town Ontario', *Health and Place*, vol 12 (not yet published).

Conradson, D. (2003) 'Editorial – Geographies of Care: Spaces, Practices, Experiences', *Social and Cultural Geography*, vol 4, no 4, pp 451-4.

Cope, M. and Gilbert, M.R. (2001) 'Introduction – Geographies of Welfare Reform', *Urban Geography*, vol 22, no 5, pp 385-90.

Coyte, P.C. and McKeever, P. (2001) 'Home Care in Canada: Passing the Buck', *Canadian Journal of Nursing Research*, vol 33, no 2, pp 11-25.

Crampton, P., Dowell, A. and Woodward, A. (2001) 'Third Sector Primary Care for Vulnerable Populations', *Social Science and Medicine*, vol 53, pp 1491-502.

Day, K. and Devlin, R.A. (1997) *The Canadian Nonprofit Sector*, Ottawa: Canadian Polity Research Networks.

Dorman, A. (2002) 'An Inventory of Past Research on the Voluntary Health Sector in Canada', in Health Canada, *Voluntary Health Sector Working Papers (Volume 1)*, Ottawa: Voluntary Sector and Strategic Frameworks Unit, Population and Public Health Branch, Health Canada.

Environment and Planning A (2003) Special issue on 'Geographies of Care and Welfare', *Environment and Planning A*, vol 35, no 5.

Evans, B.M. and Shields, J. (2002) 'The Third Sector: Neo-liberal Restructuring, Governance, and the Remaking of State–Civil Society Relationships', in C. Dunn (ed) *The Handbook of Canadian Public Administration*, Toronto: Oxford University Press, pp 139-58.

Fyfe, N.R. and Milligan, C. (2003) 'Out of the Shadows: Exploring the Contemporary Geographies of Voluntarism', *Progress in Human Geography*, vol 27, pp 397-413.

Goodwin, M. and Painter, J. (1996) 'Local Governance, the Crisis of Fordism and the Changing Geographies of Regulation', *Transactions of the Institute of British Geographers*, vol 21, pp 635-48.

Government of Canada (1984) *Canada Health Act* (Bill C-3), Ottawa: Government of Canada.

Hall, M.H. and Banting, K.G. (2000) 'The Nonprofit Sector in Canada: An Introduction', in K.G. Banting (ed) *The Nonprofit Sector in Canada: Roles and Responsibilities*, Kingston: McGill–Queen's University Press, pp 1–28.

Hall, M.H. and Macpherson, L.G. (1997) 'A Provincial Portrait of Canada's Charities', *Research Bulletin*, vol 4, nos 2–3, pp 1–12, Toronto: Canadian Centre for Philanthropy.

Hall, M.H. and Reed, P.B. (2000) 'Shifting the Burden: How Much can Government Download to the Non-profit Sector?', *Canadian Public Administration*, vol 41, no 1, pp 1–20.

Hall, M.H., McKeown, L. and Roberts, K. (2001) *Caring Canadians, Involved Canadians: Highlights from the 2000 National Survey of Giving, Volunteering and Participating*, Statistics Canada Report, Catalogue No 71-542-XIE, Ottawa: Statistics Canada.

Hall, M.H., Knighton, T., Reed, P., Bussière, P., McRae, D. and Bowen, P. (1998) *Caring Canadians, Involved Canadians: Highlights from the 1997 National Survey of Giving, Volunteering and Participating*, Statistics Canada Report, Catalogue No 71-542-XIE, Ottawa: Statistics Canada.

Hanlon, N.T. (2001) 'Hospital Restructuring in Smaller Urban Ontario Settings: Unwritten Rules and Uncertain Relations', *The Canadian Geographer*, vol 45, no 2, pp 252–67.

Hanlon, N.T. and Rosenberg, M.W. (1998) 'Not-so-new Public Management and the Denial of Geography: Ontario Health-care Reform in the 1990s', *Environment and Planning C: Government and Policy*, vol 16, pp 559–72.

Health Canada (1998) *Public Home Care Expenditures in Canada 1975-1976 to 1997-1998*, Ottawa: Health Canada, Policy and Consultation Branch.

Hollander, M.J. (2002) 'The Continuum of Care: An Integrated System of Service Delivery', in M. Stephenson and E. Sawyer (eds) *Continuing the Care: The Issues and Challenges for Long-Term Care*, Ottawa: CHA Press, pp 57–70.

James, A.M. (1999) 'Closing Rural Hospitals in Saskatchewan: On the Road to Wellness?', *Social Science and Medicine*, vol 49, pp 1021–34.

Jenson, J. and Phillips, S.D. (2000) 'Distinctive Trajectories: Homecare and the Voluntary Sector in Quebec and Ontario', in K.G. Banting (ed) *The Nonprofit Sector in Canada: Roles and Responsibilities*, Kingston: McGill–Queen's University Press, pp 29–68.

Joseph, A.E. and Knight, D.B. (1999) 'Social Sciences and Public Policy in Restructuring Societies', in D.B. Knight and A.E. Joseph (eds) *Restructuring Societies: Insights From the Social Sciences*, Ottawa: Carleton University Press, pp 1–24.

Joseph, A.E. and Martin-Matthews, A. (1993) 'Growing Old in Aging Communities', *Journal of Canadian Studies*, vol 28, pp 14–29.

Kearns, R.A. and Joseph, A.E. (1997) 'Restructuring Health and Rural Communities in New Zealand', *Progress in Human Geography*, vol 21, no 1, pp 18–32.

Kearns, R.A. and Joseph, A.E. (2000) 'Contracting Opportunities: Interpreting Post-asylum Geographies of Mental Healthcare in Auckland, New Zealand', *Health and Place*, vol 6, pp 159-70.

Keefe, J.M. (2002) 'Home and Community Care', in M. Stephenson and E. Sawyer (eds) *Continuing the Care: The Issues and Challenges for Long-Term Care*, Ottawa, CHA Press, pp 109-42.

LaPerriere, B. (1998) *Volunteerism in the Canadian Health Sector*, Ottawa: Volunteer Canada.

Lewis, N. and Moran, W. (1998) 'Restructuring, Democracy and Geography in New Zealand', *Environment and Planning C: Government and Policy*, vol 16, pp 127-53.

Lochner, K., Kawachi, I. and Kennedy, B.P. (2001) 'Social Capital: A Guide to its Measurement', *Health and Place*, vol 5, pp 259-70.

Milligan, C. (1998) 'Pathways of Dependence: The Impact of Health and Social Care Restructuring – The Voluntary Experience', *Social Science and Medicine*, vol 56, pp 743-53.

Milligan, C. (2000) '"Bearing the Burden": Towards a Restructured Geography of Caring', *Area*, vol 32, pp 49-58.

Milligan, C. (2001) *Geographies of Care: Space, Place and the Voluntary Sector*, Aldershot: Ashgate.

Milligan, C. and Fyfe, N.R. (2004) 'Putting the Voluntary Sector in its Place: Geographical Perspectives on Voluntary Activity and Social Welfare in Glasgow', *Journal of Social Policy*, vol 33, no 1, pp 73-95.

Moran, W. (1999) 'Democracy and Geography in the Reregulation of New Zealand', in D.B. Knight and A.E. Joseph (eds) *Restructuring Societies: Insights from the Social Sciences*, Ottawa: Carleton University Press, pp 33-57.

Ontario HSRC (Health Services Restructuring Commission) (2000) *Looking Back, Looking Forward: The Ontario's Health Services Restructuring Commission (1996-2000) – A Legacy Report*, Ottawa: Canadian Health Services Research Foundation.

Parr, H. and Philo, C. (2003) 'Rural Mental Health and Social Geographies of Caring', *Social and Cultural Geography*, vol 4, no 4, pp 471-88.

Pinch, S.P. (1989) 'The Restructuring Thesis and the Study of Public Services', *Environment and Planning A*, vol 21, pp 905-26.

Pinch, S. (1997) *Worlds of Welfare: Understanding the Changing Geographies of Social Welfare Provision*, London: Routledge.

Reed, P.B. and Selbee, K.L. (2000) 'Distinctive Characteristics of Active Volunteers in Canada', *Nonprofit and Voluntary Sector Quarterly*, vol 29, no 4, pp 571-92.

Reed, P.B. and Selbee, K.L. (2001a) 'Volunteering and Giving: A Regional Perspective', *Canadian Social Trends*, winter, Statistics Canada, pp 16-18.

Reed, P.B. and Selbee, K.L. (2001b) 'The Civic Core in Canada: Disproportionality in Charitable Giving, Volunteering and Civic Participation', *Nonprofit and Voluntary Sector Quarterly*, vol 30, no 4, pp 761-80.

Rekart, J. (1993) *Public Funds, Private Provision: The Role of the Voluntary Sector*, Vancouver: University of British Columbia Press.

Romanow, R.J. (2002) *Building on Values: The Future of Health Care in Canada*, Final Report of the Commission on the Future of Health Care in Canada, Saskatoon.

Rosenberg, M.W. and James, A.M. (1994) 'The End of the Second Most Expensive Health Care System in the World: Some Geographical Implications', *Social Science and Medicine*, vol 39, no 7, pp 967-81.

Selbee, K.L. and Reed, P.B. (2001) 'Patterns of Volunteering Over the Life Cycle', *Canadian Social Trends*, summer, Statistics Canada, pp 2-6.

Skinner, M.W. and Rosenberg, M.W. (2002) *Health Care in Rural Communities: Exploring the Development of Informal and Voluntary Care*, SEDAP Research Paper No 79, Program for Research on the Social and Economic Dimensions of an Aging Population (SEDAP), Hamilton: McMaster University (available at http://socserv2.mcmaster.ca/sedap).

Social and Cultural Geography (2003) Special issue on 'Geographies of Care: Spaces, Practices, Experiences', *Social and Cultural Geography*, vol 4, no 4.

Staeheli, L.A. and Brown, M. (2003) 'Guest Editorial – Where has Welfare Gone? Introductory Remarks on the Geographies of Care and Welfare', *Environment and Planning A*, vol 35, pp 771-7.

Statistics Canada (1997a) *Microdata User Guide, National Survey of Giving, Volunteering and Participating* (revised 2000), Ottawa: Statistics Canada.

Statistics Canada (1997b) *National Survey of Giving, Volunteering and Participating 1997*, Ottawa: Statistics Canada.

Statistics Canada (1998-1999a) *National Population Health Survey, 1998-1999*, Ottawa: Statistics Canada.

Statistics Canada (1998-1999b) *Microdata User Guide, National Population Health Survey*, Ottawa: Statistics Canada.

Stephenson, M. and Sawyer, E. (eds) (2002) *Continuing the Care: The Issues and Challenges for Long-Term Care*, Ottawa: CHA Press.

Vaillancourt, Y., Aubry, F., Jetté, C. and Tremblay, L. (2002) 'Regulation Based on Solidarity: A Fragile Emergence in Quebec', in Y. Vaillancourt and L. Tremblay (eds) *Social Economy: Health and Welfare in Four Canadian Provinces*, Halifax: Fernwood Publishing, pp 29-70.

White, D. (2001) 'Maîtriser un Mouvement, Dompter une Idéologie – l'État et le Secteur Communautaire au Québec' ('Harnessing a Movement, Taming an Ideology: On the State and the Third Sector in Quebec'), *Isuma: Canadian Journal of Policy Research*, vol 2, no 2, pp 34-45.

Wiles, J. (2003a) 'Informal Caregivers' Experiences of Formal Support in a Changing Context', *Health and Social Care in the Community*, vol 11, no 3, pp 189-207.

Wiles, J. (2003b) 'Daily Geographies of Care: Mobility, Routine, Scale', *Social Science and Medicine*, vol 57, pp 1307-25.

Wiles, J. and Rosenberg, M.W. (2001) '"Gentle Caring Experience" Seeking Alternative Health Care in Canada', *Health and Place*, vol 7, pp 209-24.

Williams, A.M. (2000) 'The Diffusion of Alternative Healthcare: A Canadian Case Study of Chiropractic and Naturopathic Practices', *The Canadian Geographer*, vol 44, pp 152–66.

Williams, A.M. (2001) 'Home Care Restructuring at Work: The Impact of Policy Transformation on Women's Labour', in I. Dyck, N. Davis Lewis and S. McClafferty (eds) *Geographies of Women's Health*, London: Routledge, pp 107–26.

Williams, A.M. (2002) 'Changing Geographies of Care: Employing the Concept of Therapeutic Landscapes as a Framework for Examining Home Space', *Social Science and Medicine*, vol 55, no 1, pp 141–54.

Wilson, K. and Rosenberg, M.W. (2002) 'The Geographies of Crisis: Exploring Accessibility to Health Care in Canada', *The Canadian Geographer*, vol 46, no 3, pp 223–34.

Wistow, G. (1995) 'Aspirations and Realities: Community Care at the Crossroads', *Health and Social Care in the Community*, vol 3, no 4, pp 227–40.

Wolch, J.R. (1990) *The Shadow State: Government and the Voluntary Sector in Transition*, New York, NY: The Foundation Center.

Wolch, J.R. and Geiger, R.K. (1983) 'The Distribution of Urban Voluntary Resources: An Exploratory Analysis', *Environment and Planning A*, vol 15, pp 1067–82.

Wolpert, J. and Reiner, T.A. (1984) 'Service Provision by the Not-for-profit Sector: A Comparative Analysis', *Economic Geography*, vol 60, pp 28–37.

Wolpert, J. and Reiner, T.A. (1985) 'The Not-for-profit Sector in Stable and Growing Regions', *Urban Affairs Quarterly*, vol 20, pp 487–510.

Yantzi, N. and Rosenberg, M.W. (2001) 'Exploring the Use of Home Care Services by 18 to 29 year olds: Combining Empirical Analysis with a Theoretical Framework of Citizenship', Paper presented to the annual meeting of the Association of American Geographers, February, New York.

SEVEN

Competition, adaptation and resistance: (re)forming health organisations in New Zealand's third sector

Susan Owen and Robin Kearns

Introduction

Recent changes in the health policy environment have profoundly affected 'third sector' health-related organisations in New Zealand, prompting a competitive ethic, various forms of organisational adaptation and, among some, a vehement resistance to a contractual culture. In this chapter, we trace the emergence of organisational adaptation and resistance as two responses to changes in the policy environment among third sector health providers. In particular we consider the role that key agents play in shaping the direction of these organisations. Our survey reaches into the origins of third sector activities in New Zealand. We pay particular attention to the effects of health sector restructuring during the 1980s and 1990s and the ensuing split between purchasers and providers.

Our thinking on these issues was prompted by comments made by Nowland-Foreman (1998, p 108), who depicts the forces of change that descended on third sector organisations in New Zealand during the 1980s and 1990s as being 'gentle winds of change (that) turned into a hurricane that blew through an unsuspecting voluntary sector...'. The consequences of this change were apparent in comments made by the Community and Voluntary Sector Working Group (CVSWP) in 2001. This body was established in response to requests from the third sector that the New Zealand government review its relationship with these organisations. According to the CVSWG:

> The Working Party heard a clear message that the social and economic reforms of the past two decades, particularly in the state sector, had a profound effect on the relationship between government and the community sector, leaving a residue of mistrust and tension.... (CVSWP, 2001, p 61)

In response to this observation, our chapter explores the relationship between the New Zealand government and the third sector during the 1990s, seeking to further understanding of the implications of this 'hurricane' for third sector health organisations. We contend that organisational characteristics alter with the life cycle of the organisation and the involvement of key individuals, both internally and externally. They are also influenced by social, economic and political change. The devolution of funding regimes that accompanied a neoliberally informed purchaser–provider split resulted in heterogeneous geographical experiences. Some of these experiences have occurred in subtle ways that invoke shifts in the metaphoric 'place' of organisations within the third sector landscape. In order to understand these nuances of place, we argue that it is necessary to consider the prevailing structural influences as well as the agency of particular individuals within the organisations.

The term 'third sector' is consciously used throughout this chapter. We acknowledge that in New Zealand the phrase 'voluntary and community sector' is increasingly favoured, this being a broader term than 'voluntary organisations', commonly used in the British literature. We feel that this latter term is not an adequate descriptor of the diversity of the field. The terms 'not-for-profit' and 'non-government', while variously used in the literature, are also problematic historical labels that offer a narrow conceptualisation of what, in reality, is a mosaic of organisational form and function. Drawing from Weisbrod's (1977) concept, we use the notion of the 'third sector' to encapsulate the range of organisations discussed in this chapter (Crampton et al, 2000). This term is used to encompass the assumptions of voluntarism and not-for-profit, non-governmental agencies without emphasising one or the other. Further, it allows us to juxtapose these attributes with characteristics associated with the state and market sectors.

In this chapter we consider that the functions of third sector organisations have been romanticised both in academic literature and by the state. We contend that these ideals are challenged by the mechanisms of a neoliberalising state. We briefly canvas ideas of governmentality to illustrate how shifts in organisational function and place can be linked to both the processes of the state and the role of active agents. We then grant closer attention to New Zealand's third sector health organisations and how, in sum, they represent a changed landscape of provision. We focus on the culture of contracting which fundamentally changed the relations between the third sector and state in New Zealand. We follow the trends anticipated in this section by focusing on the voices of some of those most closely involved in the sector itself, organising the narratives around the themes of competition, adaptation and resistance. We close the chapter by concluding that the neoliberally inspired purchaser–provider split and the consequential development of a 'contract culture' has deeply impacted on third sector health organisations in New Zealand. We contend that this impact is discernable through a growth in the number and diversity of health-related organisations as well as the degree to which existing organisations are reporting a diminished trust, both of state agencies and other third sector organisations. We argue that key individuals have consciously adapted to, or resisted, the governmentalities of the period and, in so doing, shaped the place of their organisation in the third sector.

Placing the third sector: idealisation and governmentality

The roles of third sector organisations are often romanticised and portrayed as a panacea to the threat of 'mass' society (van Deth, 1997). In this idealisation, the 'place' that the third sector occupies in society is arguably one that potentially buffers the disadvantaged from the forces of the state and the market sectors (Bradford and Nowland-Foreman, 2001). Constructed around notions of community building, innovation, service provision and advocacy (Salamon et al, 2000) these organisations are held up by both the political left and right as an essential part of society (Heginbotham, 1990; Halfpenny and Reid, 2002). Much of this idealisation can be directly linked to the political positioning of the state as being an inappropriate provider of welfare services. It can be argued that the range of characteristics attributed to the third sector allow for political expediency, as commentators pick and choose the elements that best support their call for changes in welfare provision (Seibel and Anheier, 1990).

We argue that the implementation of state policies underpinned by neoliberal thought is inconsistent with the reproduction of an idealised third sector. The notions of competition, professionalism and accountability that pervade the language of the neoliberalising state are incompatible with the idealised qualities of third sector agencies. These neoliberal policy mechanisms may impact on the structure and function of third sector organisations, eroding their capacity to develop trust and maintain networks (Putnam, 1995) as well as limiting their efficacy in promoting social change, thus impacting on their relative place in the third sector.

The development of neoliberal policies by various Western governments has seen the use of the market to achieve ends previously controlled by the state. This process of 'marketisation' has resulted in a move within policy analysis from the traditional concept of government as top-down state control, to the notion of devolved governance (Morison, 2000). This shift has resulted in the implementation of mechanisms such as standards, auditing and monitoring in order to ensure organisational accountability. Collectively, this 'market speak' is the new language of control and has become implanted within state governmentality (Lewis and Moran, 1998).

Governmentality describes the embedded processes that influence the implementation of governance. It is observed in the banal 'everydayness' of state bureaucracy through the process and interactions of agencies. This process, or 'mentality', therefore impacts on the outcomes and experiences of citizens engaged with agencies (Morison, 2000) and can shape experiences of citizenship (Raco and Imrie, 2000). Thus how individual agents respond to these processes can shape the place of organisations within the third sector.

Key individuals, and therefore the organisations they govern, adapt to systems and discourses in order to achieve particular ends (Rose, 2002). Alternatively these individuals may attempt to resist this process. With respect to health, the influence of the state may promote shifts in discourses that then become embedded in healthcare policies and practices. An example of this shift is the move from institutions to community settings as the preferred sites of care. State policy, which has seen individuals removed from institutions and placed within community settings, has been supported and largely promoted by individuals in consumer organisations and health professionals. Yet this process of deinstitutionalisation has also been met with resistance, especially from other stakeholders including parents and consumers (Gleeson and Kearns, 2001).

The process of governmentality can thus often be most keenly observed in the decision making of individuals placed within organisations. The role of key individuals, within the structure of the state, also needs to be accounted for. A key influence on policy implementation is the role of contractual gatekeepers who hold the 'purse strings' and make decisions about the appropriateness of organisations providing services to meet state agendas. While state intent can be set out in policy, exactly how it is implemented in society typically involves a number of permutations. For the third sector, implementation can be influenced by individual perceptions of the value of the sector as a whole, which, in turn, can be linked to personal experiences of, and interactions with, third sector organisations.

The organisational adaptation or resistance of the processes and expectations embedded in the process of neoliberal governmentality is frequently a conscious decision made by key individuals in governance roles. This process will be demonstrated later in the chapter through the use of narratives that reveal how organisations, and therefore individuals, adapt to and seek to resist state constraints. We assert that while governmentality is expressed through organisations and their forms of governance, these processes need to be adopted by key agents. In short, market-driven third sector health organisations do not just happen. Organisational adaptation or resistance can therefore be seen as an agency-level reaction to particular forms of governmentality. Adaptation and resistance are active and ongoing processes that emerge from various forms of organisational interactions, including negotiations over the conditions of contractual engagement, for example. The outcome of these responses is reflected in a pluralistic third sector. Importantly, such negotiations and the resultant place of organisations may be constrained by a need for funding.

Changing landscapes in New Zealand's third sector

Much has been written about recent changes in the New Zealand health system, documenting shifts in policy and identifying the key political drivers of these changes (for example, Barnett and Barnett, 1997; Ashton, 1999; Cheyne et al, 2000; Davis and Ashton, 2001; Gauld, 2001). Little of this material is linked explicitly to the development of New Zealand's third sector. We offer a brief summary in order to identify selected key moments in this history. Particular attention is paid to the relationship between the state and third sector health organisations during the 1980s and 1990s. In this period the neoliberal ideological drivers of policy resulted in the creation of the purchaser–provider split and the rise of the culture of contracting. These developments had implications for the shape of third sector health organisations at the time.

The provision of health services in New Zealand during the late 19th and early 20th centuries was largely undertaken by third sector organisations. These organisations tended to follow the traditional charitable model of the benevolent provision of services to the 'deserving poor' (Hay, 1989). The New Zealand state supported the actions of third sector organisations in providing health services such as hospitals and general practitioners as well as through organisations such as the Plunket Society (which provides well-child care) and the Royal New Zealand Foundation for the Blind (Tennant, 2002). This approach was pluralistic and sought market, profit and not-for-profit solutions to the provision of health and welfare. With the implementation of the Social Security Act (1938), the role of the state in the provision of health and welfare shifted, with the government becoming the key service provider in a system of universal healthcare.

The period after the passage of this landmark Act (the 1940s to 1960s) was an era of supposedly equitable health service provision. Through government funding and subsidies the population had access to basic health services. While arguably a period of relative stability, in terms of government philosophy on health service provision, there was still concern among some as to the narrow scope of the services provided. New third sector organisations emerged during this period in reaction to the narrow views of the state and the perceived limitations of established third sector organisations. In particular, organisations formed by concerned parents were established in the domains of disability and child health, challenging the institutional nature of state provision (Millen, 1999). There was also a movement in this period towards improved maternity care for women, with considerable activity by lobby groups seeking from government a centralisation of childbirth within medical facilities (Coney, 1993).

In the late 1960s and 1970s developments within third sector organisations in New Zealand mirrored international patterns. Organisations emerged in response to the trend towards deinstitutionalisation of mental health facilities. In the 1970s several key mental healthcare providers were formed to address the needs of those persons placed in the community after lengthy periods of institutional care, for instance. There was also an emerging backlash against the dominance of the medical profession within various areas of healthcare (Willis, 1989). In contrast to the approaches 30 years earlier, women sought to regain control of the birthing process and to reduce the level of medical intervention that had become the norm (Donley and Hinton, 1993). These decades were also a time during which 'consumer' groups emerged. Disability groups remained significant players but were largely controlled by parents and medical professionals. Their children, the recipients of the services, began to seek a greater say in their own destiny (Gosling, 1994).

In the 1980s and 1990s, a changing political ideology resulted in what has variously been described as the 'rolling back' of the welfare state (Kelsey, 1993) and the 'hollowing out of the state' (Barnett, 1999). This process involved the extensive, neoliberally informed restructuring of the New Zealand state as the key provider of health services. Part of this restructuring process involved the redefinition of the parameters of the public and private sectors. It was a period of considerable and rapid change, involving the introduction of a split between the roles of service purchasers and providers and, in some localities, considerable resistance by local community groups (Kearns, 1998; Coster, 1999).

The outcome was the emergence of a culture of contracting (Nowland–Foreman, 1998). In pursuit of efficiencies there was a push towards competition, which saw a purchaser–provider split and the outsourcing of service provision. The New Zealand public sector increasingly had to compete on commercial terms with the private sector for service delivery contracts (for mental health care, see Joseph and Kearns, 1999). Alongside this change was the re-emergence of the idea that the third sector is the appropriate place in which to provide efficient health and welfare services and is essential in the promotion of the political right ideals of individualism and self-reliance (Prince et al, 2004).

The resultant competitive governmentality mirrored processes already embedded in the US and the UK (Pinch, 1997; Rogers and Glasby, 2001). These changes amounted to a paradigmatic shift from a bureaucratic structure to one prioritising a competitive managerial and fiscal focus. However, this restructuring also led to significant structural change within New Zealand government agencies and a loss of institutional knowledge, as staff moved agency or were made redundant due to processes of rationalisation (Davis and Ashton, 2001).

One of the concerns emerging from the change in the nature of the relationship between the state and third sector was a perceived loss of autonomy by voluntary organisations in terms of service provision. Contracting with the state, while of financial benefit, often involves a series of non-monetary costs to organisations such as a changed place for the organisation within the third sector itself (Rogers and Glasby, 2001). The shift in focus for some third sector agencies, from providing services in a collaborative environment to working within a self-promoting bureaucratic structure, was seen to undermine long-term collective strategies and networking (Barnett and Barnett, 1997; Kearns, 1998; Nowland–Foreman, 1998). In sum, this set of outcomes resulted in a fragmentation of services and a change in the structure of the health third sector in New Zealand (Drake, 1998).

Issues of fragmentation were of particular concern to the New Zealand Council of Christian Social Services (NZCCSS), a major voice within New Zealand's third sector, which cited a lack of trust between funders and providers as impacting negatively on their attempts to work collaboratively (NZCCSS, 1998). Constituent organisations voiced concern that any criticism of state objectives would be penalised by the withdrawal of funding (Clark, 1997; Cheyne et al, 2000).

The funding of the third sector by the state to provide services has also been viewed as resulting in the sector becoming inappropriately dependent on the state. An emerging dependency means that the third sector can find itself providing services on the basis of what it is funded for rather than on its assessment of the needs of the community, families and individuals (Wilson et al, 2001). A further criticism of the purchaser–provider split is the failure to recognise the potential for providers to cut corners to gain contracts. There are also concerns that funders are not equipped with the mechanisms to ensure the quality of service provision (Cheyne et al, 2000).

Historically, New Zealand's third sector has been supported by a limited philanthropic base. This paucity of private funding can be linked to a short history of third sector initiatives and the early role of the state as a universal provider of health and welfare services (Tennant, 2004). The consequence has been that for much of New Zealand's third sector history the state has played a significant role in allocating grant-in-aid. In many cases the support of the state of individual third sector organisations has been driven by the influence of individuals in government and their acceptance of the 'worthiness' of particular causes. A key factor underlying the funding of many third sector health organisations by the state seems to be their degree of alignment with the ideology of the state at the time.

There has also been a shift in relations between organisations with some of those that began on the periphery of state acceptability subsequently receiving greater favour in light of changes in thinking within society at large. More recently this may be linked to the conscious adoption of the 'language of government' by third sector organisations, so as to facilitate engagement with the state. Ironically perhaps, the alignment of organisations with state contracts has also resulted in accusations of co-option. By way of example, the Family Planning Association not only entered a new era of favour as social views regarding gender and sexuality changed, but it also endured scorn from some more activist organisations for its move to closer relations with the state (Fenwick, 1993).

What is interesting about the growth in contracting in New Zealand is the change in relationship between the state and the third sector. While the political right argues that the third sector is best left to provide health and welfare services, it has not been left to do so in the manner of true market forces. Rather, there has been considerable government intervention in the definition of the services deemed to be necessary and the contracting of third sector organisations to meet those requirements. Indeed, the quest to gain and maintain contracts has fundamentally reshaped relations between many third sector providers, introducing hitherto foreign elements of competitiveness among providers into domains such as mental healthcare (Kearns and Joseph, 2000).

In terms of the size, shape and distribution of the third sector, change has not only been evident in the conditions of the third sector activity, but also in its diversity. Although many third sector health organisations have ceased to exist, changed their name or amalgamated with other organisations, it is nonetheless possible to trace establishment dates and note a significant increase in number since the 1980s. In particular there has been growth in the prevalence of small mutual support organisations and an increase in the number of health promotion, mental health and Maori service providers (Owen, 2003). Historically many of New Zealand's third sector health organisations started off as grassroots local initiatives and over time grew into national bodies, servicing local branch affiliates. This centralisation of decision making, accompanied by an increasingly professional ethic, has been problematic for some organisations with concerns that branch autonomy may be undermined.

The potential disparities between national organisations and their local branches have been further challenged by shifting state funding regimes. As the neoliberalising New Zealand state evolved, so did thinking on the appropriate means of allocating health funding. The result is that the geographical distribution of health funding has gone full circle. In 1983 funding was devolved regionally through 14 area health boards (AHBs). In 1993, at the time that the purchaser–provider split was initiated, funding was brought under the control of four regional health authorities (RHAs). A return to centralised funding occurred under the Health Funding Authority in 1996 and finally in 2001 there was a resumption of regional funding with the establishment of 21 district health boards (DHBs). Unlike the UK, local government bodies in New Zealand play a limited role in the provision of funding for healthcare services (Milligan and Fyfe, 2004).

These regional shifts in funding have had implications for spatial equities in service provision. Devolved funding is driven by a philosophy of the need to meet regional priorities. However, the consequence is that some regional branches of a third sector organisation may receive funding while branches in other areas may not. This situation reduces the consistency of service provision across the country and may result in areas of low service provision for some health consumers.

Third sector narratives: competition, adaptation and resistance among health providers

In 2003, 22 key individuals who had involvement with the third sector were interviewed. These interviews offered individual insights into the changes experienced in New Zealand's third sector landscape as a result of neoliberally inspired policies and the emergence of a culture of contracting in the 1990s. The interviews formed part of a broader study that involved a comprehensive review of literature on New Zealand's third sector health organisations (Owen, 2005).

The interviews were of two main types. Four were scoping conversations with key informants and involved discussions about the general nature of the third sector in New Zealand. A further 18 then focused on selected individuals' observations of changes experienced by third sector health organisations. Just over half of the respondents were located in Wellington, the national capital, with the others spread across the country in a range of other cities. The respondents had all been involved in managerial or broader governance roles in third sector health organisations. All had significant and ongoing involvement with third sector health organisations, although not all were working in the sector at the time of the interview. Of the third sector organisations that these respondents were directly associated with, the majority of organisations were engaged in health promotion activity, while the others variously addressed mental health issues, family and child health, disability issues and aged care (Owen, 2005). Many respondents had associations with more than one third sector health organisation, and collectively they were able to shed light on the experiences of over 30 such agencies during the 1980s and 1990s.

A range of methods was used to recruit respondents. Eleven individuals responded to a request for information circulated via a national health email list. Other contacts were made via email in which input from individuals in a cross-section of health organisations was sought. To ensure that respondents felt comfortable to talk frankly about their observation of change in the sector, an assurance was offered that the identities of all respondents would be masked in subsequent publications.

Several themes emerged from the conversations with these third sector respondents. These can be related to the competitive ethos of the contractual environment, and the organisational response to this changing culture. It appears that a particularly important factor in moulding the direction that organisations took in terms of their structure and function was the active agency of individuals, both in the organisation and in government. Perspectives gained from these narratives on themes of competition, adaptation and resistance will now be discussed, privileging the voices of these third sector spokespeople.

Competition

Respondents indicated that the introduction of contracting altered relationships with other third sector organisations and that there was an increased awareness of competition for funding. The result of this awareness was a diminished sense of association, with organisations seen to be in direct competition. As one respondent commented, a loss of communication between organisations resulted. The perception was that this loss was actively promoted by the state:

> 'There has sort of been that touchy touchy back off … "if I talk to you will it affect my national contract", but I think people are building up confidence with each other…. I think the Ministry [of Health] at the moment is playing us off against each other.' (manager, child health agency)

This competitive governmentality can be likened to a 'divide and conquer' scenario. There was a sense that in a contractual environment it was commercially unsound for 'competing' third sector organisations to share information. As a consequence the communication had become more guarded. This competitive culture was reproduced unequally, with Newberry and Barnett (2001) identifying geographical disparities in the way RHAs encouraged or limited third sector networks.

There were also varying levels of concern expressed at the extent of change that had been experienced by the organisations. For some respondents, organisational growth was considered to have been positive, while for others it meant a shift from what was viewed as the core purpose of the organisation. Some expressed frustration at other third sector organisations that they perceived as being insufficiently value-driven. These 'unethical' organisations were observed to adapt their services to available funding and essentially encroach on what others saw as their own niche. One respondent alluded to a fragmentation in the third sector as a result of the development of a 'them' (amoral, business-driven third sector organisations) and 'us' (moral, consumer-driven) attitude:

> 'Some of the groups coming into the sector are not really like us. They are in the same sector but they haven't got the vision, or values or the personal experience. They might be there to make money out of the contracts so they become our opposition and it's just so sad. They are a business and they are there to make money. In the end the people they are there for don't get such a good deal.' (manager, child health agency)

Some respondents also cited concerns about the duplication of services by different organisations. It was suggested that this situation resulted in confusion for consumers who were faced with a number of service providers. As suggested by one respondent, some groups of consumers in particular are potentially disadvantaged by a bewildering array of service providers:

> 'I think people are much more aware now of the existence of organisations to meet such needs. But I think the contracting regime has encouraged the growth of a large number of specialist organisations. This causes a lot of confusion, especially among older people who haven't got a clue what they are all for.' (manager, elder care agency)

This growth in the number of organisations since the advent of contracting has been observed elsewhere (Pinch, 1997). There have been suggestions in the US that having dedicated pools of money for a particular cause, particularly in the instance of AIDS service provision, has resulted in the growth of related organisations (Chambre, 1999). While there was a sense of this situation occurring in the mental health sector particularly, there was also evidence of established organisations expanding services to fit available contracts. One respondent expressed frustration at this organisational adaptation:

'... established organisations are putting in for contracts and justifying this in terms of what they do. It is painfully obvious they are trying to adapt the organisation to fit the contract.' (manager, child health agency)

Others voiced concerns about the lack of transparency of some contractual involvements. Some suggested established organisations, with a history of service provision, had missed out on contracts that had been allocated to organisations with no previous standing in the field. Again, there were concerns about the morality of 'other' organisations:

'In the contracting round I think that there are some really good ethical agencies out there that we wouldn't have any trouble working with and others we would. I find it quite interesting that some agencies that don't seem to have any previous experience or background in delivering services are suddenly contracted by the Ministry of Health to run a project.... That is when you begin not to trust those people in the sector and how they went about getting that contract, especially if it has never been in the public arena for tender.' (manager, child health agency)

Erosion of trust is therefore perceived to be a downstream effect of the increased level of competition brought about by the contracting environment. For a few, the increasingly fragmented nature of the sector and the turnover of key staff in government positions also made communication and networks difficult. Over time, the nature of change resulted in relationships being based more on procedural requirements than on interpersonal understanding. This clash of the 'culture of voluntarism' with the 'culture of contract' combined with an increasing fragmentation of the third sector impacted on interorganisational networks.

Adaptation

Adaptation is one strategy that organisations have used to ensure the smoothness of their relationship with the state. Specific strategies adopted by the organisations represented in the study included conforming to state requirements in terms of expected service provision and by communicating in government language. There was concern by some individuals that internal shifts in the direction and priorities of their organisation occurred without much forethought. There was also a sense that in order for some organisations to remain solvent it was essential for them to adapt to the contracting environment by conforming to the funder's requirements. The extent of this adaptation varied according to the structure of the funding regime of the time.

Among some respondents, this situation created a tension between the role of the advocate and the role of service provider. Several organisations had started out their life as an advocacy organisation and over time taken on the mantle of service provider. They found it difficult to gain state funding for the continuation of the original advocacy role and ultimately this role was either diminished or funding was sought from elsewhere. As one respondent stated:

> 'Services which attract funding or contracts are relatively easy to maintain and develop; others which do not attract so much money tend to wither. We have had to keep our service to the size the funder will fund, although we could expand if we had more staff time paid for. There is certainly a need.' (manager, elder care agency)

Of the organisations holding government contracts, those that expressed the least amount of tension in relationships with the state tended to be established organisations whose core purpose was in line with the objectives in the New Zealand Health Strategy. An example of 'governing by culture' (Ling, 2000), this has been an effective means for the state to promote the lifestyle-related policies that have dominated health promotion during the 1990s. Those organisations aligning with this approach may be viewed more favourably for administering programmes. While some respondents argued that organisations have come from 'nowhere' to claim contracts, there are others that have had a largely uncontentious relationship with funders. According to one:

> 'The contract relationship with the Ministry of Health has been smooth. We are an established organisation, capable of delivering services and are regarded highly for the quality of our delivery. This has been important in retaining contracts.' (manager, health promotion agency)

However, a continued contractual relationship between state and organisations is not guaranteed. Those that found themselves basing their growth on anticipated contracts could be placed in a difficult position should funding be allocated elsewhere. The loss of contracts has an effect on staffing levels and financial viability. As one respondent stated:

> 'A number of the contracts which we planned on haven't happened. This has put the whole organisation in jeopardy.' (manager, health promotion agency)

The implications for the future of organisations are significant and places further pressure on organisations to align with the direction of the state. The requirement to conform to the language of government is another process through which the state promotes organisational adaptation. When placing tenders for contracts or making submissions in response to policy documents, organisations were more effective if they forwarded correspondence couched in the terms of bureaucracy. This form of governmentality involves organisational members learning policy 'buzzwords' and understanding how to frame this language in a way that the state found acceptable. In the neoliberal, managerial regime the phrases of 'efficiency' and 'accountability' hold particular weight (Lewis and Moran, 1998). The currency of these terms has remained undiminished despite being softened by more recent 'third way' imperatives of 'participation' and 'consultation' (Prince et al, 2004). As expressed below, part of the contracting process was seen by some respondents as learning the rules of the game as a means to a financial end:

> '[In terms of] other priorities there are a lot of politics in it as well. I
> am not into playing the politics game but there are some Ministry of
> Health areas that if you play the politics right you get the funding.'
> (manager, child health agency)

In order to better ensure survival, a strategic choice on the part of third sector providers through the 1990s was to better position their organisation through 'playing the game'. Speaking the language has been central to the rules of the game. This expression of governmentality is a conscious adaptation by key individuals within some third sector organisations.

Resistance

Several respondents found that the environment created through the process of contract negotiation was not conducive to building trusting relationships. There was an expectation by funding bodies that contractual arrangements were confidential and would not be discussed between organisations. While the majority of organisations seemed to accept this model of business, some resisted this form of competitiveness. Organisations with similar aims and previously established networks communicated openly among themselves and used this knowledge of others' contractual terms as a power base to aid future funding negotiations.

Other forms of resistance to government co-option included the funding of advocacy work from separate income streams and by only accepting state funds for work that was consistent with identified values. There was talk of remaining true to the values of the organisation. One respondent said that when considering changes to services provided by the organisation the board would ask itself 'what would X [the organisation's founder] do?'. Another individual indicated the need for conscious resistance against the temptation to adapt an organisation to fit funding availability:

> 'We have been very careful not to get sucked into the funder capture.
> Many years ago it was suggested that we change our name so we
> would get Ministry of Health funding from a different pool and I just
> found that incredible. I guess we are very clear about what we need
> the funding for and we are not going to sell out our organisation to
> get it.' (manager, child health agency)

This resolve requires a strong adherence to organisational purpose. The third sector organisational response to contractual relationships with the state is therefore not a simplistic dualism of adaptation and resistance. Many organisations did not feel constrained to only undertake services that they received funding for. As one respondent commented:

> 'Yes, things like geographical boundaries mean we have to apply to two or three different committees or councils to cover the whole area or to put in separate applications for separate services. On the other hand, if we felt a service was needed we went ahead and provided it, without waiting until the funders provided the money.' (manager, elder care agency)

The insights of individuals were shaped by their unique relationships with state funders. For some individuals, dependence on the state for funding was relatively limited. However, as indicated above, others had more marked experiences of the geographical inequities in funding. The spatial disparities in funding were experienced more broadly within the health sector as a whole and were not unique to third sector organisations (Barnett and Barnett, 2003).

For many organisations the development of multiple funding streams, to address needs unmet by the state, is an important strategy. In particular, a key concern for several organisations was the balance of their roles as state-funded service providers and as advocates for their member/client base. There was a concern about their ability to operate autonomously and still be able to criticise government policy without jeopardising their funding base. As a respondent expressed, this requires a conscious strategy to navigate around potential conflicts of interest:

> 'I made up my mind that we were not going to alter what we did and the way we worked because of Ministry [of Health] contracts. I've seen it happen to other organisations. I have had organisations come to me and say "can you say this publicly – we can't as we have a Ministry contract". We have not significantly altered the way that we work because we have Ministry contracts and the way that I have dealt with that has been keeping things outside.' (manager, health promotion agency)

It is noteworthy, then, that, like adaptation, acts of resistance constitute a choice made with reference to the identity of the organisation. The agency of individuals in shaping relationships between third sector organisations and state agencies cannot be underestimated. The restructuring of state organisations coupled with the institutionalisation of neoliberal dogma contributed to the legacy of mistrust and tension that was documented by the Community and Voluntary Sector Working Party (2001).

Conclusion

Third sector health organisations in New Zealand have historically experienced varying degrees of tension in their dealings with government. The support received from the state in financial and political terms has been closely linked with the ideology of the time. Our chapter has offered evidence to support the contention that the purchaser–provider split, arising from the neoliberal restructuring of the 1980s and 1990s in New Zealand, and the consequential development of a contract culture, has deeply impacted on the idealised place of third sector organisations. There has been a growth in the number and diversity of health organisations in this period and some existing organisations have reported a shift in their experiences of trust, both of state agencies and other third sector organisations.

Historically the funding of third sector organisations by government has been undertaken through the provision of grants, which have generally provided organisations with discretion in the distribution and the development of services they provide (Drake, 1998; Bradford and Nowland-Foreman, 2001). A purchaser–provider split and a regionally devolved funding regime has resulted in geographical disparities in the funding of third sector health organisations. We see the introduction of a contracting regime as having potentially rendered third sector organisations more susceptible to political pressure. A competitive governmentality became pervasive and influenced the place of third sector health organisations. Choices by organisations have to be made as to whether they accept government funding and potentially jeopardise their independence, or take a risk and seek external funding sources. This situation implies forms of organisational adaptation or resistance to their funding environment.

The process of organisational resistance or adaptation does not occur in a vacuum. It is impossible to ignore the agency of individuals within organisations and those within state mechanisms. Those people involved in decision making on both sides of the 'fence' play a role in shaping the space that an organisation occupies. As agents of change in the third sector landscape the place and culture of organisations frequently lies in the hands of a few.

The core 'business' of third sector organisations can be considered to be as much concerned with participation and citizenship as it is about provision and services (Nowland-Foreman, 1998). It can be argued that a contract culture severely reduces the potential for this commitment. Control does not lie with the users of services despite a rhetoric that claims users will have more choice under a contracting system. The power is ultimately held by the state as funder of services (Cheyne et al, 2000). Other limitations of a contract culture include a loss of flexibility for third sector organisations and a suppression of innovation (Clark, 1997; Nowland-Foreman, 1998; NZCCSS, 1998).

Five years into the 21st century, there is a move among New Zealand's social policy stakeholders to recognise the concerns of the third sector. In 2001 the New Zealand government signed a Statement of Government Intentions for an improved community–government relationship and established good practice criteria for state employees to take heed of in their dealings with the third sector. Processes have been established (jointly managed by the third sector and the state) which are attempting to overcome some of the barriers to cooperation. Yet, two decades on from the onset of contracting, there remains a feeling of dissatisfaction with the process and a concern that core values within the sector have been sacrificed to a competitive model.

References

Ashton, T. (1999) 'The Health Reforms: To Market and Back?', in J. Boston, P. Dalziel and S. St John (eds) *Redesigning the Welfare State in New Zealand: Problems, Policies, Prospects*, Auckland: Oxford University Press, pp 134-53.

Barnett, J.R. (1999) 'Hollowing Out the State? Some Observations on the Restructuring of Hospital Services in New Zealand', *Area*, vol 1, no 3, pp 259-70.

Barnett, P. and Barnett, R. (1997) 'A Turning Tide? Reflections on Ideology and Health Service Restructuring in New Zealand', *Health and Place*, vol 3, no 1, pp 55-8.

Barnett, R. and Barnett, P. (2003) 'Back to the Future? Reflections on Past Reforms and Future Prospects for Health Services in New Zealand', *GeoJournal*, vol 59, pp 137-47.

Bradford, S. and Nowland-Foreman, G. (2001) *Mahi Tahi Working Together: Civil Society in Aotearoa/New Zealand*, Auckland: Commonwealth Foundation.

Chambre, S. (1999) 'Redundancy, Third-party Government and Consumer Choice: HIV/AIDS Nonprofit Organisations in New York City', *Policy Studies Journal*, vol 27, issue 4, pp 840-54.

Cheyne, C., O'Brien, M. and Belgrave, M. (2000) *Social Policy in New Zealand: A Critical Introduction* (2nd edn), Auckland: Oxford University Press.

Clark, J.S. (1997) 'Welfare Restructuring in New Zealand: The Changing Relationship between the State and Auckland's Voluntary Welfare Sector', Unpublished MA thesis, Auckland: University of Auckland.

Concy, S. (1993) 'Health Organisations', in A. Else (ed) *Women Together: A History of Women's Organisations in New Zealand: ngā rōpū wāhine o te motu*, Wellington: Historical Branch, Department of Internal Affairs and Daphne Brasell Associates Press, pp 241-54.

Coster, H. (1999) 'Community Responses to Changes in Delivery of Rural Health Services in Balclutha and Dannevirke', Unpublished MA thesis, Auckland: University of Auckland.

Crampton, C., Dowell, A.C. and Bowers, S. (2000) 'Third Sector Primary Health Care in New Zealand', *New Zealand Medical Journal*, vol 113, pp 92-6.

CVSWP (Community and Voluntary Sector Working Party) (2001) *Communities and Government: Potential for Partnership*, Wellington: Ministry of Social Policy.

Davis, P. and Ashton, T. (eds) (2001) *Health and Public Policy in New Zealand*, Auckland: Oxford University Press.

Donley, J. and Hinton, B. (1993) 'NZ Home Birth Association', in A. Else (ed) *Women Together: A History of Women's Organisations in New Zealand: ngā rōpū wāhine o te motu*, Wellington: Historical Branch, Department of Internal Affairs, pp 278-80.

Drake, R. (1998) 'Professionals and the Voluntary Sector', in A. Symonds and A. Kelly (eds) *The Social Construction of Community Care*, London: Macmillan Press Ltd, pp 185-91.

Fenwick, P. (1993) 'New Zealand Family Planning Association, 1936-', in A. Else (ed) *Women Together: A History of Women's Organisations in New Zealand: ngā rōpū wāhine o te motu*, Wellington: Historical Branch, Department of Internal Affairs, pp 264-6.

Gauld, R. (2001) *Revolving Doors: New Zealand's Health Reforms*, Wellington: Institute of Policy Studies and the Health Research Centre, Victoria University.

Gleeson, B. and Kearns, R. (2001) 'Remoralising Landscapes of Care', *Environment and Planning D*, vol 19, pp 61-80.

Gosling, D. (1994) *Barriers to a Dream: Issues of Power and Control in the Self-advocacy Movement of People with Intellectual Disabilities in New Zealand*, Ohope: D. Gosling and R. Gerzon.

Halfpenny, P. and Reid, M. (2002) 'Research on the Voluntary Sector: An Overview', *Policy & Politics*, vol 30, no 4, pp 533-50.

Hay, I. (1989) *The Caring Commodity: The Provision of Health Care in New Zealand*, Auckland: Oxford University Press.

Heginbotham, C. (1990) *Return to Community: The Voluntary Ethic and Community Care*, London: Bedford Square Press.

Joseph, A.E. and Kearns, R.A. (1999) 'Unhealthy Acts? Interpreting Narratives of Community Mental Health Care in Waikato, New Zealand', *Health and Social Care in the Community*, vol 7, pp 1-8.

Kearns, R. (1998) '"Going it Alone": Place, Identity and Community Resistance to Health Reforms in Hokianga, New Zealand', in R. Kearns and W.M. Gesler (eds) *Putting Health into Place: Landscape, Identity and Wellbeing*, New York, NY: Syracuse University Press, pp 226-47.

Kearns, R. and Joseph, A. (2000) 'Contracting Opportunities: Interpreting Post-asylum Geographies of Mental Health Care in Auckland, New Zealand', *Health and Place*, vol 6, no 3, pp 159-69.

Kelsey, J. (1993) *Rolling Back the State: Privatisation of Power in Aotearoa/New Zealand*, Wellington: Bridget Williams Books.

Lewis, N. and Moran, W. (1998) 'Restructuring, Democracy, and Geography in New Zealand', *Environment and Planning C: Government and Policy*, vol 16, pp 127-53.

Ling, T. (2000) 'Unpacking Partnership: The Case of Health Care', in J. Clarke, S. Gewirtz and E. McLaughlin (eds) *New Managerialism, New Welfare?*, London: Sage Publications, pp 82-101.

Millen, J. (1999) *Breaking Barriers: IHC's First 50 Years*, Wellington: IHC New Zealand (Inc).

Milligan, C. and Fyfe N. (2004) 'Putting the Voluntary Sector in its Place: Geographical Perspectives on Voluntary Activity and Social Welfare in Glasgow', *Journal of Social Policy*, vol 33, no 1, pp 73-93.

Morison, J. (2000) 'The Government–Voluntary Sector Compacts: Governance, Governmentality, and Civil Society', *Journal of Law and Society*, vol 27, no 1, pp 98-132.

Newberry, S. and Barnett, P. (2001) 'Negotiating the Network: The Contracting Experiences of Community Mental Health Agencies in New Zealand', *Financial Accountability and Management*, vol 17, no 2, pp 133-52.

Nowland-Foreman, G. (1998) 'Purchase-of-service Contracting, Voluntary Organisations, and Civil Society', *American Behavioural Scientist*, vol 42, no 1, pp 108-23.

NZCCSS (New Zealand Council of Christian Social Services) (1998) *Towards a Real Partnership: A NZCCSS Review of the Relationship between Voluntary Social Services and NZ Community Funding Agency*, Wellington: NZCCSS.

Owen, S. (2003) 'Changing Landscapes of the Third Sector: The Implications of Contracting for Health Organisations in New Zealand', in J. Gao, R. Le Heron and J. Logie (eds) *Windows on a Changing World: Proceedings of the New Zealand Geographical Society*, Auckland: NZGS, pp 224-8.

Owen, S. (2005) 'Placing Health Organisations in New Zealand's Third Sector', Unpublished PhD thesis, Auckland: University of Auckland.

Pinch, S. (1997) *Worlds of Welfare: Understanding the Changing Geographies of Social Welfare Provision*, London: Routledge.

Prince, R., Kearns, R. and Craig, D. (2004) 'Governmentality, Discourse and Space in the New Zealand Health Care System, 1991-2003', Unpublished typescript (available from second author).

Putnam, R. (1995) 'Bowling Alone: America's Declining Social Capital', *Journal of Democracy*, vol 6, no 1, pp 65-78.

Raco, M. and Imrie, R. (2000) 'Governmentality and Rights and Responsibilities in Urban Policy', *Environment and Planning A*, vol 32, pp 2187-204.

Rogers, A. and Glasby, J. (2001) 'The Tale of Two Cities: The Contract Culture in Birmingham and Chicago', *Resource Policy and Planning*, vol 19, no 3, pp 33-9.

Rose, M. (2002) 'The Seductions of Resistance: Power, Politics and a Performative Style of Systems', *Environment and Planning D: Society and Space*, vol 20, pp 383-400.

Salamon, L., Hems, L. and Chinnock, K. (2000) *The Nonprofit Sector: For What and for Whom?*, Working Papers of the Johns Hopkins Comparative Nonprofit Sector Project No 37, The Johns Hopkins Centre for Civil Society Studies, Baltimore (www.jhu.edu/~ccss/pubs/pdf/forwhat.pdf).

Seibel, W. and Anheier, H. (1990) 'The Third Sector between the Market and the State', in H. Anheier and W. Seibel (eds) *The Third Sector Comparative Studies of Nonprofit Organisations*, Berlin: Walter de Gruyter, pp 5-20.

Tennant, M. (2002) 'The Price of Partnership: Forms of Interaction between Government and the Voluntary Sector', Paper presented at the 2002 Australia New Zealand Third Sector Research Sixth Biennial Conference: Doing Well, Auckland: ANZTR.

Tennant, M. (2004) 'Mixed Economy or Moving Frontier? Welfare, the Voluntary Sector and Government', in B. Dalley and M. Tennant (eds) *Past Judgement: Social Policy in New Zealand History*, Dunedin: Otago University Press, pp 39-56.

van Deth, J. (1997) 'Social Involvement and Democratic Politics', in J. van Deth (ed) *Private Groups and Public Life: Social Participation, Voluntary Associations and Political Involvement in Representative Democracies*, London: Routledge, pp 1-23.

Weisbrod, B. (1977) *The Voluntary Nonprofit Sector: An Economic Analysis*, Lexington, MA: Lexington Books.

Willis, E. (1989) *Medical Dominance: The Division of Labour in Australian Health Care*, Sydney: Allen & Unwin.

Wilson, C., Kerslake Hendricks, A. and Smithies, R. (2001) '"Lady Bountiful" and the "Virtual Volunteers": The Changing Face of Social Service Volunteering', *Social Policy Journal of New Zealand*, vol 17, pp 124-46.

EIGHT

The difference of voluntarism: the place of voluntary sector care homes for older Jewish people in the United Kingdom

Oliver Valins

Introduction

This chapter considers the difference that voluntary sector organisations can make to the lived environments of older people in long-term institutional care. It does so through an analysis of care homes provided by the UK Jewish voluntary sector. It discusses how these institutions can create a greater sense of home than is possible in many private facilities because of the involvement of local communities and volunteers and the sense of ownership, safety and belonging of residents and families. Nonetheless, given increasing regulatory requirements and the financial realities of providing services in a highly competitive long-term care market, the chapter considers what extra dimensions the voluntary sector can still offer to highly vulnerable older people.

The UK Jewish community is used as a case study for two reasons. Firstly, the community can be said to be at the vanguard of British demographic trends. Both nationally and across the Organisation for Economic Co-operation and Development (OECD), not only is the proportion of older people relative to those of younger age increasing, but they are also living longer. While some 16% of the overall UK population is aged 65 or over, 23% of UK Jews are in this age cohort. The proportion of Jews aged 75 or over is also twice that of the UK as a whole (14% as compared with 7%). British Jewish women have a life expectancy that is two years longer than the UK average, and for men the figure is four years (Miller et al, 1996; Schmool and Cohen, 1998). In this sense, the Jewish population in Britain can be seen as 'demographic pioneers' (Valins, 2002).

Secondly, the community has a long history of voluntarism and, specifically, of providing long-term residential and nursing care home provision for older people. Indeed, some of the major Jewish social service agencies and care institutions date back to Victorian times (Alderman, 1992). Although the community (like many others) is finding it increasingly difficult to recruit volunteers, it also has reserves of social capital that can provide human and financial support in ways that other ethnic communities may find far harder to develop (see Patel, 1999). Hence, if the Jewish community is unable to make a real difference to the lives of its frail older people, then the prognosis for other voluntary sector ethnic or faith-based communities seeking to establish such provision would be even poorer.

For clarification, the Jewish voluntary sector in this chapter is understood as comprising an interlocking network of formal and informal organisations run for (and often by) Jews. These organisations are neither governmental nor commercial. They were established voluntarily and rely to some degree on voluntary contributions of human and/or financial resources (Harris, 1997). The care homes described in this chapter are not-for-profit and are all partly financed through charitable community donations. Nonetheless, these homes still charge their clients (or local authorities where clients are eligible for government support) considerable weekly sums[1]. In 2001, for example, the average fees for non-government funded clients staying at a Jewish residential voluntary sector care home in London were almost £500 per week, and £625 per week for care within a nursing home[2].

To explore the extent to which Jewish care homes do, in fact, provide an extra dimension to older people's lived experiences, this chapter reviews findings from a two-year research project (that took place between 2000 and 2002). This included undertaking more than 50 formal interviews with senior managers, nursing and care staff, a series of informal interviews with residents and their close families, as well as visits to Jewish institutional care facilities across the UK. The chapter also includes some data from a questionnaire completed by almost 3,000 Jews living in London and the South East (see Becher et al, 2002). This explored the needs and wants of Jews in relation to the overall UK Jewish voluntary sector, and included questions on their attitudes towards long-term care. Included in the survey were responses from 486 individuals aged 75 years or over.

Following this introduction, the chapter considers the place of institutional care in contemporary Britain. Institutional care has faced a long history of academic and policy criticism (see, for example, Townsend, 1962, 1981; Fisk, 1999). Concerns have been expressed that they create a culture of dependency, that there is a lack of user empowerment, with arguments raised as to how far they have really changed since the time of the Poor Law. Others, however, have highlighted the advantages of group living, criticising the seemingly automatic assumption that it is better for older people to remain in their own homes for as long as possible (Oldman and Quilgars, 1999; Johnson, 2001; Sumner, 2002). This section argues that central to the lived experiences of older people in care is the generation of a sense of home and belonging.

The third section of the chapter looks specifically at care homes provided by the UK Jewish voluntary sector. It argues that while these provide services that are generally highly regarded, they still remain places that people fear entering and are seen as a last resort. In many ways the micro-geographies of older people's lives within these environments resembles those of non-Jewish care homes. That is, these institutions operate according to national regulations, there have been strong pressures to professionalise services, and the vast majority of staff are not Jewish. Nonetheless, these homes are, to varying extents, still able to provide a Jewish ethos that feels 'safe and comfortable' to the resident and can provide for their specific religious and ethnic needs. Moreover, because Jewish care home providers are seen as being 'owned' by the community, residents have a greater sense of home than would otherwise be the case. The ability of the Jewish voluntary sector to tap into and involve local communities to help create this sense of home appears to be a critical aspect of the added value that distinguishes its service provision from that of private care home facilities.

Geographies of institutional care

There is a long history of overtly spatial critiques of institutions. Perhaps the two most important figures in these debates are Michel Foucault (1967, 1977) and Erving Goffman (1961). Foucault's and Goffman's concern with issues of power and control sought to explain how the environments of institutions and the regimes of staff acted to 'restrain, control, treat, "design" and "produce" particular and supposedly improved versions of human minds and bodies' (Philo and Parr, 2000, p 513). While also concerned with how individuals resist the system, both Foucault and Goffman explored some of the fundamental problems relating to how society deals with those no longer able (or allowed) to live independently in the community. More specifically, they argued that the institutional worlds of these asylums 'dispossess' and then try to recreate the identities and roles of inmates through the routines of their everyday lives and processes of institutionalisation.

Goffman's and Foucault's descriptions of institutions are often dark and disturbing, although neither directly investigated care homes for older people (although Goffman did include them in his list of 'total institutions'[3]). The author most associated with these institutions is Peter Townsend, whose seminal work *The Last Refuge* (1962) was highly critical of the lack of changes in British residential and nursing homes since the introduction of the Poor Law. He argued that such institutions led to isolation from family, friends and community, a collapse of self-determination and a tenuousness of new relationships with other residents and staff. In one of his most quoted passages, he describes his first visit to a former workhouse in 1957:

> The first impression was grim and sombre. A high wall surrounded some tall Victorian buildings, and the entrance lay under a forbidding arch with a porter's lodge at one side. The asphalt yards were broken up by a few beds of flowers but there was no garden worthy of the name. Several hundred residents were housed in large rooms on three floors. Dormitories were overcrowded, with ten or twenty iron-framed beds close together, no floor covering and little furniture other than

ramshackle lockers. The day-rooms were bleak and uninviting. In one of them sat forty men in high-backed Windsor chairs, staring straight ahead or down at the floor. They seemed oblivious of what was going on around them. The sun was shining but no one was looking that way.... Life seemed to have been drained from them, all but the dregs. (Townsend, 1962, p 4)

Townsend was concerned to know why so many people still lived in residential homes when, with adequate support, many could remain in the community. In a later article he argued that society associates old age with negative characteristics – infirmity, loss of intellectual ability, dementia, dependency, lack of self-worth – and this determines the expectations and the policies for how to cater for 'them'. Residential care home living, he argued, leads to 'structured dependency', where older people are presumed to be more dependent than they actually are or need to be (Townsend, 1981; see also Fisk, 1999).

Despite many criticisms of the widespread use of care institutions as structures through which society can 'lock up' people that it no longer wishes to deal with, others have argued that they have a continuing value – Johnson (2001), for example, calls for a re-evaluation of care homes as 'asylums', using the term not in the sense of 'institutions for the mad', but rather as facilities that can offer benevolent spaces of rest, salvation and shelter. In a critique of the turn to individualism, he argues that collective living can offer much that is potentially enriching to older people:

> Collective living arrangements which provide a combination of supported private space with uninhibited access to the assurances provided by shared living can be a premium option. It might be the least worst way of living at the far end of life. It could be optimal.... We need to reconstruct our thinking about institutions and to put them back in the valued spectrum of human living arrangements. (Johnson, 2001, p 17)

Oldman and Quilgars (1999) put forward a similar argument and, in particular, note the poverty of many older people's lives before they move to long-term care facilities. Hence, they maintain that a blanket rejection of group living may damage the potential of older people to mutually support and provide for each other's psychosocial needs and wants, as well as the desire of many to live in a safe and protective environment at the end of their years (see also Peace et al, 1997; Kellaher, 2000; Sumner, 2002).

While much of the recent theoretical and philosophical debates about the future of institutional care have been directly concerned with concepts of space, place and environment, geographers with an interest in institutions have tended to focus on areas such as prisons, asylums and schools (Philo, 1989, 1997; Ogborn, 1995; Valentine and Longstaff, 1998; see also the themed issue of *Geoforum*, 2000, especially Philo and Parr, 2000). Recent studies on residential and nursing homes with an explicitly geographical focus are relatively rare, often focusing on changing patterns of care home distribution at a regional or national level (Phillips and Vincent, 1986; Harrop and Grundy, 1991; Corden, 1992; Hamnett and Mullings, 1992; Smith, 1992; Smith and Ford, 1998).

In the UK the vast majority of studies on residential and nursing homes have been carried out by gerontologists, sociologists and social policy analysts – although several of these have had geographical backgrounds (see, for example, Peace et al, 1997). Arguably the most significant direct contribution geographers have made in this field has been to social gerontology, rather than within the discipline itself (for example, Warnes, 1990; Harper and Laws, 1995). There is, however, a history of behavioural and humanistic geographers who have studied the effects of environment and ageing, including life within care homes (Rowles, 1978, 1986; Rowles et al, 1996; Shawler et al, 2001; see also Milligan, 2003). There have also been some excellent sociological studies that have explored the spatialities of care within the domestic home (see especially Twigg, 2000). Nonetheless, the focus within the discipline over the last 15 years has largely been at the meso- and macro-scales. Given the large numbers of people in these institutions, the huge sums of (private and public) money being spent on the long-term care of older people, and the massive changes taking place in this sector, there is an important role for a more explicitly spatial contribution to how future provision for the day-to-day lives of older people in care should develop.

Although geographical analysis of the lived experiences of older people within care homes is limited, spatial concepts widely used within the discipline of geography – particularly those associated with understandings of place and sense of place – do provide useful avenues for examining current long-term care provision at the micro-level. Of particular relevance to this chapter are distinctions between public and private space. Often associated with feminist critiques of distinctions between private, domestic spaces traditionally assigned to women and the public, workspaces of men (see, for example, McDowell, 1983), the concept is also useful for thinking about how to categorise the internal spaces of care homes.

On the one hand, care homes are public spaces, open to residents, families, visitors and staff. There are, for example, collective dining and entertainment areas. As described by Townsend (1962), until relatively recently older people in nursing homes slept in collective, multi-bedded wards. On the other hand, care homes are moving to a model where all residents have their own bedroom, typically decorated with personal belongings and, ideally at least, a conscious effort made by staff to provide a sense of 'home' and belonging. For example, staff will be expected to knock before they enter a resident's room, an action that symbolises the crossing of the boundary between the semi-public space of the corridor and the apparently private space of an individual's bedroom. However, staff will still enter residents' bedrooms when they need to clean or to provide care, with the knock on the door often cursory and secondary to the completion of the required task. The opportunity to say 'no' within a care home is limited and this highlights the ambiguity of care homes as spaces that are neither truly public nor private (Milligan, 2005). Nonetheless, the extent to which care homes are able to personalise and deinstitutionalise the lived experiences of their residents by creating a sense of home and belonging fit with the core of current academic and policy moves to try and empower users and avoid the traps of structured dependency (see, for example, Blunden, 1998; DH, 2001a; Henwood, 2001).

This chapter argues that critical to the added value of Jewish voluntary sector care homes is that they are able to foster a sense of home and ownership. These facilities are able to mitigate the loss of private space – associated with the move to almost any institution – by generating a shared sense of Jewish collective space. It is this sense of 'home' that characterises why most Jews who require long-term care want to be looked after in a Jewish facility.

Institutional- or community-based care: policy debates on the best place to care for older people

Old age institutions in the UK can be traced back to the almshouses of the Middle Ages and in a formal sense to the 1601 Poor Law Act, which required local parishes to care for elderly paupers. By the 19th century the public workhouse was the prime source of care to those older people without alternative means, and even by 1909 a Royal Commission reported that some 140,000 older people were resident in such institutions (Peace et al, 1997).

The Labour government of the 1940s sought to remove the stigma of the workhouse with the passing of the 1948 National Assistance Act. The aim of this was to change the ethos of these institutions from one of 'inmate' and 'master', to that of a 'hotel-style' environment:

> We have decided to make a great departure in the treatment of old people. The workhouse is to go. Although many people have tried to humanize it, it was in many respects a very evil institution. (quoted in Townsend, 1962, p 32; see also Means and Smith, 1998; Thane, 2000; Means, 2001)

Despite the optimism, the reality of institutional care proved somewhat different. There was a lack of planning in the development of care and a failure to ask older people themselves what they really wanted (Townsend, 1962). Even by the 1960s accommodation was often of a poor standard, with sometimes little change from the Victorian institutions that had preceded them (Means, 2001).

The election of the Conservatives in 1979 opened up the market for the institutional care of older people. The changes implemented under the 1990 National Health Service and Community Care Act were in keeping with Conservative enthusiasm for markets and consumer-led services, a desire to deinstitutionalise care by providing services in people's own homes wherever possible, transfer the blame for apparent underfunding and service failures from central to local government, and minimise public spending to enable tax cuts (Kendall, 2000; see also Hamnett and Mullings, 1992).

The current New Labour government has largely followed the tenet of the Conservative reforms. Through a raft of legislation – some suggested by the Royal Commission on Long Term Care (1999) – the government has continued to encourage non-institutional care (see, for example, DETR, 2001; DH, 2001a). This in part recognises that the care required by most older people who need assistance is best delivered in people's own homes or in community-based centres. The Royal Commission calculated that only one in five men, and one in three women, aged 65 or over will require residential or nursing home care at some point in their lives. Nonetheless, the care home industry remains a key supplier of services to almost half a million older British people and accounts for enormous sums of money: the Royal Commission estimated the sector would be worth £14.7 billion by 2010.

The government has also increased the regulatory requirement for care homes, especially through the 2000 Care Standards Act (see DH, 2001b). This sets out detailed requirements, ranging from the qualifications required of senior management and frontline care staff, to the minimum size of clients' bedrooms. Nonetheless, despite the introduction of national minimum standards, the amounts of money available from the state to pay for those individuals who cannot fund a care home place for themselves is determined at the local level. While the government has sought to make the way that local authorities commission services from local providers more transparent and less confrontational (DH, 2001c), overall shortages in the amount they receive from central government (Henwood, 2001) has meant that locally (and especially in the South East where costs of land and staff are highest) many independent care homes have found themselves no longer profitable and have closed down (Laing, 2002).

Under the 2000 Race Relations (Amendment) Act (which explicitly includes Jews) – and reaffirmed under the *NHS Plan* (DH, 2000) and the *National Service Framework for Older People* (DH, 2001a) – the provision of culturally appropriate care is 'not just good practice but a fundamental duty for councils and other statutory bodies' (Yee and Mussenden, 2001, p 122). For the Jewish voluntary sector this has provided an opportunity to provide a network of care homes that can meet the needs of local Jewish communities. However, the legislative requirements and overall societal demands to improve services has meant that Jewish care homes have had to professionalise their operations and to follow more business-like approaches. The line between Jewish voluntary sector and privately run homes has inevitably blurred. The next section outlines how the current Jewish voluntary sector has positioned its care home services and discusses whether these still provide an added value that justifies their future.

Jewish voluntary sector care homes: the geographies of life in care

Background and location

There are currently 36 Jewish voluntary sector care homes in the UK, catering for almost 2,500 older Jews. Three fifths of these bed spaces are classed as residential, with the remainder as nursing. These homes cluster around the traditional location of Jewish communities reflecting the importance of institutions being geographically close to the communities they serve. Twenty-two homes are located in London and the South East, which reflects the preponderance of UK Jews living in the capital city. Most of these facilities are located in and around the borough of Barnet where one sixth of the entire UK Jewish population resides.

Attitudes to care

One of the major attractions of Jewish voluntary sector care homes is that they claim to meet the religious and ethnic needs of their residents. However, no evaluation of these claims has been carried out as yet. Moreover, the assumption that older Jewish people will want to go to a care home – and ones under the auspices of the Jewish community at that – have not, until recently, been tested. However, the 2002 survey of Jews living in London and the South East carried out by the Institute for Jewish Policy Research shows quite clearly that residential and nursing care is very much seen as a last option, with only 13% of 486 older respondents stating this as their first choice of long-term care (see Table 8.1).

However, it is important to distinguish between people's ideals of care and what they are willing to settle for. As such, in the survey of London Jews, respondents were also asked about their second care choice. Of those that expressed

Table 8.1: Preferences for formal and informal care among older people in the UK and older Jews living in London and the South East (n = 486)

Care preferences	Jewish respondents (%)	UK (%)
My relatives in my own home	29	15
My relatives in their home	3	3
Paid professionals in my own home	33	21
Mix of relatives and paid professionals in my own home	21	47
Nursing or residential home	13	12
Other	1	2
Total	100	100

Note: Table 8.1 compares the responses of older people in the UK with those of older Jews living in London and the South East to the question: 'Imagine that some time in the future you could no longer manage on your own and needed help with daily tasks such as getting up, going to bed, feeding, washing or dressing, or going to the toilet. How would you like to be looked after?'.

Source: UK data cited in Henwood (2001, p 43)

a preference, almost two fifths stated they would like to be looked after in a residential or nursing home. Moreover – and key to this chapter – if they did have to be looked after in such a facility, two thirds wanted this to be in a Jewish home. Furthermore, around one-in-six respondents (16%) wanted to be in a non-Jewish home, but they wanted such facilities to have a large proportion of Jewish residents.

Day-to-day living

In many ways Jewish voluntary sector care homes face the same issues as those of any other facilities including the provision of adequate care, maintaining buildings and equipment, feeding residents and providing stimulating activities. In recent years Jewish organisations have invested millions of pounds in building new care homes and updating facilities. Replacing and refurbishing facilities is an ongoing process and much work still needs to be done before all 36 Jewish voluntary sector care homes fully meet the national minimum standards of the 2000 Care Standards Act, particularly in terms of size of bedrooms. Nonetheless, homes have improved dramatically over the past 20 years, with the vast majority of residents having their own rooms (many of which are en suite), new arts and crafts centres built, eating areas and lounges redesigned, gardens redeveloped and new physiotherapy suites installed.

While bricks-and-mortar developments are important to people's quality of life, arguably, however, the primary factor is the individual care provided to residents by members of staff and volunteers. In the words of one care home employee:

> 'What matters most to people is the "caring-ness" of the individual. If somebody's taking me to the toilet – which is absolutely dominating my life because I can't do it anymore – it's the way they do it, how gentle they are, how caring, how they respect my dignity. It's that individual relationship that person forms, or doesn't form, that is the largest quality factor to somebody's life.' (care home employee)

Almost all the residents and family members who were interviewed spoke very highly about the staff working in the Jewish care homes. However, the vast majority of these staff were not Jewish: out of the 2,600 staff working in UK Jewish voluntary sector homes in 2001, less than 100 were Jewish (and most of these were in management positions). Care home managers reported an often considerable cultural gap between non-Jewish staff and their residents:

> 'There is a big cultural divide between the carers and the cared for. We run a series of lectures, for example on the Holocaust, but many of the staff had either never heard the word "Holocaust" before, or didn't know what it meant. One staff member at a recent training

session thought the Holocaust was a drug for Alzheimer's disease.'
(care home manager)

The reality of residents' day-to-day lives in Jewish voluntary sector homes is taken up with activities where being Jewish has little relevance and care is provided by professional staff (rather than volunteers) who typically have very different backgrounds to the residents.

So what difference does being in a Jewish voluntary sector home actually make, and why – if they have to go into an institution – do most Jews want one that is ethnically or faith-based?

Jewish voluntary care homes: religion, culture and home

There is no single answer as to why most Jews would want to be cared for in a Jewish voluntary sector care home. For some, Jewish care homes appear to provide modern facilities that are equivalent to, and in some cases better than, equivalent private sector homes. For others, the principal attraction of these homes is their ability to provide for their religious needs. Jewish voluntary sector care homes have a long tradition of providing kosher and Jewish-style food, as well as centring their activities around the Jewish calendar of the different festivals and the Sabbath. These care homes are – in principle at least – also able to deal sensitively with Jewish attitudes and rites relating to death and bereavement in ways that non-Jewish homes would find difficult.

For strictly observant Jews, having a home that is fully kosher and that is observant of all the rules of the Sabbath is a religious requirement. For example, the strictly Orthodox communities in Stamford Hill, London and Broughton Park, Manchester have constructed two homes specifically designed for these communities. The homes are fitted with electronic devices to ensure that the Sabbath rules are not broken, for example by having lifts that do not require buttons to be pressed, lights that are on automatic timers and food that is *glatt* kosher[4].

Other Jewish voluntary sector homes also adopt many religious Orthodox requirements. All food that is cooked will be kosher (although not *glatt* kosher), so there will be, for example, separate kitchens for the cooking of meat and dairy dishes (in Jewish law it is forbidden to mix these). The Sabbath will be observed, as far as possible, as a rest day. Communal televisions will not be turned on and music will not be played. Individuals within their own rooms can usually do whatever they please, although bringing in non-kosher food is discouraged. Jewish festivals and holy days will be observed, for example, by not eating leaven during the eight days of Passover, by the blowing of the *shofar* (ram's horn) on the Jewish New Year and the Day of Atonement, or by trying to create a carnival atmosphere on Purim (the commemoration of a foiled plot to destroy the Jewish community of ancient Persia). Larger Jewish homes are also likely to have their own synagogues for use by residents and members of the wider community.

Religion and spirituality can be significant coping resources for people suffering (or if their close relatives and friends are suffering) from chronic long-term illness or disability (Stuckey, 2001; see also Gracie and Vincent, 1998). For many Jewish residents, however, the religious components of these homes are of little relevance. What matters to them are the cultural and ethnic components of care. Many Jews are not religious and may, in fact, have had relatively little active involvement in Jewish ways of life before entering a care home. Nevertheless, in interviews many of these people described moving to a specifically Jewish residential or nursing home as being very important, reflecting a desire to 'return to what they know'. There was a feeling that these homes provided a safe and more homely environment in which they could spend the latter part of their lives with other Jews:

> 'Sometimes it's obvious, they want kosher food, access to a synagogue etc, etc, but in other cases kosher food is irrelevant, access to a synagogue is irrelevant, so one can only conclude that it's cultural reasons. Somehow they feel they can relax more and feel more comfortable with people who come from a similar background.' (care home manager)

> 'There are still lots and lots of people who have been brought up in a Jewish environment, who have been used, if not exclusively, then certainly largely, to a Jewish environment, where most of their friends are Jewish, where they've eaten kosher food, Jewish style food.' (care home manager)

One resident argued that when choosing a care home he had never even considered a non-Jewish facility, 'it would be like denying my past'. He argued that the residents of a Jewish home 'aren't strangers, they understand what I'm talking about, I don't need to explain things'. For him, the other residents were somehow the same as himself, so that even if he had thought that a non-Jewish facility had a better standard of care, he would still only have considered a Jewish institution. Residents within such an institution, he believed, are more likely to have a shared sense of humour, and perhaps to have followed similar professions:

> 'It's the difference between visiting the Vatican and my local *shul* [synagogue]. It's like wearing a shoe that fits well. Why would I want to wear a shoe that doesn't fit properly? I like my shoes to be comfortable.' (care home resident)

This particular resident was also a Holocaust survivor, and those who have directly or indirectly experienced the horrors of state-sanctioned anti-semitism were especially likely to want to live in a Jewish environment at the end of their days. It was for this reason that the Otto Schiff Housing Association (now merged with Jewish Care, British Jewry's largest social service agency) was established to care for Jewish refugees from Nazi persecution. Its care homes are specifically designed to be sensitive to the needs of these people, for example, staff do not wear uniforms in an effort to play down the institutional appearance of the home. Sixty years after the concentration camps were liberated, numbers of Holocaust survivors are inevitably declining. Nevertheless, even those who have always lived in the UK have grown up in the shadow of sometimes virulent anti-semitism, especially during the 1930s (see Alderman, 1992).

A number of interviewees pointed out that one of the key attractions of a Jewish home was the food, often not so much that it was kosher, but rather that it was of a 'Jewish' style. One interviewee described how although her father 'hated being in the home' he liked the 'nice German Jewish food, the way he was used to'. For her, there could be no thought of placing him in a care home with 'English' food: 'the sad thing about homes is that meals become the highlight of the day, hence the importance of food'.

The advantage of volunteers

Jewish care homes also have the advantage of having volunteer support to complement their professional components. Although care homes now are increasingly run as businesses, the presence of unpaid volunteers provides an added value that cannot be matched by private facilities. The UK Jewish community has an extensive network of volunteers who provide a range of services, from providing kosher meals-on-wheels to running educational services (see Institute for Jewish Policy Research, 2003). Jewish Care has 2,500 volunteers on its books, although most of these will be involved with community-based, rather than institutionally based, services. Nonetheless, larger care homes have dedicated volunteer coordinators whose job it is to arrange the different array of voluntary activities. These include befriending lonely residents and running activities, such as arts and crafts, music or theatre sessions, or religious services.

Volunteers provide a cost saving to organisations that would otherwise need to employ more paid staff. More importantly, however, they help create a Jewish atmosphere, which is extremely important given the, typically, very low numbers of Jewish staff:

> 'There's a sense in which the staffing ratios only really enable people to do the basic, minimum physical caring, they do not enable people to have that one-to-one relationship, the added value that provides quality of life.' (social services manager)

Jews appear to continue to volunteer because of a heightened level of social capital among the Jewish population stemming from a desire to contribute to and maintain a shared sense of community (see Schlesinger, 2003). This is driven by a complex matrix of factors including a sense of common history, tradition and sameness, and a belief that ultimately the community is responsible for its members. While these beliefs have been challenged as modern Jewry has evolved and split, the sense of shared identity remains a powerful unifying force (Johnson, 1987). Nonetheless, labour market adjustments, particularly the increasing proportion of women entering the workforce, have led to pressures on the traditional pool of volunteers that the Jewish voluntary sector has drawn on. Care home managers expressed considerable concern that volunteers are now increasingly elderly and frail and that younger people are failing to take on these roles. The extent to which volunteers can continue to play a central role within the Jewish community is thus in doubt. The threat to this social capital is arguably the biggest risk facing the future of the UK Jewish voluntary sector (see Institute for Jewish Policy Research, 2003).

Conclusion

Much has been written about the spatial environments of institutional care, most specifically that these have traditionally been designed to structure, control, manage and pacify. For older people, these strategies of control have − intentionally or otherwise − been achieved through the micro-geographies of people's day-to-day lives: the nature of their living spaces, the people they engage with and the places where they eat, feed, bathe and toilet. In many ways these geographies of everyday life are little different for residents living in voluntary sector homes compared to that provided by any other sector: the realities of day-to-day living are what they are. However, voluntary sector provision does appear to make a difference − at least for the case of the UK Jewish community − because they are able to create lived spaces that meet the cultural, ethnic and religious needs of their residents. The sense of community ownership allows residents to feel a sense of home that is unlikely to be as prevalent for those in private institutions. The quantitative survey of Jews in London and the South East, and the interviews with care home residents and their families, clearly demonstrates that most Jews want to be with people they see as the 'same' if they require long-term care outside of the home. Having a Jewish environment − and living in a collective Jewish space − clearly matters.

Jewish voluntary sector care homes generally enjoy a good reputation among local Jewish communities and the facilities that most (although certainly not all) provide are arguably among the best in the country. These homes have a long history of both financial and volunteer support by local Jewish communities, and are seen as key components of the Jewish voluntary sector. Care home managers frequently spoke of a sense of ownership expressed by residents and their families who may well have contributed to the organisation in charitable collections. In many ways these care homes provide a service that is highly valued by service users (and in many cases their close families too) who were struggling to cope when they were still living in their own homes. These facilities can provide services that are culturally and religiously appropriate and that are in keeping with the varied backgrounds and lifestyles of residents. Nevertheless, at the same time there are also major problems in current provision, including funding limitations and difficulties recruiting and retaining adequate numbers of paid (particularly registered nurses) and unpaid (volunteer) staff, especially in London and the South East.

Institutional care is often perceived in black-and-white terms, as either the way to solve all the problems of isolation and ill health, or else as facilities that should have been abandoned with the abolition of the Poor Law. According to Baroness Greengross (former Director General of the charity Age Concern), the future may witness the demise of residential care in its current form and the development of genuine community care and extra-care specialist housing (Brindle, 2000). While there are exciting possibilities for developing non-institutional care provision and the majority of older people will still never need to make use of their services, care homes are likely to remain at the centre of the Jewish community's provision in the foreseeable future. Institutions may never enjoy widespread public (and even academic) support, but without major advances in the medical care of older people, institutional care is here to stay. If that is the case, then the voluntary sector has the role of not only meeting the professional and legislative requirements that all providers must adopt, but offering the added dimensions that distinctive communities want and need. Even for the voluntary sector, care homes must be run as businesses with hundreds of pounds charged directly to residents or to the state, and dozens of staff from nurses to cooks have to be employed. Nonetheless, this does not negate the possibilities of such homes creating environments that do not seek to control, pacify and dispossess, but rather provide a sense of warmth, home, comfort and ease. With declining volunteer support this is increasingly difficult, but is not impossible, as the case study of the UK Jewish community shows.

Notes

[1] Eligibility for public sector-funded residential care is based on an assessment of need and capital assets. The nursing elements of long-term care (as opposed to 'personal' care, such as assistance with bathing) is, since 2001, supposed to be free.

[2] In the UK, residential homes provide meals and personal care to older people such as help with washing, dressing, getting up and going to bed. Nursing homes provide personal care *and* specialist nursing care: they must employ qualified nurses and have at least one on duty at all times.

[3] Goffman (1961, pp15-16) argued that total institutions are symbolised by their barriers to social intercourse with the outside, which are typically incorporated into their built structures. Old age homes were classed in the first of his five categories as 'institutions established to care for persons felt to be both incapable and harmless'.

[4] Glatt kosher means that food is checked by religious authorities to a 'higher' and more exacting standard than 'ordinary' kosher food.

References

Alderman, G. (1992) *Modern British Jewry*, Oxford: Clarendon Press.

Becher, H., Waterman, S., Kosmin, B. and Thomson, K. (2002) *A Portrait of Jews in London and the South East: A Community Study*, London: Institute for Jewish Policy Research.

Blunden, R. (1998) *Terms of Engagement: Engaging Older People in the Development of Community Services*, London: King's Fund.

Brindle. D. (2000) 'Grey Demands Set to Rise', *The Guardian*, 8 November.

Corden, A. (1992) 'Geographical Development of the Long-term Care Market for Elderly People', *Transactions of the Institute of British Geographers*, vol 17, pp 80-94.

DETR (Department of the Environment, Transport and the Regions) (2001) *Supporting People: Policy into Practice*, London: DETR.

DH (Department of Health) (2000) *The NHS Plan: The Government's Response to the Royal Commission on Long Term Care*, London: The Stationery Office.

DH (2001a) *National Service Framework for Older People*, London: DH.

DH (2001b) *National Minimum Standards for Care Homes for Older People*, London: The Stationery Office.

DH (2001c) *Building Capacity and Partnership in Care: An Agreement between the Statutory and the Independent Social Care, Health Care and Housing Sectors*, London: DH.

Fisk, M. (1999) *Our Future Home: Housing and the Inclusion of Older People in 2025*, London: Help the Aged.

Foucault, M. (1967) *Madness and Civilisation*, London: Routledge.

Foucault, M. (1977) *Discipline and Punish: The Birth of the Prison*, London: Penguin.

Goffman, E. (1961) *Asylums: Essays on the Social Situation of Mental Patients and Other Inmates*, London: Penguin.

Gracie, D. and Vincent, J. (1998) 'Progress Report: Religion and Old Age', *Ageing and Society*, vol 18, pp 101-10.

Hamnett, C. and Mullings, B. (1992) 'The Distribution of Public and Private Residential Homes for Elderly Persons in England and Wales', *Area*, vol 2, pp 130-44.

Harris, M. (1997) *The Jewish Voluntary Sector in the United Kingdom: Its Role and Its Future*, London: Institute for Jewish Policy Research.

Harper, S. and Laws, G. (1995) 'Rethinking the Geography of Ageing', *Progress in Human Geography*, vol 19, pp 199-221.

Harrop, A. and Grundy, E. (1991) 'Geographical Variations in Moves into Institutions among the Elderly in England and Wales', *Urban Studies*, vol 28, pp 65-86.

Henwood, M. (2001) *Future Imperfect? Report of the King's Fund Care and Support Inquiry*, London: King's Fund.

Institute for Jewish Policy Research (2003) *Long-term Planning for British Jewry: Final Report and Recommendations*, London: Institute for Jewish Policy Research.

Johnson, M. (2001) *Committed to the Asylum? The Long Term Care of Older People*, Leveson Paper No 3, Temple Balsall: The Leveson Centre for the Study of Ageing, Spirituality and Social Policy.

Johnson, P. (1987) *A History of the Jews*, London: Weidenfeld.

Kellaher, L. (2000) *A Choice Well Made: 'Mutuality' as a Governing Principle in Residential Care*, London: Centre for Policy on Ageing/Methodist Homes.

Kendall, J. (2000) *The Third Sector and Social Care for Older People in England: Towards an Explanation of Its Contrasting Contributions in Residential Care, Domiciliary Care and Day Care*, Civil Society Working Paper 8, London: PSSRU, London School of Economics and Political Science.

Laing, W. (2002) *Calculating a Fair Price for Care: A Toolkit for Residential and Nursing Care Costs*, Bristol/York: The Policy Press/Joseph Rowntree Foundation.

McDowell, L. (1983) 'Towards an Understanding of the Gender Division of Urban Space', *Environment and Planning D: Society and Space*, vol 1, pp 59-72.

Means, R. (2001) 'Lessons from the History of Long-term Care for Older People', in J. Robinson (ed) *Towards a New Social Compact for Care in Old Age*, London: King's Fund, pp 9-28.

Means, R. and Smith, R. (1998) *From Poor Law to Community Law: The Development of Welfare Services for Elderly People 1939–1971*, Bristol: The Policy Press.

Miller, S., Schmool, M. and Lerman, A. (1996) *Social and Political Attitudes of British Jews: Some Key Findings of the JPR Survey*, London: Institute for Jewish Policy Research.

Milligan, C. (2003) 'Location or Dis-Location: From Community to Long term Care – The Caring Experience', *Journal of Social and Cultural Geography*, vol 4, pp 455-70.

Milligan, C. (2006) 'Caring for Older People in the 21st Century: "Notes from a Small Island"', *Health and Place*, vol 20, pp 320-31.

Ogborn, M. (1995) 'Discipline, Government and Law: Separate Confinement in the Prisons of England and Wales, 1830-1877', *Transactions of the Institute of British Geographers*, vol 20, pp 295-311.

Oldman, C. and Quilgars, D. (1999) 'The Last Resort? Revisiting Ideas about Older People's Living Arrangements', *Ageing and Society*, vol 19, pp 363-84.

Patel, N. (1999) 'Black and Minority Ethnic Elderly: Perspectives on Long-term Care', in Royal Commission on Long Term Care, *With Respect to Old Age: Long Term Care – Rights and Responsibilities*, Research Volume 1, London: The Stationery Office, chapter 9.

Peace, S., Kellaher, L. and Willcocks, D. (1997) *Re-evaluating Residential Care*, Buckingham: Open University Press.

Phillips, D. and Vincent, J. (1986) 'Private Residential Accommodation for the Elderly: Geographical Aspects of Developments in Devon', _Transactions of the Institute of British Geographers_, vol 11, pp 155-73.

Philo, C. (1989) '"Enough to Drive One Mad": The Organization of Space in Nineteenth-century Lunatic Asylums', in J. Wolch and M. Dear (eds) _The Power of Geography: How Territory Shapes Social Life_, London: Unwin Hyman, pp 258-89.

Philo, C. (1997) 'Across the Water: Reviewing Geographical Studies of Asylums and Other Mental Health Facilities', _Health and Place_, vol 3, pp 73-89.

Philo, C. and Parr, H. (2000) 'Institutional Geographies: Introductory Remarks', _Geoforum_, vol 31, pp 513-21.

Rowles, G. (1978) _Prisoners of Space? Exploring the Geographical Experience of Older People_, Boulder, CO: Westview Press.

Rowles, G. (1986) 'The Geography of Ageing and the Aged: Towards an Integrated Perspective', _Progress in Human Geography_, vol 10, pp 511-39.

Rowles, G., Beaulieu, J. and Myers, W. (eds) (1996) _Long-term Care of the Rural Elderly: New Directions in Research, Services and Policy_, New York, NY: Springer.

Royal Commission on Long Term Care (1999) _With Respect to Old Age: Long Term Care – Rights and Responsibilities_, London: The Stationery Office.

Schlesinger, E. (2003) _Creating Community and Accumulating Social Capital: Jews Associating with Other Jews in Manchester_, London: Institute for Jewish Policy Research.

Schmool, M. and Cohen, F. (1998) _A Profile of British Jewry: Patterns and Trends at the Turn of a Century_, London: Board of Deputies of British Jews.

Shawler, C., Rowles, G. and High, D. (2001) 'Analysis of Key Decision-making Incidents in the Life of a Nursing Home Resident', _Gerontologist_, vol 41, no 5, pp 612-22.

Smith, C. (1992) 'The Geography of Private Residential Care', in K. Morgan (ed) _Gerontology: Responding to an Ageing Society_, London: Jessica Kingsley, pp 99-117.

Smith, G. and Ford, R. (1998) 'Geographical Change in Residential Care Provision for the Elderly in England, 1988-1993', _Health and Place_, vol 4, pp 15-31.

Stuckey, J. (2001) 'Blessed Assurance: The Role of Religion and Spirituality in Alzheimer's Disease Caregiving and other Significant Life Events', _Journal of Ageing Studies_, vol 15, pp 69-84.

Sumner, K. (ed) (2002) _Our Homes, Our Lives_, London: Centre for Policy on Ageing.

Thane, P. (2000) _Old Age in English History: Past Experiences, Present Issues_, Oxford: Oxford University Press.

Townsend, P. (1962) _The Last Refuge_, London: Routledge and Kegan Paul.

Townsend, P. (1981) 'The Structured Dependency of the Elderly: The Creation of Social Policy in the Twentieth Century', _Ageing and Society_, vol 1, pp 5-28.

Twigg, J. (2000) _Bathing: The Body and Community Care_, London: Routledge.

Valentine, G. and Longstaff, B. (1998) 'Doing Porridge: Food and Social Relations in a Male Prison', *Journal of Material Culture*, vol 3, pp 131-52.

Valins, O. (2002) *Facing the Future: The Provision of Long-term Care Facilities for Older Jewish People in the United Kingdom*, London: Institute for Jewish Policy Research.

Warnes, A. (1990) 'Geographical Questions in Gerontology: Needed Directions for Research', *Progress in Human Geography*, vol 14, pp 24-56.

Yee, L. and Mussenden, B. (2001) *From Lip Service to Real Service: The Report of the First Phase of a Project to Assist Councils with Social Services Responsibilities to Develop Services for Black Older People*, London: DH.

NINE

Values, practices and strategic divestment: Christian social service organisations in New Zealand

David Conradson

> ... there are now few corners of the voluntary sector still to be 'drawn in' to new social policy partnerships with governmental agencies. It was to be expected, then, that politicians would eventually turn their attention to the resources of voluntarily given time and money made available by people of faith to religious charities and religious-based charities and encourage their direction into governmentally approved policy initiatives. (Harris et al, 2003, p 96)

Since the 1990s, governments in the industrialised West have shown growing interest in faith-based organisations as welfare providers. In the US, this attention has been reflected in the formation of the White House Office of Faith-based and Community Initiatives in 2000, as well as the influential Charitable Choice legislation of 1996 (Berger, 2003; Bane et al, 2005)[1]. A similar interest in faith-based organisations has developed in the UK under New Labour (Blair, 2001; Blunkett, 2001), with specific efforts in the spheres of community development and urban regeneration for instance (Farnell et al, 2003; Lukka et al, 2003). In each country, these engagements with faith-based organisations can be read as part of ongoing neoliberal efforts to enrol non-state actors in the delivery of welfare (Peck, 2001).

Given the geography of these developments, it is unsurprising that empirical research on faith-based welfare provision to date has largely focused on the US and UK. Key themes in this literature have included:

- the extent to which faith-based welfare organisations might be considered distinctive in relation to their secular counterparts (for example, Cloke et al, 2005; Kearns et al, 2005);
- the potential of faith-based organisations for enhancing social capital and promoting community development (for example, Shaftesbury Society and DETR, 2000; Lukka et al, 2003);

- the role of faith as an impetus for volunteering and voluntarism (Cnaan et al, 1993; Lukka and Locke, 2003);
- the place of faith groups in urban regeneration (Lewis, 2002; Smith, 2002; Farnell et al, 2003).
- the variable dispositions of local and national governments regarding the funding of faith-based organisations (Ebaugh et al, 2005).

In terms of organisational forms, studies have examined both religious congregations (for example, Harris, 1995, 1998; Chaves, 1999; Cnaan, 1999) and independently incorporated faith-based organisations (for example, Harris et al, 2003; Kearns et al, 2005). The diversity of faiths considered is as yet relatively small, however, with Christianity and Judaism receiving most attention and relatively less research published – at least in the English language literature – on welfare organisations shaped by Islamic, Buddhist or Hindu belief.

As a contribution to this literature, this chapter examines the values and service practices of a set of Christian Social Service Organisations (CSSOs) in the South Pacific nation of New Zealand. As a country that once had a relatively generous welfare state (Castles, 1996), New Zealand provides an interesting social scientific context for those interested in tracing the social and economic outcomes of neoliberal reforms (Kelsey, 1996; Le Heron and Pawson, 1996; Larner and Craig, 2005). An Antipodean study also acts as a small counterweight to the Anglo-American emphasis in the current literature. The particular focus is Christchurch, a city of around 350,000 inhabitants in the country's southern island. Although not large by international standards, its examination here complements existing work on New Zealand voluntarism, as this has often been conducted at the national scale or with the largest metropolitan centre, Auckland, as its focus (for example, Whale, 1993; Clarke, 1997). The focus on Christian social services reflects the predominance of such agencies in the New Zealand faith-based welfare sector, while nevertheless recognising that research is needed on voluntary welfare that emerges from other faith traditions.

The discussion has three main sections. Firstly, and by way of context, I outline the shifting involvement of Christian organisations in New Zealand's mixed economy of welfare over time, noting the impact of neoliberal reforms in recent years. The second part of the chapter then examines the welfare philosophies circulating within four case study CSSOs in Christchurch. Noting the complex relations between articulation and enactment, I thirdly consider how these philosophies have been manifest as service practices within the city. Drawing on annual reports, occasional newsletters and interviews with senior staff in both 1996/97 and 2004, I look in particular at processes of divestment and development within organisational service portfolios. A short conclusion then follows.

Faith-based welfare provision: origins and recent developments

As is the case in many Western countries, Christian communities in New Zealand have a sustained history of involvement in welfare provision. Whether operating as congregations or independently incorporated organisations, one can observe a tradition of practical engagement with social deprivation that stretches back to the 19th century. In the early years of European settler society, when statutory welfare provision was minimal, the churches were a major player in supporting less fortunate individuals, particularly widows, unemployed men and those whose ability to work had been compromised by mining and industrial accidents. In the 1890s, as denominational structures of the church began to attain some degree of national coverage, city missions were opened in the larger metropolitan centres of Auckland, Wellington, Christchurch and Dunedin (Tennant, 1989; McClure, 1998). Against the backdrop of a welfare state, however, the rising affluence of the immediate postwar decades undoubtedly dampened demand for voluntary welfare services. But the economic downturn of the 1970s, followed by state-led restructuring during the 1980s and then welfare reform in the 1990s, gave many voluntary agencies a renewed raison d'être. Once again in the frontline of social service provision, many CSSOs in New Zealand are now multifaceted and, in some cases, multimillion dollar operations.

In order to understand the renewed prominence of these organisations, an appreciation of recent economic and social policy reform is useful. Between 1984 and 1990, in line with what Peck and Tickell (2002) have termed 'roll-back neoliberalism', a Labour government initiated a major programme of economic restructuring in New Zealand. In a similar vein, a National government from 1990 to 1999 then sought to dismantle significant elements of the postwar welfare state (Boston et al, 1999). This constellation of reforms led to sharp increases in social inequality and economic privation (Jackman, 1992; Stephens et al, 1995). For voluntary welfare agencies, this meant increased opportunity but also – from their perspective – greater obligation for active social intervention (Cheyne et al, 2004). The caseloads of many church agencies accordingly increased as they sought to support the social casualties of neoliberal reform – the unemployed, 'working poor', elderly and homeless for instance – while city-based directories show that significant numbers of new voluntary welfare organisations were also formed during the 1990s[2]. Among these, faith-based initiatives were a significant component and included foodbanks, budget advice and housing agencies, night shelters for homeless people and community development organisations.

In addition to these processes of welfare retrenchment, Christian social services in New Zealand have also been shaped by elements of 'roll-out neoliberalism' (Peck and Tickell, 2002); that is, the extension of statutory involvement in certain areas of the economy and civil society, in accordance with neoliberal imperatives. The shift from grant-based to contractual funding mechanisms has been of particular importance (Department of Social Welfare, 1990; Boston, 1995). As part of a broader programme of state sector reform guided by the nostrums of New Public Management, a contractual model for government funding of voluntary organisations was introduced. This was strongly criticised by voluntary agencies, however, with the key points of contention mirroring those noted in British and North American contexts (Wolch, 1990; Deakin, 1996). It was felt that contractual funding was accompanied by unwelcome pressures to deliver services in particular ways, that it acted to undermine interorganisational cooperation (as agencies were directly competing for the same funding streams), and that its accountability demands were incommensurate with the level of resources provided.

The contracting situation has arguably improved in recent years, however, following the publication of a *Statement of Government Intent for an Improved Community–Government Relationship* in December 2001 (Ministry of Social Policy, 2001). Issued by a Labour government (1999–), this document outlines a commitment to more respectful and less exploitative forms of partnership between the state and voluntary sector. The *Statement* has been accompanied by assurances of less intensive forms of contract monitoring and, in some cases, a willingness to make funding available over longer time periods. While staff in some voluntary organisations in Christchurch in 2004 retained a measure of scepticism regarding what it had achieved, others were prepared to acknowledge the political commitment it reflected and felt it was beginning to facilitate a more favourable operational environment for voluntary welfare provision. Mirroring wider debates regarding the capacity of neoliberalism to reinvent itself (Peck and Tickell, 2002), it is thus unclear whether the *Statement* can be adequately described as 'roll-out neoliberalism'. It might better be approached as some form of 'third way' accommodation (for differing views, see Chatterjee et al, 1999; Larner and Craig, 2005).

Philosophies of welfare: understandings and values

Having described something of the social policy background in which New Zealand's voluntary welfare organisations currently operate, I now turn to the Christchurch case study. Mirroring the diversity of the voluntary welfare sector more broadly, local CSSOs exhibit significant variation in both form and function. One can identify both small, volunteer-led agencies as well as large, relatively professionalised organisations. The discussion here focuses on four organisations of the latter type: Anglican Care, Methodist Mission, Presbyterian Support and the Salvation Army. In terms of budgets and number of clients, these are the four largest Christian social service agencies in Christchurch[3]. Each employs significant numbers of paid, professionally qualified staff, and makes varying usage of volunteers; they are voluntary organisations in the sense of being not-for-profit rather than because of any exclusive reliance on volunteer labour.

These CSSOs all sit within wider organisational structures, with a national headquarters typically located in the capital of Wellington, similar operations in other cities and regions, and some form of social policy research and evaluation unit. The latter monitor the efficacy of the organisation's service interventions, report on key developments in governmental social policy and at times lobby Parliament over specific issues. In addition, each agency is also part of the New Zealand Council of Christian Social Services (NZCCSS), a national umbrella group that represents the interests of its members to national government on a range of fronts.

Although seldom expressed in the form of a coherent written statement, each of the case study agencies can be said to operate with a particular understanding or philosophy of welfare. As a set of overlapping ideas and discourses, these philosophies encompass the rationale for the organisation's existence; conceptualisations of the needs and responsibilities of its service users; and understandings of what constitutes the most effective form of service intervention. For CSSOs, these views may be linked to particular theologies of the human condition, while nevertheless being framed in language that the agency perceives to be intelligible and acceptable to a wider public. In interpreting expressions of these philosophies, one cannot assume that a particular corporate narrative will neatly translate into enactment by individual staff and volunteers. Instead, there will always be divergence, disjunctures and slippage in this regard. Despite these limitations, an analysis of organisational discourses is able to shed some light on welfare philosophies.

As short expressions of an organisation's focus and aims, mission statements are one place to begin such analysis. While at times guiding internal decision making, these statements also work to consolidate a distinctive image for an organisation among its external stakeholders, including the general public, funding agencies and government bodies. Among the case study CSSOs, a common desire to promote social justice and well-being was evident at this level (Table 9.1). Such aspirations reflected the generally left-of-centre character of the agencies. This political positioning was widely recognised by the agencies themselves, but was also evident in public organisational newsletters and annual reports. Within these documents, the structural-economic causes of deprivation were clearly recognised, while statutory intervention was endorsed as necessary for the reduction of social inequality.

The organisations differed, however, in the degree to which Christian influences on these forms of thought and practice were signalled within mission statements. For Anglican Care, Methodist Mission and Presbyterian Support, expression of Christian faith was either absent or relatively low key at this level. Senior managers linked faith with the provision of good quality services, rather than pastoral or evangelism related activities. For the Salvation Army, the connection between the pastoral and social outreach elements of its work was relatively stronger, however, as is indicated by the clear invocation of the person of Christ as a source of authority and motivation. It should perhaps be noted, however, that

Table 9.1: Mission statements of the case study organisations

Organisation	Mission statement
Anglican Care	'In Christian love, to serve and seek justice in the community'
Methodist Mission	'To promote social justice through partnerships that strengthen families and build fair and safe communities'
Presbyterian Support	'People helping people to help themselves'
The Salvation Army	'To care for people, transform lives through spiritual renewal, and work for the reform of society by alleviating poverty, deprivation and disadvantage, and by challenging evil, injustice and oppression in the name of Jesus'

Source: Annual reports and organisational documents

the Salvation Army's government-funded work maintained an exclusive focus on material support and relief.

Beyond the mission statements, each of the agencies had identified particular values that described their preferred style of working. These were typically linked to a faith-based ethic of social service that was, in turn, inflected by particular denominational traditions of Christian faith. For Methodist Mission, these values included community and compassion; for Anglican Care, partnership and practical service; for Presbyterian Support, social justice and efficient service; and for the Salvation Army, an interest in caring for people, transforming lives and reforming society. At the broad level, these sets of values signalled something of *how* an organisation would seek to engage in a transformative fashion with marginalised individuals in New Zealand society. As the following examples illustrate, the maintenance and reproduction of values therefore attracted significant thought. The first concerns the relation between faith and personnel recruitment. The second examines the way in which service users are discursively constructed, an issue that has implications for the relational dynamics of welfare service transactions.

Reproducing organisational culture: the place of faith in recruitment

If one pushes beyond the inevitable neatness of mission statements, it is clear that the spiritual and ethical values signalled within them are taken up – as well as resisted and at times ignored – in divergent ways within an organisation. A key issue in reproducing organisational culture is thus the recruitment and retention of appropriately minded staff. For CSSOs, questions also arise regarding the *degree* to which staff and volunteers are required to identify with organisational level spirituality (and the legality of any such requirements). Should staff be required to profess a personal Christian faith, or is a broader adherence to values that are in sympathy with this faith sufficient?

Among the case study agencies a significant degree of personnel heterogeneity was permitted in these regards; indeed, most senior managers regarded it as normal and desirable. As a senior member of Anglican Care staff expressed it:

'In terms of our staffing, what we ask of staff – they don't have to be Christian, they don't have to be Anglican. But they must accept our kaupapa[4]. Not just accept it from a knowledge point of view, but from a living point of view.... we don't ask that all our people be Anglican or Christian, but we ask them to live and model Christian values.'

Similarly, a manager at Presbyterian Support noted that:

'I think some organisations employ people on the basis of how important their Christian belief might be to them. But we don't do that here. It's more around our, um, I guess we have our set of core values which are really important around how we value people, and the integrity of how we do our work. Which often has a Christian base, but not necessarily so. So that people move into this area of work, I think, on the basis of a tendency to have a strong belief system in the value of people, and the value of integrity in their work. But that may not necessarily be equal to being narrowly interpreted as Christian.'

Their faith-based organisational identity notwithstanding, managers in these agencies were thus not overly concerned whether paid staff and volunteers identified themselves as having a personal Christian faith. The issue was more that workers had a broadly Judaeo-Christian value framework, manifest as a respectful way of engaging with clients. This approach to recruitment contributed to an organisational culture in which personal faith, where present, was as much a private matter as a corporate one. In the Salvation Army, however, most if not all key staff would self-identify as committed Christians and this enabled a degree of corporate spiritual expression – collective prayer and worship for instance – that was less central to the other agencies.

It was in smaller CSSOs across the city that managers more commonly sought to attract staff with personal faith commitments. At the Supportive Family Foundation and Ellesmere House for instance – pseudonyms for a social work and community development agency respectively – it was considered important that staff had a Christian faith as well as a broad adherence to the organisation's values. This combination of qualities was pursued through recruitment practices, but also occurred to a degree on the basis of self-selection, in that individuals reflexively assessed their personal 'fit' with the local organisational culture[5]. The beliefs of volunteers were typically less amenable to such management, and in any case faith was often deemed less important than a willing attitude. Within small CSSOs, these recruitment practices nevertheless tended to support the reproduction of an organisational culture in which faith and service came together in similar ways.

In terms of engagement with service users, each of the case-study CSSOs had explicit managerial directives regarding the expression of religious faith at work. No discrimination was to be made between service users on the basis of their personal beliefs and, critically, preaching or proselytising was not permitted as part of service delivery. As a staff member at Anglican Care explained, 'our task within the diocese is not to preach, but to walk alongside [people]. It's possible to get sacked from here for proselytising'. Faith informed the work in terms of practical support and empathetic engagement, but explicit attempts to influence the spirituality of service users was forbidden.

Discursive constructions of service users

A second area of organisational reflection relates to the discursive construction of service users as individuals with particular needs and qualities. As Sibley (1995) notes in a more general argument about socio-spatial exclusion, discourses regarding social groups may act to reinforce particular ways of relating to individuals within them. If the users of a voluntary welfare agency are constructed as being needy and lacking in life skills, for example, then the service provided may seek to instil these skills in a manner that, because of its assumption of client deficiency, is at times patronising or demeaning. Alternatively, it is possible to conceive of a less hierarchical approach in which advantaged people come alongside less advantaged people to facilitate their well-being.

Among the case study agencies, the publicly expressed constructions of users – as articulated in annual reports and interview narratives – were generally of the more positive type. In particular, there was an awareness of the power relations inherent in assisting people from deprived social situations. The Director of Presbyterian Support Services thus contrasted the view of users he felt his agency enacted against that of organisations with more 'right-wing' theologies:

> 'Presbyterian Support ... has always had this emphasis on a very high understanding of humanity. That's where in my opinion, it differs from the more right-wing religious approach that says "all people are sinners, and the grace of God is the only thing that can overcome that". That is one extreme model of theology. The other is "you're made in the image of God, and the grace of God is with you". You don't have to get it, it's there. Now, depending where your theology is, it influences the kind of response you have to social need. And that's why Presbyterianism has largely said "all people have the potential to be great, thus they should be treated like that". And rather than [be] treated – as the extreme welfare model does – as casualties, or as people needing to be rescued, it's saying, "no, they don't need rescuing, they need assistance". So you get a different model of social service coming through. And Presbyterianism in my opinion is more akin to that. It is not a rescue, it would be the potential enhancing approach.

And standing alongside is very different from standing over, and lifting someone up.'

The spatial metaphor here of standing alongside an individual is instructive. It is a picture of engagement between equals, rather than the rescuing of the weak by the strong. A member of senior staff at the Methodist Mission echoed the importance of such assumptions of equal value within the service delivery environment, arguing that 'if we start with a needs based approach, then it becomes paternalistic ... and I think demeans the people that we say we then serve'. Similarly, staff at Anglican Care noted that our 'way of being is allowing each person to be given the dignity and respect humans possess'.

The 'extreme models of theology' referred to by the Presbyterian Support interviewee – presumably those of more Calvinist nature which emphasise the 'fallen nature' of humanity and associated need for redemptive transformation – were not directly encountered within the four case study agencies. This is not surprising when one considers these are large, relatively professionalised agencies with a diverse staff and relatively loose relations with their congregational roots (some of which are theologically liberal in any case). Anecdotal evidence of more conservative views was observed in a number of smaller CSSOs in Christchurch, particularly where welfare philosophy and practice were strongly shaped by the views of particular individuals and the church context was either strongly evangelical or charismatic in nature. But on the whole, the local Christian social service sector appears to reflect the general tendency of voluntary welfare organisations to be 'of the left'. Unlike the situation in the US, there was no evidence of clusterings of agencies that could reasonably be described as part of a 'religious right' in Christchurch.

Shifting portfolios of service provision

Having considered some dimensions of the welfare philosophies of CSSOs, I now turn to their practical expression as service practices. There are many different levels on which this question of enactment could be analysed (Campbell, 2002), but, within the space available here, I simply want to make some observations on the changing types of services offered. Drawing on a business metaphor, I adopt the notion of a shifting portfolio of service provision to support this analysis. The wider context, as noted earlier, is a period of strong neoliberalism and New Public Management in social policy (1990-99), followed by the emergence of a somewhat hybridised social policy approach in recent years (1999-2006). This has seen a continued commitment to workfare but also efforts to develop more productive partnerships with voluntary organisations.

We can begin by noting that each of the four CSSOs operates a diverse portfolio of services, including care for older people, social work and counselling, various forms of emergency relief and charity shops (Table 9.2). These services are offered both from fixed sites and directly to individuals in their homes or on the streets.

Table 9.2: Organisational social service portfolios in 2004

Organisation	Date founded in Christchurch	Key service divisions	Summary of services provided
Anglican Care	1952	• Anglican Aged Care • Christchurch City Mission • Family and Community Division	• Care for older people • Material support for disadvantaged inner-city residents • Work with disadvantaged families/groups via a community development model
Methodist Mission	1939	• Childwise • ER (Emergency Relief) • 4C (Advocacy Programme) • Wesley Care (Aged Care) • Social Policy Advocacy	• Social work with children and families • Emergency food and budget advice • An advocacy programme to facilitate ER client independence • Hospital, respite care and independent accommodation facilities • Quarterly newsletter and participation in local and national forums
Presbyterian Support	1908	• Services for Older People • Youth, Children and Families • Mental Health	• Supporting the frail elderly in their own homes • Supporting the family in the task of raising children • Residential care for people with chronic mental illness, including dementia
The Salvation Army	1883	• Community and Family Service Centres • Youth work • Street Outreach Services • Addiction Services and Supportive Accommodation	• Foodbank services, budgeting advice, advocacy, training and support services • Support, advocacy and employment training • On street support for sex workers and homeless people • Supporting people with drug and alcohol addictions, including residential support

Source: Annual reports and organisational websites

Within the Family and Community Division of Anglican Care, for example, there are a series of Community Cottages – encompassing drop-in and advice services – located in the city's poorer neighbourhoods. The City Mission then provides food, overnight accommodation and other material support for vulnerable people in the city centre. Similar lists of activities can be constructed for the other case study agencies. Taken together, the four CSSOs provide a significant proportion of the voluntary welfare provision in Christchurch.

The service portfolios of the CSSOs reflect the intersection of collective aims, internal dynamics and the external environment. Processes of competition and cooperation between agencies have been important, as these have contributed to degrees of specialisation and niche service provision (cf Rao, 2002). Anglican Care offers the broadest portfolio of services, stretching from the City Mission through to various forms of aged care services and community development interventions. The Salvation Army comes close for breadth, with services that similarly extend from material support and emergency relief through to social work and counselling. Methodist Mission operates a somewhat smaller, but nonetheless significant, 'emergency relief' operation, focusing on budgetary advice and food support. This is accompanied by advocacy work, aged care services and social policy evaluation. Presbyterian Support is almost entirely focused on professionalised services such as social work and counselling and, as such, does not offer any emergency relief. It intentionally leaves this to other agencies.

Between 1999 and 2003, the case study agencies faced at least four challenges in seeking to operate as faith-based welfare organisations. First, demand for their assistance consistently outstripped available resources, such that rationalisation of activities was inevitably required. Second, at least in the early part of this period (prior to the *Statement of Government Intent*), competitive contractualism continued to bring pressures around compliance and monitoring. Third, revenue from charitable giving had been declining[6]. Finally, the government's desire to encourage a diversity of welfare providers had seen competition not only between voluntary sector agencies, but also between voluntary organisations and private sector companies.

Taken together, these challenges led to reduced operating margins, with all four of the agencies experiencing degrees of fiscal constraint between 1999 and 2003 (Table 9.3). With the exception of the Salvation Army, all agencies in fact ran deficit budgets at some point, thereby eating into their financial reserves. This has generated pressure to review service portfolios, with an eye both to core organisational values and financial sustainability (Table 9.4). Two case study agencies consequently engaged in significant rationalisation. Methodist Mission sold a number of aged care facilities to emerging private sector providers, as well as divesting its telephone counselling service and charity shops. In an effort to reconcile organisational values more fully with financial reality, the charity shops were not deemed to contribute sufficiently directly to the core social justice mission. Presbyterian Support undertook a similar though more comprehensive divestment of its residential care facilities in 2001, moving instead to a model of

Table 9.3: Overall financial performance (1999-2003)

Organisation	Net surplus/deficit as of 30 June (thousands of New Zealand dollars)				
	1999	2000	2001	2002	2003
Anglican Care	−33	143	455	−61	−250
Methodist Mission	−252	−996	−141	−188	155
Presbyterian Support[a]	1,499	1,266	4,622	−234	466
Salvation Army[b]	15,736	13,301	12,533	4,867	4,751

Source: Annual reports.

Notes:

[a] Figures for the upper South Island region, including Christchurch.

[b] National figures, and thus disproportionately larger than those of other agencies that record expenditure/income at the city or regional level. The general trend of a declining annual surplus is nevertheless evident.

supporting aging people in their homes and non-residential environments. The sale of its homes is reflected in a large net surplus. Although Anglican Care and the Salvation Army also experienced financial constraints, neither organisation made any significant adjustments to their service provision portfolios during the analysis period.

The centrality of residential aged care to the divestment strategies of both Methodist Mission and Presbyterian Support reflects in part its expense, but an important broader structural influence has been the growth of private sector providers of aged care. In Christchurch, one firm in particular has expanded aggressively into the care sector. Well capitalised, it has been able to build new properties from scratch, thus obtaining a competitive advantage in terms of the quality of residential environment it can offer. Achieving a similar quality of residential setting has been increasingly (and prohibitively) expensive for some of the CSSOs, principally because of the age of their housing stock. Staff at both Methodist Mission and Presbyterian Support thus spoke of an emerging consensus in which residential aged care was no longer perceived to be a financially sustainable or strategic area of service. Interestingly, Anglican Care was also reconsidering its involvement in this area, not in terms of divestment but rather cost savings. These shifts also reflect a wider preference in governmental policy for home- rather than institutionally-based aged care.

Alongside these divestments, a number of new service developments can be noted across the case study agencies. First, Methodist Mission has restructured its emergency relief activities. In an effort to address concerns over becoming complicit in service dependency, the foodbank was expanded to encompass a fuller advocacy and mentoring service. The analysis underlying this shift did not emerge from a neoliberal or right-wing standpoint, but rather managerial observations over a period of years regarding the 'revolving door' status of some long-term service users. Second, as noted above, both Methodist Mission and Presbyterian Support have started to develop new forms of home-based aged

Table 9.4: Rationalisation of service provision portfolios (1999-2004)

Agency	Service divestments	Other service developments
Anglican Care	• Nothing significant noted	• Currently seeking efficiencies in aged care services
Methodist Mission	• Closure of all charity shops • Sale of Lifeline Counselling Service • Divestment of selected residential aged care facilities	• General review of welfare service philosophy • Supplementing ER[a] with advocacy and mentoring work • Development of alternative aged care facilities
Presbyterian Support Services	• Divestment of all residential aged care facilities • Internal restructuring of staff divisions	• New focus on home-based care services for older clients • Increasing focus on family-based interventions
The Salvation Army	• Nothing significant noted	• Formation of a new national social policy evaluation unit • Seeking more effective service interventions

Source: Annual reports and organisational documents.

Note: [a] Emergency Relief

care services. Finally, the Salvation Army has set up a national social policy evaluation unit, in an effort to develop a strong research basis for effective service interventions and for lobbying government. These initiatives all point to the ongoing efforts of individual agencies to realise their faith-based service provision goals in the wider context of financial and political challenges.

Given the scale of these adjustments, it is fair to say that the period 1999-2003 has been challenging for CSSOs in Christchurch. While these changes have been narrated with reference to financial headlines, it is important – if perhaps obvious – to note that these CSSOs are not conventional businesses, seeking to maximise profit and returns for shareholders. Faith-based values, rooted in both denominational traditions and the perspectives of individual employees, arguably function as a second form of bottom line. The precise ways and extent to which these values matter of course differs by individual organisation, but a strong desire to work in partnership with disadvantaged individuals and communities to enhance their well-being was nonetheless common. The following excerpt from the 2002 Annual Report of Presbyterian Support expresses this divergence from straightforward business ethics rather well:

> While Presbyterian Support organises its affairs in a businesslike way, it is not a business. Generally businesses manage income and expenditure to provide the surplus expected by shareholders. We do not of course provide a dividend return. Those who 'invest' in Presbyterian Support do so for philanthropic reasons, knowing their donation will provide a different kind of return.... In situations like this it is important to remember there is another way we are different from commercial business – we're driven by our mission. We are here to make a difference in people's lives and particularly to those at risk in our communities. This is what Presbyterian Support's Mission Statement calls us to do.

One can, of course, be sceptical regarding the degree to which such narratives are able to be realised in practice (Cloke et al, 2005). Moreover, as debates regarding the shadow state have highlighted, the autonomy that voluntary sector agencies enjoy to realise such aspirations is often not as great as they would like (Wolch 1990; Fyfe and Milligan, 2003; see also Owen and Kearns, Chapter Seven, this volume). And yet as the examples here suggest, CSSOs in Christchurch are managing to draw on their faith-based values to offer distinctive and important forms of voluntary welfare service.

Conclusion

In considering four relatively large CSSOs, a number of conclusions can be drawn regarding the place of faith-based welfare organisations in contemporary New Zealand. Firstly, as one might expect, the diversity of faith positions articulated by these agencies are in turn manifest as a diversity of social welfare practices. There are also differences in the degree of professionalisation and extent to which volunteer labour is used. At one end of a spectrum, Presbyterian Support exhibits a high degree of professionalisation, with significant numbers of paid staff with social work, psychological and therapeutic qualifications. Other agencies, such as Anglican Care and Methodist Mission, make a little more use of volunteers in terms of their city mission and community based ministries, while still incorporating significant numbers of qualified social work and mental health staff. Each approach has its benefits, and neither is incontrovertibly better than the other, but it is important to observe this diversity and consider how its erosion might impact on service users.

Secondly, it can be seen that CSSOs have faced, and will continue to face, challenges in their efforts to articulate their core values as service providers. It is one thing to declare an interest in restorative models of justice or caring for the marginalised, but such generosity and empathetic engagement inevitably requires motivated labour, whether voluntary or paid, as well as sufficient finance and appropriate infrastructure. Within a competitive socio-political environment and amidst financial pressures, CSSOs are inevitably involved in processes of negotiation and contestation regarding what constitutes a desirable and sustainable portfolio of activities. The agencies considered here have sought to address the tensions that arise in a number of ways, including activity and asset divestment, internal restructuring, reformulation of welfare philosophies and service reviews. In an effort to identify areas for greater efficiencies these are all elements of the business of voluntary welfare.

Thirdly, it is possible to argue that faith-based organisations in general – and CSSOs in particular – function as social repositories for values and perspectives that are to some degree oppositional to those of neoliberal social policy (cf Boston, 1994). The four agencies considered here each expressed an understanding of poverty as having significant structural causes for instance, and this sits uneasily with workfarist approaches that continue to characterise New Zealand's unemployment policy. On a range of fronts, CSSOs in New Zealand have thus been active in lobbying government. Published reports have engaged with issues such as benefit reform (Auckland Methodist Mission, 1991; Dalziel, 1993), rising poverty and inequality (Jackman, 1992), the privatisation of state housing (Young, 1995; Gunby, 1996), as well as tensions relating to service contracting (Nowland-Foreman, 1995; NZCCSS, 1998). In contributing to broader left-of-centre critiques of neoliberal social policy, this work highlights the fact that CSSOs are about more than welfare service provision. They are also important in terms of enlarging our social policy horizons, taking us beyond the imperatives of instrumental economics and New Public Management theory.

Notes

[1] This legislation seeks to encourage private and religious charitable organisations to deliver welfare services, whilst ensuring they need not compromise their religious freedom or organisational integrity in doing so.

[2] One such directory is CINCH (Community Information Christchurch), an online list of community and voluntary sector agencies in Christchurch, New Zealand. There are limitations, of course, to the use of such registers, as inclusion is typically voluntary and dependent on a response to an enquiry or questionnaire. Smaller agencies without permanent addresses or sufficient administrative capacity are thus likely to be under-represented.

[3] There are a number of Catholic social service initiatives in Christchurch, although collectively these are relatively small. They have been excluded here because it was not possible to obtain equivalent levels of interview or documentary access. There are also a number of influential Baptist social service initiatives, but as congregationally based activities these have been excluded because of the focus here on independent organisations.

[4] *Kaupapa* is the Maori word for 'statement of being' and roughly corresponds to the English 'mission statement'.

[5] By this I mean to summarise the way volunteers and staff assess institutional cultures and, in the process of intuitively evaluating their 'fit' with an organisational culture, seek work in environments with which they feel most comfortable. This dynamic is arguably particularly significant for volunteers, where the usual imperatives of remuneration operate less strongly.

[6] A number of voluntary welfare managers saw the initiation of a national lottery as a strong possible cause of this financial attenuation. Because the lottery organisation had been widely advertised as contributing funds to voluntary sector causes, they were concerned its activities might thereby be eroding public motivation for independent charitable giving.

References

Auckland Methodist Mission (1991) *Just Another Experiment? A Critical Analysis of the 1991 Budget*, Auckland: Social Policy Unit of Auckland Methodist Mission.

Bane, M.J., Coffin, B. and Higgins, R. (eds) (2005) *Taking Faith Seriously*, Cambridge, MA: Harvard University Press.

Berger, J. (2003) 'Religious Non-Governmental Organizations: An Exploratory Analysis', *Voluntas: International Journal of Voluntary and Nonprofit Organizations*, vol 14, no 1, pp 15–39.

Blair, T. (2001) 'The Faith Communities and the Labour Government', Speech to the Christian Social Movement at Westminster Central Hall, 29 March (www.number10.gov.uk/output/page3243.asp, accessed January 2005).

Blunkett, D. (2001) 'Partnership with Faith Communities Vital to Civil Renewal', Home Office Press release, 19 June.

Boston, J. (1994) 'Christianity in the Public Square: The Churches and Social Justice', in J. Boston and A. Cameron (eds) *Voices of Justice: Church, Law and State in New Zealand*, Palmerston North: Dunmore Press, pp 11-36.

Boston, J. (1995) *The State Under Contract*, Wellington: Bridget Williams Books.

Boston, J., Dalziel, P. and St John, S. (eds) (1999) *Redesigning the Welfare State in New Zealand: Problems, Policies and Prospects*, Auckland: Oxford University Press.

Campbell, D. (2002) 'Beyond Charitable Choice: The Diverse Service Delivery Approaches of Local Faith-related Organisations', *Nonprofit and Voluntary Sector Quarterly*, vol 31, no 2, pp 207-30.

Castles, F.G. (1996) 'Needs-Based Strategies of Social Protection in Australia and New Zealand' in G. Esping-Andersen (ed) *Welfare States in Transition: National Adaptations in Global Economies*, London: Sage Publications, pp 88-115.

Chatterjee, S., Conway, P., Dalziel, P., Eichbaum, C., Harris, P., Philpott, B. and Shaw, R. (1999) *The New Politics: A Third Way for New Zealand*, Palmerston North: Dunmore Press.

Chaves, M. (1999) 'Religious Congregations and Welfare Reform: Who Will Take Advantage of "Charitable Choice"?', *American Sociological Review*, vol 64, no 4, pp 836-46.

Cheyne, C., O'Brien, M. and Belgrave, M. (eds) (2004) *Social Policy in Aotearoa New Zealand: A Critical Introduction* (3rd edn), Auckland: Oxford University Press.

Clark, J.S. (1997) *Welfare Restructuring in New Zealand: The Changing Relationship Between the State and Auckland's Voluntary Welfare Sector*. Unpublished Masters thesis, Auckland: Department of Geography, University of Auckland.

Cloke, P., Johnsen, S. and May, J. (2005) 'Exploring Ethos? Discourses of "Charity" in the Provision of Emergency Services for Homeless People', *Environment and Planning A*, vol 37, pp 385-402.

Cnaan, R. (1999) 'Our Hidden Safety Net: Social and Community Work by Urban American Religious Congregations', *Journal of Brookings Institution*, vol 17, no 2, pp 50-3.

Cnaan, R., Kasternakis, A. and Wineburg, R. (1993) 'Religious People, Religious Congregations and Volunteerism in Human Services: Is there a Link?', *Nonprofit and Voluntary Sector Quarterly*, vol 22, no 1, pp 33-52.

Dalziel, P. (1993) *Taxing the Poor: Key Assumptions behind the 1991 Benefit Cuts. What are the Alternatives?*, Working Paper, Lincoln: Department of Economics, Lincoln University, New Zealand.

Deakin, N. (1996) 'The Devil's in the Detail: Some Reflections on Contracting for Social Care by Voluntary Organisations', *Social Policy and Administration*, vol 30, no 1, pp 20-38.

Department of Social Welfare (1990) *Contracting for Social Services: Principles and Guidelines*, Wellington: New Zealand Department of Social Welfare.

Ebaugh, H.R., Chafetz, J.S. and Pipes, P.F. (2005) 'Faith-based Social Service Organisations and Government Funding: Data from a National Survey', *Social Science Quarterly*, vol 86, no 2, pp 273-92.

Farnell, R., Furbey, R., al Haqq Hills, S., Macey, M. and Smith, G. (2003) *'Faith' in Urban Regeneration: Engaging Faith Communities in Urban Regeneration*, Bristol/York: The Policy Press/Joseph Rowntree Foundation.

Fyfe, N. and Milligan, C. (2003) 'Space, Citizenship and Voluntarism. Critical Reflections on the Voluntary Welfare Sector in Glasgow', *Environment and Planning A*, vol 35, no 11, pp 2069-86.

Gunby, J. (1996) *Housing the Hungry: The Third Report*, Wellington: NZCCSS.

Harris, M. (1995) '"Quiet Care": Welfare Work and Religious Congregations', *Journal of Social Policy*, vol 24, no 1, pp 53-71.

Harris, M. (1998) *Organizing God's Work: Challenges for Churches and Synagogues*, Basingstoke: Macmillan.

Harris, M., Halfpenny, P. and Rochester, C. (2003) 'A Social Policy Role for Faith-Based Organisations? Lessons from the UK Jewish Voluntary Sector', *Journal of Social Policy*, vol 32, no 1, pp 93-112.

Jackman, S. (1992) *Windows on Poverty: A Report from the New Zealand Council of Christian Social Services*, Wellington: NZCCSS.

Kearns, K., Park, C. and Yankosi, L. (2005) 'Comparing Faith-based and Secular Community Service Corporations in Pittsburgh and Allegheny County, Pennsylvania', *Nonprofit and Voluntary Sector Quarterly*, vol 34, no 2, pp 206-31.

Kelsey, J. (1996) *Economic Fundamentalism*, London: Pluto Press.

Larner, W. and Craig, D. (2005) 'After Neoliberalism? Community Activism and Local Partnerships in Aotearoa New Zealand', *Antipode*, vol 37, no 4, pp 402-24.

Le Heron, R. and Pawson, E. (eds) (1996) *Changing Places: New Zealand in the Nineties*, Auckland: Longman Paul.

Lewis, J. (2002) *Faiths, Hope and Participation: Celebrating Faith Groups' Role in Neighbourhood Renewal*, London: New Economics Foundation and Church Urban Fund.

Lukka, P. and Locke, M. (2003) 'Faith, Voluntary Action and Social Policy: A Review of the Research', *Voluntary Action*, vol 3, no 1, pp 25-41.

Lukka, P., Locke, M. with Soteri-Proctor, A. (2003) *Faith and Voluntary Action: Community, Values and Resources*, London: Institute for Volunteering Research, University of East London.

McClure, M. (1998) *A Civilized Community: A History of Social Security in New Zealand, 1898-1998*, Auckland: Auckland University Press.

Ministry of Social Policy (2001) *Communities and Government: Potential for Partnership: Whakato-pu- Whakaaro*, Wellington: Communications Unit, Ministry of Social Policy.

Nowland–Foreman, G. (1995) *Neither Mendicants Nor Deal-Makers: Contracting, Government Funding and Voluntary Organisations*, Wellington: NZCCSS.

NZCCSS (New Zealand Council of Christian Social Services) (1998) *Towards a Real Partnership: A NZCCSS Review of the Relationship between Voluntary Social Services and the New Zealand Community Funding Agency*, Wellington: NZCCSS.

Peck, J. (2001) 'Neoliberalising States: Thin Policies/Hard Outcomes', *Progress in Human Geography*, vol 25, no 3, pp 445-55.

Peck, J. and Tickell, A. (2002) 'Neoliberalising Space', *Antipode*, vol 34, no 3, pp 380-404.

Rao, H. (2002) 'Interorganisational Ecology', in J.A.C. Baum (ed) *The Blackwell Companion to Organisations*, Oxford: Blackwell, pp 541-56.

Shaftesbury Society and DETR (Department of the Environment, Transport and the Regions) (2000) *Faith Makes Community Work*, London: Shaftesbury Society.

Sibley, D. (1995) *Geographies of Exclusion*, London: Routledge.

Smith, G. (2002) 'Religion and the Rise of Social Capitalism: The Faith Communities in Community Development and Urban Regeneration in England', *Community Development Journal*, vol 37, no 2, pp 167-77.

Stephens, R., Waldegrave, C. and Frater, P. (1995) 'Measuring Poverty in New Zealand', *Social Policy Journal of New Zealand*, vol 5, pp 88-113.

Tennant, M. (1989) *Paupers and Providers: Charitable Aid in New Zealand*, Wellington: Allen and Unwin/Department of Internal Affairs.

Whale, A. (1993) 'Voluntary Welfare Provision in a Landscape of Change: The Emergence of Foodbanks in Auckland', Unpublished Masters thesis, Auckland: Department of Geography, University of Auckland.

Wolch, J. (1990) *The Shadow State: Government and Voluntary Sector in Transition*, New York, NY: The Foundation Centre.

Young, M. (1995) *Housing the Hungry: The Second Report. A Survey of Salvation Army Foodbank Recipients to Assess the Impact of the Government's Housing Reforms*, Wellington: Salvation Army and NZCCSS.

TEN

Faith-based organisations and welfare provision in Northern Ireland and North America: whose agenda?

Derek Bacon

Introduction

This chapter draws on research evidence from two national contexts that, although distinctly different, are selected because they show signs not only of a similar apparent convergence between government aspirations and some of the purposes of faith communities but also of attempts to harness the resources of such communities to policy aims. That there should be government interest in faith communities is unsurprising, given that the most cursory survey of a landscape of voluntarism reveals religion at the heart of much voluntary action 'providing the initial and continuing impetus for activities ranging from small-scale parish-based social and health services to major international emergency relief and development efforts' (Kendall and Knapp, 1996, p 1). Thus one of the debates within the non-profit or voluntary sector that currently engages policy makers in the US and, perhaps in a more low key way, in the UK, centres on moves to encourage greater involvement of faith-based organisations[1] in a range of community-benefit programmes through initiatives to broaden the access of these organisations to government support.

A growing body of empirical studies into the strengths and weaknesses of faith-based voluntary action now informs this debate on both sides of the Atlantic (Harris, 1994, 1995; Wineburg, 1994; Cameron, 1998; Cnaan, 2000; Sherman, 2000). In the US a White House Office of Faith-based and Community Initiatives (OFBCI), set up in February 2001, pursues a policy that includes: adjusting the law to allow faith-based and community organisations to compete for federal funding; eliminating barriers to such organisations being included in the provision of social services; and encouraging greater corporate and philanthropic support for faith-based and community organisations through public education and outreach activities. In the UK a Faith Communities Unit (FCU), formed at the Home Office in June 2003, is evidence of a similar trend and also marks a significant step towards involving representatives of the major world faiths found in Britain in policy development. There is perhaps a more oblique approach to faith groups by the UK government, focusing less on their potential for direct service provision than on activities that strengthen social cohesion or that sustain and renew local communities. To date there are few signs that the implementation of newer policy initiatives in relation to participation by local faith communities in the work of neighbourhood regeneration and civil renewal has penetrated to Northern Ireland. Despite, or perhaps because of, the continuing significance of religion in the province, the policy dialogue there has been somewhat 'more cautious' than elsewhere in the UK (Shannon, 2004).

The chapter offers commentary and analysis on these trends across two national contexts. It begins by outlining developments in government support for faith-based welfare provision in the US, and then provides an overview of a similar trend towards government utilisation of the experience, skills and diversity of faith communities in the UK. Against this backdrop, analysis then focuses on the emerging dialogue between government and religious interests within the specific context of the Northern Irish voluntary sector.

Faith-based welfare provision in North America and 'Charitable Choice'

In the US the process of seeking to plug gaps in community provision through government use of faith-based organisations is well advanced. The Reagan administration (1981-89) began the cutting of social spending and shifting the burden of welfare towards the non-profit sector, giving responsibility to states and localities for the design and delivery of services. As a consequence the need for knowledge about non-profit organisations, including faith-based ones, became urgent. Early research identified the range of service provision of over 2,000 congregations across the country (Salamon and Teitelbaum, 1984). A study of the funding arrangements of Protestant social service agencies in a Midwestern city exposed the kind of problems of organisation and accountability that still feature in the contemporary literature (Netting, 1982, 1984). Research into churches and religious institutions as non-profit organisations began to receive more systematic attention in 1990, when the multidisciplinary Program on Non-Profit Organizations (PONPO) at Yale University gave birth to the Project on Religious Institutions and Society. This aimed to develop new levels of understanding of the changing place of religion in society and, specifically, to examine the degree to which voluntarism and religion are aligned (Demerath et al, 1998). The PONPO project engaged a strong team of researchers from North American universities and also included input from research that was underway in the UK. The project director, Peter Hall, had already demonstrated the religious roots of many non-profits and presented statistics that underline the significance and value of the contribution of religious organisations to the activity of the sector. His studies revealed the inadequacy of understanding religious organisations like churches simply as voluntary non-profits supported by donations. They were better viewed, he argued, as complex entrepreneurial public-serving organisations, often funded by government, for provision of education, health and human services (Hall, 1982, 1996). Any assumption, however, that government underpinning of human services could be replaced by non-profit agencies, religious or otherwise, was questioned by Queen (1998). His reservations were echoed by Chaves (2001) and Smith and Sosin (2001) among others. The resulting debate gathered momentum throughout the 1990s as rising support for religious agencies in the US was evident in welfare reform legislation. The promotion of faith-based agencies, on the basis of their hypothesised benefits, stimulated increasing and more widespread investigation of their activities (Wineburg, 1998; Cnaan and Boddie, 2002).

In the US context, a number of researchers have argued for the positive value of faith-based organisations. Among these, the work of Ram Cnaan and Robert Wineburg has become particularly well known. Cnaan's (2000) quantitative and qualitative investigation into the social and community involvement of religious congregations in Philadelphia found them to be at the centre of social and community service delivery, forming a significant part of both the institutional and the informal safety net. His survey instrument listed some two hundred categories of social and community programmes that congregations might possibly operate. Of these only 11 programmes were not found among the congregations he studied, and only 21 were geared specifically towards congregational members and not to the community at large. This, for Cnaan, was clear evidence not of member-serving organisations but of other-serving organisations concerned with the welfare and the quality of life of those in the wider community. Using the independent sector assessment of the monetary value of a volunteer hour, Cnaan estimated that the 181 responding congregations in the Philadelphia survey were contributing in volunteer work over four million dollars a year to their communities.

Wineburg's (1994, forthcoming 2007) research unpicked the complicated social and political functions of religious congregations in North Carolina, also demonstrating that they are more than member-benefit organisations only. However, he questions the capacity of such bodies to meet the expectations being put upon them by proponents of the White House faith-based and community initiative, and he warns that the effect of this legislation will be to cut housing for the poor, children's programmes and rural health centres, while shifting that money to the nation's churches. Wineburg's thinking builds on insights from long-term working relationships with religious practitioners in his own locality. These relationships enable him to trace the impact of welfare reform legislation on the ground in North Carolina, exploring the response of the religious community to rapid change, and analysing the assets it can bring to local service provision. Partnerships involving religious communities are often the only viable way to get help and maintain stability in a time of great programmatic change. Wineburg cites examples of congregations joined in partnerships where the goal is to create a service delivery system that meets community need in a way that promotes self-sufficiency and the development of healthy families and individuals. He argues that the religious community holds the bulk of private charitable resources in an increasingly shrinking store of such goods, and identifies seven assets that local religious congregations bring to the public arena. These are: a mission to serve the poor; a pool of volunteers; useable and sacred space; potential for raising and distributing discretionary funds; potential for political strength; a reservoir of moral authority; and creativity and experimentation (Wineburg, 1996). Presenting evidence from over two decades of research, he contends that the agenda of the current North American administration is driven more by political expediency than by policy imperatives, and is less concerned about meeting the needs of deprived individuals and communities than about buttressing an alliance with the religious right and co-opting the resources of the religious community (Wineburg, forthcoming, 2007).

The agenda that Wineburg has in mind is familiarly known as 'Charitable Choice', a label that refers to Section 104 of the Personal Responsibility and Work Opportunity Reconciliation Act of 1996 (Center for Public Justice, 1996). Paragraph b of Section 104 reads:

> The purpose of this section is to allow States to contract with religious organizations, or to allow religious organizations to accept certificates, vouchers, or other forms of disbursement under any program described in subsection (a)(2), on the same basis as any other nongovernmental provider without impairing the religious character of such organizations, and without diminishing the religious freedom of beneficiaries of assistance funded under such programs.

The Charitable Choice provisions have been presented by the administration as a way to level the playing field and remove barriers that impede religious organisations seeking to serve the common good in collaboration with federal government. Two statements by the President give the tone. 'The paramount goal is compassionate results, and private and charitable groups, including religious ones, should have the fullest opportunity permitted by law to compete on a level playing field, so long as they achieve valid public purposes' (Bush, 2001, p 1). 'The Administration today eliminated more barriers that have kept faith-based charities from partnering with the Federal government to help Americans in need' (Bush, 2002, p 1).

Of course government had for a long time been involved with faith-based organisations, having contracted for the delivery of human and social services with agencies like Catholic Charities, Jewish Family Services and Lutheran Social Services, and providing around 50% of their funding. Using data from the National Congregations Study, Chaves and Tsitsos (2001, p 680) show that congregational social services in North America were already embedded within the secular non-profit world, often receiving substantial portions of their budgets from government sources. A major point of contention about the new legislation, however, was that local religious congregations were to be encouraged to compete in the mix of social service providers, or, in the language of the Act, they were now not to be discriminated against. Government funding was not to be denied them for welfare service provision. Previously, in order to contract with government, a religious-based organisation had to remove all religious symbols from the room where the service was provided, omit prayers at meal times, and accept as clients (and hire as staff) people opposed to the spirit and belief system of the organisation, but these conditions no longer applied.

This raised issues of employment practice and civil rights and disturbed the guardians of the line between church and state. It also gave sharper focus to the question of whether religious organisations are to be seen as different, and what exactly 'faith-based' now means. Smith and Sosin (2001) suggest using the term 'faith-related' instead of 'faith-based' to indicate a broader universe of service organisations that are of interest to policy makers in the US. A Senate-based working group sought to differentiate such organisations further, proposing a typology of characteristics along a spectrum from 'faith-saturated' to 'secular' (US Senate, 2002). Between these two extremes, they identify organisations that are 'faith-centered', 'faith-related', those that have a 'faith background' and those in a 'faith–secular partnership'. The typology takes a step beyond the common and simplistic antithesis of 'faith-based' and 'secular', illuminating the variety to be found among such organisations, and provides a starting point for understanding different kinds of connection to faith.

Clarifying the nature of an organisation's faith connections becomes important in a context where it is necessary to make reasonable and testable judgements about any claims it makes to be 'religious', especially where this forms the basis for application to the Federal resources available on President Bush's level 'playing field' of Charitable Choice. For Wineburg (2000), such finer points obscure the realities of local politics on the ground, where a cost shifting exercise may lock a local faith-based organisation into a contract that is to its own detriment but to the taxpayers' benefit. This is not the most effective and workable way to address complex community concerns. He argues that:

> Many who want the government to give the money away to faith based groups may not actually care whether those organizations have good plans to use the money or not. If faith based organizations fail, none will see or hear the policymaker, the expert, or bureaucrat volunteering to take responsibility for poor planning. The competition for the scarce funds, coupled with the politics of needing to shrink welfare rolls without necessarily addressing poverty, undermines the requirements for thoughtful planning and coordination to handle the changes brought on by welfare reform and the devolution of responsibility. (Wineburg, 2000, www.arnova.org)

The North American experience appears to be one of a rediscovery of the potential of the reserves of energy and commitment that faith communities have been willing to put to the service of others. This rediscovery has come at a time when the political will to provide such resources through government agency is diminished, a time when the administration judges it both salutary to give careful attention to the place of faith in the life of North American citizens and politically expedient to cultivate alliances with powerful religious groups. While the significance of the assets and the large dollar value of the activities of faith-based organisations are now readily perceived, the capacity of these bodies to meet government aspirations for them without losing the essential and distinctive qualities that drive them is less clear.

Faith-based voluntary activity and policy developments in the UK

UK policy is some way from the directness of North American engagement with faith-based organisations and the accompanying controversy over who benefits, who is using whom and for what purpose. But as the voluntary sector has been 'mainstreamed' into public policy through mechanisms like the Compact and the Active Community Unit, so churches and other faith-based organisations have come more fully into the frame of government interest as the significance of the local initiatives in which they are often engaged has become clearer. Westminster policy makers now recognise a potential synergy between the aims and practices of faith groups and policy objectives relating to neighbourhood renewal and social inclusion. Growing awareness of the importance of faith communities was apparent in the positioning of political parties before the 1997 General Election. Since then they have featured in speeches by senior politicians (Brown, 2000; Blair, 2001); in training materials produced by government departments (Chester et al, 1999); in reports of the Policy Action Teams set up by the Social Exclusion Unit (Home Office, 1999, 2000); and in the Local Government Association publication *Faith and Community* (LGA, 2002). The Social Exclusion Unit report refers explicitly to a place for faith communities on local strategic partnerships (Cabinet Office, 2001, ch 5). The *Compact Code of Good Practice on Community Groups* includes an appendix setting out reasons for, and the value of, bringing faith groups into the compact process at local level (Home Office, 2003, pp 35-6). Guidelines have been published for encouraging interfaith understanding and cooperation at the local level (IFN, 2003a, 2003b). An Inner Cities Religious Council (ICRC), in existence since 1992, advises on the faith dimensions of government regeneration policy. Building on this work, an FCU formed at the Home Office in 2003 conducted a review of the government's interface with faith communities with the specific aim of including them in the development of policy across the range of Home Office responsibilities, and encouraging and facilitating their involvement in the voluntary sector and in active citizenship (Home Office, 2004). The Home Office, itself supporting research into the role and contribution of faith groups to local communities (for example Cairns et al, 2005), launched a Faith Communities

Capacity Building Fund specifically for faith groups and organisations in England and Wales in September 2005. The government is apparently treating faith-based voluntary action as seriously as it is taking the voluntary sector as a whole.

There is a growing response from faith communities. A Faith-Based Regeneration Network was launched in the Muslim Cultural Heritage Centre in London in September 2002. Funded and supported by faith communities, its purpose is to develop a support network for people working as professionals or as volunteers for faith-based neighbourhood and renewal bodies. In 2004 a Commission on Urban Life and Faith (CULF) was formed in the Church of England with a remit similar to that which produced *Faith in the City* (ACUPA, 1985). CULF will publish its findings on poverty and the needs of minority ethnic groups in urban areas across Britain at the end of 2005 to coincide with a government report *The State of our Cities and Towns* (*Church of England Newspaper*, 5 February 2004). A number of groups from within the faith sector responded to the Home Office consultation document on community capacity building (CCWA, 2004).

Much of the government's policy approach is premised on ideas about social capital. Labour's 'third way' thinking recognises a need to invest in social capital as well as in the human and financial capital that dominated past regeneration agendas (Szreter, 2000; Aldridge et al, 2002). The UK government's stated perception of faith communities (ODPM, 2000, para 3.45) is in keeping with Putnam's assertion that 'faith communities in which people worship together are arguably the single most important repository of social capital in America' (2000, p 66). Studies of English religious congregations would support this perception, reporting them as places where people can 'experience a sense of belonging, of being valued, of being protected and of being at home' (Harris, 1998, p 197). Harris's research:

> ... provided numerous examples of people being socialized into group decision-making processes, learning the implications of voluntarism, being helped to develop leadership competence, being encouraged to speak in public, and learning the realities of achieving organisational change. Through their welfare projects congregations also raised members' awareness of broader social problems (homelessness, for example). All these experiences are applicable and transferable to other contexts. And as people develop confidence in their own abilities, they are more likely to be willing to engage in collective activities beyond their immediate congregational context. (1998, p 199)

This potential capacity of religious congregations to counterbalance contemporary trends towards social fragmentation is prized by government. Margaret Harris is one of the first British academic researchers of voluntary organisations in recent times to draw attention to it, and to the growing and largely unrecognised welfare and caring activities of congregations in England (1994). Her empirical work distinguishes six forms of congregational welfare provision in what she terms welfare projects, indirect welfare, informal care, informal care in an organised framework, mutual aid and social integration. Underpinning these forms, she identifies a 'religion factor' (what Uphoff (2000) would include under his 'cognitive' social capital) that opens a ready-made channel for the expression and communication of a particular quality of care. Significantly, she notes that this care is set within the framework of other priorities. With potentially limitless demand and often slender resources, the difficulty for congregations is one of boundary setting, of sustaining commitment and of coping with the results of welfare projects.

Harris reveals a significant investment of volunteer time in congregations that is given both to members and to people in the wider community. But she is cautious about any policy of expanding the formal welfare role of religious congregations in the context of the UK, seeing instead room for further development of their informal 'quiet care'. Quiet care falls somewhere on the spectrum between informal self-help at one end and formally organised volunteering at the other (Harris, 1995). Some volunteers take on heavy responsibility in an 'inner circle' and many more take on smaller commitments. Overload and dropout are real dangers, yet her congregations provide a forum within which people are socialised into voluntary roles and caring activities. They can be important contributors to the mixed economy of care and to the development and maintenance of civil society. But they are too dependent on individual enthusiasm to be suitable for mounting long-term systematic projects. Here Harris is in broad agreement with North American researchers who see much value in what congregations may contribute to the public good, but who urge that policy makers should be cautious about their expectations of congregations (1998, p 193). Unlikely to have the organisational capacity to sustain formal welfare projects, congregations may perhaps be seen as 'nurseries' for them, 'hospitable environments in which new ideas and appropriate organisational structures can be nurtured in response to social needs at the local community level' (1998, p 194). There are data to suggest that 77% of congregations in the UK, comparing favourably with 87% in the US, are involved in human service programmes. The lesson from those that undertake this activity is that it adds significantly to the pressure and complexity of congregational life (Cameron, 1998). This measured assessment is echoed in research by Smith into faith communities, community development and neighbourhood regeneration (2002).

As in the North American literature, there is a sense here of something being uncovered in the life of faith communities that may be of value to, and may be made available to, society beyond those communities. Through the FCU, the British government is offering funding and training in community leadership skills for ministers of religion among other means of facilitating their involvement in the voluntary sector. For faith-based organisations, a door stands wide in Britain that is barely ajar in Northern Ireland.

The Northern Ireland context for faith-based voluntary action

Northern Ireland, with a population approaching 1.7 million people and a geographical area of about one sixth of the island, came into being when the Anglo-Irish treaty of 1921 formalised the partition of Ireland. Twenty-six of the old 32 counties became a republic, now with the conventional short name of Ireland. The remaining six continued within the jurisdiction of the United Kingdom of Great Britain and Northern Ireland, with a local Parliament at Stormont. By the 1960s this Unionist-controlled regional government was perceived to be unresponsive to the grievances of the Catholic section of the population, and a civil rights campaign began to involve increasing numbers of people in mass public demonstrations. Events spun out of control during 1969, paramilitaries became engaged, and the situation worsened to a point where political progress seemed unlikely and everyday security could not be guaranteed. The Stormont Parliament was prorogued in March 1972 and responsibility transferred from the Home Office to a new department, the Northern Ireland Office (NIO). The arrangement, known as Direct Rule, was to hold until a more representative system of regional government was devised. It was 1998 before this appeared to be realised and the Belfast (Good Friday) Agreement[2] paved the way for elections to a power-sharing devolved government for the province. In the event, this Northern Ireland Assembly has remained suspended since 2002 with the fragile political process in stalemate. The struggle to emerge from a 30-year period of violent political upheaval continues.

Throughout the period of conflict and disruption, euphemistically known as 'The Troubles', some 3,500 people died and around ten times that number suffered serious injury. Community and voluntary organisations provided support and services to social casualties (Acheson and Williamson, 1995). With the fragmentation of the region's political institutions between 1972 and 1999, these organisations expanded into the space left by the absence of political representation. They took on representative and advocacy functions for both geographical communities and communities of interest.

It became received wisdom that the development of an organisational structure within segregated communities would enable more confident communication across the community divide and contribute to the cohesion of those communities at least, if not to that of wider society. Although that philosophy is now being questioned (Morrow, 2004), it remains the case that previously existing structural differences between the two main ethnic religio-political blocs in the province have hardened and the alienation of one from the other has been reinforced. This has in turn hampered, and led to huge diseconomies in the delivery of mainstream social services in some of the areas where they are most needed. It has inhibited local development and has necessitated a return to serving the Protestant and Catholic communities separately, despite official policy assumptions about the existence of a single voluntary sector. These assumptions result from the impact of the Committee of Enquiry, chaired by Lord Wolfenden and set up in 1974 to review the future role and functions of voluntary organisations in the UK. The Wolfenden Report (1978) triggered a consultative exercise by government that dealt separately with Northern Ireland and had a significant influence on the development of structures of voluntary action there. Since Wolfenden, promoting the voluntary sector as a single entity has been seen as a mechanism for managing the conflict, giving government a way of managing the demands of voluntary and community organisations, although it still has to deal practically with institutions embedded in each of the two main communities.

During the period of Direct Rule, as relations between government and voluntary action were formalised, a large-scale transfer of resources from the state, and the European Union and other international sources, institutionalised the voluntary sector in the governance of Northern Ireland and enabled it to deliver welfare services at a time when the relationship between the voluntary and community sector and government was being fundamentally redefined by successive administrations. The Conservative government tried to broker a new relationship with Northern Ireland's Nationalist community, and by implication, with Republicans. Diplomats began to lay the foundation for reconfigured relationships that led, in 1994, to paramilitary ceasefires. Developments in policy towards the voluntary and community sector paralleled these events. From a situation in which there was no recognisable policy to govern relations between the voluntary and community sector and government, by 1998 a compact between government and the voluntary sector was in place and new structural arrangements recognised and shaped the sector's partnership role with government (DHSS, 1998).

As noted above, the Northern Ireland Assembly, elected in June 1998, was suspended in October 2002, but not before the Executive had set out a key role for the sector and recognised the importance of involving it in policies and programmes aimed at strengthening community well-being (NIE, 2001). Understandably, perhaps, Belfast was slow to follow London's expectation that each devolved administration within the UK would carry out a review of the government's interface with faith communities. While central government had been 'increasingly exploring ways of using the experience and resources of faith communities "on the ground" to deliver services' (Home Office, 2004, p 8), there was little indication either of a similar exploration in Northern Ireland or of the new policy initiatives observable in Britain. It might be speculated that there were other and greater priorities, or that the hesitation related to perceptions about religious traditions being socially reactionary and divisive, or to the way that religion solidifies the opposing political alliances. For some in Northern Ireland, religion indicates a life of faith grounded in spiritual values. For many it means allegiance by birth and upbringing to one of the two communities, Protestant or Roman Catholic, an allegiance that does not necessarily require active religious belief (Doherty and Poole, 1995). In this second sense, what goes by the name of religion in Northern Ireland divides in the most fundamental way. It becomes the marker of specific and separate loyalties that bear directly on the legitimacy of the state. This 'two communities' theory illuminates the point that, while a strong network of voluntary and community organisations exists in the province, projects are delivered in the context of two separate and distinct communities.

Although it may therefore seem unreal in the circumstances to speak of it, officially the Northern Ireland voluntary sector includes some 4,500 voluntary and community organisations employing around 29,000 people and generating an estimated income of £650 million. The current strategy for government support of this activity is set out in *Partners for Change* (DSD, 2003a). This document commits all departments in the Executive to a programme of practical actions designed to encourage greater partnership working, to enable the sector to contribute more fully to policy making and build the capacity of the sector to strengthen its sustainability. Of two related initiatives launched in 2003, the first is the Northern Ireland version (DSD, 2003b) of the UK-wide National Strategy Action Plan (Cabinet Office, 2001). The second, the government's consultation paper, *A Shared Future: Improving Relations in Northern Ireland*, acknowledges that churches and other faith-based organisations 'have a particularly important role to play' in neighbourhood regeneration (OFMDFM, 2003, p 2).

It should be remembered that, whereas both in the US and in Britain a wide plurality of churches, religious bodies and faith groups compete and coexist, especially in the multicultural urban areas, this is less true of Northern Ireland. There the faith-based organisation and the congregation will usually be from the Christian tradition. Indeed Christian churches, among the most continuous indigenous cultural institutions, are part of the historic fabric of society. The 2001 Northern Ireland Census Religion figures show roughly 86% of a total population of 1,685,267 people owning attachment to a Christian church and a further 0.30% indicating affiliation with another religion (NISRA, 2001). When adjustment for the community background question in the Census is made, the official figure given for religious affiliation in the province is 96.89% Christian, 0.39% other religions and philosophies and 2.72% who cannot be allocated. Although this should be tempered by awareness that respondents to the religion question in the Census may interpret it in terms of 'tribal designation' referred to above, it is self-evident that religious tradition continues to have significance even for people who are not church members, especially in the field of voluntary action and the provision of community facilities.

Churches form the largest voluntary institutions in Northern Ireland, with the largest voluntary economies in terms of money and time and probably the richest resources to bring to bear on some of the most intractable problems of the present. Despite this, there is no corpus of research focused specifically on the voluntary community benefit activity of churches in Northern Ireland to provide knowledge and guide policy as in the US or in Britain. Apart from this author's studies of voluntary action in congregations and other faith-based organisations, most academic research to date has tended to trace the links between religion and politics, to weigh the churches against the background of the years of violence, or to assess their contribution to community relations, conflict resolution, or peace building. The churches have done some valuable work on themselves (IICM, 1990, 2000; Harrison, 2000; PCI, 2001). The Churches Community Work Alliance, with the support of the Department for Social Development, has provided good practice examples of church-related community development (Bacon et al, 2004). Beyond the churches, Making Belfast Work commissioned an examination of the role of churches in community development, mainly in the north Belfast area (Speight, 1997). The results expose the gulf between the world of social welfare and public policy in which local government and statutory services operate and wider society as it is known by the churches. A report commissioned by the Link Family and Community Centre in Newtownards, an independent faith-based community development organisation, reveals that communication between churches and the community sector in the town is 'generally poor' and that there is a 'gap in understanding and trust between churches and community' (Macaulay, 2003, p 6). A practitioner study identifies a similar gap and a loss of place by the Protestant churches in north Belfast, with the urban community 'no longer seeing itself as needing the local church in the way it once did' (Hamilton, 2002, p 48). The literature shows a mixed and partial picture of a significant level and range of voluntary welfare activity in congregations and other faith-based organisations in response to social need in the community. Extensive, important, and full of potential it may be, but the fact that it is so deeply split into two separate communities makes for a dynamic that at times works against a single voluntary sector policy and renders it problematic to harness to the concerns of government.

Whose agenda?

On either side of the Atlantic the policy-making community is now alert to a need to nurture channels of communication with local faith groups of all kinds. Research has made it increasingly clear that not only does religion continue to motivate many people in their public lives, but also that faith groups can and still do play significant roles in the wider community. The attack on the World Trade Center in New York, measures against what is perceived as a global terrorist initiative, racial unrest in English cities, increasing volumes of economic and political migration, these are some of the other sensitising factors also in play. The North American context might be described as one in which a rampant administration has been setting the pace for faith-based welfare provision, going so far as to drive new legislation by presidential executive order. In Britain, government has been actively seeking dialogue and engagement with the faith communities. The Northern Irish scene continues to be pervaded by a degree of wariness. Although government may woo faith communities (Harris, 2001), policy makers have to deal with the fact that such communities are not inert resources to be harnessed by official programmes to an external agenda. They have other business, which is about the transmission of values across generations, about creating space for cultural and aesthetic expression as well as about the exploration of religious ideas and human concerns. In relation to programmes for neighbourhood renewal in particular, they are 'active in investing the idea of "regeneration" with distinctive meanings, and bringing values and working styles to the practice of regeneration that challenge official assumptions and approaches' (Farnell et al, 2003, p 2). Such critical interaction may be creative, and is promoted as one of the advantages of partnership. Partnership between faith communities and public agencies may be good for both and healthy for society at large if it educates faith communities as it educates the policy makers, obliging each to take the other more seriously (Williams, 2003). The British Prime Minister is an open advocate of partnerships between faith communities and central and local government. In a recent speech to the Faithworks Movement he referred to the critical role of the voluntary sector in Labour's programme to recast the 1945 settlement on public services and the welfare state for the modern age. Of the churches and faith communities he stated: 'I would like to see you play a bigger, not a lesser role in the future' (Blair, 2005, p 1). Faithworks, here so enthusiastically addressed, is active in Northern Ireland, having been 'invited by the Office of the First Minister to continue its work with the denominations, overseeing the creation of community projects that bring churches together for the purpose of regenerating the community' (*Faithworks News*, issue 4, p 12). This initiative may be welcomed, even embraced, by churches where the possibility of working collaboratively with other agencies for the wider community fits within their mission as they understand it. However, the challenges facing faith-based organisations in this work that have been identified in the US and in Britain are also factors in Northern Ireland (Bacon, 2003). In addition there is the hardening effect of the years of conflict, resulting in suspicion and bitterness from which the churches are not immune. In view of the magnitude of the task of social transformation in the province, the value of the combined resources of the churches and the lack of baseline information about the activities into which they put their volunteering energy, it would take a dedicated agency with research muscle and the long-term capacity for a full range of professional, advisory and technical services to release the latent potential of faith-based organisations. But then whether, and if so how, the churches in Northern Ireland might be willing to work together systematically on local issues within an agreed one community strategy that would challenge sectarianism in the long term is a question that only they can answer.

Notes

[1] 'Faith-based' is used in this chapter as a broad umbrella term to cover a range of religious organisations. Among these is included 'congregation', understood as a formally organised group of people with a name and a membership who gather together regularly

for what they know as worship. Greg Smith adds that the Judaeo-Christian definition serves 'reasonably well' for other faith traditions. He adds:

> Congregations may (but sometimes do not) own and manage resources such as buildings and paid staff. There are many models of organisation from independent, self-managing local, democratic membership groups, to branches of wider national or international denominations under a hierarchical authority structure. They may also have associated sub groups such as women's organisations or youth groups, and may in some cases have set up arms length agencies such as community projects or charitable trusts with a separate legal identity but broadly identical membership on the various governing bodies. (Smith, 2001, p 5)

[2] The Belfast (Good Friday) Agreement, reached on Friday, 10 April 1998, 'sets out a plan for devolved government in Northern Ireland on a stable and inclusive basis and provided for the creation of Human Rights and Equality commissions, the early release of terrorist prisoners, the decommissioning of paramilitary weapons and far reaching reforms of criminal justice and policing'.

References

Acheson, N. and Williamson, A. (eds) (1995) *Voluntary Action and Social Policy in Northern Ireland*, Aldershot: Avebury.

ACUPA (Archbishop's Council on Urban Priority Areas) (1985) *Faith in the City: A Call for Action by Church and Nation*, London: Church House Publishing.

Aldridge, S. and Halpern, D. with Fitzpatrick, S. (2002) *Social Capital: A Draft Discussion Paper*, London: Performance and Innovation Unit, Cabinet Office, March.

Bacon, D. (2003) *Communities, Churches and Social Capital in Northern Ireland*, Coleraine: Centre for Voluntary Action Studies, University of Ulster.

Bacon, D., Groves, K., McDowell, E. and Robertson, J. (2004) *Acting in Good Faith: Churches, Change and Regeneration*, Belfast: CCWA Northern Ireland.

Blair, T. (2001) 'Faith in Politics', Speech to the Christian Socialist Movement, London, 29 March.

Blair, T. (2005) Speech to Faithworks, 22 March (retrieved March 2005 from www.number-10.gov.uk/output/Page7375.asp).

Brown, G. (2000) *Civic Society in Modern Britain*, Seventeenth Arnold Goodman Charity Lecture, London.

Bush, G.W. (2001, 2002) Statements by the President (retrieved September 2001 from www.whitehouse.gov/news/releases/2001/08/unlevelfield.html and www.whitehouse.gov/infocus/faith-based/).

Cabinet Office (2001) *A New Commitment to Neighbourhood Renewal: National Strategy Action Plan*, Report by the Social Exclusion Unit, London: The Stationery Office.

Cairns, B., Harris, M. and Hutchison, R. (2005) *Faithful Regeneration: The Role and Contribution of Local Parishes in Local Communities in the Diocese of Birmingham*, Birmingham: CVAR, Aston Business School.

Cameron, H. (1998) 'The Social Action of the Local Church: Five Congregations in an English City', PhD thesis, LSE.

CCWA (Churches' Community Work Alliance) (2004) 'Churches help government to help local communities' (retrieved as from www.ccwa.org.uk/ccwa/news.htm).

Center for Public Justice (1996) 'A Guide to Charitable Choice' (retrieved in December 2001 from http://cpjustice.org/charitablechoice/guide).

Chaves, M. (2001) 'Religious Congregations and Welfare Reform', *Society*, vol 38, no 2, pp 21-8.

Chaves, M. and Tsitsos, W. (2001) 'Congregations and Social Services: What They Do, How They Do It, and With Whom', *Nonprofit and Voluntary Sector Quarterly*, vol 30, no 4, pp 660-83.

Chester, M., Farrands, M., Finneron, D. and Venning, E. (1999) *Flourishing Communities: Engaging church communities with government in New Deal for Communities*, London: Church Urban Fund.

Cnaan, R.A. (2000) *Keeping Faith in the City: How 401 Urban Religious Congregations Serve their Neediest Neighbors*, Philadelphia, PA: Center for Research on Religion and Urban Civil Society, University of Pennsylvania.

Cnaan, R.A. and Boddie, S.C. (2002) 'Charitable Choice and Faith-based Welfare: A Call for Social Work', *Social Work*, vol 47, no 3, pp 235-47.

Demerath, N.J., Hall, P.D., Schmitt, T. and Williams, R.H. (eds) (1998) *Sacred Companies: Organizational Aspects of Religion and Religious Aspects of Organizations*, New York, NY: Oxford University Press.

DHSS (Department of Health and Social Services) (1998) *Compact between Government and the Voluntary and Community Sector in Northern Ireland*, Belfast: DHSS.

Doherty, P. and Poole, M.A. (1995) *Ethnic Residential Segregation in Belfast*, Colearine: Centre for the Study of Conflict, University of Ulster.

DSD (Department for Social Development) (2003a) *Partners for Change: Government's Strategy for the Support of the Voluntary and Community Sector 2001-2004*, Belfast: DSD.

DSD (2003b) *People and Place: A Strategy for Neighbourhood Renewal*, Belfast: DSD.

Farnell, R., Furbey, R., Hills, S., Macey, M. and Smith, G. (2003) *'Faith' in urban regeneration?*, Bristol/York: The Policy Press/Joseph Rowntree Foundation.

Hall, P.D. (1982) *The Organization of American Culture, 1700-1900*, New York, NY: New York University Press.

Hall, P.D. (1996) 'Founded on the Rock, Built upon Shifting Sands: Churches, Voluntary Associations, and Nonprofit Organizations in Public Life, 1850-1990', Paper for the ARNOVA conference, New York, November 1996.

Hamilton, N. (2002) *Church and Community in North Belfast*, Coleraine: Centre for Voluntary Action Studies, University of Ulster.

Harris, M. (1994) 'The Work and Organisation of Local Churches and Synagogues: Four English Congregations in the 1990s', PhD thesis, London School of Economics and Political Science.

Harris, M. (1995) '"Quiet Care": Welfare Work and Religious Congregations', *Journal of Social Policy*, vol 24, no 1, pp 53-71.

Harris, M. (1998) *Organizing God's Work: Challenges for Churches and Synagogues*, London: Macmillan.

Harris, M. (2001) 'Politicians Go A-Wooing', *The Tablet*, 20 January.

Harrison, J. (2000) *Protestant Churches in Areas of Disadvantage: A Series of Case Studies in Belfast*, Belfast: Belfast Churches' Urban Development Committee.

Home Office (1999) *National Strategy for Neighbourhood Renewal: Policy Action Team 9 – Community Self-help*, (www.socialexclusion.gov.uk/page.asp?id=102).

Home Office (2000) *National Strategy for Neighbourhood Renewal: Policy Action Team 17 – Joining it up Locally*, (www.socialexclusion.gov.uk/page.asp?id=111).

Home Office (2003) *Compact Code of Good Practice on Community Groups*, (http://communities.homeoffice.gov.uk/activecomms/suppvcs/compact-codes/).

Home Office (2004) *Working Together: Co-operation between Government and Faith Communities*, London: Home Office Faith Communities Unit, February.

IFN (Inter Faith Network) (2003a) *Local Inter Faith Activity in the UK*, London: IFN.

IFN (2003b) *Partnership for the Common Good: Inter Faith Structures and Local Government*, London: IFN.

IICM (Irish Inter-Church Meeting) (1990) *The Challenge of the City: A Report to the Churches*, Belfast: IICM, Department of Social Issues.

IICM (2000) *Being Church in the New Millennium*, Belfast: IICM, Department of Theological Questions.

Kendall, J. and Knapp, M. (1996) *The Voluntary Sector in the United Kingdom*, Manchester: Manchester University Press.

LGA (Local Government Authority) (2002) 'Faith and Community: A Good Practice Guide for Local Authorities' (retrieved in March 2002 from www.lga.gov.uk/Publication.asp?lsection=28&id=SX9D67-A7806AE2).

Macaulay, T. (2003) *Inter-Church and Church-Community Relations in Newtownards*, Report by the Link Family and Community Centre, Newtownards.

Morrow, D. (2004) 'On the Far Side of Revenge?', Speech at the Shared Future Conference, Belfast, 27 January.

Netting, F.E. (1982) 'Secular and Religious Funding of Church-Related Agencies', *Social Service Review*, vol 56, no 4, pp 586-604.

Netting, F.E. (1984) 'Church-Related Agencies and Social Welfare', *Social Service Review*, vol 58, no 3, pp 404-20.

NIE (Northern Ireland Executive) (2001) *Programme for Government 2001-2004*, Belfast: OEMDPM, NI Executive.

NISRA (Northern Ireland Statistics and Research Agency) (2001) 'Northern Ireland Census 2001 Key Statistics' (retrieved December 2002 from www.nisranew.gov.uk/census/Census2001Output/KeyStatistics/keystatrep.html).

ODPM (Office of the Deputy Prime Minister) (2000) 'Our Towns and Cities: The Future – Delivering an Urban Renaissance' (retrieved February 2006 from www.odpm.gov.uk/index.asp?id=1127167).

OFMDFM (Office of the First Minister and Deputy First Minister) (2003) *A Shared Future*, Belfast: Castle Buildings, Stormont.

PCI (Presbyterian Church in Ireland) (2001) *Engaging with the Community: The Challenge of Mission in the 21st Century*, Belfast: Presbyterian Board of Social Witness.

Putnam, R.D. (2000) *Bowling Alone: The Collapse and Revival of American Community*, New York, NY: Simon & Schuster.

Queen II, E.L. (1998) 'Civil Society? Uncivil Religion?', Paper given at ISTR conference, Geneva, July 1998.

Salamon, L.M. and Teitelbaum, F. (1984) 'Religious Congregations as Social Service Agencies: How Extensive Are They?', *Foundation News*, vol 25, no 5, pp 62-5.

Shannon, A. (2004) 'Foreword' by the Permanent Secretary, Department for Social Development, Northern Ireland, in D. Bacon, K. Groves, E. McDowell and J. Robertson (2004) *Acting in Good Faith: Churches, Change and Regeneration*, Belfast: CCWA Northern Ireland.

Sherman, A.L. (2000) *The Growing Impact of Charitable Choice: A Catalogue of New Collaborations between Government and Faith-based Organizations in Nine States*, Washington, DC: Center for Public Justice.

Smith, G. (2001) 'Faith Based Groups in Partnership with the State' (retrieved in June 2001 from http://homepages.uel.ac.uk/G.Smith/BRIEFING.htm).

Smith, G. (2002) 'Religion, and the Rise of Social Capitalism: The Faith Communities in Community Development and Urban Regeneration in England', *Community Development Journal*, vol 37, no 2, pp 167-77.

Smith, S.R. and Sosin, M.R. (2001) 'The Varieties of Faith-Related Agencies', *Public Administration Review*, vol 61, no 6, pp 651-70.

Speight, P. (1997) *The Role of Churches in Community Development*, Unpublished report commissioned by Making Belfast Work, Belfast.

Szreter, S. (2000) *A New Political Economy for New Labour: The Importance of Social Capital*, Political Economy Research Centre Policy Paper 15, Sheffield: University of Sheffield.

Uphoff, N. (2000) 'Understanding Social Capital: Learning from the Analysis and Experience of Participation', in P. Dasgupta and I. Serageldin (eds) *Social Capital: A Multifaceted Perspective*, Washington, DC: World Bank, pp 215-49.

US Senate (2002) 'Finding Common Ground: Recommendations of the Working Group on Human Needs and Faith-Based Community Initiatives' (retrieved March 2002 from www.sfcg.org/programmes/us/us_faith.html).

Williams, R. (2003) 'Christian Theology and Other Faiths', Birmingham, lecture at the University, 11 June (retrieved September 2003 from www.archbishopofcanterbury.org/sermons_speeches/index.html).

Wineburg, R.J. (1994) 'A Longitudinal Case Study of Religious Congregations in Local Human Services', *Nonprofit and Voluntary Sector Quarterly*, vol 23, no 2, pp 159-69.

Wineburg, R.J. (1996) 'Religion, Politics and Social Services: Looking Ahead with Rearview Mirrors', Paper for ARNOVA conference, New York, November 1996.

Wineburg, R.J. (1998) 'Review of Carlson-Thies and Skillen (eds) "Welfare in America: Christian Perspectives on a Policy in Crisis"', *Nonprofit and Voluntary Sector Quarterly*, vol 27, no 1, pp 98-107.

Wineburg, R.J. (2000) in a contribution to the ARNOVA-List Discussion Group dated 8 March (retrieved September 2004 from www.arnova.org).

Wineburg, R.J. (forthcoming, January 2007) *Faith-based Inefficiencies: The Follies of Bush's Initiatives*, Westport, PO: Praeger.

Wolfenden, L. (1978) *The Future of Voluntary Organisations*, London: Croom Helm.

ELEVEN

Government restructuring and settlement agencies in Vancouver: bringing advocacy back in[1]

Gillian Creese

Introduction

The election of a series of neoliberal governments in the 1980s and 1990s led to a sea change in government relations with voluntary organisations in Canada (Brock and Banting, 2001). The Canadian government has funded voluntary organisations since the 1940s, when it first recognised their potential for nation building by funding activities related to 'citizenship training' (Phillips, 2001). Funding expanded over the next three decades: charities were supported through the tax system, direct funding was provided to groups promoting aspects of 'Canadian identity' and voluntary organisations were included in public consultations (Brock and Banting, 2001; Phillips, 2001). Relations began to deteriorate in the 1980s, however, with the election of two Conservative governments under Brian Mulroney (1984 and 1988). The Conservatives launched selective cuts to the voluntary sector, attacking advocacy-oriented organisations critical of neoliberal policies and branding them as 'special interest groups' (Phillips, 2001). The subsequent election of a Liberal government under Jean Chretien (1993) ushered in deeper funding cuts, a shift from core to short-term project funding, and voluntary organisations were firmly shut out of further policy consultations (Phillips, 2001).

During the second Chretien term (1997), however, the federal government changed its stance on voluntary organisations. The Liberals adopted Tony Blair's 'third way' approach and began to forge a new relationship with the sector (Phillips, 2001). Funding cuts continued, but public policy soon hinged on an enhanced role for the voluntary sector, now envisioned as 'a vital third pillar in Canadian society, working alongside the public and private sectors to make Canada a more humane, caring and prosperous nation' (Canadian Privy Council, cited in Chappell, 2001, p 118). The Voluntary Sector Initiative followed, bringing together representatives of government and voluntary organisations to draft a new Accord (Phillips, 2003a, 2003b). Phillips (2003a, 2003b) observes that the Voluntary Sector Initiative marks a shift from a model of top-down 'government' to a model of 'governance' where the state works collaboratively with partners. Still, it must be noted, the voluntary sector does not enter this partnership on an equal footing with government.

The Canadian voluntary sector depends on 1.6 million volunteers and over 1.3 million employees, providing paid employment to 9% of the country's workforce (Hall and Banting, 2000, p 15; Chappell, 2001, pp 114, 118). With nearly two thirds of voluntary sector revenues coming from government, funding cuts created a deep 'fiscal crisis' in the sector (Chappell, 2001, p 116)[2]. Federal funding cuts dramatically reduced funding to the provinces, which in turn launched cuts to social programmes, and both levels of government downloaded services to voluntary organisations (Cohen, 1997; Brock and Banting, 2001; Mitchell, 2001)[3]. Increased demand for services coincided with substantially reduced levels of funding, however, leaving the voluntary sector feeling as if it were 'under siege' (Browne, 1996; Brock and Banting, 2001, p 5; Chappell, 2001).

Welfare state restructuring in Canada has heightened debates about the independence of voluntary organisations, about the meaning of distinctions between the public, private and third sectors, and about the nature of the welfare state (Rekart, 1993; Hasson and Ley, 1994; Brown, 1997; Phillips and Graham, 2000; Mitchell, 2001; Brock, 2003). Successive cuts in government spending threaten the viability of the voluntary sector and have generated more competition for scarce resources (Rekart, 1993; Browne, 1996). At the same time, voluntary organisations are recognised as having a crucial role in building 'social capital' and enhancing 'social cohesion', and are thus in great demand as community partners (Pal, 1997; Phillips, 2003a). Moreover, mediating the divergent demands of government and grassroots community needs can increase tensions between service provision and the (increasing) need for advocacy during periods of restructuring (Ng, 1990; Hasson and Ley, 1994; Brown, 1997)[4].

Downloading responsibility for welfare provision from the state to the voluntary sector also threatens to exacerbate existing inequalities in the geography of social welfare provision (Wolch, 1990; Brown, 1997; Fyfe and Milligan, 2003). While public programmes can be designed to ameliorate existing social inequalities, the voluntary sector develops in an ad hoc and piecemeal manner, responding to available resources as much as to needs in the community (Milligan, 2001, p 162). Moreover, as Brock (2003) points out, the new state–voluntary sector relationship casts the voluntary sector as a 'buffer' between the state and the citizenry, with service organisations bearing the brunt of citizen dissatisfaction with deteriorating services. As a consequence, the credibility of the voluntary sector has been called into question. Brock (2003) argues that the sector has two possible ways to respond to its loss of credibility: it can coordinate the delivery of services to enhance efficiency within various subsectors, or form coalitions to publicly respond to government initiatives.

Decades of neoliberal governance in Canada have heightened the challenges voluntary organisations face as they become more tightly interwoven into what Wolch (1990) refers to as the 'shadow state'. The voluntary sector faces a potential loss of autonomy, distortion of agency mandates, dangers of increased bureaucratisation and commercialisation, greater difficulty responding to community needs and decreasing ability to undertake advocacy, all of which potentially result in a loss of legitimacy (Rekart, 1993; Browne, 1996; Brown, 1997; Salamon, 1999; Mitchell, 2001). Wolch argues that increasing state penetration of the non-governmental sector 'could ultimately shackle its potential to create progressive social change' (1990, p 15). Salamon (1999), on the other hand, suggests that the crisis of legitimacy can only be addressed through voluntary sector 'renewal' by 'working collaboratively with government and the business sector to respond to societal needs' (p 21). While Salamon's strategy of 'holding the centre' requires stronger links with government, Wolch (1999) argues against legitimising neoliberal governments and corporations. Instead she suggests that the voluntary sector should 'decentre' itself and move away from partnerships with the very governments and corporations responsible for orchestrating increased social inequality on a global scale. Wolch argues that the voluntary sector should become a site of resistance by 'join[ing] the margins in an effort to weave a new, more humane and inclusive social contract' (1999, p 25). As the following discussion of settlement organisations in Vancouver suggests, however, Brock's (2003) call for coalitions may provide an alternate strategy to mount effective resistance without either 'holding the centre' or abandoning it for resistance from the margins.

The changing landscape of settlement services in Canada

Immigration is a significant ongoing process creating new and diverse landscapes in the major urban centres in Canada. Between 1991 and 2000, for example, 2.2 million immigrants were admitted to Canada (Statistics Canada, 2001a, p 6). Of those arriving in the last decade, 58% came from Asia, 20% from Europe, 11% from the Caribbean, Central and South America, 8% from Africa and 3% from the US (Statistics Canada, 2001a, p 6). The vast majority of new immigrants, nearly three out of every four, settle in one of three cities: Toronto, Vancouver or Montreal (Statistics Canada, 2001a, p 7). According to the 2001 Census, the proportion of all residents who are immigrants is 37.5% in Greater Vancouver, and immigrants who arrived since 1991 now make up 17% of the total population (Statistics Canada, 2001a, p 8; 2001b). This large and diverse population of recent immigrants face many challenges as they experience the processes of (re)settlement in Canada. Programmes to aid various dimensions of (re)settlement can ease the multiple transitions immigrants experience and enhance processes of belonging.

Settlement services began to develop in Canada in the 1970s as postwar immigration shifted away from traditional European sources and became more diverse[5]. Programmes to provide English language training (and French in Quebec), interpretation services, employment training and orientation services for new immigrants emerged as volunteer-based, and largely women-led, grassroots community organisations sprang up in major cities across the country (Ng, 1990,

1993). By the 1990s, the landscape of settlement services was dominated by a large network of voluntary organisations, both ethno-specific and multicultural in orientation, concentrated in the major cities and staffed largely by poorly paid immigrant women and volunteers (Lee, 1999a, 1999b). As the following case study of Vancouver will illustrate, welfare state restructuring in the late 1990s fundamentally reshaped settlement services in Canada.

Restructuring and settlement services in Vancouver

This study is based on research conducted in Vancouver from the fall of 1996 through the spring of 1998 during the process of 'settlement renewal' that saw the restructuring of settlement programmes prior to their devolution from federal to provincial responsibility. Funding for settlement programmes was cut, core funding was replaced by short-term funding for specific projects, and agencies were encouraged to develop partnerships and find new sources of funding. In addition, agreements were later negotiated with the provinces to oversee settlement programmes in exchange for a fixed transfer payment at the new reduced level of funding[6]. This study examines how settlement agencies negotiated this critical period of initial restructuring.

The research focused on three large non-profit agencies that dominated settlement service provision in the Vancouver area: the Immigrant Services Society (ISS), the Multilingual Orientation Service Association for Immigrant Communities (MOSAIC) and the United Chinese Community Enrichment Services Society (SUCCESS)[7]. ISS, MOSAIC and SUCCESS each developed in the mid-1970s from volunteer-based, grassroots community efforts to meet the needs of new immigrants. SUCCESS developed as an ethno-specific organisation providing services to the Chinese immigrant community. ISS and MOSAIC began as broader multicultural settlement organisations. By the mid-1990s each organisation had grown to encompass over 100 paid staff, in addition to volunteers, running dozens of different programmes, including English-as-second-language training, interpretation services, employment training and orientation services, with annual budgets of at least five million Canadian dollars apiece, most of which came from government sources.

Prior to restructuring, ISS, SUCCESS and MOSAIC had little trouble adhering to their core missions and retained responsiveness to community needs in spite of reliance on government funding. Although there were some differences among the three settlement agencies[8], the impact of restructuring was very similar: increased bureaucratisation, tighter incorporation into the 'shadow state' and programme developments that threatened to undermine agency missions (as resources were increasingly diverted to state-defined priorities that did not necessarily fit with community needs).

As part of a process of 'settlement renewal', the three core settlement programmes – settlement orientation programmes (ISAP)[9], English-as-second-language programmes (LINC)[10] and programmes for government sponsored refugees

(AAP)[11] – were redesigned to be more targeted, efficient and accountable (Gruno and Stovel, 1996; Citizenship and Immigration Canada, 1998). Other federal programmes underwent restructuring at the same time, including employment programmes run by Human Resources Development Canada (HRDC, 1995). HRDC employment programmes had long been a core element of settlement services, but soon became inaccessible to most immigrants.

Overall the two-year process of 'settlement renewal' was marked by considerable uncertainty. Funding directions often changed quickly and with little consultation. New eligibility requirements were imposed that defined services more narrowly. Funding became scarcer and more piecemeal, with the shift from funding full positions or programmes to partial funding, and specific short-term projects rather than core funding. New demands for accountability intensified the management responsibilities of settlement staff. Paradoxically, shifting priorities also saw funding open in some new areas less relevant to community needs.

Changes in employment programmes provide a good example of the way restructuring altered the landscape of settlement services. In 1995 the Consolidated Revenue Fund, an HRDC programme aimed at helping the 'severely disadvantaged' enter the labour market, was suddenly cancelled. Overnight the three settlement agencies each lost around one million dollars in employment programmes, between one fifth and one quarter of their annual budgets. Staff delivering employment programmes, many with years of specialised expertise, were laid off[12]. More important, the Consolidated Revenue Fund allowed agencies to develop a number of specific skills training programmes for immigrants – for example, bridging programmes for foreign trained nurses, accountants and engineers – and these programmes disappeared. HRDC later provided short-term funding for programmes that provided the most basic employment assistance, such as job clubs and resumé (or CV) services, but not funding to run skills-based programmes to integrate foreign-trained immigrants into the labour market.

Obtaining employment is the single most important issue facing new immigrants so programmes in this area were critical (Gibbens and Associates and Martin Spigelman Research Associates, 1997; Martin Spigelman Research Associates, 1998). In the scramble to replace the employment programmes that were cancelled, settlement agencies contracted with the federal government to provide employment programmes for recipients of Employment Insurance (EI), and with the provincial government to provide employment programmes for recipients of Income Assistance or welfare. This was done even though very few recent immigrants could qualify for either. To qualify for EI a newcomer to the labour market (someone with less than two years' work experience) must have 910 insured hours in the previous year; while other unemployed workers must have between 420 and 700 insured hours of work depending on the local unemployment rate (HRDC, 1995; Pulkingham, 1998). Given the difficulties most new immigrants have finding full-time, long-term employment, few were eligible to collect EI when unemployed (Martin Spigelman Research Associates, 1999). Similarly, employment programmes that targeted recipients of Income

Assistance were little use to most recent immigrants because few were able to qualify for provincial welfare payments[13]. Thus, in response to fiscal instability, settlement agencies began to run employment programmes for which few recent immigrants could ever hope to qualify.

Employment contracts quickly inflated agency coffers, often beyond the original budget cuts, but the impact on immigrants was less beneficial. Restructuring widened the gap between community needs and services provided for employment and threatened to compromise the mandate of settlement agencies in an effort to pursue fiscal solvency.

Employment programmes were not the only core areas subject to restructuring. English-language classes were cut at every agency. One agency was reduced from 206 class hours per week to 161 hours, and lost more than $100,000 in one year. Another was reduced by $300,000 over three years. Settlement agencies also lost funding for bilingual settlement counsellors. In one case, although the number of counsellors increased from 8 to 10 over two years, there was also a shift from full to partial funding. In 1995, 7 of 8 counsellors were fully funded by the federal government; in 1997 only 3 of 10 were fully funded.

Along with decreased funding came tighter eligibility criteria, closer monitoring and new accountability structures, which widened gaps in services for immigrants while increasing unfunded, and often unpaid, workloads for settlement staff. As one settlement worker commented:

> 'I have to serve the same or more clients in the same time which I have, and that would affect the effectiveness of the service we provide. Well to tell you the truth, that makes me sacrifice my time for them.... I come early in the morning and I go later in the evening in order to cover that area because I see the need for the people. However, I know that the budget is cut, but it's hard for them to understand because they need help. So when they are here, they are newcomers and I have been in the same shoes and I know how they feel. So it's hard for me to tell them there is no such service ... so because of that I have to sacrifice my time.' (interview 12)

Time limits for service eligibility were particularly problematic for women:

> 'Say for example they are women. They have to look after their kids when they are still very young ... so they cannot really go out and take classes.... And when their kids get older and then it's about the time they also become Canadian citizen, so that means they are not eligible to take LINC [English language] classes'. (interview 25)

Some language centres provided on-site daycare, but spaces were few and waiting lists were usually long. Moreover, subsidised daycare was not available for employment programmes, remaining a critical barrier for many women.

Restricted eligibility for settlement services coincided with reductions in many other social services as the welfare state was cut back. The result was an intensification of settlement work as immigrants brought new needs to settlement agencies that had previously been met elsewhere:

> 'There are more and more people coming to us for services in areas we're not supposed to be providing service – help to fill out forms from immigration, asking about classifications of immigration and that kind of thing. Whereas it was normally done at the office – the CIC office – it's being handed over to the community or at least pushed out the door.' (interview 2)

> 'Well to tell you the truth, some of the services it provides for the clients, if you go by the rules and regulations which government is giving as guidelines, we are not supposed to do it. So it means that we will, we are being limited to providing those services.... I must tell them "no" ... or we have to charge them for those services you know, when we know that people don't have a job. This newcomer here, whether immigrants or refugees, how can we charge them when they just hardly survive here?' (interview 12)

Most noticeably, issues of poverty, hunger and homelessness increased among immigrants. One settlement worker talked about collecting food from the foodbank for distribution in class; another ran clothing drives to provide running shoes and other clothing for work practicums; many recounted the mounting number of clients suffering emotional stress and depression, and family conflict and spousal abuse, with few resources available for referral:

> 'So much that's happened within Canadian society, the cuts in the Liberals' move to balance the budget, not only the devolution of federal government responsibilities but also the, you know, the massive cuts to transfer payments has really raised poverty issues within the immigrant and refugee communities.... So what's happening is that we're kind of caught between a rock and a hard place because in particular settlement services and community settlement services there's this push for further accountability, there's this push for more and more quantitative evaluation analysis, how many clients you serve. But on the other hand the clients that are coming to us for service require longer interventions, they're more complex cases. The problems that they're bringing to the frontline staff are not just nice and neat settlement pieces, they touch on a myriad of poverty issues.' (interview 3)

Unemployment, underemployment, poverty, stress and lack of services to help with these key issues, was noted in increased levels of frustration and anger among clients. As one settlement worker commented:

> 'They're also very angry, they're often angry when they come. They're angry with the government and they're angry with us. We can usually bring their anger down to a point and bring them to a point of accepting like, "okay you're here now so let's get going we'll help you do whatever we can". But this is all we can do, you know, and it's very crushing for many people.' (interview 8)

All three agencies provided services well beyond the time frame funded by government programmes. As a consequence there was a struggle to find ways to fund the shortfall, and increasing pressure to expand, with greater or lesser success in different agencies, in the areas of fee-for-service, partnerships with business, fundraising and increased use of volunteers. These trends affected the geography of settlement agencies. It was rare for smaller agencies, and those outside the major metropolitan centres, to be able to draw on a large constituency for volunteering, fundraising or successful fee-for-service ventures. Moreover, smaller agencies were less likely to command a public profile that a potential business partner might be drawn to, or possess the resources needed to continuously explore potential new avenues of funding. In this new funding environment, smaller settlement agencies – often more specialised agencies serving women or smaller ethno-cultural communities – became much more marginal. Larger agencies, and SUCCESS in particular, enjoyed considerable growth.

As Lee (1999b) points out, the line between paid and unpaid work within settlement agencies also became more blurred. In her study of 10 immigrant settlement agencies in 1998, Lee found that paid staff were under pressure to increase their volunteer hours for the good of the agency. Sometimes this pressure emerged from efforts to keep a programme going during times of transitional funding, other times it resulted from the increased need for fundraising, or community development work that no longer received any funding.

ISS, MOSAIC and SUCCESS each offered some fee-for-service programmes at the time of the study, but service fees had not been adopted in what were considered core settlement areas. One agency, for example, ran a very successful fee-for-service translation department that helped to fund other programmes. There were a few partnerships with private sector businesses and trade unions, usually fee-for-service contracts to provide programmes such as multicultural workplace training or English-as-second-language programmes in the workplace. Less often corporate sponsorship could be found for a specific settlement programme, such as a family violence prevention programme run by one agency. All agencies were searching for ways to increase fee-for-service activities and fundraising to offset the loss of federal funds.

Increased competition for funding, combined with less stable funding, required constant production of programme proposals. The never-ending treadmill of funding proposals took considerable agency resources:

> 'We did ten full proposals and those proposals are about eighty pages long so we did ten proposals in the first year, in '95, and ended up getting five, which was extraordinary because we did better than we ever anticipated. And five projects was a very, very good number, but that was an enormous amount of work. Last year we did the same thing ... we did eight proposals to get four contracts.' (interview 4)

Needless to say, the time required to prepare programme proposals was not paid for by funders. The push towards more partnerships and collaboration also required more time in administration, especially for the growing number of programmes funded by more than one source:

> 'The enhanced complexity of managing collaborative programs takes an enormous amount of administrative time. For example you have X kind of program which has five funders, three partners, and so every decision that has to be made is made with your partners, there are issues around staff supervision and performance appraisal and all that angle. There's also the fact that you're working with different funders who have a different fiscal year, different deadlines throughout the year.' (interview 3)

Employment programmes saw the most aggressive downloading of management and accountability functions from the federal government to voluntary agencies, while simultaneously reducing government services. Both measures increased the workload of settlement workers and their integration into the 'shadow state':

> 'Recently we have seen that HRDC has stopped employment counselling at all from their office ... and they have shifted that to immigrant societies.... Secondly, there have been a lot of changes like case management, which is going to be by centralized computer where the person who is coming to [my agency] will not be duplicated by [another agency].... It's going to double my work. I have to, like I have to give the information to HRDC in their computers, then I have to do my other D [data] base computer where we have to provide the [internal agency] report every month because in the government computer, which is Contact 4, I cannot do the report [for my agency].' (interview 9)

In addition, narrowly framed accountability measures changed the way some settlement workers provided services by affecting programme recruitment. As two workers explained, this trend was counterproductive for the mission of the settlement agencies:

> 'Programs are looking at marketability, they're looking at results so in the process of recruitment and selection there could be subconsciously, you're going to go for the client who is marketable. Be able to get the job, be employable you know.' (interview 5)

> 'Which means in my next in-take in September I am forced to take, like between a woman who needs more daycare and someone who has a school age or no kid, I'll take that [latter] woman. There's less chance that woman will drop out of the program…. [So it's affecting] my recruitment and my ability to reach people who really need it. This person who has younger kids probably needs the program more because she's really isolated and motivated, but I know that she cannot afford to have an extra hundred dollars every month.' (interview 7)

Settlement work was performed largely by women with immigrant backgrounds and, as we might predict, it was relatively low paid. In the settlement sector in British Columbia 80% of employees were women, 75% were first generation immigrants and 70% were people of colour (Lee, 1999b, p 98). This marginalised 'flexible' workforce experienced the further deterioration of working conditions through the processes of restructuring: jobs became more insecure (more part-time and limited-term contracts), workloads intensified and work became more stressful as immigrants brought more complex issues but faced increasing barriers to finding services to meet their needs:

> 'Well you know I love working in this field but I also find it very discouraging as a worker in the field who feels overwhelmed sometimes by the needs of the clients that we can't meet. I feel like we don't keep up.' (interview 8)

> 'I can't think of an English word although I know there is one, and I don't want to say "humiliating" because it's not humiliating…. [It is] really unsettling and almost to the point where it disrespects the individual who does the work. I mean, I don't know what the word is, but it just feels really disrespectful to us as workers who do front-line work. And to think that our contracts are, we don't know until two days before the year [end] whether we're going to have a job or not, or what kind of job. Is it going to be half-time? Full-time? Three days? Four days? You know? I think that's really unsettling. Dehumanizing. Yes, that's probably closer to the word I was looking for.' (interview 20)

Not surprisingly, this combination of high stress, low pay and limited job security contributed to high staff turnover (Lee, 1999b).

In summary then, restructuring changed the landscape of settlement services in several important ways. It created a more uneven geography of the programmes provided by settlement agencies, both within Vancouver (by creating conditions that further marginalised smaller agencies) and across the country (as provinces set different levels of service provision when they began to take over settlement services[14]); brought settlement work more firmly within the parameters of the 'shadow state'; increased the gap between community needs and services provided; contributed to the deterioration of working conditions within the sector; and threatened to distort the mission of settlement agencies. Effects were also contradictory, however, and for some settlement workers political activism and advocacy became a key way to reconnect to community needs and reclaim the value of settlement work.

Bringing advocacy back in

Advocacy has always been an important part of settlement work. Settlement workers talked about how they advocate for their clients, to get them into social housing, onto social assistance, into employment programmes, access to emergency funds for medical or dental care, eyeglasses, clothing for work, food, interpreters, assistance with family sponsorships, refugee claims, children's schools, to name but a few of the examples provided. As one settlement worker argued:

> 'It's essential that as workers we advocate for them because of whatever limited power that we may have, but that power is certainly more than our clients' power.' (interview 20)

Even at this level of individual advocacy, the need for advocacy was perceived to be increasing as restructuring expanded needs while services declined.

The most significant change, however, was the growing importance of what one settlement worker referred to as 'big advocacy':

> 'I believe in advocacy big-time and I think it's everybody's responsibility. It's part of our work.... There's small advocacy and there's big advocacy right. I mean the small advocacy we're all doing in our own little ways ... but big-time advocacy [is] in terms of issues that will really affect our ability to deliver services.' (interview 7)

'Big advocacy' involved challenging government policies that adversely affect immigrants and refugees. There was some controversy about engaging in more political forms of advocacy, so agencies differed in how active they were in 'big advocacy'. As a high-ranking manager in one agency argued:

> 'Advocacy is important. I think that there's a real role for it but I don't
> think you can do it when you're on government funding ... I mean
> you can do it up to a point and then you realize that if you continue
> to do it you'll get into trouble.' (interview 2)

The tension between 'big advocacy' and adverse government reaction was
mediated through participation in coalitions organised around specific issues.
Working within a coalition was always preferable to standing alone:

> 'At the senior management level [we do] write letters proposing
> changes to policies but ... we would never take that to the media and
> say we do not believe in this policy. We would not design our campaign
> to change that policy and include a media briefing on an issue. [But]
> if we were involved with a group of agencies we would probably be
> willing to be quoted.' (interview 4)

One settlement agency, MOSAIC, was less reticent than others about 'big
advocacy' and increasingly set itself apart by taking a strong leadership role in
this area. MOSAIC was more likely than the others to form and lead a coalition
of settlement service agencies:

> 'We sell ourselves as advocates here and we sell the organization as an
> advocacy-based organization.... None of the other organizations do
> because they have some convoluted view that it's got to do with your
> charitable status when it really doesn't. I mean, you can do advocacy
> for the purposes of your client. You can't do partisan politics but you
> can participate in non-partisan type activities, and we do that, on
> behalf of the clients.' (interview 22)

At the time of this research at least, its higher-profile advocacy position did not
hurt MOSAIC's fiscal health, which, like the other large agencies in this study,
continued to improve. Whether an organisation was willing to offer leadership
or simply join a coalition, however, coalitions were central to 'big advocacy' in
the settlement sector.

One forum for such advocacy occurred through the Affiliation of Multicultural
Society and Service Agencies of British Columbia (BC) (AMSSA). AMSSA was
a coalition of 75 multicultural and settlement service agencies in British Columbia.
In the late 1990s AMSSA endorsed a strong advocacy role and revised its mission
statement to pursue 'major social justice issues of multiculturalism, anti-racism,
and immigration' (AMSSA, 1998, p 1). As part of this commitment, for example,
AMSSA organised an all-day community forum to critically assess proposed
changes to immigration and refugee legislation. The forum helped to raise political
awareness in the sector and produced a collective response to the federal
government.

Much of settlement workers' 'big advocacy' in the late 1990s focused squarely on poverty. As restructuring increased poverty issues among immigrants, anti-poverty work become central to politicising settlement workers and to forging new alliances outside the sector. The most important expression of this was the formation of the Working Group on Poverty (WGP). In 1996 MOSAIC helped organise a one-week tent camp to protest homelessness amongst refugee claimants. The tent camp protest resulted in the elimination of a three-month waiting period for eligibility for Income Assistance. That protest forged new connections with 'mainstream' anti-poverty groups, who then agreed to put the situation of refugee claimants at the centre of an issue that affected all newcomers to British Columbia, the majority of whom were Canadians from other provinces. Building on this experience MOSAIC spearheaded a new broad based coalition against poverty, the WGP.

The WGP grew to include over 70 member organisations, including settlement agencies, 'mainstream' anti-poverty groups, other community groups, healthcare providers, teachers and unions, as well as representatives from all three levels of government. The mandate of the WGP focused specifically on immigrant and refugee poverty. It was a grassroots coalition that acted as a bridge between the settlement and 'mainstream' community groups. In 1998 its objectives were fivefold: affordable housing, food security, equal access to employment and language training, eliminating barriers for immigrants and refugees and advocating for social justice[15].

The WGP accomplished a number of initiatives by the end of the 1990s. It organised an anti-poverty conference at the People's Summit opposing the Asia Pacific Economic Cooperation meetings held in Vancouver in the autumn of 1997. It successfully lobbied the British Columbia Human Rights Commission to recommend wide-ranging human rights protection for the poor, and won changes to welfare regulations such that refugee claimants awaiting landed immigrant status gained access to full Income Assistance[16]. The WGP attained government funds for research on poverty among immigrants in British Columbia[17], and it organised a conference on affordable housing.

Two things made the WGP noteworthy. First, immigrants were placed at the centre of a broad anti-poverty coalition, helping to redraw poverty issues in a way that incorporated immigrants as part of the 'mainstream' citizenry, while at the same time redrawing settlement issues by connecting them to broader trends in welfare state restructuring. Second, all levels of government and community groups participated in the coalition, but leadership of the WGP remained with settlement workers. The WGP provided settlement workers with an effective forum through which to challenge government policies, without undermining either its ability to offer services or its grassroots commitment to immigrant communities.

Conclusion

Welfare state restructuring during the 1990s changed the landscape of settlement services in Vancouver, creating a more uneven geography of provision, increasing gaps between community needs and the services available, bringing settlement work more firmly within the parameters of the 'shadow state', adversely affecting working conditions in the sector and threatening to distort the mission of settlement agencies. At the same time, the legitimacy crisis engendered by these changes produced heightened levels of advocacy that helped bring immigrants from the margins to the centre of debates over poverty, equality and the welfare state. Thus settlement workers in Vancouver followed neither Salamon's (1999) advice to 'hold the centre', nor Wolch's (1999) entreaties to abandon the centre for resistance from 'the margins'. Instead, as Brock (2003) suggests, they used coalitions to publicly challenge neoliberal policies while continuing to partner with government to provide essential services. The experience of settlement agencies suggests that reclaiming an advocacy stance, which is both more difficult and more necessary in a neoliberal environment, can be marshalled through coalitions as an effective mode of resistance without abandoning 'the centre'.

Notes

[1] I would like to thank the Vancouver Centre for Research on Immigration and Integration in the Metropolis (RIIM) for funding this research, my research assistants, Arthur Ling and Timothy Welsh, the Executive Directors of ISS, MOSAIC and SUCCESS, the settlement workers who agreed to be interviewed, and the funders who provided programme information. I would also like to thank David Ley, David Conradson and Christine Milligan for comments on earlier drafts.

[2] Sixty per cent of voluntary sector funds come from government, 26% from earned income and 14% from donations (Brock, 2003, p 11).

[3] In the Canadian federal system the federal government maintains most powers of taxation, but the provinces are constitutionally responsible for such things as health, education and social services. A complex system of transfer payments to the provinces allows the federal government to claim a role in these areas, and equalisation payments make it possible for poorer provinces to offer social programmes similar to those in wealthier provinces. When the federal government cut funding for welfare programmes it did so largely by cutting transfer payments and equalisation payments to the provinces, and therefore 'downloaded' the fiscal crisis to the provinces (Cohen, 1997).

[4] In Canada the definition of a charity is regulated through the Income Tax Act, which adopts a very narrow definition of allowable advocacy and political activity (Phillips, 2003a; Pross and Webb, 2003).

[5] Restrictive immigration legislation in the late 19th and early 20th centuries closed most immigration to non-Europeans. Immigration was liberalised with the adoption of a universal points system in 1967 and a formal refugee system a decade later. As a result of these policy changes immigration patterns changed in the late 1960s, quickly shifting from European sources to countries in Asia, the Caribbean, Latin America and Africa (Li, 2003).

[6] Unlike other social programmes, settlement services were funded directly by the federal government because immigration is constitutionally a federal responsibility. However, these responsibilities were also 'downloaded' to the provinces. In 1998, just as this research ended, an agreement to transfer responsibility for settlement programmes was struck with the province of British Columbia (Citizenship and Immigration Canada, 1998).

[7] Research was based on analysis of agency annual reports, programme documentation, interviews with 27 staff at ISS (13 interviews), MOSAIC (10 interviews) and SUCCESS (4 interviews), and a focus group. Interviewees were drawn from a wide range of positions including frontline staff, such as receptionists, bilingual counsellors and English-as-second-language teachers, as well as programme managers and all three executive directors. In addition, this research draws on the author's five years as a member of the board of directors of MOSAIC, and both research assistants' many years of experience working in the settlement field. In response to agency concerns over confidentiality, general identifiers are used in the text – such as 'one settlement agency' – and individual interviewees are cited only by interview number and not by organisation. The only exception to this practice is naming MOSAIC for its leadership role in 'big advocacy'.

[8] ISS, MOSAIC and SUCCESS each carved out some degree of specialisation, although all three ran English-as-second-language programmes, employment programmes and settlement services in a wide range of languages. SUCCESS was the largest of the organisations, experienced the greatest growth and was least dependent on government funding with more than 40% of its funds generated through fundraising.

[9] The Immigrant Settlement and Adaptation Program (ISAP) met settlement needs within the first three years in Canada, providing orientation services, bilingual counsellors in numerous languages, family programmes, women's programmes and community development programmes.

[10] Language Instruction for Newcomers (LINC) was a programme for English as a second language (French in Quebec) open to all landed immigrants prior to becoming Canadian citizens.

[11] The Adjustment Assistance Program (AAP) provided temporary settlement services for government-assisted refugees. Those who arrived and claimed refugee status under the terms of the United Nations Convention on Refugees were ineligible for these services.

[12] Termination compensation, in lieu of adequate notice for long-term employees, forced agencies to shift to short-term fixed contracts for all employees.

[13] Sponsorship clauses for family members prevented access to government income support for a period of 10 years. In addition, refugee claimants were excluded from full Income Assistance (welfare) and only qualified for 'hardship allowance', a maximum $550 per month regardless of the size of the family (interview 22).

[14] So, for example, the province of British Columbia only funds English-language training to a level of basic comprehension, while Ontario and Manitoba include English-language training to higher 'work ready levels' (BC Coalition for Immigrant Integration, undated, p 2).

[15] Personal communication with the chair of the WGP.

[16] Along with more money, access to Income Assistance provided entitlement to healthcare, pharmacare, dental benefits and access to employment programmes designed for Income Assistance recipients (*Vancouver Sun*, 21 July 1998, p A3).

[17] The study documented the high levels of poverty that settlement workers identified in interviews. Among immigrant and refugee families who arrived between 1991 and 1996, 51% lived in poverty, compared to 11.2% of non-immigrant families (Martin Spigelman Research Associates, 1998, executive summary).

References

AMSSA (Affiliation of Multicultural Societies and Service Agencies of British Columbia) (1998) 'AMSSA Adopts Advocacy Policy', *AMSSA Update*, January 6.

Brock, K. (2003) 'The Nonprofit Sector in Interesting Times', in K. Brock and K. Banting (eds) *The Nonprofit Sector in Interesting Times*, Montreal: McGill-Queen's University Press, pp 1-16.

Brock, K. and Banting, K. (2001) 'The Nonprofit Sector and Government in a New Century: An Introduction', in K. Brock and K. Banting (eds) *The Nonprofit Sector and Government in a New Century*, Montreal: McGill-Queen's University Press, pp 1-20.

Brown, M. (1997) *Replacing Citizenship: Aids Activism and Radical Democracy*, New York, NY: The Guilford Press.

Browne, P.L. (1996) *Love in a Cold World? The Voluntary Sector in An Age of Cuts*, Ottawa: Canadian Centre for Policy Alternatives.

Chappell, R. (2001) *Social Welfare in Canadian Society* (2nd edn), Scarborough: Nelson Thompson Learning.

Citizenship and Immigration Canada (1998) *Agreement for Canada–British Columbia Co-operation on Immigration, Backgrounder, Immigration by Province, 1995-1997*, 19 May. Ottawa: Citizenship and Immigration Canada.

Cohen, M.G. (1997) 'From the Welfare State to Vampire Capitalism', in P. Evans and G. Wekerle (eds) *Women and the Canadian Welfare State*, Toronto: University of Toronto Press, pp 28-67.

Fyfe, N. and Milligan, C. (2003) 'Out of the Shadows: Exploring Contemporary Geographies of Voluntarism', *Progress in Human Geography*, vol 27, no 4, pp 397-413.

Gibbens, A. and Associates and Martin Spigelman Research Associates (1997) *Enhancing Opportunity: Meeting the Employment Training Needs of Recent Immigrants to British Columbia*, prepared for the Ministry Responsible for Multiculturalism and Immigration, BC, Ministry of Education, Skills and Training, BC, Citizenship and Immigration Canada and Human Resources Development Canada.

Gruno, V. and Stovel, S. (1996) *Settlement Renewal in British Columbia Phase III: Constituent Assemblies and Final Recommendations to the Federal and Provincial Governments*, March. Unpublished manuscript.

Hall, M. and Banting, K. (2000) 'The Nonprofit Sector in Canada: An Introduction', in K. Banting (ed) *The Nonprofit Sector in Canada: Roles and Relationships*, Montreal: McGill-Queen's University Press, pp 1-28.

Hasson, S. and Ley, D. (1994) *Neighbourhood Organizations and the Welfare State*, Toronto: University of Toronto Press.

HRDC (Human Resources Development Canada) (1995) *A 21st Century Employment System for Canada: Guide to the Employment Insurance Legislation*, December, Ottawa: Human Resources Development, Canada.

Lee, J.-A. (1999a) *Immigrant Settlement and Multiculturalism Programs for Immigrant, Refugee and Visible Minority Women: A Study of Outcomes, Best Practices and Issues*, Report submitted to the British Columbia Ministry Responsible for Multiculturalism and Immigration.

Lee, J.-A. (1999b) 'Immigrant Women Workers in the Immigrant Settlement Sector', *Canadian Woman Studies*, vol 19, no 3, pp 97-103.

Li, P. (2003) *Destination Canada: Immigration Debates and Issues*, Don Mills: Oxford University Press.

Milligan, C. (2001) *Geographies of Care: Space, Place and the Voluntary Sector*, Aldershot: Ashgate.

Mitchell, K. (2001) 'Transnationalism, Neo-liberalism, and the Rise of the Shadow State', *Economy and Society*, vol 30, no 2, pp 165-89.

Ng, R. (1990) 'State Funding to a Community Employment Center: Implications for Working with Immigrant Women', in R. Ng, G. Walker and J. Muller (eds) *Community Organization and the Canadian State*, Toronto: Garamond Press, pp 165-83.

Ng, R. (1993) 'Racism, Sexism and Immigrant Women', in S. Burt, O. Code and L. Dorney (eds) *Changing Patterns: Women in Canada* (2nd edn), Toronto: McClelland and Stewart, pp 279-301.

Pal, L. (1997) 'Civic Re-Alignment: NGOs and the Contemporary Welfare State', in R. Blake, P. Bryden and F. Strain (eds) *The Welfare State in Canada: Past, Present and Future*, Toronto: Irwin Publishing, pp 88-104.

Phillips, S. (2001) 'From Charity to Clarity: Reinventing Federal Government-Voluntary Sector Relationships', in L. Pal (ed) *How Ottawa Spends 2001-2002: Power in Transition*, Don Mills: Oxford University Press, pp 145-76.

Phillips, S. (2003a) 'Voluntary Sector–Government Relationships in Transition: Learning from International Experience for the Canadian Context', in K. Brock and K. Banting (eds) *The Nonprofit Sector in Interesting Times*, Montreal: McGill-Queen's University Press, pp 17-70.

Phillips, S. (2003b) 'In Accordance: Canada's Voluntary Sector Accord from Idea to Implementation', in K. Brock (ed) *Delicate Dances: Public Policy and the Nonprofit Sector*, Montreal: McGill-Queen's University Press, pp 17-61.

Phillips, S. and Graham, K. (2000) 'Hand-in-Hand: When Accountability Meets Collaboration in the Voluntary Sector', in K. Banting (ed) *The Nonprofit Sector in Canada: Roles and Relationships*, Montreal: McGill-Queen's University Press, pp 149-90.

Pross, P. and Webb, K. (2003) 'Embedded Regulation: Advocacy and the Federal Regulation of Public Interest Groups', in K. Brock (ed) *Delicate Dances: Public Policy and the Nonprofit Sector*, Montreal: McGill-Queen's University Press, pp 63-121.

Pulkingham, J. (1998) 'Remaking the Social Divisions of Welfare: Gender, "Dependency" and UI Reform', *Studies in Political Economy*, vol 56, Summer, pp 7-48.

Rekart, J. (1993) *Public Funds, Private Provision: The Role of the Voluntary Sector*, Vancouver: UBC Press.

Salamon, L. (1999) 'The Nonprofit Sector at the Crossroads: The case of America', *Voluntas*, vol 10, no 1, pp 5-23.

Spigelman, Martin, Research Associates (1998) *Unfulfilled Expectations, Missed Opportunities: Poverty among Immigrants and Refugees in British Columbia*, Report prepared for the Working Group on Poverty, October. Victoria: Ministry Responsible for Multiculturalism and Immigration.

Spigelman, Martin, Research Associates (1999) *Transitions: An Analysis of the Impact of Funding Purchase and Case Management Changes on Immigrants, Employment Eligible Refugees and Immigrant Serving Organizations*, Prepared for Immigrant Services Society of BC, MOSAIC and SUCCESS, January, Unpublished manuscript.

Statistics Canada (2001a) *Canada's Ethnocultural Portrait: The Changing Mosaic*, 2001 Census: Analysis series, Catalogue no 96F0030XlE2001008.

Statistics Canada (2001b) *2001 Census of Canada* (www.statcan.ca).

Vancouver Sun (1998) 'Refugees Get Job Training Help', 21 July, A3.

Wolch, J. (1990) *The Shadow State: Government and Voluntary Sector in Transition*, New York, NY: The Foundation Center.

Wolch, J. (1999) 'Decentering America's Nonprofit Sector: Reflections on Salamon's Crisis Analysis', *Voluntas*, vol 10, no 1, pp 25-35.

TWELVE

Developing voluntary community spaces and Ethnicity in Sydney, Australia

Walter F. Lalich

Introduction

Public places and facilities are highly significant features of any urban landscape, yet in the country of arrival, many immigrants find such places to be unfamiliar and unwelcoming. They may be experienced as inadequate, inappropriate, inaccessible or even unfriendly to their needs (Lewis, 1978; Kraus, 1994). The development of community facilities through collective action by immigrant populations is thus often initiated as a way of reproducing the familiar plazas, streets, places of worship and leisure that defined everyday habitus in a place of origin. In this way, immigrant communities come to play an important role in the development of a nation's social infrastructure. They contribute to changes in the urban landscape through the development of diverse communal places designed to satisfy their collective needs.

As a way of exploring these issues, this chapter explores the development of voluntary[1] and non-commercial communal spaces by non-English speaking immigrants in Sydney, Australia. Since the early 1950s, Sydney has been a city in which diverse ethnic communities have sought to establish their own places of worship, education, welfare and leisure and recreation[2]. These developments have changed the urban landscape of a society that had previously been largely defined by cultural traditions imported from Britain (Connell, 2000; Burnley, 2001). The concern, here, is to consider how such developments play a crucial role in helping immigrants to settle in to their new social environment. While the chapter draws on a specific case study, it is argued that parallels can be found in many other places of migrant destination.

The chapter begins by examining the notion of 'communal home' as a key outcome of voluntary collective immigrant endeavour. Communal places or homes are considered, unlike public goods, to have a particular significance for specific segments of the community, in this case an ethnic collective. Many ethnic communities feel the need to establish such places, in part to address the cultural challenges encountered during settlement in the new environment. The resulting sites are thus of both symbolic and material significance. To ground this argument in the Australian context, the chapter outlines the key elements of postwar demographic and cultural change in Sydney. Drawing on survey data obtained from local ethnic organisations between 1999-2001, the discussion then explores how Sydney's immigrant communities have reacted to cultural shock through various forms of collective action. The data provide insights into the efforts of 393 ethnic collectives over a 50-year period, and illustrates the diverse material outcomes and social effects of such voluntary, collective endeavours.

Making communal places

Immigrant organisations are central to the process of adaptation to a new social environment; they play a key role in expression of identity, cultural transfer and maintenance[3]. In many instances, these organisations centre around regular access to a particular physical site, such as a club, place of worship or nursing home. It is in this coming together of a social community and a particular physical site that we can speak of a *communal place*. Such places support immigrants' everyday activities and are important in helping to preserve their cultural integrity, they assist their settlement and act as a source of a collective memory. Like many public buildings, they are often distinguishable by their design, patterns of use, applied artefacts and symbolic significance and, as such, they make a visible impact on the landscape (Parsons and Shils, 1962). The diversity in appearance and consumption of these new urban forms not only reflects their origin, but also reflects a process of cultural encounter.

The development of ethnic communal spaces in a destination country not only denotes the organisational capabilities of the immigrant population, but also reflects processes of cultural transfer and the setting down of new communal roots (Weil, 1978). Ethnic communal spaces help to provide a new address and an anchor to the social world (Zukin, 1992). Moreover, they reflect a collective cultural identity, potentially acting as a site of resistance against hegemonic structures and assimilation pressures (Creswell, 1996). They are also places of social exchange and communication, not only with other co-ethnic immigrants, but also with other social groups in the host city.

Historically, in addition to providing family support, migrant remittances were used to develop public spaces in the place of origin. However, many postwar refugees and immigrants to Australia had neither a straightforward place of origin nor family to send money to. Hence, the settlers' new milieu became a matter of greater concern and the focus of action. Immigrants became conscious that it was only through their joint or collective efforts that they could hope to improve their own well-being. As a result, the development of their own communal places became a matter of greater priority. Direct intervention in the development of urban space has been shown to have a major impact on the welfare, quality of life, culture transfer and maintenance of new ethnic communities.

Communal places are voluntarily developed and communally owned collective goods that serve to advance communal interests and address human and social needs; without immigrants' collective action they would not have been produced (Olson, 1965; Hechter et al, 1982). Research suggests that the development of ethnic communal places:

- reflects the human capability to act collectively in a purposeful and productive manner under the constraints of migration and settlement in a new environment;
- highlights the magnitude, diversity and significance of immigrants' direct intervention in the development of the social and urban infrastructure; and
- leads to the creation of relatively permanent nodes on the city landscape – many such places will be relatively enduring and hence become important points of reference in a culturally diverse society.

New relationships and associations need to be developed to shore up these spaces, and this requires a process of cultural interaction between immigrants and their receiving societies. To understand this process in Sydney, an appreciation of the experience of Australian migration and settlement patterns provides an important contextual background.

Placing immigration patterns in Australia

Continuous large-scale immigration had a significant impact on the postwar economic and social development of Australia. This immigration has been characterised by ethnic heterogeneity and predominantly urban settlement patterns. These characteristics, in turn, were induced by the needs of defence, industrialisation, construction and housing growth that demanded both labour and markets (Burnley, 1974; Collins, 1984). In 1947, the first postwar boat-loads of new settlers to Australia encountered a society in which the share of non-English speaking settlers amounted to only 1.8% (Price, 1979). Immigration continued over the following decades, however, and in 2001 the share of settlers of non-English speaking background had risen to 13.5% (ABS, 2001) (Table 12.1).

From 1948 onwards, Australian immigration intake shifted from heavily subsidised British immigration to a gradual acceptance of continental European immigrants. This resulted in the breakdown of the White Australia policy that had effectively excluded non-white immigrants during the first 60 years of the 20th century. By the early 1970s, immigrants from other parts of the world were arriving in increasingly significant numbers. The 2001 Census data showed that over a million and a half Australian inhabitants had been born in Africa, Asia, Latin America and the Pacific Islands. This complex immigration structure included the intake of several waves of refugees (most notably after the Second World War and the Vietnam War), the renewal of chain migration with an initial predominance of male immigrants, humanitarian entrants and immigrant family

Table 12.1: Australian population born in non-English speaking countries, by regions (1954-2001)[a]

Regions	1954	1971	1978	2001
Western Europe	147,118	281,874	279,133	272,997
Eastern Europe	148,493	166,047	160,261	140,612
Southern Europe[b]	197,427	669,450	696,570	633,587
Middle East[c]	7,871	70,348	115,150	213,942
Southern Asia[d]	na[g]	35,028	57,737	186,612
South East Asia	na[g]	35,940	63,913	497,076
China, Hong Kong[e]	11,831	23,184	43,672	234,404
Korea, Japan	966	4,929	10,363	64,427
Latin America	1,719	12,879	38,131	75,691
Pacific Islands	4,426	17,461	21,563	99,361
Africa[f]	na[f]	21,054	26,066	141,696
Total	519,851	1,338,194	1,512,499	2,560,405
NESB as % share of population	5.79	10.49	10.61	13.50
Total population	8,986,530	12,755,638	14,263,078	18,972,350

Notes:

[a] excluding British Isles, Canada, USA, New Zealand, Caribbean and South Africa; [b] including countries of the former Yugoslavia; [c] including Egypt; [d] including Central Asia from 2001; [e] Singapore in 1978; [f] excluding South Africa; [g] data for 1954 not available: assumed non-indigenous emigration.

NESB: non-English speaking background.

Source: Lalich (2004)

reunions. More recent emphasis has focused on skilled, professional and business immigrants, as well as various forms of transnational and temporary immigration[4].

Immigrants to Australia gravitated to the major coastal cities. Sydney, in particular, was one of the most preferred destinations. The first major change in its demographic structure occurred in the period 1950-60, with the large arrival of continental European migrants. Between 1947-71, 258,000 people from continental Europe settled in Sydney, including some 50,000 postwar refugees (Price and Pyne, 1977; Spearritt, 2000). As a consequence, the proportion of non-English speakers in Sydney increased from 2.2% of its population in 1947 to 23.4% in 2001 (Spearritt, 2000; ABS, 2001). By 1997 it was estimated that over 54% of the total population in Sydney consisted of first and second generation people from a non-English speaking background (Burnley et al, 1997).

Australia found itself unprepared for the effects of its own ambitious immigration programme. For years policy makers had either ignored or been unaware of the many subtle issues generated by the arrival of large numbers of immigrants and they showed little political interest in solving the attendant settlement issues (Martin, 1978; Cox, 1987; Jupp, 1991). Despite a change in policy in the 1970s and the contemporary emphasis on multiculturalism, non-English speaking migrants are still not readily accepted by many segments of the host society (Hage, 1998; Jupp, 2002).

Dynamic cultural change

The arrival of over three million settlers from a non-English speaking background since 1948 has had a major impact on the cultural and social life of Australia. The resultant cultural diversity can be seen in data on language use and religious diversity. In 1996, 734,000 people in Sydney, over five years of age, were using one of 20 major (non-English) languages on a daily basis. An additional 175,000 inhabitants were found to speak other non-English languages on a daily basis. In 2001, these non-English speakers represented approximately 27% of the city's inhabitants (EAC NSW, 1998; ABS, 2001).

Changes in Australia's religious structure also provides a useful indicator of cultural change. Australia now hosts all major world religions. As the data in Table 12.2 indicate, there has been an increase in religions other than the initially established Western Protestantism, Roman Catholicism and Judaism[5]. The large-scale arrival of continental Europeans and later settlers from Asia and Latin America greatly increased the number of Roman Catholics, amplifying pressure on existing religious and educational systems developed by earlier (predominantly Irish) Catholic settlers. Although some from these new Roman Catholic communities used the existing Catholic churches, others developed their own places of worship (for example, those of Croatian, Korean, Lebanese, Slovak, Slovenian, Syrian and Ukrainian origin). Similarly, while the postwar arrival of refugees sustained and continued the immigration of Jewish people, it also acted to change the local Jewish community social structure, as manifest in the construction of the first

Table 12.2: Religion in Australia: changes in denominational affiliation (1947-2001) (%)

Religion/denomination	Australia (1948)	Australia (1971)	Australia (2001)	Sydney (2001)
Anglican	39.0	31.0	20.7	19.8
Roman Catholic	20.9	27.0	26.3	28.8
Other Protestant[a]	24.6	20.4	17.6	12.8
Judaism	0.4	0.5	0.4	0.8
Subtotal	84.9	80.9	58.8	62.2
European Orthodox		2.7	2.9	4.2
Oriental Christian			0.4	1.5
Islam		0.2	1.5	3.4
Buddhism			1.9	3.4
Hinduism and Sikh			0.4	1.4
Other Non-Christian			0.4	0.3
Other	3.8	5.4	1.2	1.7
No religion	0.3	6.7	15.3	11.7
Not stated	10.8	6.1	10.3	9.0
Inhabitants	7,579,358	12,755,286	18,972,350[b]	3,997,322[b]

Notes: [a] includes data for Lutheran, Methodist, Presbyterian, Reformed, Uniting Churches and other Western Christian denominations; [b] includes visitors (1.1% and 1.2% respectively).

Source: Lalich (2004)

Sephardi synagogue in Sydney (Rutland, 1997). The appearance of new religious communities also resulted in a new demand for facilities, reviving the demand for church buildings that had been closed or abandoned.

The dynamics of the settlement process brought with it new forms of leisure, sport, media, art, food, building styles and gardening. Sydney, however, was not well endowed with public places and access to those that did exist was further limited due to cultural and linguistic differences (Spearritt, 1978; Sant and Waitt, 2000). Australian pubs, for example, with their gender segregation and early closing time were, for many years, not the easiest meeting places for immigrant settlers, corner milk bars were often below the standards of those in their countries of origin, and there were few easily accessible restaurants (Kraus, 1994; Connell, 2000; Sayer and Nowra, 2000).

With needs that differed from the established local customs and a cultural environment defined by transplanted British social patterns, immigrants could, initially, find little satisfaction or solace in the Sydney suburbs outside the workplace. In Patrikareas's (2000) drama *The Promised Woman*, for example, he illustrates how gender imbalances caused by the early immigration of single male immigrants were addressed through a government initiative in the early 1960s. The initiative resulted in a mass arrival of Italian and Greek women. Hence, in the drama, an Italian immigrant informs a new arrival, a young Greek woman, that the only available choices for Saturday afternoon outings are the races and the pub – social activities that are at odds with those that are seen as acceptable for women within her own culture. Several years later, in the 1970s, Thomas (1999) drew attention to the unease that Vietnamese refugee immigrants – individuals used to open and communal spaces – felt in an Australian suburban landscape, with its streets fragmented by fenced housing and the absence of places of social interaction.

The collective experience of Sydney's immigrant settler groups differed considerably during the postwar period. Some were able to participate in the social and spatial mobility offered by the city's sprawling suburbs, so benefiting from improved living conditions. In some instances housing and employment opportunities led to the spatial concentration of settlers, although no 'ghetto' settlements developed (Jupp, 1990). In 1976, the largest ratio of concentration was found among Greek immigrants in the inner Sydney suburb of Marrickville, the only suburb where more than 40% of all inhabitants were born overseas (Burnley, 1976). In 1996 the largest concentration of settlers were Vietnamese immigrants located in the western suburb of Fairfield, representing 25% of all those born overseas. However, in 1996 only five out of 39 suburbs had more than 40% of inhabitants of non-English speaking origin (NSW EAC, 1998).

Ethnic collective action

The postwar development of ethnic communal places illustrates the intensity of immigrants' preoccupation with communal well-being. Settlers had to provide their own answers, to find products and services and to establish communal places (Unikoski, 1978; Jupp, 1991). The magnitude of immigrant investment into communal places is dependent on many factors, including the number of immigrants, psychological and social pressures and their investment capability (that is, access to human, material, financial and organisational resources). It is also dependent on exogenous factors, most notably on the level of awareness of immigrant welfare needs and subsequent policy responses (Galbally, 1978; OMA, 1994). The focus of ethnic communal action can also change due to social and spatial mobility; increasing encounters with other segments of the local social structure; the ageing process; and generational changes. Hence, ethnic collective action and outcomes can take different forms over space and time.

In Australia, the emergence of ethnic communal places preceded any form of governmental assistance or even the solution of household problems, as immigrants resorted to mutual help to solve collectively experienced problems. Immediate, private, self-interests were sublimated to collective interests (Putnam, 1993), with this shift supported by the enhanced levels of social capital acquired during immigration and settlement. As Durkheim (1964) maintained, although many immigrants arrive with no previous mutual contacts, the common settlement experience can generate a strong sense of solidarity among those coming from the same cultural background and who share a similar fate in a new environment. This solidarity facilitates the establishment of networks among the people on the basis of a shared language, culture and settlement experience.

Social capital, understood as a joint interaction of norms, networks and trust (Bourdieu, 1993; Portes, 1995), is thus very significant in the early period of immigrant settlement. It is at this point that immigrant communal development evolves in response to unsatisfied needs, deprivation and the paucity of appropriate social infrastructure. Immigrant solidarity, social networks and trust are key factors behind the mutuality and voluntary collaboration inherent to these developments. A high level of mutual trust within such groups encourages individuals to join forces to find solutions to perceived problems. Social capital, then, can be seen as a bonding thread, facilitating communal investment in important infrastructure, although social capital is itself also a product of successful community development.

The combined outcome of these voluntary, collective actions is the establishment of new ethnic communal places in the urban landscape. The dynamics of participation, mobilised resources and spatial dispersion in the particular case of postwar Sydney are discussed in more detail in the next section.

The development of ethnic communal places in Sydney

During the period 1950–2000 it is estimated that at least 450 diverse ethnic organisations (formed by members of over 60 ethnic communities) established their own communal places in Sydney. These included places of worship, social and sporting clubs, community halls, schools, childcare facilities, aged care hostels and nursing homes. These developments arose as a consequence of a growing awareness that community needs could be satisfied only through the development of adequate facilities. New immigrants continued the pattern of prewar settlement in Sydney, where those from non Anglo-Celtic backgrounds had constructed 30 communal places in the city, some of which still continue to serve their original function (Lalich, 2004).

The increased consciousness of disadvantage among postwar settlers – alongside awareness of their own potential – facilitated collaboration and the accumulation of the material resources needed for local investment. This was the case even for smaller and financially insecure migrant communities. Many developments began on a modest scale: some of those initiated in the 1950s, for example, began with less than one hundred pounds in the bank. In other cases, organisations either purchased or leased available land in semi-rural suburbs, and in several instances the land was donated by benefactors. Still other organisations purchased and adapted abandoned halls, churches (sometimes with the help of the parent organisation), houses and even squash courts in older suburbs as former residents departed to new housing being developed in distant suburbs. In this way it has been estimated that around 80 churches in Sydney, some dating from the 19th century, acquired a new lease of life (Lalich, 2004).

As the majority of immigrants were initially single males and used to different types of entertainment, many new ethnic social and sporting clubs were initiated. These were often communal ventures. For example, new immigrants revived football in Australia[6]. This was much more than a recreational pastime for young male immigrants. It has been argued that football 'saved' many immigrants, providing after-work recreation and socialisation opportunities, companionship, opportunities for communication with other sectors of the community, for the display of organisational and leadership skills, and a path for inclusion into the new society (Caldwell, 1987; Mosely et al, 1997).

In a series of ways, immigrants were thus able to create places of action and commitment, where communal needs could be met. They were also sites of cultural exchange and social intercourse where immigrants communicated in their own languages. Such places accordingly helped to engender a sense of attachment and belonging – a *feeling of home* – that many immigrants were unlikely to have possessed in their initial experiences of Sydney. Collectively developed communal places not only provided a necessary feeling of stability and a continued link with the homeland, but they also helped immigrants to set down roots in the new environment. The sense of attachment developed in relation to these communal places and participation in communal life to some degree compensated for the dislocation.

The material effects and the social significance of collectively established communal places can be identified through research data obtained between 1999 and 2001. This provides insights into voluntary participation, job creation, financial involvement, associated activities, feelings of attachment and diverse linkage effects. The analysis of immigrant voluntary collective (non-commercial) intervention in Sydney's urban space clearly incorporates an economic dimension, but the full impact of immigrant contribution to urban infrastructure is difficult to ascertain, and thus does not form a major focus here. As indicated above, collective action by immigrant communities has contributed to the development of at least 450 communal places, differentially expanding and contracting across a range of functions between 1950 and 2000. Table 12.3 illustrates the development of 393 of those organisations that provided information on the development of their own places.

These voluntarily developed communal places occupy over 470,000m² of functional urban space. Immigrants developed at least 313,000m² of this space for spiritual and leisure use, mostly through their own resources. The development of educational and welfare places, however, did receive some public assistance. The outcome of this voluntary human effort has been the emergence of a new and culturally diversified urban landscape, facilitating the development of immigrants' spiritual life, leisure, sport, entertainment, education, childcare and welfare of their older people. This means that at any given moment, over 180,000 (immigrant) people in Sydney can be accommodated within voluntarily and communally developed places appropriate to their cultural needs. This includes room for 120,000 people in places of worship, 49,151 in social clubs, 10,792 students and 2,270 beds in aged care.

The dynamics of this communal development reflect changes in immigration patterns, as well as the socioeconomic environment and processes within the ethnic communities. A threshold of sufficiently large numbers of immigrants of the same origin and cultural background has been achieved in many instances, although this is structured not only by age and gender, but also by ideological, class, regional, cultural and educational differences. This impacts on perceived communal priorities and on the dynamics of development.

This process of development also needs to be understood within the context of two different time periods: the initial period, prior to 1980, was characterised by a lack of public support for immigrant-generated initiatives; and the period after 1980, which saw the development of schools, childcare and aged care facilities to meet the needs of immigrant communities, with significant public support and funding. Public financial support arose as a consequence of a growing

Table 12.3: Development of ethnic communal places: respondents by type and periods of development, Sydney, 1950-2000 (units)

Type/period	1950-60	1961-70	1971-80	1981-90	1991-2000	Total
Religious[a]	28	31	31	51	67	208
Clubs[b]	12	15	21	31	15	94
Education[c]	2	5	11	18	8	44
Aged care[d]	6	6	4	17	14	47
Total	48	57	67	117	104	393

Notes: [a] includes halls and Sunday school classrooms; [b] includes sports clubs; [c] includes childcare, day schools and tertiary institutions; [d] includes general welfare organisations.

Source: Lalich (2004)

awareness during the 1970s of the unsatisfactory social conditions facing immigrants, as identified by the Whitlam Labour government (1972-74), the Green Paper (APIC, 1977) and, finally, the Galbally Commission in 1978. Major policy changes were recommended and consequently introduced with bipartisan support. This change in governmental attitude led to a fuller recognition of the role that ethnic organisations played in the provision of services to immigrant communities. Multicultural policies, based on cultural identity, social justice and economic efficiency, developed to secure equality of access to social resources and greater social cohesion (NMAC, 1995, 1997). These principles established grounds for the public funding of multicultural resource centres to facilitate settlement; the employment of social workers by ethnic organisations; the development of English language classes; cultural activities; and the development and continuous financing of ethnic educational and aged care facilities. Access to public funding was based on an assessment of merit or need, the benefit to Australia, social justice and equity.

While Table 12.3 illustrates the intensity of the development of ethnic communal spaces over a 50-year period, it also indicates changes in development priorities. The importance of clubs and sports facilities during the first four decades (from 1950-90), for instance, declined during the last decade of the 20th century, while the development of places of worship significantly increased from the 1980s due to diverse trends in immigration. At the same time, the development of schools, childcare and aged care facilities became a focus of immigrant social interest after 1970, reflecting the appearance of public support for the development of educational and aged care capacities.

It is important to note that patterns of development differ among ethnic groups in Sydney. Some key points are that:

- European immigrants built over 90% of all leisure capacities;
- all day schools and the majority of childcare centres were developed by European (Mediterranean) and Muslim immigrants;
- the development of places of worship is spread across previously non-existing religious denominations;
- language and culturally specific Catholic churches have been developed despite the long tradition of an Australian/Irish-dominant local Roman Catholic Church;
- Asian and Pacific Island Christian communities were involved primarily in the development of places of worship; and
- non-European Christians, Buddhists, Hindus and Muslims played a major role in the development of places of worship during the last two decades of the century.

Ethnic communal places are spatially distributed right across the metropolitan area of Sydney. Although many postwar European settlers have moved away from their first inner-city residences, they maintain ties to communal spaces developed in these areas, with these sites forming a reminder of the beginning of their lives in a new country. The movement of individuals out of the centre was primarily determined by factors such as the availability of property, accessibility and price. The proximity to railway stations has been an important influence behind many developments. Only a few cases of development in particular areas were as a direct result of governmental influences (that is, through the long-term lease of land, the initial lease and later sale of land, or the sale of land at a low price).

For the most part, communal places in Sydney centre consist of individual buildings, but in some instances they form a cluster of such structures, usually along a main railway line or within a neighbourhood. In some suburbs, ethnically diverse communal places are concentrated within a very small area, well within walking distance. Nevertheless, only two clusters in Sydney could be considered to be mono-ethnic and only two such concentrations could be considered as mono-functional – one with five social clubs situated around a football field, the other comprising seven places of worship belonging to different religious denominations and ethnic groups, but all within walking distance. The other 15 clusters, widely dispersed throughout the metropolitan area, have diverse densities of ethnic communal content.

Voluntary participation

To develop communal places immigrants rely primarily on their own voluntary input of time, skills, energy and on various material contributions. These collective acts enhance empowerment, community satisfaction and create new social capital that further acts to expand the communal life of the immigrant community. The resulting places constitute a major element of ethnic institutional completeness[7], but their significance often extends beyond ethnic boundaries to impact on the local environment and transnational social space more generally (Smith and Guarnizo, 1998). The processes involved in these voluntary collective acts can be briefly illustrated through two case studies – the Italian Club *Marconi* and the Lao *Wat Phrayortkeo*.

This grassroots development has been characterised by significant voluntary involvement of people at diverse stages of the organisation's life and at diverse hierarchical levels. *Wat Phrayortkeo* represents a communal effort where there are few, if any, 'free riders' (Coleman, 1990). While such contributions are rarely registered and identified, many communal places were erected by voluntary physical labour, so minimising financial expenditure[8]. At *Wat Phrayortkeo*, people contributed not only their physical and creative labour but also material resources. They cleared the land, cleaned and laid bricks, cooked meals, participated in committees, taught languages and religion and joined in diverse social and religious activities. Individuals were able to volunteer not only their practical skills and finances, but also to express their leadership abilities and organisational and business acumen. The contemporary construction of ethnic educational and aged care

Plate 12.1: Christina Lounge

Plate 12.2: Club Marconi

Club *Marconi*

The first Italian gardeners settled in the western Sydney rural suburbs before the Second World War; however, large-scale immigration of Italian settlers did not occur until the postwar period. At this time, Italian immigrants had no familiar space of their own in which they could socialise, have a glass of wine, play bocce or football. As a consequence, two Italian brothers offered eight acres of land to the community at a price of £3,500, but on delayed payment. The first 100 members, including some Anglo neighbours, raised £5,000 to start the club, constructing the first building in 1958. A further addition, the Christina lounge, was built in 1962. Following the purchase of additional blocks of land, diverse social and recreational premises were also developed to meet the growing needs of its 23,000 members. This included a football stadium for 12,000 spectators, parking for 1,800 cars, tennis grounds, a magnificent multifunctional indoor *Boccedromo* and childcare facilities. While the club mainly supports traditional Italian recreational activities, it also supports netball and was one of the first clubs to establish female membership. Having grown from a small Italian communal association, Marconi is now a meeting place for many local associations, and is now a major, professionally managed institution in western Sydney. It stands as a recognisable feature of the urban landscape and represents a unique cultural space developed to meet the recreational needs of the Italian diaspora. While its development is now wholly based on support from financial institutions, at times of crisis its members, and many individuals who are not of Italian background, still come forward to provide crucial support.

Wat Phrayortkeo

Arriving with other South-East Asian refugees in 1976, Lao refugees had no governmental or institutional support in Australia. They invited the first Buddhist monk from Paris in 1984, collected money and purchased a house for community meetings in 1985. In early 1993 a temple, *Wat Phrayortkeo*, and residence were built in Bonnyrigg, a semi-industrial suburb of western Sydney. The block of land was acquired on a long-term lease from the state government, with financial support from the federal government. A new community hall and cultural centre was later built through voluntary labour and donations given by this small community. *Wat Phrayortkeo* provides a cultural home to the Lao community and provides a site for communal festivities such as the Lao New Year celebrations. However, it is also a place that helps to define the cultural texture of the diverse city of Fairfield. As Map 12.1 indicates, together with other nodes in the Bonnyrigg cultural cluster (ranging from the Assyrian Club *Nineveh*, the Croatian Club *Jadran-Hajduk*, the Hungarian *Magyar* Club, to the Khmer and Vietnamese Buddhist temples, to name but a few) *Wat Phrayortkeo* contributes to a fascinating cultural experience of Sydney.

Map 12.1: Locations of ethnic communal places: Cluster Bonnyrigg (2000)

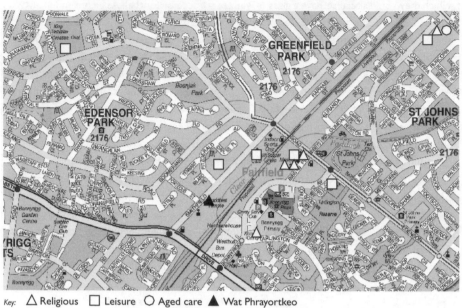

Key: △ Religious   ▢ Leisure   ○ Aged care   ▲ Wat Phrayortkeo

Source: UBD Sydney 2001 Street Directory on CD-ROM, Sydney, Universal Press

places, however, and even of some clubs and places of worship has now mostly phased out volunteer input. The development of education and aged care places, in particular, are partly financed by the authorities and as such require construction and management according to government-stipulated requirements.

Investment

To establish these communal spaces, immigrants had to turn to their own resources, with particular emphasis placed on voluntary material contributions at the expense of household consumption and savings. In financial terms, the investment of Sydney's ethnic communities in communal spaces is estimated to be over a billion Australian dollars during this 50-year period (see Table 12.4). However, this financial estimate only partly records the full extent of material involvement by many thousands of immigrants.

Although immigrant collectives initiated the development of educational and aged care facilities, public authorities (state and federal) have provided various forms of direct and indirect assistance, including capital investment and financing part of the current expenditure since the 1980s. Public sources supported the development of schools/childcare and aged care places with an estimated 17% and 31% of investment respectively (Lalich, 2004). The estimated public financial involvement in ethnic community capital development, together with very limited overseas public and private funding, amounted to around 13% of the total

Table 12.4: Ethnic communal places: estimated total investment, by type and periods, Sydney, 1950-2000 (%, A$'000s, 2000=100)

Type/period	1950-60	1961-70	1971-80	1981-90	1991-2000	Total = 100
Religious	18.88	22.18	15.28	23.41	20.25	338,926
Leisure[a]	19.39	27.19	23.89	22.62	6.91	215,466
Education[b]	...	11.00	20.60	54.10	24.30	147,394
Aged care	16.07	23.29	6.39	25.76	28.49	224,110
Total ('000s)	141,773	187,408	148,013	265,472	183,230	925,896
Decade (%)[c]	15.31	20.24	15.99	28.67	19.79	100.00

Notes: [a] includes sports facilities; [b] includes childcare, dayschools and tertiary institutions; [c] % by decade of period 1950-2000.

Source: Lalich (2004)

investment of nearly a billion dollars over the 1950–2000 period. On the other hand, many organisations experienced difficulties in securing bank loans, encountered unfriendly neighbours and inflexible local councils, dissipating energy and resources on court litigations (Dunn, 2001).

The collective actions and consequent investment undertaken by Sydney's ethnic communities were arguably the only way to satisfy their perceived needs, to enable pursuit of a 'normal life' (Jamrozik, 1983). The diversity of communal space in the city today reflects the diversity of collectively perceived needs, as well as the variability of available resources, local constraints and the impact of government strategies ranging from assimilation policy to the provision of active support. The personal sacrifice, financial investment and voluntary contribution of time inherent to communal spaces is compensated by their social utility, and the potential to facilitate empowerment in the new environment. This investment facilitated the realisation of a communal intent: the provision of diverse services to meet the needs of ethnic community members.

The intensity of a newly established field of social interaction is best observed in established functions and activities that take place at or from these places. As ethnic organisations respond to changes in society and to the perceptions of communal needs, many organisations claim more than one function. Furthermore, ethnic communal places provide the setting for more than 5,500 estimated diverse activities, thereby satisfying the different needs of many Sydney residents. This is perhaps the best description of the social value and social capital inherent to such places.

Immigrants' volunteer contributions are typically a key feature in all stages of the life cycle of ethnic communal organisations, whether expressed through work, consumption or financial and other material contributions. For many small organisations, such contributions are central to their existence and, in some cases, form the sole source of income and survival. Today, over 4,800 people are employed by those organisations managing ethnic communal places in Sydney, providing employment opportunities to many people with specific language and other skills.

The extent of volunteer participation, although of paramount importance at all stages of the organisational life cycle (from initial deliberations and voluntary physical labour input to current management and everyday assistance), is probably the most difficult aspect of development to be assessed, due to the incomplete nature of basic records and data, and more general difficulties in estimating the value of volunteer input in Australian society (Ironmonger, 2000; Lyons, 2001). The ethnic organisations in this survey registered at least 17,150 regular volunteers at the time of research. If the reported lower estimate of national weekly participation of approximately 2.3 hours per volunteer (Lyons, 1994; Ironmonger, 2000) is applied to these 17,150 volunteers, it can be estimated that they, alone, voluntarily contributed at least 2.1 million hours in the year 2000 (Lalich, 2004).

Respondent organisations also claim that over 320,000 people regularly participated in the diverse activities offered within their communal places. However, as some participants frequently appear in multiple roles and at different places, such an estimate necessarily has its limitations. Still, even the conservative estimate based on developed user capacity of 183,000 places at any given time indicates that one fifth of all immigrants from a non-English speaking background in Sydney can, at any time, access a voluntary developed communal place for a specific purpose.

Conclusion

The voluntary development of ethnic communal places in Sydney reflects the successful transfer of immigrant cultures, customs and lifestyle to a new city. The presence of such places in the city landscape is an important signifier of immigrant involvement in urban changes and in the provision of social and welfare services. Alongside other forms of ethnic involvement in city life, ethnic communal places form a permanent indicator of the growth of Sydney from a colonial outpost with inadequate public space and semi-rural suburbs to a global and multicultural city (Powell, 1993; Burnley, 2000).

Ethnic communal spaces have arisen as a result of fragmented collective action, undertaken with the aim of satisfying unmet human and cultural needs within immigrant communities. They have been primarily realised through voluntary contributions of labour, time and money. As a product of immigrants' goodwill and voluntary action during the difficult years of settlement, they are clearly differentiated from other forms of investment in social and urban infrastructure. Although development patterns differ in specific cases, in the early postwar period these communal places typically developed autonomously through individual contributions, without always enjoying governmental support. While many organisations encountered various impediments during this process, the subsequent provision of public support facilitated the development of educational and aged care facilities and acted to secure continuity of the required level of service.

Through voluntary collective action, immigrant communities have been able to enrich the social, cultural, religious and sporting life of many of the old and new suburban areas of Sydney, creating signifiers of cultural diversity in the process. The resulting communal sites – rooted in voluntary action, self-reliance and mutual help of less privileged community segments – also often have a significance that transcends their initial ethnic, collective and suburban limits. As the efforts of people who initially arrived on the now forgotten steamships and refugee boats in the mid-20th century, these ethnic communal spaces are now central to the cosmopolitan vibrancy of contemporary Sydney.

Notes

[1] For the purposes of this chapter, voluntary activity is understood to be activity that is undertaken by an individual of his or her own free will, of benefit to the wider community and organised through a not-for-profit organisation (Cordingley, 2000; Lyons, 2001).

[2] In the Australian context, 'ethnic' indicates first or second generation immigrants of non-English speaking background or origin (Martin, 1981). In this chapter, the term *ethnic* is often used interchangeably with the term *immigrant*.

[3] There is a diverse literature on the importance of migrant organisations, including: Park (1967); Baureiss (1982); Rex et al (1987); Rex (1994); Jupp (1991).

[4] Among many other sources analysing major features of the postwar Australian immigration experience are: Viviani (1984); Collins (1991); Cutts (1991); Kunz (1988); Coughlan and McNamara (1997); Jupp (2001, 2002).

[5] Although immigration of Orthodox, Muslim and Buddhist believers to Sydney occurred in the 19th century, they were barely recorded in the 1947 statistics due to the entry restrictions.

[6] Football is, in Australian terminology, *soccer*. Data illustrate the predominance of immigrant organised soccer clubs (players were not segregated, and many local born people joined these clubs) in the Sydney Championships in the 1950s and 1960s when rare clubs had names of local Sydney origin. In the Sydney First Division in 1967 Pan Hellenic teams competed from Hakoah, Prague, Apia, Polonia, Yugal, Croatia, St George-Budapest, Melita Eagles and Manly, a local beach suburb (Korban, 1994).

[7] Institutional completeness is used by Breton (1964) to indicate the extent of organisational development among ethnic communities, including the development of various religious, communal, commercial and media organisations; however, only some appropriate their own property.

[8] In some instances, voluntary work was registered during the construction of ethnic communal places. Examples include the construction of the Russian Orthodox *Archangel*

Michael Church (2,670 donated hours registered between 1959 and 1965); the Macedonian Orthodox church, *St Petka*, with at least 597 voluntary work days in addition to contracted labour during four months of construction in 1977 (Cirevski, 1999). Also, Kalinski (1985) notes that the Polish House in nearby Maitland was built in 1978 for 64,000 dollars, although the real cost was 120,000 dollars. Local brickworks gave 9,000 bricks free of charge, roofing was bought for 1,000 instead of 3,000 dollars, while 12,000 dollars and 8,500 hours were donated by dozens of people.

References

ABS (Australian Bureau of Statistics) (2001) *Clib 2001 Census Statistics*, Canberra: ABS.

APIC (Australian Population and Immigration Council) (1977) *Immigration Policy and Australia's Population, A Green Paper*, Canberra: Australian Government Printing Services (AGPS).

Baureiss, G. (1982) 'Towards a Theory of Ethnic Organisations', *Canadian Ethnic Studies*, vol 14, no 2, pp 21-42.

Bourdieu, P. (1993) *Sociology in Question*, London: Sage Publications.

Breton, R. (1964) 'Institutional Completeness of Ethnic Communities and the Personal Relations of Immigrants', *American Journal of Sociology*, vol 70, no 2, pp 193-205.

Burnley, I.H. (ed) (1974) *Urbanization in Australia: The Postwar Experience*, Cambridge: Cambridge University Press.

Burnley, I.H. (1976) *Social Environment: A Population and Social Geography of Australia*, Sydney: McGraw Hill.

Burnley, I.H. (2000) 'Diversity and Difference: Immigration and the Multicultural City', in J. Connell (ed) *Sydney*, Melbourne: Oxford University Press, pp 244-72.

Burnley, I.H. (2001) *The Impact of Immigration on Australia: A Demographic Approach*, Melbourne: Oxford University Press.

Burnley, I.H., Murphy, P. and Fagan, R. (1997) *Immigration and Australian Cities*, Sydney: The Federation Press.

Caldwell, G. (1987) 'Leisure', in S. Encel and M. Berry (eds) *Selected Readings in Australian Society: An Anthology*, Melbourne: Longman Cheshire, pp 279-310.

Cirevski, K. (1999) *Makedoncite vo Novata Tatkovina*, Sydney.

Coleman, J.S. (1990) *Foundations of Social Theory*, Cambridge, MA: Belknap, Harvard University Press.

Collins, J. (1984) 'Immigration and Class', in G. Bottomley and M. de Lepervanche (eds) *Ethnicity, Class and Gender in Australia*, Sydney: Allen & Unwin, pp 1-27.

Collins, J. (1991) *Migrant Hands in a Distant Land – Australia's Post-war Immigration*, Sydney: Pluto Press.

Connell, J. (ed) (2000) *Sydney: The Emergence of a World City*, Melbourne: Oxford University Press.

Cordingley, S. (2000) 'The Definition and Principles of Volunteering', in J. Warburton and M. Oppenheimer (eds) *Volunteers and Volunteering*, Sydney: The Federation Press, pp 73–82.

Coughlan, J.E. and McNamara, D.J. (eds) (1997) *Asians in Australia: Patterns of Migration and Settlement*, Melbourne: Macmillan.

Cox, D. (1987) *Migration and Welfare: An Australian Perspective*, Sydney: Prentice Hall.

Creswell, T. (1996) *In Place Out of Place: Geography, Ideology and Transgression*, Minneapolis, MS: University of Minnesota Press.

Cutts, L. (1991) *Immigration and Local Government Budgets*, Canberra: BIR/AGPS.

Dunn, K. (2001) 'Representations of Islam in the Politics of Mosque Development in Sydney', *Tijdschrift voor Economische en Soziale Geografie*, vol 92, no 3, pp 291–308.

Durkheim, E. (1964) *The Division of Labor in Society*, New York, NY: The Free Press.

EAC NSE (Ethnic Affairs Commission New South Wales) (1998) *The People of New South Wales: Statistics from the 1996 Census*, Sydney: New South Wales Government.

Galbally, F. (1978) *Migrant Services and Programs: Report of the Review of Post-Arrival Programs and Services for Migrants*, Canberra: AGPS.

Hage, G. (1998) *White Nation: Fantasies of White Supremacy in a Multicultural Society*, Sydney: Pluto Press.

Hechter, M., Friedman, D. and Appelbaum, M. (1982) 'A Theory of Ethnic Collective Action', *International Migration Review*, vol 16, no 2, pp 412–34.

Ironmonger, D. (2000) 'Measuring Volunteering in Economic Terms', in J. Warburton and M. Oppenheimer (eds) *Volunteers and Volunteering*, Sydney: The Federation Press, pp 56–72.

Jamrozik, A. (1983) *The New Polish Immigrants: A Quest for Normal Life*, Sydney: Polish Task Force/EAC NSW.

Jupp, J. (1990) *Ghettoes, Tribes and Prophets*, Canberra: OMA.

Jupp, J. (1991) *Immigration, Australian Retrospectives*, Sydney: Sydney University Press.

Jupp, J. (ed) (2001) *The Australian People: An Encyclopedia of the Nation, Its People and their Origins*, Melbourne: Cambridge University Press.

Jupp, J. (2002) *From White Australia to Woomera; The Story of Australian Immigration*, Melbourne: Cambridge University Press.

Kalinski, M. (1985) *The Poles in Australia*, Melbourne: Australasian Educational Press.

Korban, R. (1994) *40 Lat Klubu Sportowego – Polonia*, Sydney.

Kraus, P. (1994) *A New Australian, A New Australia*, Sydney: The Federation Press.

Kunz, E.F. (1988) *Displaced Persons: Calwell's New Australians*, Sydney: The ANU Press.

Lalich, W. (2004) 'Ethnic Community Capital: The Development of Ethnic Social Infrastructure in Sydney', Unpublished PhD thesis, Sydney: University of Technology Sydney.

Lewis, F.W. (1978) *The Myth of the Universal Church*, Canberra: ANU Press.

Lyons, M. (1994) *Australia's Nonprofit Sector*, Working Paper Series, No 13, Sydney: University of Technology Sydney/CACOM.

Lyons, M. (2001) *Third Sector: The Contribution of Nonprofit and Cooperative Enterprises in Australia*, Sydney: Allen & Unwin.

Martin, J. (1978) *The Migrant Presence*, Sydney: Allen & Unwin.

Martin, J. (1981) 'Ethnic Pluralism and Identity', in S. Encel (ed) *The Ethnic Dimension*, Sydney: Allen & Unwin.

Mosely, P.A., Cashman, R., O'Hara, J. and Weatherburn, H. (eds) (1997) *Sporting Immigrants: Sport and Ethnicity in Australia*, Sydney: Walla Walla Press.

NMAC (National Multicultural Advisory Council) (1995) *Multicultural Australia: The Next Steps Towards and Beyond 2000*, Canberra: NMAC/AGPS, vol 1, cat no 95.0571 7.

NMAC (1997) *Multicultural Australia: The Way Forward*, Canberra: NMAC/AGPS.

OMA (Office of Multicultural Affairs) (1994) *Achieving Access and Equity*, Canberra: AGPS.

Olson, M. (1965) *The Logic of Collective Action*, Cambridge, MA: Harvard University Press.

Park, R.E. (1967) *On Social Control and Collective Behaviour: Selected Papers*, edited by R.H. Turner, Chicago, IL: University of Chicago Press.

Parsons, T. and Shils, E. (eds) (1962) *Towards a General Theory of Action, Theoretical Foundations for Social Sciences*, New York, NY: Harper and Row.

Patrikareas, T. (2000) *Antipodean Trilogy: The Promised Woman*, Melbourne: Royal Melbourne Institute of Technology/Greek-Australian Archive Publications.

Portes, A. (ed) (1995) *The Economic Sociology of Immigration: Essays on Networks, Ethnicity, and Entrepreneurship*, New York, NY: Russell Sage Foundation.

Powell, D. (1993) *Out West, Perceptions of Sydney's Western Suburbs*, Sydney: Allen & Unwin.

Price, C. (ed) (1979). *Australian immigration: A bibliography and digest, No 4*, Canberra: ANU, Department of Demography: A, pp 92-5.

Price, C. and Pyne, P. (1977) 'The Immigrants', in A.F. Davies, S. Encel and M.J. Berry (eds) *Australian Society: A Sociological Introduction*, Melbourne: Longman Chesire, pp 331-55.

Putnam, R.D. (1993) *Making Democracy Work: Civic Traditions in Modern Italy*, Princeton, NY: Princeton University Press.

Rex, J. (1994) 'Ethnic Mobilisation in Multi-Cultural Societies', in J. Rex and B. Drury (eds) *Ethnic Mobilization in a Multi-Cultural Europe*, Aldershot: Ashgate, pp 3-12.

Rex, J., Joly, D. and Wilpert, C. (eds) (1987) *Immigrant Associations in Europe*, Aldershot: Gower/European Science Foundation.

Rutland, S. (1997) *Edge of the Diaspora: Two centuries of Jewish Settlement in Australia*, Sydney: Brandl & Schlesinger.

Sant, M. and Waitt, G. (2000) 'Sydney: All Day Long, All Night Long', in J. Connell (ed) *Sydney*, Melbourne: Oxford University Press, pp 189–221.

Sayer, M. and Nowra, L. (eds) (2000) *In the Gutter... Looking at the Stars*, Sydney: Random House.

Smith, M.P. and Guarnizo, L.E. (eds) (1998) *Transnationalism from below*, New Brunswick, NJ: Transaction.

Spearritt, P. (1978) *Sydney since the Twenties*, Sydney: Hale and Iremonger.

Spearritt, P. (2000) *Sydney's Century*, Sydney: UNSW Press.

Thomas, M. (1999) *Dreams in the Shadows: Vietnamese-Australian Lives in Transition*, Sydney: Allen & Unwin.

Unikoski, R. (1978) *Communal Endeavours: Ethnic Organisations in Melbourne*, Canberra: The ANU Press.

Viviani, N. (1984) *The Long Journey: Vietnamese Migration and Settlement in Australia*, Melbourne: Melbourne University Press.

Weil, S. (1978) *The Need for Roots*, London: Routledge.

Zukin, S. (1992) 'Postmodern Urban Landscape: Mapping Culture and Power', in S. Lash and J. Friedman (eds) *Modernity and Identity*, Oxford: Blackwell, pp 221–47.

THIRTEEN

The voluntary spaces of charity shops: workplaces or domestic spaces?

Liz Parsons

Introduction

The UK government has recently turned attention towards the voluntary sector and volunteering is now high on the social policy agenda. The value of volunteers has been recognised primarily as a means of providing services in the emerging mixed economy of welfare, but also in less concrete terms as contributing to an active and participatory society (Davis Smith, 1998). A number of authors have discussed the links between volunteering and active citizenship (Kearns, 1995; Turner, 2001), but some have recently argued that while the government is encouraging and supporting volunteering, changes in policy and regulatory procedures could actually be discouraging it (for example, Milligan and Fyfe, 2005). Authors have argued strongly that the voluntary sector is being transformed by the increasing encroachment of new managerial concepts and tools (Bondi, 2005; Fyfe, 2005), for example, the Labour government voluntary sector compacts launched in 1998, which require new standards, guidelines and reporting mechanisms for voluntary organisations (Home Office, 1998). The attendant push towards increasing professionalism and bureaucratisation faced by these organisations is placing pressures on their relationships with both volunteers and the wider community. This chapter explores these changing relationships in the context of charity shops in contemporary Britain.

This chapter also aims to contribute to a wider project of exploring the spatial dimensions of voluntarism. It takes on a perspective that acknowledges that spaces are brought into being, negotiated and interpreted through social practices and discourses. An exploration of the organisational spaces of charity shops on these terms views them as key sites where government policy, public discourse and volunteer experiences come together and are transformed. As such the chapter begins with a consideration of recent volunteer-focused government policies. It then examines recent changes within the charity retail sector, focusing in particular on the (re)formation of the spaces of charity shops themselves. There has been a tendency for what were once relatively informal (domestic) sites of voluntary activity to be recast as professional, work-inflected sites. The chapter then focuses on the volunteers' experiences and interpretations of volunteering in these evolving environments. The core of volunteers tends to value the informal 'domestic' character of these spaces and prioritise the social benefits of volunteering. Such experiences suggest that government discourses around volunteering as a form of active citizenship may be problematic.

Volunteering as 'active citizenship'

Recent government initiatives have begun to harness voluntary activity in new ways. While voluntary action has been seen as a key constituent of citizenship since the Second World War, as elaborated in Beveridge's *Voluntary Action* (1948), the links between volunteering and formal employment have never been as explicit as they now are. The New Deal for the Unemployed, which was rolled out across the UK in 1998, is a good example. This programme targets young people aged 18-24 who are in receipt of Jobseeker's Allowance (JSA), aiming to improve their long-term employability and ultimately to match them with jobs. It begins with a gateway where jobseeking advice and support is offered for up to four weeks. At the end of this period, if the individual has not found an unsubsidised job, they are offered one of four options: (1) a subsidised job; (2) full-time education and training; (3) work with a voluntary sector organisation; and (4) work with an environmental task force. Each option lasts for six months, apart from the full-time education and training option, which can last for up to 12 months. Failure to take up an option may lead to the loss of benefit, such that there is therefore an element of coercion. At the end of December 2004, 10,570 young people were participating in the job training aspects of the scheme (options 2, 3 or 4) and of these 2,440 (23%) were working with a voluntary sector organisation (Department for Work and Pensions, National Statistics website).

In the late 1990s New Labour launched their *Millennium Volunteers* initiative, and this has seen the establishment of a range of projects designed to promote volunteering among young people. In England by the end of March 2002 53,768 young people had started as Millennium Volunteers (separate arrangements exist in Wales, Scotland and Northern Ireland) (Institute for Volunteering Research, 2002). A speech by the then Home Secretary, David Blunkett, at the National Council for Voluntary Organisations (NCVO) conference in 2001 clearly demonstrated Labour's commitment to volunteering as a form of active citizenship. Blunkett also emphasised the perceived potential of volunteering in the 'local community' for countering social exclusion among young people:

> Millennium Volunteers is offering thousands of young people who have often felt isolated from wider society a way of channelling their energies into something positive. New research shows that volunteers are carrying out crucial local work – such as setting up youth and drugs projects, tackling racism, helping younger children with reading, conservation and a range of cultural activities. That first step towards

active citizenship is enormously important. For some it will be the start of a journey that sees them become key figures in local communities. (David Blunkett, NCVO Annual Conference, February 2001)

New Labour have placed a continued emphasis on the social benefits of voluntary action, emphasising volunteering as having positive transformative powers in promoting both economic development and social cohesion. 'The Compact Code of Volunteering Good Practice', which was launched in October 2005 and forms an element of the original 1998 government voluntary sector compact, states that:

> Volunteering is a powerful force for change, both for those who volunteer and for the wider community. Volunteers offer support, expertise and innovation to any organisation, enhancing impact and adding value. (Home Office, 2005, section 3.2)

Authors have argued that such discourse is indicative of broader attempts to incorporate the voluntary sector into a hegemonic neoliberal model (Bondi, 2005; Fyfe, 2005; Jenkins, 2005). Jenkins observes: 'a growing sense of the encroachment of neoliberal processes and practices, one associated with purely economic development, into almost every aspect of our lives' (2005, p 613). Such encroachment has had serious consequences for the charity retail sector; on the one hand, the sector has restructured and reorganised in attempts to become increasingly 'professional' but this has also impacted on the role of shops in providing alternative spaces for sociality, belonging and identity construction. These changes to the structure of charity retail organisations and the associated changing nature of charity shops as voluntary spaces are explored below.

Changes in charity retail organisations: the move to professionalise

Over the past 10 years the charity retail sector has experienced a raft of organisational changes moving from a set of locally coordinated operations managed entirely on voluntary effort, to a series of national chains of shops with attendant management hierarchies and increased sets of regulatory policies designed to promote accountability and standardisation. This move to professionalise has been observed by a series of authors (Horne, 1998, 2000; Goodall, 2000a, 2000b; Maddrell, 2000; Gregson et al, 2002; Horne and Maddrell, 2002; Broadbridge and Parsons, 2003a, 2003b; Parsons, 2004). Broadbridge and Parsons (2003a) found that this professionalisation consisted of four interrelated trends: the replacement of volunteer shop managers with paid staff; the introduction of head office management from senior management positions in commercial retail; the centralisation of control and standardisation of policies; and an overall 'trading up' of the shop environment (see also Horne, 2000).

Moves to replace volunteer managers with paid managers in charity shops have been underway for some time. Traditionally, charity shops relied solely on volunteer work teams to manage and run them. Throughout the 1980s and 1990s an increasing number of charities have recognised the potential of charity shops as a fundraising mechanism. In 1992 there were around 3,480 charity shops in the UK, for instance, but by 2003 this number had increased to around 5,860 (Charity Finance, 2003). Charities thus began to introduce paid managers to coordinate and focus their fundraising efforts. In 1995 the average wage bill of British charity retail organisations as a percentage of turnover was 21.8%, but this had grown to 29.3% in 2003 (NGO Finance, 1995; Charity Finance, 2003). The investment and overall belief in the benefits of paying managers are highlighted by a comparison with commercial retailing where the wage budget is typically only between 6.5% and 9.5% of turnover (Broadbridge, 2002).

The payment of managers has been accompanied by a trading up of the shop environment. This has involved standardisation of merchandising and general shop layouts. Other measures have been introduced to both build a corporate brand and encourage customers into the shops. These include the use of new shop fittings and fixtures, the use of campaign advertising posters and corporate logos on shop frontages, bags, staff uniforms and badges. Charities have begun to develop both shop and product branding, 'creating a distinct image in the minds of consumers through their merchandising, shop design, corporate image and own branding' (Mintel, 1997, p 51). Even the smaller charities and local hospice charities are starting to use branding as a way of identifying themselves among other charity shops. Probably the most successful brand name is Oxfam, with its distinctive yellow and blue logo. Awareness of this brand is so widespread, that the Oxfam shop is often used as a generic term for 'charity shop'. Other charities have begun to follow suit, redesigning their logos and shop fronts. This branding extends to goods in the shops. Oxfam even brands some of their second-hand goods for instance. 'Origin' labelled clothes are donations that have been selected for their originality or style, aiming to attract a more fashion conscious customer.

One of the biggest drivers of change in the sector has been the employment of senior management 'professionals' who have tended to transfer management practices and policies developed in the for-profit sector across to the charity sector (Broadbridge and Parsons, 2003a; Parsons, 2004). Broadbridge and Parsons (2003a) found in interviews with head office managers that they relied heavily on discourses developed in the for-profit retail sector to describe changes with little or no mention of the strong voluntary cultures that underpin the whole operation. These managers have introduced a number of measures to produce uniformity across the charity retail chain and to maintain tight head office central control on policy making over the shops. This has resulted in the hierarchy of much charity retailing following a similar pattern to many commercial retail chains. It is now usual for operational decisions regarding issues such as store layout, merchandising and in-store promotional materials to be made at head office level.

Thus head offices have been seeking to reposition or recast charity shops in discursive terms as 'charity retail'. Gregson et al (2002, p 1661) explore the specific means through which this is achieved, examining how 'charity retailing has been re-imagined and reworked in head offices and how this is displaced through charity retail chains'. Similarly Goodall (2000b) has also examined the agency of head office staff in shaping understandings of the charity retail operation. In doing so he questions the extent to which managerial cultures and practices applied outside the voluntary sector can be applied to voluntary sector organisations. Indeed, Gregson et al (2002) question the ability of head office staff to effect change at shop floor level, observing that their attempts are significantly hampered by the presence of multiple understandings of charity. They focus on three specific understandings: charity as gift, as acting charitably and as fundraising. In doing so they emphasise the 'tensions, contradictions, juxtapositions, clashes, and ruptures of discourse as these occur within and constitute various charity retail spaces' (2002, p 1662). In this spirit the sections below explore the understandings and experiences of charity shop volunteers of charity retail spaces, examining how and why they are significant in their daily lives and questioning the extent to which broader moves to professionalise such spaces impact on the quality of these volunteers' experiences.

Researching the experiences of volunteers

Discussion of volunteers' experiences of charity shops is informed by a range of research activities in the vicinity of Bristol, UK, during the period 1996 to 2000. At the core of this work was a four-year period of participant observation, centring around working one morning a week as a charity shop volunteer. This work facilitated a broad-based and in-depth understanding of the sector. More specifically, research included a round of focus groups with groups of volunteers from three different charity shops. The three charities were of slightly different organisational sizes and structures. St Peter's Hopsice is a local charity, which operates 38 shops in the greater Bristol area, and these are also overseen by a trading manager at head office. CLIC (Cancer and Leukaemia in Childhood) is a regional charity with its roots in the South West, with 25 shops in the South West region, overseen by a trading manager at head office. Barnardo's is typical of a large national charity and operates 330 shops across the UK, with a series of area, regional and head office managers. All three charities employed paid managers at store level who oversee teams of volunteer assistants.

The first focus group, in a St Peter's Hospice charity shop, consisted of four volunteers, all of whom were women in their late sixties and early seventies. The second group, from a CLIC charity shop, consisted of five volunteers: three women in their late fifties and early sixties and a couple in their thirties. The third group, in a Barnardo's charity shop, consisted of four volunteers, all of whom were women in their late fifties and early sixties. We met for an hour in the backrooms of the charity shops where they worked and discussed their motivations and experiences of volunteering.

Creating spaces of charity retail: the experiences of volunteers

The focus groups highlighted a series of overlapping and conflicting experiences of the voluntary spaces of charity shops, including the importance of the shops in creating spaces for sociality and belonging in the local community, spaces for the expression of social concern and spaces which offer an important alternative to paid work environments. Each of these constructions of charity retail spaces are explored below. The volunteers' names have been replaced with pseudonyms to retain a degree of anonymity.

Before exploring the focus group findings it is worth outlining the findings of previous studies on charity shop volunteers. These studies highlight in particular the importance of these spaces in countering social exclusion, especially for elderly and retired women. Broadbridge and Horne's (1994) survey of 810 volunteers in a chain of charity shops in Scotland found that two thirds of these volunteers were retired, and 98% were female. The picture of the charity shop volunteer as an older, retired woman is also borne out by Whithear's (1999) survey of 74 volunteers in Ruislip (a small town 30 miles west of London in England) and Maddrell's (2000) study of 136 volunteers from 17 shops in the Oxford area in England. In both cases over 80% of volunteers were female and 70% over 60 years of age.

Spaces of sociality and belonging

It has been argued that voluntary welfare environments – whether oriented around service provision or mutual support – allow volunteers a greater freedom to explore and develop social relationships than workplaces organised along more formal lines (Pearce, 1993). This is indeed the case in charity shops, as Whithear's (1999) research noted there is often a 'club-like' atmosphere in charity shops. For some of the volunteers I talked to and worked alongside, it was certainly clear that their voluntary work provided an important source of social contact. The following excerpt is illustrative of this perspective:

> Dorothy (Barnardo's): 'I think working with people is the thing that I like in a way and I think you've got the, both the aspects which Anita said, of the other volunteers and people in the shop you're working with and the people who come in.'
>
> Anita: 'It's companionship.'

The relatively informal and relaxed atmosphere in charity shops makes it easy to build up relationships and make friends in the shops. As the following extract from a focus group illustrates, volunteering in a team encourages camaraderie:

> Anita (Barnardo's): 'And then there are those, that couple that we avoid don't we? [laughs]'

> Pauline: 'Oh yes, you get that in every business don't you? [laughs]'

> Anita: 'And though they find things that are really bargains, they still want to knock you down a bit.'

> Pauline: 'Yes, though you always get that type of customer don't you.'

> Anita: 'I can think of one lady in particular.... I have disappeared when I've seen her coming through the door and I know Pauline has as well [laughs]. They always want it reduced, they find a little hole somewhere. [laughs]'

These spaces provide a feeling of togetherness that is encouraged by working together for a common cause. Interestingly, the declared motivations for this charitable behaviour may include helping 'needy' customers as well as raising funds for the parent charity. In my research, feelings of belonging and inclusion were at times linked to this sense of assisting a 'needy other', here, the customer:

> Author: 'What do you get out of volunteering?'

> Elaine (Barnardo's): 'I suppose a certain amount of personal satisfaction. You feel you're helping, you're doing some good and helping to contribute. Again it's rather nice to meet friends. We've made friends haven't we? Since we've been here.'

> All: 'Yes.'

> Elaine: 'And there's that feeling of togetherness I suppose, and we also have a laugh as well. You get to know people and definitely helping some that really are needy people that come in.'

Elaine comments that she is 'helping to contribute', which suggests that she views her volunteer work as contributing to a bigger project or wider cause. Volunteers typically highlighted their work as making them feel involved and included in something that extends beyond their usual social sphere.

Spaces for the expression of social concern

Charity shops offer spaces for belonging, but they are also spaces that foster and encourage expressions of altruism. That is, spaces in which 'acting charitably' both with respect to a distant other (the beneficiaries of the charity's work) and a more immediate other (fellow volunteers and customers), are prioritised by volunteers.

Many volunteers said that they were motivated to 'give something back'. In this sense volunteering could be said to be a demonstration of reciprocity. This reciprocity appears to be largely undirected though, as volunteers rarely specified what they were giving back or to whom. This sentiment of wanting to give something back might thus be interpreted in a more general sense as a form of philanthropy. Sheard (1995, p 122) suggests that:

> Volunteering clearly taps into a natural urge which people have to help their fellow citizens. At the same time, it enables individuals to place boundaries around their involvement, and thus provides a 'safe' and structured outlet for their altruism and social concern.

As two respondents from CLIC put it:

> Jan (CLIC): 'I just like helping out other people.'

> Amy: 'That's it, that's the bottom line. No matter what you do and which way you do it, it's all the same. Comes out in the end, don't it.'

This comment by Amy highlights that the specific form of charitable activity is not necessarily of primary importance to volunteers. What is important to them is the benefit to others, however unspecified these others may be. Volunteers typically placed significant emphasis on meeting the needs of others. The shops were seen as providing cheap clothing for people on low incomes, for instance, with volunteers' altruism and social concern often extending to the shop customers:

> Pauline (Barnardo's): 'Take Daisy for example.'

> Anita: 'Oh yes.'

> Pauline: 'Eighty-nine isn't she, and she goes around the charity shops trying to look for things, and she isn't very well off is she? [...] I know in next door, because I only went in there the other day, and she was saying to the manager "I'm looking for a cardigan".'

> Anita: 'She's always looking for a cardigan.'

Pauline:'When she comes in here we look around for her, you know. We know more or less what she likes and she's chuffed to bits if she finds something useful like that. I think that's something which we like about the charity shop isn't it?'

All: 'Yes.'

Pauline:'That a person like that can find a little bargain. And of course the manager here and in the next shop – in the other shop – I noticed they reduce it a bit for her, which is a good thing, I think so.'

Some volunteers couched their desire to 'give something back' in terms of their underlying beliefs and ideologies. The relationship between religion and voluntary activity has been researched in a range of contexts. Bales suggests that 'people are moved to volunteer for several possible reasons tied to their overt social background and less visible psychological orientations and attitudes' (1996, p 212). One volunteer made direct reference to her beliefs when explaining her commitment to volunteering:

Janice (St Peter's Hospice):'Another reason why I work here is because I believe it's doing God's work, helping the unprivileged: you know people who can't afford clothes and things like that you know.'

Commentators have observed that religious involvement does help to explain engagement in voluntary work particularly within church-related organisations where volunteers are drawn in both through social networks and organisational identities (Park and Smith, 2000; Becker and Dhingra, 2001). Bales (1996) found that those individuals with some involvement with an organisation, such as receiving services or having friends in it, were more likely to volunteer. Hospice charities consequently rarely have problems recruiting and retaining volunteers. As one respondent noted:

Tracey (St Peter's Hospice): 'When you go in and out of there and you realise what wonderful work they do, it just stays with you, you know. You think *well, it must continue.*'

In their survey of charity shop volunteers, Horne and Broadbridge (1994) found that nearly half of their respondents (48%) had a personal affiliation with the cause of the charity, while a further quarter believed the mission of the charity to be a worthwhile cause. They also suggested that motives for volunteering may be based on empathy, as the charity that they researched sought to assist the elderly and also attracted elderly volunteers.

Domestic spaces: an alternative to workplaces?

Many of the volunteers contrasted their experiences of voluntary work with previous paid work, often referring to the relative informality and relaxed familiarity of the space of the charity shop. This relaxed familiarity combined with the practices of washing, steaming and ironing of clothing in preparation for sale allows parallels to be drawn between the spaces of charity shops and those of the domestic sphere. In Gregson et al's (2002) account of the in-store geographies of charity shops they note that the back regions of the shops were seen as relatively private spaces – typically for volunteers only. As well as being spaces where clothes were prepared for sale these back regions of shops also often had a kitchen area, typically used for the making and consumption of copious cups of tea and coffee by volunteers. Of course the strongly gendered make-up of the voluntary workforce reinforces such notions of domesticity:

> Pauline (Barnardo's): 'I suppose one thing I haven't said about, or to do with why I came to the charity shop, I mean I think I'd always previously been in and out of charity shops, always quite enjoyed it and always looked for bargains. I mean I used to find things in sales and used to make my own clothes and that sort of thing…. I'd be in and out of charity shops and I think that's what's made me suddenly think, "well, perhaps I could cope with that. I couldn't go into an ordinary work situation, but maybe I could cope with a charity shop", and I have.'

Pauline contrasts the environment of the charity shop favourably with an 'ordinary work situation'. She associates the space of the shop with a familiarity gained from previous shopping experiences and therefore feels less intimidated by working in this space, suggesting that she could 'cope with a charity shop'. This familiarity means that it has none of the unknown associated with other imagined work situations, in particular those associated with paid employment.

Many people find it difficult to adjust when the structure and routine created by a particular role are removed, be it paid employment or the task of caring for a child or elderly relative. This is especially the case for those who have retired, been made redundant or reached a particular life stage where tasks that previously took up substantial amounts of time and energy have come to an end. As one individual explained when asked why she volunteered, '[my] husband's working, [my] children are grown up'. Certain aspects of volunteering in charity shops make the work quite ideal for those who have not worked for a long time. Working in a team provides a supportive structure and the level of involvement is up to the individual volunteer, from working a few hours a week and undertaking one or two different tasks, to working a full week with responsibility for supervising the shop.

Volunteering in charity shops is thus flexible, with volunteers often able to do as little or as much as they want. The flexibility of working in a team is especially important for those who are elderly and/or whose health is unpredictable, as making a fixed commitment may be difficult. Indeed, volunteering through an organisation provides both structure and stability, and volunteers can reduce their commitment or withdraw it altogether if necessary. As Pauline noted:

> Pauline (Barnardo's): 'And it's different because I've always worked behind a desk and a pile of work and it's still there the next day in the in-tray. Whereas here you say bye–bye and that's it. Half past three you disappear and that's it. And it's quite pleasant and you can forget about it.'

Many volunteers are nervous when starting work in the shops, and for some this may be due to a lack of self-confidence, especially if they have been out of work situations for a long time. In general volunteers felt that the support of paid staff was thus very important, both personally and in their work. Some individuals preferred to work behind the scenes in the shop, preparing stock for the shop floor. Over time, however, many found that volunteering gave them confidence and improved their self-esteem:

> Author: 'Do you find that you've learnt a lot from volunteering here?'

> Tracey (St Peter's Hospice): 'Well I think it's given me a bit more confidence. Because I find, and I did find for many years when I was at home bringing up the family, you lose confidence in yourself and your ability to do things. After I had been home for quite a few years with my family I then got a job. I was well, so scared for ages, but that gave me confidence and then to go out and do something, once I realised I wasn't sort of, as stupid as I thought, I went out and got a job.'

> Maggie: 'I like to be needed. I think that gives you confidence. Having worked with people for thirty–seven years, people's problems, I wanted a break from that. That's why I took early retirement, *but I still needed to be needed, you know.*' (emphasis added)

Conclusion

This research into volunteers in the charity retail sector underlines the continued importance of charity shops in creating spaces for sociality and belonging in the local community, spaces for the expression of social concern and spaces which offer an important alternative to paid work environments. Spaces where those that may traditionally have been marginalised from the workforce have the freedom and support to build up the self-esteem gained from a feeling that they are contributing to a project much bigger than themselves. However, continued changes to the formation of these spaces through discourses and practices of professionalism do question the scope for the organisational spaces of charity shops to continue to act as 'alternative spaces' to traditional workplaces.

Despite broader moves to formalise and professionalise charity retail operations it is clear that charity shops continue to play a pivotal role in encouraging active citizenship. Within the three charity shops examined in Bristol, volunteers' primary interpretation of their work was as a channel for social concern. They also recognised that their relationship with the organisation was a reciprocal one, identifying the social and personally rehabilitative benefits of their work. Interpretations of voluntary work as helping 'needy others' were also evident among the charity shop volunteers. However, these 'needy others' were most often viewed as other volunteers and customers than as the beneficiaries of the parent charity (such as recipients of Oxfam's support in the developing world). This suggests that volunteers' interpretations of their work and the value of this effort are firmly rooted in the actual experience of volunteering. While fundraising is a clear goal of their efforts, the charitable acts they perform towards their fellow volunteers and regular customers provide them with a much more accessible interpretation of their voluntary work.

Volunteers frequently referred to their voluntary work as gainful employment but seldom as a goal-oriented exercise. They also frequently alluded to the personally rehabilitative role of volunteering; this was not necessarily with a view to re-entering paid employment but more simply about building up their confidence and/or enabling them to feel socially useful. This demonstrates a clear difference between using volunteer opportunities as a means of 'keeping in touch' with the world of work or as a way of merely keeping busy and getting out of the house, and using volunteering as a stepping stone into paid employment. The former interpretation of volunteering was dominant and underlines the importance of this activity in countering social exclusion.

Overall, the government appears to view volunteering as another training resource, focusing on what volunteers can gain from their voluntary activity rather than what they can contribute (Zimmeck, 1998). The presence of New Deal (and other) work placements has the potential to dilute the strong volunteer culture in British voluntary sector organisations. One of the documented benefits of voluntary sector service spaces is the genuine freedom they offer to construct relationships outside of profit imperatives (Pearce, 1993). Additionally commentators have argued that training-based voluntary schemes have undoubtedly exacerbated the lack of clarity of the relationship between the 'professional' and the 'volunteer' (Zimmeck, 1998).

To conclude, this discussion has highlighted two key tensions between these volunteers' experiences of the spaces of charity shops and governmental discourse on voluntarism. The first is the informal and localised nature of much voluntary activity, even within formalised environments such as charity shops. As other authors have observed, at present informal modes of voluntary action such as caring for relatives, friends and neighbours remains largely invisible in dominant discourses of active citizenship. In addition this type of activity also remains largely hidden in discussions of volunteering. As Lukka and Ellis (2001) observe, the term volunteering itself is a potentially exclusionary one. They support the use of 'bottom-up' definitions of volunteering such as 'giving', 'sharing' and 'duty', which encompass more fully both the wide scope and type of voluntary activities and the range of social, cultural and political positions from which volunteers come.

Second, the above discussion highlights that more often than not volunteering is non-goal oriented or non-instrumental in ethos. This does not mean that volunteers are unmotivated by the outcomes of their efforts. Indeed many charity shop volunteers 'need to be needed'; it is important that they feel their effort and skills are being put to good use. But Gay's (2000) study of the role of volunteering in improving employability found that formal qualifications figured only very insignificantly as key benefits of voluntary work for unemployed volunteers. Benefits perceived by both the volunteers and the organisations focused around enhancing the person, offering psychological/emotional support and giving volunteers the chance to be part of a team. Giving a sound training for the tasks required and providing a 'work-like' environment did feature, however, as important aspects of volunteering. This raises the question as to what constitutes a 'work-like' environment, and the extent to which voluntary spaces are able to fulfil this role without losing the qualities that attract volunteers and enhance their lives in the first place.

Returning to the question posed in the title of this chapter, as to whether the voluntary spaces of charity shops represent workplaces or domestic spaces, the answer is undoubtedly both. However, for the core of charity shop volunteers, these spaces offer benefits and opportunities more akin to a domestic space as opposed to a traditional workplace environment. The volunteers considered in this study thus prized these spaces as arenas for social interaction, with their voluntary work narrated as an outlet for social caring and concern. This cautions against an over-formalisation of these spaces both through management practices and government policy. At present, the relative insensitivity of government policy to the importance and fragility of often highly localised voluntary cultures has allowed us to proceed too far down the professionalisation path. Indeed, Horne (2000) emphasises the importance of recognising both the local support and strong voluntary cultures that facilitate the continuing existence of charity shops.

References

Bales, K. (1996) 'Measuring the Propensity to Volunteer', *Social Policy and Administration*, vol 30, pp 206-26.

Becker, P.E. and Dhingra, P.H. (2001) 'Religious Involvement and Volunteering', *Sociology of Religion*, vol 62, no 3, pp 315-35.

Beveridge, W. (1948) *Voluntary Action*, London: Allen and Unwin.

Bondi, L. (2005) 'Working the Spaces of Neoliberal Subjectivity: Psychotherapeutic Technologies, Professionalisation and Counselling', *Antipode*, vol 37, no 3, pp 497-514.

Broadbridge, A. (2002) 'Rationalising Retail Employment: A View From the Outside Looking In', *International Journal of Retail and Distribution Management*, vol 30, no 11, pp 536-43.

Broadbridge, A. and Horne, S. (1994) 'Who Volunteers for Charity Retailing and Why', *The Service Industries Journal*, vol 14, pp 421-37.

Broadbridge, A. and Parsons, E. (2003a) 'Still Serving the Community? The Professionalisation of the UK Charity Retail Sector', *International Journal of Retail and Distribution Management*, vol 31, no 8, pp 418-27.

Broadbridge, A. and Parsons, E. (2003b) 'UK Charity Retailing: Managing in a Newly Professionalised Sector', *Journal of Marketing Management*, vol 19, nos 7-8, pp 729-48.

Charity Finance (2003) *Annual Charity Shops Survey*, London: Plaza.

Davis Smith, J. (1998) 'Making a Difference: Can Governments Influence Volunteering?', *Voluntary Action*, vol 1, no 1, pp 7-20.

Department for Work and Pensions, UK government's National Statistics website (www.dwp.gov.uk/asd/ndyp.asp).

Fyfe, N. (2005) 'Making Space for "Neo-communitarianism"? The Third Sector, State and Civil Society in the UK', *Antipode*, vol 37, no 3, pp 536-57.

Gay, P. (2000) *Getting into Work: The Role of Volunteering in Improving Employability*, London: Institute for Volunteering Research.

Goodall, R. (2000a) 'Charity Shops in Sectoral Contexts: The View from the Boardroom', *International Journal of Nonprofit and Voluntary Sector Marketing*, vol 5, no 2, pp 105-12.

Goodall, R. (2000b) 'Organising Cultures: Voluntarism and Professionalism in UK Charity Shops', *Voluntary Action*, vol 3, no 1, pp 43-57.

Gregson, N., Crewe, L. and Brooks, K. (2002) 'Discourse, Displacement and Retail Practice: Some Pointers From the Charity Retail Project', *Environment and Planning A*, vol 34, no 9, pp 1661-83.

Home Office (1998) *Getting It Right Together: Compact on Relations between Government and the Voluntary and Community Sector in England*, London: Home Office.

Home Office (2005) *The Volunteering Compact Code of Good Practice*, London: Home Office.

Horne, S. (1998) 'Charity Shops in the UK', *International Journal of Retail and Distribution Management*, vol 26, no 4, pp 155-61.

Horne, S. (2000) 'The Charity Shop: Purpose and Change', *International Journal of Nonprofit and Voluntary Sector Marketing*, vol 5, no 2, pp 113-24.

Horne, S. and Broadbridge, A. (1994) 'The Charity Shop Volunteer in Scotland: Greatest Asset or Biggest Headache?', *Voluntas*, vol 5, no 2, pp 205-18.

Horne, S. and Maddrell, A. (2002) *Charity Shops, Retailing, Consumption and Society*, London: Routledge.

Institute for Volunteering Research (2002) *UK Wide Evaluation of the Millennium Volunteers Programme*, Nottingham: DfES Publications.

Jenkins, K. (2005) 'No Way Out? Incorporating and Restructuring the Voluntary Sector within Spaces of Neoliberalism', *Antipode*, vol 37, no 3, pp 613-18.

Kearns, A. (1995) 'Active Citizenship and Local Governance: Political and Geographical Dimensions', *Political Geography*, vol 14, no 2, pp 155-75.

Lukka, P. and Ellis, A. (2001) 'An Exclusive Construct? Exploring Different Cultural Concepts of Volunteering', *Voluntary Action*, vol 3, no 3, pp 87-109.

Maddrell, A. (2000) 'You Just Can't Get the Staff these Days: The Challenges and Opportunities of Working with Volunteers in the Charity Shop – An Oxford Case Study', *International Journal of Nonprofit and Voluntary Sector Marketing*, vol 5, no 2, pp 125-39.

Mintel (Marketing Intelligence) (1997) *Charity Shop Retailing*, London: Mintel.

Milligan, C. and Fyfe, N. (2005) 'Preserving Space for Volunteers: Exploring the Links between Voluntary Welfare Organisations, Volunteering and Citizenship', *Urban Studies*, vol 42, no 3, pp 417-34.

NGO Finance (1995) *Annual Charity Shops Survey*, London: Plaza.

Park, J.Z. and Smith, C. (2000) '"To Whom Much Has Been Given…" Religious Capital and Community Voluntarism Among Churchgoing Protestants', *Journal for the Scientific Study of Religion*, vol 39, no 3, pp 272-87.

Parsons, E. (2004) 'Charity Shop Managers in the UK: Becoming More Professional?', *The Journal of Retailing and Consumer Services*, vol 11, no 5, pp 259-68.

Pearce, J.L. (1993) *Volunteers: The Organizational Behaviour of Unpaid Workers*, London: Routledge.

Sheard, J. (1995) 'From Lady Bountiful to Active Citizen: Volunteering and the Voluntary Sector', in J. Davis Smith, C. Rochester and R. Hedley (eds) *An Introduction to the Voluntary Sector*, London: Routledge, pp 114-27.

Turner, B.S. (2001) 'The Erosion of Citizenship', *British Journal of Sociology*, vol 52, no 2, pp 189-210.

Whithear, R. (1999) 'Charity Shop Volunteers: A Case for Tender Loving Care', *Nonprofit and Voluntary Sector Marketing*, vol 4, no 2, pp 107-20.

Zimmeck, M. (1998) *To Boldly Go: The Voluntary Sector and Voluntary Action in the New World of Work*, London: Royal Society of Arts.

FOURTEEN

The changing landscape of voluntary sector counselling in Scotland

Liz Bondi

In 1989 the Scottish Health Education Group and the Scottish Association for Counselling compiled a directory of counselling services in Scotland. When asked if they offered counselling, the great majority of voluntary sector organisations in the welfare field said that they did, and they were therefore included in the directory, generating over 500 entries in total, including, among others, all the Citizens Advice Bureaux in Scotland. In 2001, I was involved in the implementation of another survey of voluntary sector counselling, which provided an updated snapshot of provision across the whole of Scotland, and offered the possibility of examining how the availability of voluntary sector counselling had changed since the late 1980s (Bondi et al, 2003a). The 2001 survey solicited a rather different response from the earlier one. Several of the organisations listed in the 1989 directory responded to the 2001 survey by telephoning or writing to stress that they did not offer counselling. For example, a paid worker from Victim Support contacted us to ask us to ignore any returns from local Victim Support groups, insisting that any of them who claimed to offer counselling were wrong. A note from another agency manager stated that 'X does not deliver counselling ... and no service user is ever given this impression'. In a similar vein, when an interview was conducted with a member of the Samaritans, he began the interview by saying, 'I must state now that Samaritans are not counsellors'. These responses provided graphic evidence of a substantial shift in the place of counselling within the voluntary sector between the late 1980s, when it had been embraced as a description of a vast array of services designed to meet welfare needs, and the beginning of the 21st century, when it was understood in much narrower terms from which many organisations actively sought to distance themselves.

This chapter contextualises and explores this shift. I begin by exploring the evolution of voluntary sector counselling in Scotland that led up to the picture summarised in the 1989 directory in the context of shifts that have characterised the voluntary sector more generally. In so doing I illuminate how and why counselling was eagerly taken up by voluntary sector organisations in the 1980s. I then consider how and why counselling was redefined in rather narrower terms in the 1990s. Against this background, I examine the changing geography and the changing role of volunteering in voluntary sector counselling provision in Scotland. This account illustrates how processes at work within the voluntary sector in general – especially those associated with professionalisation – are played out within one arena of voluntary sector action.

My account draws on the surveys to which I have referred, together with a series of research interviews conducted in 2001 and 2002 with approximately 100 people involved in the provision of voluntary sector counselling, including counsellors and service managers. The survey was distributed very widely and sought to identify all voluntary sector agencies in Scotland that offered counselling services. The interviewees were drawn from four geographical areas (two urban and two rural) and were recruited primarily via agencies identified in the survey, supplemented by the use of personal networks. The research was conducted in close collaboration with the field of voluntary sector counselling in Scotland. The research team included two very experienced counselling trainers with strong and long-standing links to the voluntary sector, while I too brought direct involvement with voluntary sector counselling as a part-time volunteer counsellor. In addition, the research was supported by an advisory group that included representatives of nine different voluntary sector counselling agencies. It led directly to my co-option to the governing body of COSCA (Counselling and Psychotherapy in Scotland) and the International Research Committee of the British Association for Counselling and Psychotherapy. During and since the formal life of the project, my understanding of the field has been greatly enriched by numerous informal conversations with others involved in the field, whose paths I crossed in the course of my own volunteering, and my wider formal and informal participation in the field of counselling training. Either through interviews or through such conversations, the research has been informed by key actors, many of whom have played crucial roles in the evolution of voluntary sector counselling in Scotland at some point over the past half-century.

Modest beginnings: marriage counselling as a supplement to the welfare state in the Scottish cities

The first counselling services to be developed in Scotland were set up soon after the Second World War by voluntary sector agencies concerned with the causes and effects of marriage breakdown. As the current manager of what is now Lothian Couple Counselling explained:

> 'We were the first organisation in Scotland. I've got the first Annual Report here, and it says the Edinburgh Marriage Guidance Council was founded in the summer of 1946, and the first Annual Report was 1947. It was set up by "the great and the good": the Faculty of Advocates, the Education Institute of Scotland, the Council of Social Service, and a lot of quite well known people. At that time the concern

was to save marriages, and … I think it was because at the end of the war there were a lot of people coming back ….'

A similar organisation was set up in Glasgow in 1947, and in 1948 the Scottish Marriage Guidance Council came into being to deliver training to volunteers recruited by all the local Marriage Guidance Councils (Mitchell, no date).

As their names suggest, these organisations initially offered 'guidance' rather than 'counselling'. However, they established a foundation from which counselling soon grew. As Jane Lewis, David Clark and David Morgan (1992) have described in relation to the marriage guidance movement in England, one of the key ideas contributing to this foundation was that neither practical advice nor expert advice from lawyers, church leaders or other professionals was what people struggling with difficulties in their marriages most needed. Instead the marriage guidance movement argued that what was needed was the support and guidance of ordinary people in untroubled (or at least less troubled) marriages. The Marriage Guidance Councils provided these ordinary people by recruiting volunteers – men, and more often women, who were themselves married – who offered a few hours a week during which they provided those in need with 'someone to turn to' (Wallis, 1968). Volunteers were provided with training. By the early 1950s those involved in the provision of training began to pick up on ideas advanced by the American psychologist Carl Rogers (1942, 1951), whose 'client-centred counselling' emphasised the importance and benefits of non-hierarchical client–practitioner relationships. Those involved in training enthusiastically embraced these ideas, combining them with other inputs to develop 'marriage guidance counselling' which has since evolved into 'relationship counselling' (Lewis et al, 1992).

The moment at which the Edinburgh Marriage Guidance Council came into being was, in some ways, rather inauspicious for a new voluntary sector organisation. The dawn of the British welfare state was expected by many 'to have rung down the curtain on the central role of voluntary action in meeting social needs' (Smith et al, 1995, p 1). Although the welfare role of the voluntary sector did not, in fact, disappear, in the early postwar period, it was viewed as supplementary to statutory provision, funded through charitable giving and providing non-essential services (Deakin, 1995; Lewis, 1999). Developing in this context, the Marriage Guidance Councils found a niche, successfully appealing to benefactors drawn from both morally conservative and morally liberal quarters (Lewis et al, 1992). In these early years, volunteer recruitment also benefited from continuing resistance to employing married women, as one early volunteer explained:

'When we married [1952], in those days you got a dowry from the Civil Service and I got £100 dowry, and then you were out you see…. I was going to climb the walls [not working]. I got myself a part-time job, which I really didn't like at all. [Husband] came home with this advert [for training in marriage guidance counselling...]. I think that was the turning point for me....'

Until the mid-1960s – some two decades after marriage guidance counselling began – there was no hint that voluntary sector organisations in the welfare field would flock to embrace counselling. While the marriage guidance movement, which successfully consolidated its position outside the new welfare state, had taken it up, it remained a specialist field, apparently without wider relevance. Geographically, the reach of counselling services remained limited, and access uneven. Councils were successfully established in the four largest Scottish cities (Edinburgh, Glasgow, Dundee and Aberdeen) by the early 1950s. While efforts to establish services in other areas followed, several either failed to come to fruition or swiftly faltered. For example, discussion began in Orkney in 1954 but no service was established until 1984; a local Council opened in Dumfries in the same year but two years later had only one counsellor and in 1958 had none (Mitchell, no date). While services did develop in several more substantial towns in the late 1950s and early 1960s, coverage remained patchy and strongly urban in character. Positioned as a supplement to the welfare state, this patchiness was not regarded as a cause for concern.

Expansion and popularisation: the rise and spread of counselling in voluntary sector welfare

In the 1960s a significant shift in the relationship between the state and the voluntary sector was underway. Driven in part by economic crises that interrupted expectations of the progressive expansion of welfare provision, much closer forms of collaboration between the state and the voluntary sector developed, and the 1970s witnessed an upsurge in the number and range of voluntary sector organisations (Deakin, 1995; Kramer, 2000). It was in this context that new players entered the field of voluntary sector counselling.

The training provided to marriage guidance counsellors emphasised the value of the careful use of ordinary interpersonal skills in helping and supporting others. These included listening attentively, responding empathically, refraining from judging or directive advice giving and emotional honesty. As the voluntary sector expanded, many organisations in the welfare field recognised the value of such skills in their work helping and supporting service users. Among the first on the scene in Scotland were local Alcohol Councils, which developed as an alternative to the twelve-step programme and strict abstinence of Alcoholics Anonymous groups, and offered counselling services to people experiencing difficulties connected to alcohol, whether their own drinking or the impact on them of other people's drinking. One of those involved in this development recounted that:

'... the Scottish Council on Alcohol had just been formed, 1973....

> They wanted me to take over [the training of] a number of people
> who had been doing counselling in the Glasgow Council on Alcohol
> [which was established in 1965] who were all ex-drinkers …, people
> who had fallen out with the AA, disliked AA and that's why they
> were with the Glasgow Council on Alcohol.'

The idea of counselling was soon taken up by others involved in the wider
upsurge of voluntary action within the welfare field during the 1970s. Examples
include services developed by the women's liberation movement around issues
of domestic abuse and rape (which became Women's Aid Centres and Rape
Crisis Centres), by the gay liberation movement (some of which evolved into
telephone helpline and counselling services like Gay Switchboard), by people
seeking to innovate in the field of community-based mental healthcare
(contributing to the development of local Associations for Mental Health), and
in the field of bereavement (through Cruse Bereavement Care Scotland). In due
course specialist counselling services developed for other groups including adult
survivors of sexual abuse, minority ethnic groups, people with disabilities, people
diagnosed with serious illnesses (such as cancer, HIV/AIDS and MS), women
seeking advice about unintended pregnancy, people who have been adopted
and people who care for ill or disabled relatives.

The appeal of counselling continued to grow through the 1980s and into the
1990s, despite the progressive reduction in grants available for social welfare
interventions, as the British government shifted the emphasis of urban policy to
economic initiatives (Atkinson and Moon, 1994; Kramer, 2000). One factor was
undoubtedly the utility of a flexible definition of counselling that allowed it to
be assimilated into a wide range of services; another was a broadly sympathetic
cultural and political context. Counselling draws attention to and engages the
subjective experience of the individual service user. It is therefore often interpreted
as bound up with the intensification of individualism associated with the rise of
neoliberalism (Rose, 1990). Although this interpretation underplays the emphasis
counselling places on relationships (Bondi, 2003, 2005), it helps to account for
the enormous appeal of counselling in the closing decades of the 20th century.
During this period more and more organisations described the services they
offered as including counselling. For example, because the advice work of Citizens
Advice Bureaux involved attentive empathic listening to service users, it could
be described as 'counselling'. So too could the work of Women's Aid in supporting
women fleeing domestic abuse, Rape Crisis telephone lines, ChildLine's work
with children in distress, and so on.

The geographical patterning of voluntary sector counselling provision changed
as the sector expanded. Whereas marriage guidance counselling began in the
relatively middle-class city of Edinburgh, alcohol counselling began in the more
working-class city of Glasgow, giving early expression to a class contrast between
the two fields[1]. Moreover, the Scottish Council on Alcohol was more actively
involved in the development of a network of local councils across Scotland than

was the Scottish Marriage Guidance Council. One consequence of this was that, while alcohol counselling services were established in the four largest cities of Scotland only two decades after marriage counselling services had achieved the same coverage (the early 1970s as opposed to the early 1950s), in several more rural localities in Scotland, alcohol counselling services arrived before marriage or relationship counselling services, and in some instances remain the only counselling services available. A key factor underlying this difference was a long-standing concern with alcohol issues in rural Scotland, in contrast with a tendency (at least in the 1950s and 1960s) to view marital and relationship troubles as more closely linked to urban lifestyles. Moreover, those involved in the development of alcohol counselling services embraced the ideal of universal provision more explicitly and energetically than those involved in marriage counselling. Thus, although geographical unevenness persisted its form changed, and the tension between reliance on local voluntary action and universal welfare began to be addressed (compare Milligan, 2001; Bryson et al, 2002; Fyfe and Milligan, 2003a).

The directory of counselling services in Scotland published in 1989 captured the enthusiasm for counselling that had developed among organisations involved in voluntary sector welfare provision during the 1970s and 1980s. However, changes in the character and definition of counselling were already afoot, which would soon lead to a significant shift in how many of these organisations described their services.

Professionalisation: redefining voluntary sector counselling at the turn of the millennium

Although its contours have changed, the influence of neoliberalism is generally understood to have increased rather than waned since the 1980s (Peck and Tickell, 2002). Why then had so many voluntary organisations in Scotland backed away from counselling as a description of their services by 2001? A key factor lies in the complex processes of professionalisation to which counselling has been subject from the early 1970s, and which gathered pace significantly during the 1990s (Bondi, 2004).

While the organisations that first developed counselling services focused on particular issues – such as marriage, alcohol and bereavement – some of those involved were swiftly aware of common interests related to the training of volunteers and the delivery of services. As a result, networks began to develop that focused specifically on counselling. One of the most influential within and beyond Scotland was the Standing Council for the Advancement of Counselling, which came into being in 1971, and led to the founding of the British Association for Counselling in 1976. These networks cut across the specific concerns and constituencies of voluntary sector organisations that focused on particular issues or particular groups of people. In so doing, they began to separate counselling as a distinctive approach and practice from the contexts in which it was applied.

While this was important in enabling the rapid popularisation of counselling described above, it also paved the way for the emergence of generic counselling services and generic counselling training, which had the converse effect of fostering the distinctiveness of counselling as something different from other interventions.

Those involved in the provision of counselling services organised around particular issues or around the needs of specific groups often found that the issues that people brought to counselling were wide-ranging and complex. For example, what began as counselling about a relationship issue or an alcohol problem might uncover other issues such as low self-esteem, or a history of sexual abuse. In addition, services were sometimes asked to see people who did not fit their explicit purpose but who clearly needed help of a related kind. For these reasons, by the 1980s, generic counselling services began to develop.

The separation of counselling training from the remits of specific voluntary sector organisations, together with the development of generic counselling services, created opportunities for new players to enter the field of counselling training. Those that did included institutions of further and higher education (colleges and universities). The linkage of counselling training to academic qualifications was one expression of processes of professionalisation. In due course, it impacted on voluntary sector organisations that offered counselling training. Some withdrew from training and others entered into partnerships with universities. For example, the counselling training courses offered by Couple Counselling Scotland (successor to the Scottish Marriage Guidance Council) and Alcohol Focus Scotland (successor to the Scottish Council on Alcohol) are both now validated by universities and carry university-level academic credit.

Umbrella organisations concerned with counselling, including especially the British Association for Counselling (renamed the British Association for Counselling and Psychotherapy in 2000), and the Confederation of Scottish Counselling Agencies (founded in 1990 and subsequently renamed COSCA[2]), promoted other processes of professionalisation, and described themselves as professional bodies for counselling. They sought to raise and monitor standards of training and practice through the development of codes of ethics, course validation, service recognition and practitioner accreditation. They also developed independent complaints procedures to enhance public safety and practitioner accountability.

These frameworks and mechanisms required clarity about when counselling was being used and when it was not. During the 1980s, in the context of generic counselling training and the development of codes of practice, a distinction began to develop between counselling and the use of counselling skills within other tasks. It was soon promoted by the British Association for Counselling, which published its first Code of Ethics and Practice for Counsellors in 1984 (British Association for Counselling, 1984). In 1985 it published a definition of terms, and by 1989 it had produced a Code of Ethics and Practice for Counselling Skills (British Association for Counselling, 1985, 1989). Through these documents the organisation developed and disseminated a distinction that reserved the term 'counselling' for work in which (a) there is an explicit agreement between the recipient and the practitioner to enter into a counselling relationship, and (b) both the recipient and the practitioner understand their work together to involve no other tasks or roles. By contrast, practitioners were deemed to be using 'counselling skills' if their work with a service user was not explicitly contracted, and/or was framed by another caring, supporting or professional role (such as advice giving, befriending, nursing or teaching) (Bond, 1989).

Although these definitions were being promoted from the mid-1980s onwards, they were not immediately absorbed by voluntary sector organisations. Indeed, because counselling had strong links with mutual aid, organisations like the British Association for Counselling could not necessarily claim the authority needed to determine what did and what did not constitute counselling. One of those who had been deeply involved in the development of standards of practice for counselling suggested that if professionalisation narrowed the definition of counselling too much, people would just invent another name for a practice grounded in the use of what are fundamentally ordinary interpersonal skills:

> Respondent: '… it will fossilise, just like other professions fossilise. And there will come after it, there'll be another wave of people who call themselves befrienders or something like that. And there'll be cowboy chaos in that area for a while, and then all those will begin to come and it will fossilise too and then there'll be another wave.…'

> Interviewer: 'And so it's just a case of what's the next thing that will be used to identify ordinary skills?'

> Respondent: 'Yes. The next vehicle for unlocking the talents of the population. And at the moment, it's counselling, that's fine. And I have every sympathy with people who want to.… I mean I've been, well, not an enforcer, but I've been an encourager and developer of standards right from the beginning, and I still am. But the whole thing can go top heavy, and totally bureaucratic, and obsessional, and everything else.'

Notwithstanding the potential for resistance, processes of professionalisation did impact on perceptions and practices of counselling in the voluntary sector. In response to the survey conducted in 2001, one organisation informed us that:

> … we ceased offering a counselling service in August 1999. We had run this service since we started in 1976 but over the years the implications of providing counselling altered dramatically.

Responses by local Women's Aid groups (37 of which had been listed in the 1989 directory) provided an illustration of the range of positions taken in relation to claims about counselling. Some groups responded by stating that they did not offer counselling, while others stated that they did. In their descriptions of their services, some of the latter were clearly holding onto an inclusive understanding of counselling undifferentiated from other tasks. However, others explained how they offered service users counselling as something distinct from other forms of support work, whether delivered 'in-house' by a qualified counsellor, or through interagency referral arrangements.

Reconfiguring the geography of voluntary sector counselling

While the 1989 directory of counselling services listed over 500 organisations, as definitions changed, the number of voluntary sector agencies delivering counselling services declined. Applying the definition of counselling promulgated by the British Association for Counselling, the 2001 survey identified just over 200 voluntary sector agencies involved in the provision of face-to-face counselling[3]. Among the voluntary sector organisations that had withdrawn from the field were Citizens Advice Bureaux, the Samaritans, Victim Support, most Women's Aid Centres, most voluntary sector family planning services, some Associations for Mental Health and many agencies providing advice and support to people affected by serious illnesses. The organisations involved in counselling provision in 2001 fell into four broad groups, as summarised in Table 14.1.

Table 14.1: Voluntary sector counselling agencies in 2001

Type of service	Type of agency	Number of agencies
Generic counselling	Mainly small autonomous local organisations	40
Loss and bereavement counselling	Mainly local branches of Cruse Bereavement Care Scotland	31
Alcohol, drugs and/or addictions counselling	Mainly local affiliates of Alcohol Focus Scotland	44
Relationship counselling	Local affiliates of Couple Counselling Scotland or local branches of Scottish Marriage Care	25
Other specialisms[a]	Some small autonomous local organisations and some projects of large voluntary sector organisations	64

Note: [a] This category includes counselling for a wide range of specific groups including disabled people; people from black and ethnic minority backgrounds; gay, lesbian, bisexual, transgendered and transexual people; children and young people; women affected by domestic abuse; adult survivors of sexual abuse; women seeking advice about unintended pregnancy; people who have been adopted; people affected by mental health problems; people suffering from serious illnesses; and people who care for ill or disabled relatives.

The geographical distribution of counselling provision in Scotland also changed with this reconfiguration of the field. Although the absolute number of organisations involved declined, the distribution across Scotland became less concentrated. This occurred because of changes in both urban and rural areas. On the one hand, both the absolute numbers and the proportion of counselling agencies declined most markedly in the two largest cities, Edinburgh and Glasgow: in 1989 the two health boards centred on these cities included 47% of all agencies listed in the directory, compared to 35% of those identified in the 2001 survey. Conversely, the health boards covering the most remote, rural areas in Scotland (three island areas in northern and western Scotland), which had included 9 of the agencies listed in 1989 (2% of the total), had 10 (5% of the total) in 2001. Thus, at the scale of Scotland as a whole, the tendency for voluntary sector action to produce some areas with many voluntary sector organisations and others with very few, was reduced rather than intensified in the process of redefining counselling more narrowly (cf Wolch, 1990).

As Map 14.1 shows, in 2001, voluntary sector counselling agencies were, in fact, still strongly concentrated in the central belt of Scotland. The paucity of services in many parts of rural Scotland indicates that provision does not in any sense approach universal coverage. Nevertheless, the overall pattern does broadly reflect population density, with two island health board areas rivalling the health board areas covering the two largest cities (Glasgow and Edinburgh) for the largest number of clients seen per head of population (see Map 14.2). The pattern suggests that, by 2001, voluntary sector counselling had diffused across the whole of Scotland. Lanarkshire Health Board stands out as the area with the lowest number of clients per 1,000 population. This is probably a result of two factors: on the one hand, it is likely that people living in some parts of Lanarkshire make use of voluntary sector counselling services in neighbouring health board areas, especially Greater Glasgow; on the other hand, Lanarkshire Health Board has a relatively high level of counselling provision in primary healthcare.

Notwithstanding the relative dispersion of voluntary sector services identified above, in the major cities people are likely to have access to several different services, while in the rural areas, they may have to travel very large distances to access any face-to-face voluntary sector counselling service at all. Moreover, as Table 14.2 shows, most of the agencies located in rural areas offer counselling either for issues relating to alcohol, drugs and/or addictions, or for loss and bereavement. The involvement of the Scottish Council on Alcohol in supporting the development of alcohol counselling in rural areas has already been mentioned. The great majority of voluntary sector counselling agencies offering loss and bereavement counselling are local branches of Cruse Bereavement Care Scotland. Cruse originated as a self-help organisation of and for widows. Its history in Scotland is not well documented, but it seems likely that its relatively strong representation in rural areas is linked to these origins, sharing with organisations like the Women's Institute a particular capacity to mobilise rural women (Little, 1997).

Map 14.1: Counselling agencies in Scotland (2001)

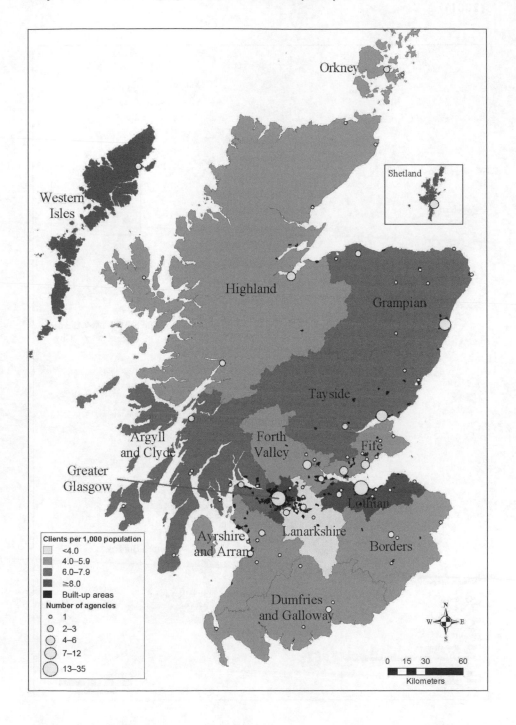

Map 14.2: Population density versus counselling services in Scotland (2001)

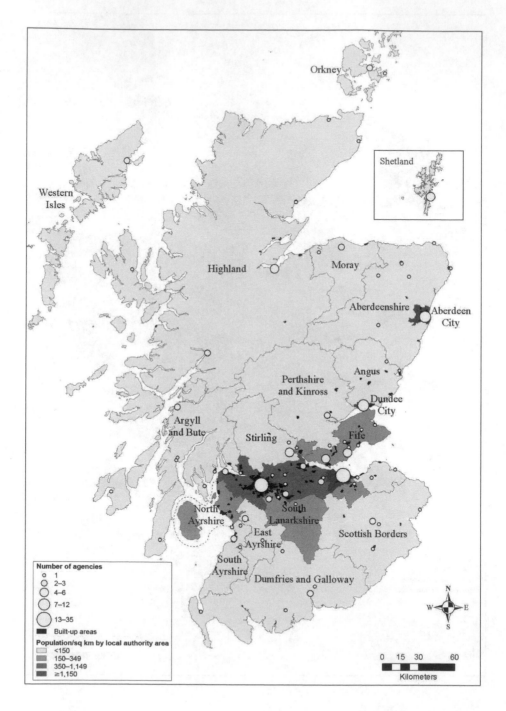

Table 14.2: Types of counselling agency in urban and rural Scotland in 2001

Type of voluntary sector counselling offered	Number of agencies in rural areas	Number of agencies in urban areas
Generic (anyone any issue)	6	34
Loss and bereavement	12	19
Alcohol, drugs and/or addictions	14	30
Relationship issues	4	21
Other specialisms	6	58
Total	42	162

Turning to the local, neighbourhood level, the geography of counselling provision is complicated by the importance attached to offering service users a resource they can access anonymously. Because of this emphasis, agencies run services from two kinds of premises: either those located in busy city centre areas or multi-use buildings, both of which people access for a variety of reasons (cf Fyfe and Milligan, 2003b). One service manager involved in the development of a new rural service was thrilled to find a building beside an isolated hotel:

'It's so rural and ... anywhere in X seemed so public that everyone would know everyone who was going to counselling because it was all in the one wee main street. How do you find and overcome some of those ethical dilemmas of working in rural communities? How do we overcome travel and how do we overcome all sorts of things? So those were all the questions going on in my mind and I had to meet [some local people] in a hotel in ... and when I got out of the car ... I said to myself "gosh, this would make a perfect counselling centre, it's so quiet, so peaceful, people could come here and really take time". And so at the end of my meeting I asked if I could speak to the manager of the hotel and I said "you wouldn't want to rent me your hotel so I could make it into a counselling centre?" And he said "no ... but I have another place out the back that was purpose built as an overflow facility and we've never used it".'

Another service manager in an urban area described how a surprising proportion of service users effectively bypass more local services because of their intense concern about being seen by someone they know. Given these considerations, it is very difficult to assess patterns of provision at a local level in ways that are adequately sensitive to the logic of locational choices.

Volunteering, regulation and the future of voluntary sector counselling in Scotland

The association between volunteering and the voluntary sector is a complex one. As Rob Paton (1991) has noted, the term 'voluntary' originated in the notion of independence from government, but has subsequently come to be associated with the idea of volunteering. However, the extent to which voluntary sector organisations depend on or deploy volunteers varies enormously. At one extreme, organisations are major employers and their only 'volunteers' are members of management committees; at the other extreme, organisations may depend entirely on volunteers (Milligan and Fyfe, 2005).

As I have described, counselling originated as a form of voluntary action in which all counsellors were volunteers. The professionalisation of counselling that gathered pace during the 1980s and 1990s was accompanied by its diffusion beyond the voluntary sector, into the public sector (especially into educational institutions like universities and into primary healthcare) and the private sector (through in-house counselling services in large organisations, Employee Assistance Programmes and private practice). In these contexts counsellors were paid, either as salaried staff or as hourly-paid freelancers. Similar opportunities have developed in the voluntary sector. However, the sector also continues to mobilise substantial numbers of volunteers. The survey conducted in 2001 found that approximately 2,100 counsellors work in voluntary sector counselling services in Scotland, three quarters of whom do so as unpaid volunteers (Bondi et al, 2003a, 2003b).

Traditionally, voluntary sector organisations have provided counselling training free of charge to people they recruit, who are expected to give their time as volunteers in return. This kind of arrangement has come under enormous pressure and has partially broken down. As counselling training courses began to develop in the education sector, some voluntary sector organisations sponsored their volunteers to train. However, the dominant trend has been for an increasing proportion of the costs of training, whether delivered by voluntary sector organisations, universities or colleges, to be passed on to the trainees themselves[3]. The capacity of the voluntary sector to cover the costs of training has come under increasing pressure as minimum standards of training have risen, and, not surprisingly, the more that trainees have paid for their own training, the more they have sought payment for their counselling work, whether delivered in voluntary sector contexts or elsewhere. A 'mixed economy' is now in evidence within the voluntary sector: in 2001, two fifths of voluntary sector counselling services in Scotland reported that all counselling was delivered by volunteers, a quarter reported that all counselling work was paid, and one third reported that the counselling was delivered by a mixture of paid and unpaid counsellors (Bondi et al, 2003a, 2003b). Among those organisations in which some counselling work is paid and some is not, many have one paid employee who delivers some of the counselling and manages a team of volunteers. Another pattern has been adopted by the successors to the original Marriage Guidance Councils (mainly called Couple Counselling centres), which require all their counsellors to deliver a minimum of 120 hours of counselling per year unpaid, in addition to which some counsellors may be recruited to deliver counselling at an hourly rate of pay.

Those involved in the organisation and management of voluntary sector welfare services interpret the erosion of volunteer counselling in different ways. The survey conducted in 2001 solicited some highly critical comments about the professionalisation of counselling, which suggested that volunteer status is viewed by some as a defining feature of counselling. The survey asked only for information about counselling services, and so the fact that people bothered to reply with such critical remarks highlights the strong feelings it generates. One respondent made clear his view that professional status and counselling are mutually incompatible. His point was that the counselling depends on the practitioner and the recipient being peers, whereas professionals have to maintain greater distance and cannot be peers to their clients. However, as I have argued elsewhere (Bondi with Fewell, 2003), counselling has itself developed more complex understandings of the practitioner–recipient relationships. In brief, within the field the issue of the relative positions of practitioners and service users has been reframed to place less emphasis on objectively non-hierarchical relationships, and more on the idea that one of the tasks of practitioners is to facilitate service users to explore their subjective experiences of relationships with others, including their counsellors. Thus, while many of those involved in the management of voluntary sector counselling services express regret that it is getting harder to recruit and retain volunteer counsellors, most would be happy to pay their counsellors if they could afford to do so, and express few qualms about the consequences of this shift away from the origins of counselling as a practice undertaken by non-professional volunteers.

Volunteer counselling faces further pressures as a result of other aspects of professionalisation. By January 2001 it had become clear that the promotion of voluntary self-regulation by the professional bodies for counselling was influencing the British government. This became apparent in the context of the second reading of a Private Member's Bill to regulate psychotherapy. The author of the Psychotherapy Bill, Lord Alderdice, had explicitly excluded counselling from the remit of the Bill, arguing that it lacked sufficient coherence and delimitation to make its regulation possible. However, in the debate that ended with the falling of the Psychotherapy Bill, the government explicitly included counselling in a statement expressing its 'wish to work with health professionals to strengthen the system of professional regulation, using the order-making power in the Health Act' (Lord Burlison, Government Peer, *Hansard*, 19 January 2001). In other words, the government articulated its desire to build on systems of voluntary self-regulation in order to limit entitlement to practice to registered practitioners including counsellors as well as psychotherapists, thereby creating a clearly delimited body of professionals (Bondi, 2004). Since then, a timescale for government regulation has begun to emerge, with 2007/08 identified as a likely target for the regulation of counselling and psychotherapy.

The survey of voluntary sector counselling provision was conducted in early summer 2001 and the questionnaire was sent out with a flier that summarised the rationale for the research. The flier included reference to the possibility that counselling might be subject to government regulation. Some voluntary sector bodies responded by saying that they 'were not aware of the government's intention to legislate', while others made evident their dismay at the implications in comments like this:

> ... as a voluntary organisation which may in the future wish to deliver counselling services ... we would ... like to be in a position to have all counsellors ... accredited, but if the government were to ... legislate for this, the cost to the voluntary sector and small voluntary organisations would probably mean that some would have to disband.

As I have discussed elsewhere (Bondi, 2004, 2005), those involved in the provision of voluntary sector counselling services within the ethical frameworks of the professional bodies for counselling are themselves ambivalent about the prospect of government regulation. At this stage, the requirements for registration are not yet known; nor are the arrangements that will apply to pre-registration counsellor training. While those involved in the organisation and delivery of voluntary sector counselling services generally welcome the recognition that regulation would bring, they are concerned about the potential exclusion of those lacking sufficiently formal, and especially academic, qualifications, and the potential that it will become impossible to recruit volunteer counsellors (with the possible exception of students in counselling placements).

While the consequences of the regulation of counselling and psychotherapy for voluntary sector counselling in Scotland remain unclear, there is little doubt that the shape of the sector will change further in years to come. Perhaps the volunteer counsellor integral to the original development of counselling will become extinct. However, given the importance accorded to volunteering by government in Scotland and elsewhere in the UK (Milligan and Fyfe, 2005), organisations committed to volunteer counselling are poised to resist this scenario by highlighting tensions between different strands of public policy. If they are successful, voluntary sector counselling may become an increasingly influential example of how voluntary sector organisations can enable professionalisation and volunteering to coexist. The geography of voluntary sector counselling will change too. Although successful in diffusing far beyond its original urban origins, it remains typical of numerous other voluntary sector activities in its reliance on local initiatives that do not add up to universal coverage. The British government's commitment to regulate counselling has not been accompanied by a parallel commitment to ensure universal access within the public sector. Consequently, whether the regulation of counselling will ameliorate or intensify inequities in access within and beyond the voluntary sector remains to be seen.

Acknowledgements

The research on which this chapter draws was funded by the Economic and Social Research Council (R00239059). My thanks also to project co-investigators Judith Fewell and Colin Kirkwood, those who participated in the project whether by responding to the questionnaire survey, giving interviews or participating in the project advisory group, and all those others who have enriched my understanding of counselling since I first entered the field.

Notes

[1] The association between marriage counselling and middle-class 'do-gooding' was partially offset by the arrival of another marriage counselling organisation in the late 1960s: the Scottish Catholic Marriage Advisory Council (now Scottish Marriage Care). The organisation's religious affiliations linked it to the predominantly working-class Catholic communities of the west of Scotland.

[2] Founded as the 'Confederation of Scottish Counselling Agencies', the organisation subsequently changed its name to COSCA and then made a further change to add the strapline 'Counselling & Psychotherapy in Scotland in 2001'.

[3] Telephone counselling services were excluded because the great majority of telephone counselling work does not involve explicit contracting into a counselling relationship as required within the British Association for Counselling's definition.

[4] There is, of course, considerable concern about the exclusionary effects of this trend. A recent request by COSCA to the Scottish Executive for support for an initiative to enhance inclusivity in training was rejected. Moreover, there is no routine monitoring in place to track changes in the sociodemographic mix of either counsellors or recipients of counselling (see Bondi et al, 2003a).

References

Atkinson, R. and Moon, G. (1994) *Urban Policy in Britain*, Basingstoke: Macmillan.

Bond, T. (1989) *Standards and Ethics for Counselling in Action*, London: Sage Publications.

Bondi, L. (2003) 'A Situated Practice for Resituating Selves: Trainee Counsellors and the Promise of Counselling', *Environment and Planning A*, vol 35, pp 853-70.

Bondi, L. (2004) '"A Double Edged Sword?" The Professionalisation of Counselling in the United Kingdom', *Health and Place*, vol 10, pp 319-28.

Bondi, L. (2005) 'Working the Spaces of Neo-liberal Subjectivity: Psychotherapeutic Technologies, Professionalisation and Counselling', *Antipode*, vol 37, pp 497-514.

Bondi, L. with Fewell, J. (2003) '"Unlocking the Cage Door": The Spatiality of Counselling', *Social and Cultural Geography*, vol 4, pp 527-47.

Bondi, L., Fewell, J. and Kirkwood, C. (2003b) 'Working for Free: A Fundamental Value of Counselling', *Counselling and Psychotherapy Research*, vol 34, pp 291-9.

Bondi, L., Fewell, J., Kirkwood, C. and Árnason, A. (2003a) *Voluntary Sector Counselling in Scotland: An Overview*, Edinburgh: Counselling and Society Research Team.

British Association for Counselling (1984) *Code of Ethics and Practice for Counsellors*, Rugby: British Association for Counselling.

British Association for Counselling (1985) *Counselling: Definitions of Terms in Use with Expansion and Rationale*, Rugby: British Association for Counselling.

British Association for Counselling (1989) *Code of Ethics and Practice for Counselling Skills*, Rugby: British Association for Counselling.

Bryson, J.R., McGuiness, M. and Ford, R.G. (2002) 'Chasing a "Loose and Baggy Monster": Almshouses and the Geography of Charity', *Area*, vol 34, pp 48-58.

Deakin, N. (1995) 'The Perils of Partnership', in J.D. Smith, C. Rochester and R. Hedley (eds) *An Introduction to the Voluntary Sector*, London: Routledge, pp 40-65.

Fyfe, N.R. and Milligan, C. (2003a) 'Out of the Shadows: Exploring Contemporary Geographies of Voluntarism', *Progress in Human Geography*, vol 27, pp 397-413.

Fyfe, N.R. and Milligan, C. (2003b) 'Space, Citizenship and Voluntarism: Critical Reflections on the Voluntary Welfare Sector in Glasgow', *Environment and Planning A*, vol 35, pp 2069-86.

Kramer, R. (2000) 'A Third Sector in the Third Millennium', *Voluntas*, vol 11, pp 1-23.

Lewis, J. (1999) 'Reviewing the Relationship between the Voluntary Sector and the State in Britain in the 1990s', *Voluntas*, vol 10, pp 255-70.

Lewis, J., Clark, D. and Morgan, D.H. (1992) *Whom God Hath Joined Together: The Work of Marriage Guidance*, London: Routledge.

Little, J. (1997) 'Constructions of Rural Women's Voluntary Work', *Gender, Place and Culture*, vol 4, pp 197-209.

Milligan, C. (2001) *Geographies of Care. Space, Place and the Voluntary Sector*, Aldershot: Ashgate.

Milligan, C. and Fyfe, N.R. (2005) 'Preserving Space for Volunteers: Exploring the Links between Voluntary Welfare Organisations, Volunteering and Citizenship', *Journal of Urban Studies*, vol 42, no 3, pp 417-34.

Mitchell, A. (no date) *Picking Up The Pieces*, Edinburgh: Scottish Marriage Guidance Council.

Paton, R. (1991) 'The Social Economy: Value-based Organisations in the Wider Society', in J. Batsleer, C. Cornforth and R. Paton (eds) *Issues in Voluntary and Nonprofit Management*, Wokingham: Addison-Wesley, pp 3-12.

Peck, J. and Tickell, A. (2002) 'Neoliberalizing Space', *Antipode*, vol 34, pp 380-404.

Rogers, C. (1942) *Counseling and Psychotherapy*, Boston, MD: Houghton Mifflin.

Rogers, C. (1951) *Client-Centered Therapy*, Boston, MD: Houghton Mifflin.

Rose, N. (1990) *Governing the Soul*, London: Routledge.

Smith, J.D., Rochester, C. and Hedley, R. (eds) (1995) *An Introduction to the Voluntary Sector*, London: Routledge.

Wallis, J.H. (1968) *Marriage Guidance: A New Introduction*, London: Routledge and Kegan Paul.

Wolch, J. (1990) *The Shadow State: Government and Voluntary Sector in Transition*, New York, NY: The Foundation Centre.

FIFTEEN

Volunteering, geography and welfare: a multilevel investigation of geographical variations in voluntary action

John Mohan, Liz Twigg, Kelvyn Jones and Steve Barnard

Volunteering and voluntarism have recently been characterised as a 'lost continent' of social life (Salamon et al, 2000), in that relatively little appears to be known about the patterns and determinants of voluntary activity. Yet voluntary activity has rarely had such salience in political debate. Firstly, from a range of political perspectives, it is argued that political institutions are failing to engage citizens and that the consequence is a retreat into the private sphere of the home and the family and an absorption in individualised consumption. The remaking of citizenship will therefore involve a transition from passive and limited participation in the formal institutions of democracy to active citizenship through participation in civil society (Brown et al, 2000, p 55).

Furthermore, fiscal pressures on welfare systems have led governments to rely to a greater extent on the voluntary sector as a means of obtaining greater flexibility and responsiveness in the welfare state. Regardless of the contrasting interpretations of this development (for example, Johnson, 1987; Wolch, 1989; Whelan, 1996) the implication is a greater reliance on volunteers and unpaid carers to buttress the core services of the welfare state. A specific example would be the 'new' Labour government in the UK, a distinctive characteristic of which has been its determination to distance itself from 'old' Labour by constantly reminding citizens that there are limits to what government can do and that the corollary is a much greater degree of partnership, entailing an expansion of voluntary support for welfare provision, or of voluntary involvement in governance.

The extent to which such programmes and policies will succeed depends on the response by people in local communities to such calls for voluntary effort. There are strong grounds for the view that the extent of voluntary activity is a function of context (the characteristics of a place) as well as composition (the type of people who are resident in a place). There is much work on geographies of voluntarism using aggregate statistical sources (see Chapter One, this volume), which has broadly lent support to the view that the safety net represented by the voluntary sector had a 'mesh of varying size', so that the probability of slipping through it varied, depending on location (for example, Wolch and Geiger, 1983;

Wolch, 1989; Wolpert, 1990). Other national and international comparisons confirm these differences in capacity (Salamon, 1995; Kendall and Knapp, 1996).

However, these studies did not have much to say about our central concern, which is the geography of voluntarism: to what extent is the probability of volunteering mediated by the kind of place in which people live? If such place effects exist, one could not presume that a call for voluntary effort would be met with an undifferentiated response in all communities. Instead, the probability of success of such policies would be contingent on local circumstances. Understanding influences on variations in volunteering is therefore an important task. However, while there has been much work on social variations in the propensity to volunteer, there is rather less on spatial variations.

We might nevertheless expect such variations for several reasons. First, political participation and volunteerism vary by age, class, ethnicity and gender (Davis-Smith, 1998) and so, at a minimum, one would expect compositional effects to produce spatial variations. Analyses of national survey datasets in the UK have consistently revealed substantial regional variations in volunteering (Goddard, 1994; Lynn, 1997; Davis-Smith, 1998; Coulthard et al, 2002; Attwood et al, 2003), but a question we explore here is whether, and to what extent, regional variations in reported volunteering can be explained by variations in the composition of those living in different areas.

Second, there is evidence that the extent and character of political and civic participation varies from place to place. There is ample historical evidence for this from studies of the formation of charitable or voluntary associations (Gamm and Putnam, 2000), and of contemporary patterns of political participation (for example, Parry et al, 1992; Verba et al, 1996; Miller et al, 1996), which are attributed to local contextual factors. Thus Parry et al (1992) contended that after allowing for compositional effects, 'locality counts': in other words, there were locality-specific variations in the form and extent of participation in the six localities studied (p 347). This conclusion finds echoes in Chanan's (1993, p 144) suggestion that the nature of voluntary activity would be 'bound up with the conditions and history of the locality', Deakin's (2001, p 14) emphasis on the 'rediscovery of the significance of the local' in studies of civil society, and the studies of Little (1997), Macdonald (1996) and Milligan (2001), which indicate the effect of local contexts on the propensity to volunteer and on the nature of the volunteering that takes place.

Finally, institutional structures can influence levels of participation in voluntary activity. Examples might include the former Greater London Council's populist programmes aimed at enlisting a rainbow coalition (Mackintosh and Wainwright, 1987) and the many other efforts by central and local government in the UK to mobilise the voluntary sector (Hall, 1999; Maloney et al, 2000; Milligan, 2001). Consequently, Skocpol (1997) emphasises the symbiotic relationship between institutional structures and voluntarism.

All these influences underline Fyfe and Milligan's (2003) recent call for greater attention to the geography of volunteering, but there is an element of wheel reinvention here because as long ago as 1978 the Wolfenden Report argued that 'some social and geographical contexts seem to provide a much more fertile soil for voluntary action than others' (Committee on Voluntary Organisations, 1978, p 58). Picking up this theme, Williams (2002) has summarised the results of recent national surveys of volunteering in the UK. He was mainly concerned with differences between what he termed 'formal' and 'informal' volunteering. His argument was that middle-class respondents were more likely to recall and report participation in formal voluntary activities undertaken for, or on behalf of, established organisations, whereas informal exchanges between neighbours, although a routine part of everyday life in working-class areas, were not recorded. He pointed out that the latter was far more common in disadvantaged areas and among disadvantaged groups. But he also observed that, within what was defined as 'formal' volunteering, there were still substantial variations between places. Both the General Household Survey (GHS) and the Home Office Citizenship Survey (HOCS) demonstrated a consistent social gradient between areas in the proportion of residents who were volunteers (Prime et al, 2002). Coulthard et al (2002) also demonstrated significant variations between places in the propensity to be active in neighbourhood organisations. Thus, in the most deprived decile of wards in England, only 14% of the population participated in voluntary groups compared to 29% in the most affluent decile. This led Williams to hint at the possibility of 'contrasting regional and local cultures of community engagement' (Williams, 2003, p 536).

However, those analyses presented an aggregate picture and could not distinguish contextual from compositional influences. The patterns summarised by Williams could therefore reflect variations between places in the composition of the population rather than being a true measure of contextual differences. In contrast we wish to explore whether the relationship between individual characteristics, and the probability of specific behaviours or attitudes, varied between places. This is important because an aggregate rate of volunteering is made up of individual decisions to participate. If those decisions – and the context in which those decisions are made – vary between individuals (for example, if individuals of similar socioeconomic status exhibit divergent behaviour in different circumstances), then it is clearly important that policies to encourage volunteering take account of such variations. We suggest that the overall likelihood that an individual will act as a volunteer in their local community will partly reflect individual characteristics (age, gender, ethnicity, material circumstances) and it will also reflect ecological or contextual influences. We therefore need a modelling strategy which can capture both individual and area effects simultaneously, and which can analyse interactions between the two. For example, there may be place effects which serve to depress or raise the probability of volunteering that would be predicted from an individual's personal characteristics. Here, we are echoing a broader debate in the literature on health inequalities which has engaged with the composition–context distinction, exploring the question of whether geographical variations in health outcomes are a function of the characteristics of a place or the characteristics of those who live in that place (Gatrell, 2002; Macintyre et al, 2002). The response by scholars working in that area has characteristically been to draw on multilevel models as a means of handling the distinction between composition and context, and we adopt a similar approach here. Whereas numerous previous studies of volunteering have concentrated on composition – who volunteers, and why (for example, Cnaan et al, 1996; Clary and Snyder, 1999; Wardell et al, 2000) – our aim is to show how those individual characteristics interact with context – the place in which people live.

In this study we therefore explore the relationship between individual and area characteristics and the probability that an individual will be what we define as a 'committed volunteer': someone who is, according to the GHS, engaged in voluntary activity on at least 11 days in a year. Of course, this is an arbitrary cut-off point, but it does allow us to exclude those who perhaps have volunteered on a very occasional basis. By using this terminology we do not imply that irregular or occasional volunteers are any less committed to voluntary activity.

The bulk of this chapter consists of a description of the modelling strategy used to explore these issues. We first describe the data source we have used and explain the modelling strategy we devised. We then discuss the results from a multilevel analysis of the determinants of volunteering. In the conclusion we explain why we believe this approach yields novel insights and discuss the practical implications of the results.

Data sources and analytical strategies

Information on voluntary activity was gathered from combining two annual rounds of the GHS (OPCS, 1989, 1994). The GHS is a multipurpose continuous survey now undertaken by the Social Survey Division of the Office for National Statistics (ONS) and has been carried out since 1971, except for breaks in 1997-98 when the survey was reviewed, and 1999-2000 when the survey was redeveloped. Currently the GHS samples approximately 13,000 addresses each year and aims to interview all adults at every household in the sampled address. The sample of addresses is selected using a multistage, stratified and clustered design and uses postcode sectors as the primary sampling unit (PSU). The details of the strata currently used are provided by Insalaco (2000) and an outline of the sample design is given by Walker et al (2002). The survey collects information on a range of core topics from people living in private households in Great Britain including household and family information, employment, education and health. Additional topics are investigated each year and in 1987 and 1992 a schedule focusing on voluntary activity was included. All individual respondents aged 17 and over were asked to provide information on the extent and nature of any voluntary activity that they had undertaken over the preceding 12 months. The definition of voluntary activity differed slightly between the two surveys. In 1987, work for a political or trade union organisation was included in the definition but was omitted for the 1992 definition. A screening question in the

1987 survey allowed such activity to be identified and so a consistent definition of volunteering was employed in this analysis that does not include political or trade union work. Also in this analysis we focus on those individuals who stated that they had engaged in such activities on 11 days or more. We are therefore not concerned with 'one-off' offers of unpaid help for a particular group or organisation. Instead we hope to shed some light on the factors associated with a more committed approach to volunteering. More recent sources of data, such as the HOCS of 2001 (Home Office, 2003) or the results from the social capital module of the 2000 GHS (ONS, 2002), would have permitted an updated version of this analysis but not for such a large sample[1]. Combining survey data for 1987 and 1992 gives a large sample size; adding 2001 to that would, however, have been problematic due to changing socioeconomic circumstances (sustained economic growth following exit from the Exchange Rate Mechanism [ERM] in 1992). In any case our purpose here is to draw on a large pooled dataset to make general observations about place effects, if any, on volunteering. It is not to provide the most up-to-date assessment of the pattern of volunteering. In total 19,104 individuals provided information on voluntary activity in the 1987 GHS and 17,927 provided similar information during the 1992 survey, giving us a total of some 37,000 respondents and, crucially, this enables us to analyse within-region variations in volunteering as well as between-region variations.

Information on the socioeconomic characteristics of these people was also derived from the survey and these are listed in Table 15.1 with the base categories (that is, the individual and areal characteristics that the constant in the subsequent models will represent) italicised. The GHS identifies the standard region in which respondents live, but it does not (for reasons of confidentiality) release details of their local authority district, let alone electoral ward. Given this constraint, how can we take account of within-region variability? We do so by exploiting the clustered sampling design of the GHS. As outlined above the design uses PSUs that are based on postcode sectors. Although we do not know the actual locations of these postcode sectors (and hence the respondents within them), the survey does, however, indicate whether individuals are located within the same PSU. We can therefore use survey results to estimate a number of variables that summarise the characteristics of the PSU.

We can derive, for example, the percentage of respondents in each PSU who are in private or in public rented tenure. This allows us to include 'ecological' or contextual variables as well as individual variables in our multilevel analysis of volunteering, thus allowing us to assess the relative impact of individual and areal influences on an individual's propensity to be a 'core' volunteer (for legibility and to avoid repetition, we may use the terms 'committed volunteers' or 'frequent volunteers' in subsequent discussion; this does not imply that other volunteers are not 'committed'). In total, five variables were generated that were thought to be (a priori) of potential influence on volunteering. These were the percentage of individuals in social class I or II, the percentage of individuals in social class IV or V, the percentage of individuals who are non-white, the percentage of individuals

Table 15.1: Individual and contextual covariates

Variable name	Definitions
Individual characteristics	
Age	*17-24*, 25-34, 35-54, 55-64, 65+
Gender	*Male*, Female
Marital status	*(Married/cohabiting)* or (Single, Widowed, Divorced, Separated [SWDS])
Ethnicity	*Non-white*, White
Economic status	*Unemployed*, Employed, Inactive
Social class	*IV/V*, I/II, III non-manual, III manual
Household composition	*Couple without dependants*, Single-person household, Couple with dependants, Lone parent with dependent children
Car ownership	*0 or 1 car*, 2+ cars
Tenure	*Public renting*, Owner-occupied, Private renting
Areal characteristics	**Centred on mean value of**
Percentage in social class I or II	28.7
Percentage in social class IV or V	22.6
Percentage non-white	4.2
Percentage in public rented tenure	23.1
Percentage without a car	26.6

in public rented housing and the percentage of individuals who do not have access to a car. Previous work had shown these variables to be useful and distinctive in terms of characterising socioeconomic differences between places, for example, in studies of between-place variations in health-related behaviour.

Using survey-derived percentages in the model has obviously introduced possible sources of error but due to the constraints already outlined, this is our only way of characterising the neighbourhoods within which the individuals live. Over the two GHS sweeps there are a total of 993 PSUs. The minimum number of respondents in any one PSU was 4 and the maximum number was 66 (average = 33.8, standard deviation = 6.1). A sensitivity analysis was undertaken to exclude all those individuals in areas where there were less than 25 people living. There were no differences in the results and so the full sample was used in the analysis described here.

Turning to analytical approaches, binary logistic regression modelling was used to assess the relative impacts of individual and areal characteristics on the log-odds of being a regular volunteer. Multilevel approaches were used to develop these models using MLwiN software (Rasbash et al, 1998). Multilevel models are particularly suited to analysing hierarchical data such as those found in the GHS, whereby individuals are nested within PSUs, within standard regions. Standard errors may be underestimated when observations are clustered and this is taken into account in the multilevel approach. Factors operating at an individual level and those operating at higher levels such as at the level of PSUs can be modelled simultaneously. The resultant models allow us to assess the proportion of total variation occurring at each of the levels and provide some indication of the relative importance of each explanatory variable in accounting for this variation. Importantly, they also allow us to assess 'cross-level' interactions. For example, there may be an increase in the likelihood of volunteering among individuals who are of a high social class (that is, an individual main effect). Also there may be an additional effect for the surrounding neighbourhood having a high concentration of high social class individuals (that is, an area or contextual main effect). Using multilevel approaches, we can assess whether there is a separate, independent effect for being both high social class at the individual level and living in a high social class area (the cross-level interaction)[2].

In this analysis two stages of modelling are described. The first stage represents a null model where the constant value represents the log-odds of being a 'core' volunteer for all types of people nationally. Also in this null model, the higher-level variances provide an estimate of the extent to which such volunteering varies between the PSUs and regions before any individual characteristics have been taken into account. Indeed such geographical variation may simply reflect spatial variation in the compositional variables that are associated with volunteering such as age, gender, social class or marital status, and so the fully adjusted model reports the changes in these higher-level variances once these compositional variables have been accounted for. The results of this fully adjusted model will also allow us to investigate the relative size of the between-area variations after taking account of the effect of these compositional variables on the propensity to volunteer.

As already noted, the multilevel structure models individual volunteering operating at three levels: the individual, the unidentifiable PSU and the standard statistical region[3]. PSUs were used as crude analogues of the local community; they are approximately the same size as electoral wards and can therefore be regarded as the areas providing the context for individual voluntarism. Standard statistical regions offer an identifiable level at which to take account of broader 'regional' variation. It is debatable whether these areas can in any sense be regarded as communities but no alternatives are available from the dataset we are using.

Results

Within this chapter we are attempting to unpack the aggregate (that is, regional) variations that exist in the propensity to volunteer. Before doing so, it is first useful to look at the extent of these spatial variations. Table 15.2 shows that lowest rates are found in the metropolitan areas of the Northern and West Midlands regions of England, parts of Inner London and Wales. Highest rates are found in the South West, South East and the non-metropolitan area of the West Midlands. These are substantial variations, which are broadly consistent with the findings

Table 15.2: Volunteering across the regions: results from the 1987 and 1992 General Household Survey

% of survey respondents defined as 'committed' volunteers	Region	Number of respondents
8.97	Northern metropolitan	825
9.47	West Midlands metropolitan	1,752
11.10	Greater London – inner	1,468
11.33	Wales	1,818
12.20	Northern non-metropolitan	1,352
12.33	Yorkshire and Humberside metropolitan	2,344
13.41	Yorkshire and Humberside non-metropolitan	1,014
14.10	Scotland	3,299
14.23	East Midlands	2,685
14.38	North West metropolitan	2,622
14.80	North West non-metropolitan	1,682
15.72	Greater London – outer	2,755
15.81	East Anglia	1,385
16.46	West Midlands non-metropolitan	1,731
17.58	South East outer metropolitan area	3,760
18.20	South East remainder	3,351
19.07	South West	3,188

of earlier studies, but what happens when allowance is made for individual characteristics?

At first sight, these initial variations are also highlighted in the results of the null multilevel model shown in Table 15.3. The null results indicate that there is significant variation in rates of volunteering across PSUs and regions. The constant for this null model is given as −1.909 (expressed as a logit) and when an antilogit is taken, we find that the chances of being a frequent volunteer are approximately 13% *generally*. Using this constant value and the variance values shown in Table 15.3, we can estimate that 95% of the time, volunteering rates will range between 5% and 28% across PSUs and between 9% and 19% across regions.

Table 15.3: Variance (standard error), credible interval and percentage of total unexplained variance in the multilevel model of volunteering at the individual, household and primary sampling unit (PSU) level for the null model

	Variance (standard error [SE])	95% credible interval (CI)	p for a Wald test	% of unexplained variation
Level 3 (Region)	0.054 (0.023)	0.026-0.097	0.02	1.5
Level 2 (PSU)	0.253 (0.024)	0.216-0.293	<0.00	7.0
Level 1 (Individual)	3.29			91.5

However, Table 15.3 also indicates that 7% and 1.5% of the total variation in volunteering is estimated to occur at the level of PSU and region, respectively. The bulk of the variation occurs at the individual level (91.5%), not at a higher level of spatial aggregation.

Of course some of this initial PSU and regional variation is due to variation in the types of people living in these areas. For example, Table 15.2 indicates that we have more reporting of committed volunteers in the South West compared to the Northern region but this may reflect the possibility that the South West comprises a higher percentage of people who are more likely to undertake voluntary work. Table 15.4 shows the results of a fully adjusted model and we can note the individual and areal characteristics that impact on the likelihood of volunteering. Table 15.4 reports the logit value and standard error for the model terms, the odds ratio (OR) and the accompanying 95% confidence interval around the OR. The constant in this fully adjusted model (–3.99) indicates that the chances of being a 'core' volunteer are approximately 1.8% for someone who possesses the characteristics of the base category individual[4]. By 'base category' we mean, conventionally, the category for which the prevalence of the dependent variable is lowest; other groups are contrasted with this category. The results suggest, however, that there are statistically significant gender differences (albeit small) with the odds of volunteering increasing to 1.23 if you are female. Therefore if you possess the characteristics of the stereotypical respondent (that is, the base category) but happen to be female, as opposed to male, the chances of volunteering are increased to around 2.2%. The model indicates that age tends to increase the likelihood of volunteering with a positive gradient evident until retirement ages when the increase in likelihood decreases slightly. Interestingly, however, the 65+ age group still have greater odds of volunteering than the 25 to 34 year old age group.

There are also significant differences based on ethnicity with non-whites reporting less volunteering than whites. Employment status does not appear to significantly impact on the chances of volunteering. Although positive logits (representing increased levels of volunteering) are reported for the employed and economically inactive groups, the terms are not statistically significant.

There appears to be a strong socioeconomic gradient to volunteering, with social classes I through to III non-manual, as well as the 'class missing' group, all reporting increased odds of volunteering compared to social class IV or V. All of these are statistically significant apart from the social class III manual group. To illustrate the effect of class, we have already noted that the chances of being a frequent volunteer in social class IV or V (and possess all other characteristics of the base individual) are around 1.8%. However, this probability increases to around 4.3% if you happen to be from social class I or II. Similarly the chances are around 3.0% for those in social class III non-manual and 2.8% in the 'class missing' group.

Using tenure as an indicator of socioeconomic status, highest rates of volunteering (around 2.9%) are estimated for those who are in owner-occupied

Table 15.4: Results of fully adjusted multilevel logistic model of volunteering

Variable	Logit estimate	Standard error	Odds ratio and 95% CI
Intercept	−3.99	0.11	
Individual characteristics			
Gender			
Male			1.0
Female	0.21	0.03	1.23 (1.15-1.31)*
Marital status			
Couples			1.0
Single, widowed, divorced or separated	0.05	0.05	1.05 (0.95-1.16)
Age categories			
17-24			1.0
25-34	0.17	0.06	1.19 (1.05-1.35)*
35-54	0.57	0.06	1.77 (1.58-2.00)*
55-64	0.69	0.07	2.00 (1.75-2.29)*
65+	0.37	0.07	1.44 (1.25-1.66)*
Ethnicity			
Non-white			1.0
White	0.50	0.08	1.64 (1.39-1.94)*
Economic activity			
Unemployed			1.0
Employed	0.04	0.07	1.05 (0.91-1.21)
Inactive	0.08	0.08	1.08 (0.92-1.26)
Individual social class			
IV and V			1.0
I and II	0.90	0.05	2.45 (2.22-2.70)*
III non-manual	0.53	0.05	1.70 (1.53-1.88)*
III manual	0.04	0.05	1.05 (0.94-1.16)
Missing	0.46	0.09	1.59 (1.33-1.90)*
Household composition			
Couple without dependent children			1.0
Single-person household	0.11	0.06	1.12 (0.99-1.26)
Lone parent dependent children	0.43	0.12	1.54 (1.22-1.94)*
Couple with dependent children	0.36	0.04	1.43 (1.33-1.54)*
Car ownership			
0 or 1 car			1.0
2 plus cars	0.21	0.04	1.23 (1.14-1.32)*
Tenure			
Local authority renting			1.0
Owner occupier	0.49	0.05	1.63 (1.48-1.80)*
Private sector renting	0.25	0.07	1.29 (1.11-1.49)*
Areal characteristics			
% in social class I/II in PSU	0.01	0.00	1.01 (1.00-1.01)*

Note: * Statistically significant ($p \leq 0.05$)

accommodation but who otherwise possess the characteristics represented by the constant in the model. The chances of volunteering are reduced slightly if such an individual lives in the private or public rented sector. Similarly, using car ownership as an indicator of wealth, those individuals who have access to 2 or more cars indicate statistically significant increased odds of volunteering (OR = 1.23, $p < 0.05$), with a probability of approximately 2.2%.

There appears to be no significant differences between couples and single people in terms of the probability of volunteering. However, both lone parents and couples with dependent children appear to volunteer more than their childless counterparts, with statistically significant odds of 1.54 (2.7% chance of volunteering) and 1.43 (2.6% chance of volunteering), respectively. This may reflect the opportunities to volunteer that are associated with schooling (for example, Parent–Teacher Associations) and other child-related activities (for example, children's clubs and societies such as Scouts, Guides and various sports clubs). Many schools, for example, now rely on unpaid parent helpers to assist with regular activities such as 'breakfast clubs' and reading schemes. These activities may also help explain the positive (but statistically insignificant) logit recorded for the 'inactive' group noted above. Often, a parent who decides to stay at home to care for small children may declare themselves as inactive rather than unemployed because they are unable to seek work because of childcare commitments and may also be involved with volunteering work associated with these children.

The base category in the model reported in Table 15.4 represents the group of people who report the lowest rates of volunteering. Hence all other terms in the table of results show positive logits and odds that are greater than 1. In contrast, if we look at the other extreme and estimate the rate for a white, single, female, aged 55-64, from social class I or II, who has access to 2 or more cars, lives in owner-occupied accommodation and is classed as economically inactive but with dependent children, then we find that the chance of such an individual being a frequent volunteer is around 39%.

In terms of areal characteristics, the only statistically significant term was that provided for the percentage of people in the PSU who were in social class I or II. The OR is given as 1.01 for a unit increase in this percentage. To explore the impact of this, the 39% figure reported above refers to the chances of being a committed volunteer for a respondent (as described) living in an area with an *average* level of social class I and II households (28.7%). If that level is reduced to 0%, the chances of volunteering for that type of individual are reduced to 33%. Conversely if the level is 100%, the chances of being a committed volunteer are approximately 55%.

A number of cross-level interactions were tested in the model (results not shown). Specifically, the individual social class terms were interacted with the areal social class I/II variable. This would allow us, for example, to examine whether there are effects for being low social class (or middle or high social class) but living in an area where there was a high percentage of social class I/II.

There was some indication that the interaction between individual high social class and area high social class had a very marginal negative effect on volunteering. This implies that although volunteering is higher among high social class individuals and also in areas with high percentages of high social class individuals, the positive impact of each of these is reduced slightly if an individual is both high social class and lives in a high social class area. This interaction, however, was not significant using conventional levels of statistical significance.

The impact of time was also investigated in the modelling process. As already noted this dataset comprised respondents surveyed in 1987 and 1992. If we include time in the model as a dummy variable, we find that although the logit value is negative (-0.027), its impact is relatively small and is statistically insignificant. There is a 0.3% difference in the chances of volunteering in 1992 compared to 1987 for the base individual (results not shown). It would appear that the propensity to volunteer over the time period has not altered to any significant extent. Furthermore, there were no significant interactions between time and any of the other individual or areal characteristics and the variation between places did not appear to change with time. This provides further justification for our decision to combine two sweeps of the GHS.

We now need to examine the extent to which the individual characteristics and areal characteristics explain the differences in volunteering reported across the areas in Table 15.2 and summarised in the null model of Table 15.3. Table 15.5 indicates that indeed the variation at both the PSU and the regional level has now reduced. Furthermore at the regional level the variation does not quite reach conventional levels of statistical significance. Estimates from the model suggest that the range in volunteering rates across the regions is just over 3% once the types of people living in the regions has been taken into account (that is, just under 10% in Inner London and slightly less than 13% in the South East outer metropolitan area). Contrast this with Table 15.2, where the range is from 9% to 19%. At the PSU level the variation remains statistically significant using conventional thresholds of statistical significance and the variance value for the PSU level indicates that 95% of the time, volunteering rates for such an individual will range between 6% and 26% across PSUs, even after taking account of the compositional and contextual characteristics of such areas. As with the null model

Table 15.5: Variance (standard error), credible interval and percentage of total unexplained variance in the multilevel model of volunteering at the individual, household and primary sampling unit (PSU) level for the fully adjusted model

	Variance (se)	Credible interval	p	% of unexplained variation
Level 3 (Region)	0.017 (0.010)	0.005-0.036	0.11	0.5
Level 2 (PSU)	0.186 (0.020)	0.154-0.221	<0.00	5.3
Level 1 (Individual)	3.29			94.2

we see that the bulk of the unexplained variation remains at the individual level (94%). Using the method described by Snijders and Bosker (1999), we estimate that the proportion of the total variation that has been accounted for by the variables included in Table 15.4 is approximately 11%. There is still much variation to be accounted for, the bulk of which relates to individual characteristics.

Conclusion

This analysis has indicated that regional variation in rates of committed volunteering across the English regions and across Wales and Scotland can be explained largely by differences in the compositional characteristics of the people in those areas and by differences in the social class make-up of local neighbourhoods. Highest rates are found among the 35- to 64-year-olds and for individuals in households with dependent children. Similarly, higher rates are found among those who have a higher socioeconomic status as measured through social class, tenure and car ownership. Also women tend to volunteer more than men, as do individuals whose ethnicity is recorded as 'white' compared to non-whites. In addition the findings show that there are spatial differences in the propensity to volunteer, but they are not statistically significant at the regional level. Put another way, the findings of Williams (2003) are not supported by our analysis. Regional differences are largely a function of composition. If 'geography matters' it is at the subregional scale, where neighbourhood social status does appear to explain some of the variation at the PSU level, but there remain substantial differences between places after having done so. Our explanatory variables are therefore less successful at explaining the disparities that remain at the level of local neighbourhood as captured via the primary sampling unit (that is, postcode sector) used in the GHS sampling process. Although the variation at this level is reduced after adjusting for these explanatory variables, a significant amount still remains. There may be individual or area characteristics, which impact on volunteering, that are not captured in this modelling process. Although area effects were explored in the analysis, area characteristics were summarised using aggregated information for survey respondents. We were not provided with the identification details of the PSUs and so could not link in more accurate Census information or any other geodemographic information to explore further the disparities in area rates of volunteering, but we are developing new work, which will do so[5].

We have already suggested that varying rates may be related directly to differences in the opportunities to volunteer, such as those associated with children and schooling. Variations may similarly reflect differential opportunities based on proximity to the volunteering activity in question or may reflect patterns of geographical targeting for recruitment of individuals. There is some support for this from North American work on blood donation and registration as potential organ donors (Piliavin and Callero, 1992; Grubesic, 2000) and our own work on the geography of blood donation (Mohan et al, forthcoming) provides support for this view. The patterns we have demonstrated may reflect, to a lesser or greater extent, variations in targeting. We could also argue that volunteering may have different meanings and interpretations for different cultures. What is seen as voluntary work for one culture or one group may be regarded as a duty, a leisure pursuit or a social activity for another. In terms of the distribution of such groups across space, what appear as spatial variations in the probability of volunteering may therefore really be spatial variations in what is characterised and reported as volunteering. It may also be that volunteers are recruited through other sources and networks – workplace-based programmes associated with corporate social responsibility, or church-based networks of voluntary activity. But it is difficult to see why such opportunity and recruitment structures would be expected to operate in such a way as to produce strong regional differentials. Within-region variation seems inherently more plausible, and consistent with comments from authors cited in our introduction regarding the significance of the local scale.

The implications of this work are that we do not share Williams' (2003) argument that regional 'cultures' of voluntary activity can be identified. This is because of the analytical framework he used, which cannot distinguish between composition and context; when allowance is made for composition, contextual differences – his 'regional cultures' – disappear. There is some support for spatial variations at the smaller scale of PSUs, which might give qualified support at least for the Wolfenden Committee's comment about the comparative fertility of the soil for volunteering, but further work is necessary on this. Linking our findings to wider debates on social capital, we believe that this work demonstrates that considerable caution should be taken in attributing social outcomes to comparative levels of social capital. This contradicts the position of Putnam (2000, 2002) and of enthusiastic supporters such as Labour's Performance and Innovation Unit, now known as the Strategy Unit (PIU, 2002). Once allowance is made for social composition, variations in volunteering largely disappear, and this would imply that outcomes (for example, improved health or educational performance) which appear to be due to variations in social capital are in fact largely due to variations in the composition of the population. We would conclude by suggesting that, on the basis of this analysis, there is some evidence that geography matters to volunteering – but not at the scale of regions, and certainly not as much as individual socioeconomic characteristics.

Notes

[1] Furthermore the chapter describes work undertaken as part of a Health Development Agency funded project that pre-dates the publication of these additional surveys.

[2] Multilevel analyses were undertaken using a logit link function based on the notion of a continuous latent variable, in which a threshold defines the binary outcome (see Snijders and Bosker, 1999, p 223). We therefore assumed an underlying standard logistic

distribution for the binary outcome (volunteer or not) at the individual level (Level 1). The Level 1 variance on this latent variable was always standardised to the standard logistic variance of $\pi^2/3 = 3.29$. When unexplained random variance at Level 2 was indicated as r_0^2, the proportion of the total unexplained variance occurring at this level was estimated (from a two-level null random intercept model as $r_0^2/(r_0^2 + 3.29)$. In the logistic models, parameters were estimated using second-order Taylor expansion with predictive quasi-likelihood (PQL). This estimation procedure is considered superior to first- or second-order marginal quasi-likelihood (MQL) when clusters such as PSUs are small (see Goldstein, 1995, chapter 7). Statistical significance of individual fixed estimates was tested using a Wald test against a χ^2 distribution. While approximate Wald tests can be used to assess the higher-level variances, difficulties are encountered due to the distribution of parameter estimates when the variances are close to zero (negative variances cannot exist). Therefore the 95% interval estimates (the 'credible interval') derived from Markov Chain Monte Carlo (MCMC) procedures are also reported for the random parameters of the models.

[3] The term 'regions' is used loosely and comprises 15 standard statistical regions across England, plus Wales and Scotland.

[4] The base category individual is a non-white, married, unemployed male, aged between 17 and 24, in social class IV or V, living in a household as part of a couple without dependent children. He either has no access to a car or to only one, lives in local authority rented accommodation and lives in a local area with an average percentage of social class I or II households.

[5] In the analysis reported here we did not have access to socioeconomic data for PSUs for reasons of confidentiality, but such data can now be attached to individual survey data, albeit without naming the PSUs, with the agreement of the organisation carrying out the survey.

References

Attwood, C., Singh, G., Prime, D., Creasey, R. et al (2003) *2001 Home Office Citizenship Survey: People, Families and Communities*, Home Office Research Study 270, London: Home Office.

Brown, K., Kenny, S., Turner, B. and Prince, J. (2000) *Rhetorics of Welfare: Uncertainty, Choice and Voluntary Associations*, London: Macmillan Press.

Chanan, G. (1993) 'Local Voluntary Sectors: The Hidden Dynamic', in S. Saxon-Harold and J. Kendall (eds) *Researching the Voluntary Sector*, West Malling: Charities Aid Foundation, pp 143-55.

Clary, E.G. and Snyder, M. (1999) 'The Motivations to Volunteer: Theoretical and Practical Considerations', *Current Directions in Psychological Science*, vol 8, no 5, pp 156-9.

Cnaan, R.A., Handy, F. and Wadsworth, M. (1996) 'Defining Who is a Volunteer: Conceptual and Empirical Considerations', *Nonprofit And Voluntary Sector Quarterly*, vol 25, no 3, pp 364–83.

Committee on Voluntary Organisations (1978) *The Future of Voluntary Organisations: Report of the Wolfenden Committee* (London: Croom Helm).

Coulthard, M., Walker, A. and Morgan, A. (2002) *People's Perceptions of their Neighbourhood and Community Involvement: Results from the Social Capital Module of the General Household Survey 2000*, London: The Stationery Office.

Davis Smith, J. (1998) 'Volunteering in the UK: Some Findings from a New National Survey', in C. Pharaoh and M. Smerdon (eds) *Dimensions of the Voluntary Sector 1998*, West Malling: Charities Aid Foundation, pp 207–13.

Deakin, N. (2001) *In Search of Civil Society*, Basingstoke: Palgrave.

Fyfe, N. and Milligan, C. (2003) 'Out of the Shadows: Exploring Contemporary Geographies of Voluntarism', *Progress in Human Geography*, vol 27, pp 397–413.

Gamm, G. and Putnam, R. (2000) 'The Growth of Voluntary Associations in America 1840-1940', *Journal of Interdisciplinary History*, vol 29, pp 511–57.

Gatrell, A. (2002) *Geographies of Health*, Oxford: Blackwell.

Goddard, E. (1994) *Voluntary Work*, OPCS series, GHS 23, supplement A, London: HMSO.

Goldstein, H. (1995) *Multilevel Statistical Models*, London: Edward Arnold.

Grubesic, T. (2000) 'Driving Donation: A Geographical Analysis of Potential Organ Donation in the State of Ohio', *Social Science and Medicine*, vol 51, pp 1197–210.

Hall, P.A. (1999) 'Social Capital in Britain', *British Journal of Political Science*, vol 29, no 3, pp 417–61.

Home Office (2003) Communities Research and BMRB International, *Home Office Citizenship Survey, 2001*, Colchester, Essex: UK Data Archive, SN: 4754.

Insalaco, F. (2000) 'Choosing Stratifiers for the General Household Survey', *ONS Social Survey Division, Survey Methodology Bulletin*, No 46, January.

Johnson, N. (1987) *The Welfare State in Transition: The Theory and Practice of Welfare Pluralism*, Brighton: Wheatsheaf.

Kendall, J. and Knapp, M. (1996) *The Voluntary Sector in the UK*, Manchester: Manchester University Press.

Little, J. (1997) 'Constructions of Rural Women's Voluntary Work', *Gender, Place and Culture*, vol 4, no 2, pp 197–209.

Lynn, P. (1997) 'Measuring Voluntary Activity', *Non-Profit Studies*, vol 1, no 2, pp 1–11.

Macdonald, R. (1996) 'Labours of Love: Voluntary Working in a Depressed Local Economy', *Journal of Social Policy*, vol 25, pp 19–38.

MacIntyre, S., Ellaway, A. and Cummins, S. (2002) 'Place Effects on Health: How Can We Conceptualise, Operationalise and Measure Them?', *Social Science and Medicine*, vol 55, pp 125–39.

Mackintosh, M. and Wainwright, H. (eds) (1987) *A Taste of Power: The Politics of Local Economics*, London: Verso.

Maloney, W., Smith, G. and Stoker, G. (2000) 'Social Capital and Urban Governance: Adding a More Contextualised Top-down Perspective', *Political Studies*, vol 48, pp 802-20.

Miller, W., Timpson, A. and Lessnoff, M. (1996) *Political Culture in Contemporary Britain*, Oxford: Clarendon Press.

Milligan, C. (2001) *Geographies of Care: Space, Place and the Voluntary Sector*, Aldershot: Ashgate.

Mohan, J., Jones, K., Twigg, L. and Barnard, S. (forthcoming) *Mapping the Gift Relationship: An Analysis of the Geographical Distribution of Blood Donors in England*, mimeo, Portsmouth: Geography Department, University of Portsmouth.

ONS (Office for National Statistics) (2002) Social Survey Division, *General Household Survey, 2000-2001* [computer file] (2nd edn), Colchester, Essex: UK Data Archive [distributor], SN: 4518.

OPCS (Office of Population Censuses and Surveys) Social Survey Division (1989) *General Household Survey, 1987* [computer file], Colchester, Essex: UK Data Archive [distributor], SN: 2679.

OPCS, Social Survey Division (1994) *General Household Survey, 1992-1993* [computer file], Colchester, Essex: UK Data Archive [distributor], SN: 3166.

Parry, G., Moser, G. and Day, N. (1992) *Political Participation in Britain*, Cambridge: Cambridge University Press.

Piliavin, J. and Callero, P. (1992) *Giving Blood: The Development of an Altruistic Identity*, Baltimore, MD: Johns Hopkins University Press.

PIU (Performance and Innovation Unit) (2002) *Social Capital: A Discussion Paper*, London: PIU.

Prime, D., Zimmeck, M. and Zurawan, A. (2002) *Active Communities: Initial Findings from the 2001 Home Office Citizenship Survey*, London: Research Development and Statistics Department, Home Office.

Putnam, R. (2000) *Bowling Alone: The Collapse and Revival of American Community*, New York, NY: Simon & Schuster

Putnam, R. (ed) (2002) *Democracy in Flux: The Evolution of Social Capital in Contemporary Society*, New York, NY: Oxford University Press.

Rasbash, J., Browne, W., Goldstein, H., Yang, M., Healy, M., Woodhouse, G., Draper, D., Langford, I., Lewis, T. and Plewis, I. (1998) *A User's Guide to MlwiN*, London: Institute of Education, University of London.

Salamon, L. (1995) *Partners in Public Service*, Baltimore, MD: Johns Hopkins University Press.

Salamon, L., Sokolowski, S. and Anheier, H. (2000) *Social Origins of Civil Society: An Overview*, WP-38, Johns Hopkins Comparative Nonprofit Sector Project, Baltimore, MD: Johns Hopkins University.

Skocpol, T. (1997) 'The Tocqueville Problem: Civic Engagement in American Democracy', *Social Science History*, vol 21, pp 455-79.

Snijders, T. and Bosker, R. (1999) *Multilevel Analysis: An Introduction to Basic and Advanced Multilevel Modeling*, London: Sage Publications.

Verba, S., Schlozman, K. and Brady, H. (1996) *Voice and Equality: Civic Voluntarism in American Politics*, Boston, MD: Harvard University Press.

Walker, A., O'Brien, M., Traynor, J., Fox, K., Goddard, E. and Foster K. (2002) *Living in Britain: Results from the 2001 General Household Survey*, London: The Stationery Office.

Wardell, F., Lishman, J. and Whalley, L. (2000) 'Who Volunteers?', *British Journal of Social Work*, vol 30, pp 227-48.

Whelan, R. (1996) *The Corrosion of Charity: From Moral Renewal to Contract Culture*, London: Civitas.

Williams, C. (2002) 'Harnessing Voluntary Work: A Fourth Sector Approach', *Policy Studies*, vol 23, pp 247-68.

Williams, C. (2003) 'Developing Community Involvement: Contrasting Local and Regional Participatory Cultures in Britain and their Implications for Policy', *Regional Studies*, vol 37, pp 531-41.

Wolch, J. (1989) *The Shadow State*, New York, NY: The Foundation Center.

Wolch, J. and Geiger, R. (1983) 'The Distribution of Urban Voluntary Resources: An Exploratory Analysis', *Environment and Planning A*, vol 15, pp 1067-82.

Wolpert, J. (1990) 'Generosity and Civic Commitment: The Local Public and Voluntary Sector', in R. Bennett (ed) *Decentralisation, Local Government and Markets*, Oxford: Oxford University Press, pp 172-93.

SIXTEEN

Reflections on landscapes of voluntarism

David Conradson and Christine Milligan

As the social and political significance of voluntarism has grown in Western states since the 1980s, social scientists have increasingly recognised the voluntary sector as an important focus for research. As a consequence, we now have a better understanding – at a variety of spatial scales – of the nature and dynamics of the community and voluntary sector. Research has documented the sector's diversity in particular national settings (for example, Kendall and Knapp, 1996; Anheier and Seibel, 2001; Lyons, 2001), while also looking at the changing nature of charitable giving (for example, Andreoni et al, 2003; Bowman, 2004; Charities Aid Foundation, 2004; Sargeant and Lee, 2004). Studies have tracked the experiences of voluntary organisations engaged in contracts for service provision, noting the tensions and difficulties associated with many of these arrangements (Deakin, 1996; Lewis, 1996; Morison, 2000; Majumdar, 2004; NCVO, 2004; Phillips and Levasseur, 2004). Recent efforts to achieve more egalitarian, even-handed forms of partnership between the state and voluntary sector have also been noted (Home Office, 1998; Welsh Office, 1998; Ministry of Social Policy, 2001).

In this volume, our aim has been to draw out one particular strand of this scholarship – research shaped by geographical perspectives – and to demonstrate what this approach might bring to the work conducted within disciplines such as sociology, social policy and political science. Most contributors to this book actively work within the discipline of geography, while others have had their work shaped by its conceptual and methodological debates. In this conclusion, we reflect on their work as a means of responding to two main questions. Firstly, what do the chapters indicate about a geographical approach to voluntarism? We address this question in terms of analytical perspectives. Secondly, what does this geographically inflected research tell us about contemporary landscapes of voluntarism? This is about material trends and developments within particular cities, regions and nations. We finish with some suggestions for future research.

Analytical perspectives

In relation to other social scientific scholarship, a geographical perspective on voluntarism has a number of dimensions. At a general level, we can reiterate that human geography is a discipline characterised by an attentiveness to the complex ways in which social, political and economic processes are played out within – and indeed modified by – the terrains of particular localities and regions. It is this concern for *emplacement* and the variable operation of social processes across space that arguably distinguishes geographical research from some of the more abstract or aggregate scale investigations in economics or political science. This is not to suggest that geographers object to abstraction per se, but rather that they are interested in place both as an integrative analytic framework and as an important domain of social experience. Elements of the geographical perspective thus resonate with the strands of other disciplines such as the community studies tradition in sociology (Bell and Newby, 1971; Wright, 1992). Here, a common interest can be discerned in terms of how sociopolitical processes and governmental initiatives become implicated in the character of particular localities. The concern is with how places are made and remade.

For a geographer interested in voluntarism, this interest in emplacement unfolds in at least two further ways. Firstly, it invites attention to what is happening to voluntary organisations 'on the ground', whether within particular localities or at the scale of regions and nations. Geographically inflected research is thus inclined to consider the nature and influence of voluntarism within the substantive configurations of economy, culture and society that comprise places. The scale of investigation may vary, stretching from small rural communities through to metropolitan boroughs, regions and provinces, but 'groundedness' remains an important focus. Secondly, a geographical perspective on voluntarism will consider the way in which voluntary activity varies between places. How does voluntary welfare provision differ between southern and northern Britain, for instance, within regions in New Zealand or across provinces in Canada? Such variation has important implications for the nature and scope of social services available to particular communities. This, in turn, has implications for social welfare and well-being.

Combining these lines of thought, a geographical perspective on voluntarism thus invites us to consider issues such as:

- the contribution of voluntarism to the ongoing evolution of particular localities;
- the uneven distribution of volunteering and voluntary activity within and between cities, regions and nations;
- the links between the geographic distribution of voluntary activity and the spatial structure of governmental initiatives (such as regeneration policy) and governance arrangements (such as regional assemblies and partnership boards);

- the international circulation of particular governmental approaches to voluntarism, as part of a broader transnational trade in social policy ideas (cf Peck and Theodore, 2001);
- the nature of voluntary sector organisational 'spaces' and their service environments.

This list is indicative only – we intend it to be suggestive rather than prescriptive. Nevertheless, it identifies some of the broad types of questions that concern geographers in their engagements with voluntarism, many of which are evident in this volume. Reflecting the heterogeneity of the discipline itself, there is no canonical agreement over which of these avenues of enquiry is more important; indeed, they often sit alongside each other within specific projects. The point of consensus, however, is that such questions are able to generate valuable insights regarding the nature of contemporary landscapes of voluntarism.

As suggested earlier, this interest in emplacement is not necessarily confined to scholars working within the discipline of geography. It has also been evident within some sociology and social policy research. Lupton's (2001) interrogation of area deprivation in Britain, *Poverty Street*, is a good recent example. While drawing on the empirical traditions of social policy research, this monograph demonstrates a persistent concern with the intersection of social and economic processes 'on the ground'. It examines how this intersection contributes to localities with varying levels of wealth, ethnic diversity, educational achievement and opportunity. The analysis engages, in a more than metaphorical sense, with notions of space and place. Moreover, if one looks at the points of reference in Lupton's work, it is clear that her approach has been shaped by the work of geographers such as Doreen Massey, Richard Meegan and Chris Philo. For us, this engagement underlines the analytical utility of geographical perspectives, while also demonstrating their capacity – indeed propensity – to travel across traditional disciplinary boundaries. It points to the added value that geographical questions bring to voluntary sector research.

Contemporary developments

Thus far, we have considered some of the analytical perspectives that characterise geographical research into the voluntary sector. But what do the studies compiled here tell us about contemporary landscapes of voluntarism? In answering this question, it is important to note that the nations examined – the UK, New Zealand, Canada, Australia and, to a lesser extent, the US – have all undergone a transition from some form of social democratic welfare state towards a neoliberal model of welfare pluralism during the 1980s and 1990s (Esping-Andersen, 1996). The statutory retrenchment involved saw both opportunity and, in most cases, social need for greater levels of private and voluntary sector involvement in welfare provision (Kendall, 2000). Since the late 1990s, two of the countries – the UK and New Zealand – have arguably moved from a strongly neoliberal social policy programme towards some form of 'third way' position (Chatterjee et al, 1999; Powell, 2000). As we discuss below, however, whether this should be seen as a positive development for statutory–voluntary relations is unclear.

The specificities of these national contexts notwithstanding, a number of common points emerge regarding their landscapes of voluntarism. Firstly, contracting continues to be a significant issue across these countries. A strong theme within the social policy literature of the mid-1980s to mid-1990s was that voluntary organisations were in some sense being co-opted by their statutory funders and, in the process, ceding elements of their distinctiveness and political autonomy. Although of serious political importance, this observation became something of a familiar refrain and, perhaps as a result, contracting has suffered a certain attenuation of interest among voluntary sector researchers in recent years. But the work reported on here underlines the degree to which contracts and funding constraints remain a challenging area of organisational life for voluntary agencies. In many cases, acceptance of funding continues to bring significant compliance costs in the form of institutional monitoring and accountability. This may limit the ability of an agency to set its own service provision agenda and, more particularly, to engage in campaigning and advocacy activities.

While funders and voluntary sector providers typically negotiate the terms of these service contracts, there also remain significant imbalances of power at the bargaining table. The precise form of these asymmetries differs by the size and nature of actors involved, with large professionalised voluntary organisations typically faring somewhat better in their engagements with external funders than small community organisations. Such asymmetries also vary geographically, reflecting the different approaches taken by central and local governments to working with the voluntary sector. Any generalised narrative that frames all state–voluntary sector partnerships as inherently exploitative and the state as villainous is thus insufficiently nuanced. Equally problematic, however, is an undifferentiated optimism which suggests that Wolch's (1990) concerns about the emergence of a shadow state are no longer relevant. Reality, in most places, lies somewhere between these two poles. The analytical challenge is to understand the social and political dynamics that lead to particular, emplaced forms of statutory–voluntary relations.

Secondly, the work reported on here highlights the efforts of some governments to move beyond the difficulties evident in contractual funding relationships with voluntary organisations during the 1990s. Initiatives such as the UK's Voluntary Sector Compacts and New Zealand's Statement of Government Intent are good examples. Each programme has sought to foster more positive forms of dialogue and engagement between government and the voluntary sector. The parallels between these British and Antipodean developments arguably reflect a shared engagement with 'third way' political strategies. In both countries, signs of more positive partnership relations between government and the voluntary sector are evident. At the same time, there remain significant variations in the experiences of individual organisations in this regard. It is also clear that new partnership arrangements are giving rise to governance structures that sit outside traditional political formations, raising new sets of questions about political legitimacy and democratic accountability. Hence, these developments cannot be accepted uncritically; there remains a need for ongoing research to monitor their outcomes.

Thirdly, our contributors underline the shift towards professionalisation within the sector. Whether in relation to voluntary sector counselling in Scotland, the internal dynamics of charity shops in England, or settlement agencies in Vancouver, professionalisation is having significant impacts on the personnel and operation of voluntary organisations in Western states. The growing emphasis on credentialism and professional qualification in some quarters has tended to marginalise more informal types of volunteering, with knock-on effects for the viability of very small community agencies. The 'amateur' nature of some organisations has come under pressure as the requirements of professionalisation have been imposed. In some instances, professionalisation has arguably facilitated *positive* developments for service users, in terms of improving service quality. But it is also something of a double-edged sword, as it has the potential to alienate the informal 'traditional volunteer' and, at the same time, undermine the flexibility and responsiveness that many small to medium-sized voluntary agencies consider to be central to their distinctiveness.

Taken together, contracting and professionalisation represent significant drivers for voluntary sector organisational change. In the process of competing for limited funds, some organisations inevitably struggle to obtain sufficient operational resources and may have to rationalise their activities accordingly. In this regard, concerns regarding bifurcation within the community and voluntary sector remain significant (Milligan and Fyfe, 2005). There is still an ongoing discussion to be had regarding the emergence of a 'two-tier voluntary sector', characterised by relatively large and resource-rich organisations on the one hand, and smaller, relatively resource-constrained organisations on the other. A key driver in the perceived divergence of these two groups is the differential allocation and accrual of funds to larger, more professionalised agencies. Large providers are typically well placed to liaise and interact with statutory agencies, as their size and resourcing enables them to deal with complex administrative requirements more effectively. As such, they perhaps parallel the 'shadow state' agencies that Wolch (1990) identified in the US and UK voluntary sector. At the same time, however, new voluntary organisations continue to emerge, as is evident from organisational directories for particular cities or regions. These new entrants to the sector to some degree offset its potential ossification into established players and marginalised others. Such grassroots developments arguably represent 'signs of life' in terms of their vitality and capacity for innovation.

Alongside these three key trends, the work in this volume also highlights the geographically uneven nature of voluntary sector provision. In contrast to positive narratives regarding its independence, informality and responsiveness to community needs, one of the clear limitations of voluntary health and welfare provision – at least historically – has been its unplanned nature, generating potential for significant unevenness in service provision across space. This issue is addressed in a number of chapters in the book, moving the debate beyond earlier observations regarding the apparently positive connections between local affluence and levels of volunteering and voluntary service provision. Indeed, as MacDonald (1996) illustrates, relatively deprived communities may also be significant contexts for the emergence of collective voluntary action. Christine Milligan and Nicholas Fyfe (Chapter Three, this volume) thus examine the ways in which the spatial organisation of public sector regeneration strategies in Glasgow, Scotland have led to quite striking geographic differences in the nature of voluntary welfare provision between different areas of the city. Similarly, Pauline Barnett and Ross Barnett's work in New Zealand (Chapter Five, this volume) shows how the transition from a centralised system of health funding to a more regionally devolved model has led to significant interregional variations in the fortunes of health non-governmental organisations (NGOs). The chapters by Mark Skinner and Mark Rosenberg (Chapter Six) and John Mohan et al (Chapter Fifteen) offer some interesting observations about the scale at which any kind of contextual effect between place and levels of volunteering can be observed. Each of these contributions is strongly shaped by a geographical perspective; indeed, the questions asked depend closely on notions of scale and areal differentiation. This enables authors to examine the connections between the spatiality of government initiatives and the geographical patterning of voluntarism. As a potentially unintended outcome of area-based interventions, this is a matter that resonates strongly with the interests of contemporary policy makers.

A further dimension of analytical attention to spatiality in the volume has concerned voluntary sector 'organisational spaces'. Here contributors have examined the nature and dynamics of organisational environments within voluntary agencies, considering the interactions between staff, volunteers and service users in both service settings and organisational 'back regions' (Goffman, 1969). A recurring observation is how the values and philosophies of agencies and actors *external* to a voluntary agency can have a significant bearing on the dynamics of its organisational spaces. A service contract, for example, may function as a relational conduit for the transmission – and possibly imposition – of certain ways of doing welfare, not all of which may accord with those of the voluntary agency involved. When translated into organisational dynamics, these pressures may have important implications for the homeless person or aging woman (for example) who presents for assistance. Issues of professionalisation are also significant in this regard. Liz Parsons' analysis (Chapter Thirteen, this volume) of the changing nature of charity shops – one particular form of voluntary sector organisational space – illustrates this point well, in that she traces the tensions between conceptions of charity shops as businesses and those volunteers who approach them as something more akin to a domestic environment, characterised by informality and relaxed sociality. The individuals who work and manage charity shops become involved in the negotiation of these divergent visions; their daily resistance, deflection or acceptance of external imperatives is a significant determinant of the experiential texture of charity shops. Although they examine different types of voluntary activity, the contributions of Liz Bondi (Chapter Fourteen, this volume) and David Conradson (Chapter Nine) both demonstrate a similar interest in the changing constitution of voluntary sector organisational spaces.

Future directions

In offering a conclusion to *Landscapes of Voluntarism*, we have not sought to offer a neat account of all the insights and contexts involved. Such strategies are often exercises in imposing an arbitrary sense of order, and in any case the diversity of our material resists such narration. Instead, we have highlighted a number of the themes that run through the contributions, while at the same time recognizing that there are points of tension and difference between the arguments they advance. For us, these differences reflect the vitality of recent geographical interest in voluntarism. After a period in the early 1990s when the voluntary sector appeared to enjoy limited geographical attention, it is now once again an active topic for research, with studies drawing on a diversity of analytical approaches and theoretical perspectives. In our view, this scholarship has a significant part to play in advancing social scientific understanding of voluntarism.

In closing, we would like to highlight three issues we think worthy of future investigation. First, there remains a need for research into the changing nature of community and voluntary sector organisations in particular places. What mix of providers exists in a given landscape of voluntarism, and how are processes of contracting, professionalisation and partnership working influencing both the heterogeneity of this landscape and the individual organisations within it? These matters have important implications for service users, especially in terms of the kind of services available to address their needs: whether professionalised or informal, small or large scale, free or user-pays and so on. Second, further work is needed on the geographically uneven distribution of voluntary health and welfare provision, both within and between cities and regions. Given the increasing role of voluntary and private sector actors in contemporary welfare configurations, there is now arguably less central oversight of the spatial and social equity of welfare and health provision. For those concerned with social well-being, monitoring the unevenness of voluntary provision is thus an important political and academic task.

Finally, given the parallels between the development trajectories of the voluntary sector in countries such as the UK, New Zealand, Canada and Australia, we believe there remains much value in internationally comparative work on voluntarism (Salamon and Anheier, 1996a, 1996b). While such research is challenging and the experience of one country is never simply transferable to another, comparative analysis enables us to more fully appreciate the evolving position and different expectations of voluntarism within contemporary societies. Insights derived in this way have the potential to contribute positively to debates regarding the most effective way to organise welfare provision. At the same time they furnish researchers with an evidential basis on which to critically evaluate existing policies.

References

Andreoni, J., Brown, E. and Rischall, I. (2003) 'Charitable Giving by Married Couples – Who Decides and Why Does it Matter?', *Journal Of Human Resources*, vol 38, no 1, pp 111-33.

Anheier, H.K. and Seibel, W. (2001) *The Nonprofit Sector in Germany: Between State, Economy and Society*, Manchester: Manchester University Press.

Bell, C. and Newby, H. (1971) *Community Studies*, London: Unwin.

Bowman, W. (2004) 'Confidence in Charitable Institutions and Volunteering', *Nonprofit And Voluntary Sector Quarterly*, vol 33, no 2, pp 247-70.

Charities Aid Foundation (2004) *Charity Trends 2004: 25th Anniversary Edition*, London: Charities Aid Foundation.

Chatterjee, S., Conway, P., Dalziel, P., Eichbaum, C., Harris, P., Philpott, B. and Shaw, R. (1999) *The New Politics: A Third Way for New Zealand*, Palmerston North: Dunmore Press.

Deakin, N. (1996) 'The Devil's in the Detail: Some Reflections on Contracting for Social Care by Voluntary Organizations', *Social Policy & Administration*, vol 30, no 1, pp 20-38.

Esping-Andersen, G. (1996) *Welfare States in Transition*, London: Sage Publications.

Goffman, E. (1969) *The Presentation of the Self in Everyday Life*, London: Penguin.

Home Office (1998) *Compact: Getting Right Together. Compact on Relations between Government and the Voluntary Sector in England*, Cm 4100, London: Home Office, November.

Kendall, J. (2000) 'The Mainstreaming of the Third Sector into Public Policy in England in the Late 1990s: Whys and Wherefores', *Policy & Politics*, vol 28, pp 541-62.

Kendall, J. and Knapp, M. (1996) *The Voluntary Sector in the UK*, Manchester: Manchester University Press.

Lewis, J. (1996) 'What Does Contracting Do to Voluntary Agencies?', in D. Billis and M. Harris (eds) *Voluntary Agencies: Challenges of Organisation and Management*, Basingstoke: Macmillan, pp 98-113.

Lupton, R. (2001) *Poverty Street: The Dynamics of Neighbourhood Renewal and Decline*, Bristol: The Policy Press.

Lyons, M. (2001) *Third Sector: The Contribution of Nonprofit and Cooperative Enterprises in Australia*, Sydney: Allen and Unwin.

McDonald, R. (1996) 'Labours of Love: Voluntary Working in a Depressed Local Economy', *Journal of Social Policy*, vol 25, pp 19-38.

Majumdar, D. (2004) 'The Community Funding Agency and the Voluntary Sector: Purchase of Service Contracting in Otago/Southland', *Australian Journal Of Public Administration*, vol 63, no 3, pp 88-98.

Milligan, C. and Fyfe, N. (2005) 'Preserving Space for Volunteers: Exploring the Links between Voluntary Welfare Organisations, Volunteering and Citizenship', *Urban Studies*, vol 42, no 3, pp 417-33.

Ministry of Social Policy (2001) *Communities and Government: Potential for Partnership. Report of the Community and Voluntary Sector Working Party*, Wellington: Ministry of Social Policy.

Morison, J. (2000) 'The Government–Voluntary Sector Compacts: Governance, Governmentality, and Civil Society', *Journal of Law and Society*, vol 27, pp 98-132.

NCVO (National Council for Voluntary Organisations) (2004) *Voluntary Sector Strategic Analysis 2004/05*, London: NCVO.

Peck, J. and Theodore, N. (2001) 'Exporting Workfare/Importing Welfare-to Work: Exploring the Politics of Third Way Policy Transfer', *Political Geography*, vol 20, pp 427-60.

Phillips, S. and Levasseur, K. (2004) 'The Snakes and Ladders of Accountability: Contradictions between Contracting and Collaboration for Canada's Voluntary Sector', *Canadian Public Administration-Administration Publique Du Canada*, vol 47, no 4, pp 451-74.

Powell, M. (2000) 'New Labour's Third Way in British Social Policy: A New and Distinctive Approach?', *Critical Social Policy*, vol 20, no 1, pp 39-60.

Salamon, L. and Anheier, H. (1996a) *The Emerging Nonprofit Sector: An Overview*, Manchester: Manchester University Press.

Salamon, L. and Anheier, H. (1996b) *Defining the Nonprofit Sector: A Cross-sectional Analysis*, Manchester: Manchester University Press.

Sargeant, A. and Lee, S. (2004) 'Donor Trust and Relationship Commitment in the UK Charity Sector: The Impact on Behavior', *Nonprofit And Voluntary Sector Quarterly*, vol 33, no 2, pp 185-202.

Welsh Office (1998) *Compact between the Government and the Voluntary Sector in Wales*, Cm 4107, Cardiff: The Stationery Office.

Wolch, J. (1990) *The Shadow State: Government and Voluntary Sector in Transition*, New York, NY: The Foundation Center.

Wright, S. (1992) 'Image and Analysis: New Directions in Community Studies', in B. Short (ed) *The English Rural Community. Image and analysis*, Cambridge: Cambridge University Press, pp 195-217.

Index

Page numbers in *italic* refer to figures or tables.

A

access to government
  campaigning and lobbying activities 46,
    80-1, 201-3
  see also governance arrangements
accountability of voluntary sector 66, 68
  Canada 199-200
  New Zealand 74, 78-81
  see also regulation of voluntary sector
Acheson, N. and Williamson, A. 181
Active Communities Initiative 34
Active Community Unit (Home Office) 17
advocacy work 80-1, 201-3
  see also campaigning activities
age and volunteering 275, *276*
Alcock, P. et al 22
Alderdice, Lord 261
Alderman, G. 135, 146
Aldridge, S. et al 179
Alexander, T. 97
Allan, V. 74
AMSSA (Affiliation of Multicultural Societies
    and Service Agencies) 202
Andreoni, J. et al 285
Andrews, G.J. 93
Anheier, H.K. 2-3
Anheier, H.K. and Salamon, L.M. 2
Anheier, H.K. and Seibel, W. 285
Annesley, C. 25
Antipode (Bondi and Laurie) 5
APIC (Australian Population and Immigration
    Council) 218
Areas of Priority Treatment (APTs) 38-9
Aronson, J. and Neysmith, S.M. 97
Ashton, T. 118
Atkinson, R. and Cope, S. 55
Atkinson, R. and Moon, G. 251
Auckland Methodist Mission 167
Australia and voluntarism 209-10
  ethnic collective action 214-15
  development of meeting places 215-35
  gender studies 6
  immigration patterns 211-12, *212*
  religious and cultural changes 213-14, *213*
Australian Bureau of Statistics (ABS) 211-13
Australian Population and Immigration
    Council (APIC) 218

B

Bacon, D. 185
Bacon, D. et al 184
Bailey, N. et al 55
Bales, K. 239
Bane, M.J. et al 153
Barber, B. 54

Barnett, P. and Barnett, R. 77-9, 82, 84, 118,
    120, 128
Barnett, P. and Clayden, C. 77, 80, 84
Barnett, P. and Malcolm, L. 78
Barnett, P. and Newberry, S. 77, 79-80, 82
Barnett, R. 91, 120
Barnett, R. et al 77
Becher, H. et al 136
Becker, P.E. and Dhingra, P.H. 239
Bell, C. and Newby, H. 286
Berger, J. 153
Beveridge, W. 232
Billis, D. and Harris, M. 85
Black and Minority Ethnic (BME) issues 6,
    43-4
  experiences of partnership working 47-8
Black, J. 75
Blair, Tony 15-16
  on citizenship 54
  on community renewal 16
  on faith-based organisations 153, 178, 185
  on local authorities 20
  on voluntary sector 16
Blunden, R. 140
Blunkett, David 17, 153, 232-3
BME issues *see* Black and Minority Ethnic
    (BME) issues
Boateng, P. 35
Bond, T. 254
Bondi, L. 233, 251-2, 261-2
Bondi, L. and Fewell, J. 261
Bondi, L. and Laurie, N. 5
Bondi, L. et al 247, 260
Bonnyrigg (Australia), ethnic communal places
    221, *222*
Boston, J. 156, 167
Boston, J. et al 75, 155
Bourdieu, P. 215
Bowman, W. 285
Bradford, S. and Nowland-Foreman, G. 117,
    129
Brenton, M. 54
Brindle, D. 148
British Association for Counselling 253
Broadbridge, A. 234
Broadbridge, A. and Horne, S. 236
Broadbridge, A. and Parsons, E. 233-4
Brock, K. 192-3, 204
Brock, K. and Banting, K. 191-2
Brown, Gordon 33-5, 178
Brown, K. et al 2, 267
Brown, M. 1, 5, 37, 41, 92-3, 192-3
Browne, P.L. 192-3
Bryson, J.R. et al 5, 252
*Building the Future Together: Labour's Policies for
    Partnership between the Government and the
    Voluntary Sector* (Labour Party 1997) 34

Burlison, Lord 261
Burnley, I.H. 209, 211, 214, 224
Burnley, I.H. et al 212
Bush, George W. 176-7

C

Cabinet Office publications 34, 178, 183
Cabinet Office Strategy Unit, review of
    charitable law 17
Cairns, B. et al 178
Caldwell, G. 216
California, poverty and voluntarism studies 4
Cameron, H. 173, 180
campaigning activities 46
  and conflicts of interest 128
  see also advocacy work
Campbell, D. 161
Canada Health Act 1984 (CHA) 96-7
Canada and voluntarism
    government policies 94-6, *95*, 100, 191-3
    healthcare systems 96-8
    history of state–civil society relations 106-7,
      191-3
    home care services
      geographic variation *99*, *101*, 102
      levels of 'need' *99*, *103*, *104*
      and voluntarism trends 98-105, *101*
      research studies 94-6
Canadian Privy Council 191
capacity building, partnership initiatives 21
Castles, F.G. 154
Center for Public Justice 176
'Challenge Funds' 20
Chambre, S. 124
Chanan, G. 268
Chandler, D. 40
Chappell, R. 191-2
'Charitable Choice' provisions (US), defined
    176
charities
    fundraising pathways 234-5
    retail outlets 233-43
Charities Aid Foundation 285
Charity Finance 234
Chatterjee, S. et al 156, 288
Chaves, M. 154, 175
Chaves, M. and Tsitsos, W. 176
CHCA (Canadian Home Care Association)
    106
Cheyne, C. et al 118, 120-1, 129, 155
child-related voluntary activities 277
Christian Social Service Organisations
    (CSSOs) 154-67
Christina Lounge (Sydney) *220*, 221
Citizens Advice Bureau 62-3
citizenship 25-6, 35, 54, 231-3, 267
'civil renewal' agenda 17, 34-5, 54
Civil Renewal Unit 25
Clark, J.S. 120, 129, 154
Clarke, J. and Newman, J. 24-5, *24*

Clarke, J. et al 33
Clary, E.G. and Snyder, M. 270
CLIC (Cancer and Leukaemia in Childhood)
    charity 235-41
Cloke, P. et al 153, 166
Cloutier-Fisher, D. and Joseph, A.E. 94, 106
Cloutier-Fisher, D. and Skinner, M.W. 106
Club Marconi (Sydney) *220*, 221
Cnaan, R. 154, 173, 175, 270
Cnaan, R. and Bodie, S.C. 175
Cnaan, R. et al 154
Cohen, M.G. 192
Coleman, J.S. 219
Colenutt, B. and Cutten, A. 55
Collins, J. 211
Commission on Urban life and Faith (CULF)
    179
Committee on Voluntary Organisations 269
'communal home' concepts 209-11
    development of ethnic meeting places
      (Australia) 215-23
'communitarianism' 16, *24*, 25-6
community councils *see* local level councils
Community Empowerment Funds 21
'community governance paradigm' (Osborne
    and McLaughlin) 55, 58
    see also governance arrangements
Community Planning Partnerships (CPPs) 49
community safety initiatives, Scotland 44-7
'community turn'
    background 15-17
    defined 15
    development trajectories 23-8, *24*
    and 'neocommunitarianism' 27-8, 33-5
    geographical consequences 28-9
    mechanisms and tools 17-22
    see also voluntarism; voluntary sector
*Compact Code of Good Practice on Community
    Groups* (Home Office) 178
Coney, S. 119
Connell, J. 209, 214
Conradson, D. 105
Conservative government
    and European Structural Funds 18
    policies on voluntarism 33, 54
contracting arrangements
    bid proposals 22, 38, 41-3, 198-9
    and conflicts of interest 128
    criticisms 128, 156
    as drivers for change 288-9
    in New Zealand 78-81, 121-2, 123-5, 155-6
    see also funding pathways
Cope, M. and Gilbert, M.R. 91
Corden, A. 139
Coster, H. 120
Coulthard, M. et al 268-9
councillors, parish and town communities
    63-4
counselling services
    background and contexts 247-54
    development of standards 253-4

evolution of terms 247–8, 253–5
pay and conditions 260–2
Scotland 247–63
training 253
costs 260
Cox, D. 212
Coyte, P.C. and McKeever, P. 97
CPPs *see* Community Planning Partnerships (CPPs)
Craig, G. et al 17
Crampton, C. et al 116
Crampton, P. 83, 85
Crampton, P. et al 77, 92
Creswell, T. 210
crime prevention initiatives, Scotland 44–7
cross-cultural comparison studies 4–5
see also geographies of voluntarism
CSSOs (Christian Social Service Organisations) 154–67
CULF *see* Commission on Urban life and Faith
culture and voluntarism 280
see also citizenship; geographies of voluntarism
CVSWP (Community and Voluntary Sector Working Party) (New Zealand) 115

D

Dahrendorf, R. 37
Dalziel, P. 167
Davis, P. and Ashton, T. 118, 120
Davis Smith, J. 231, 268
Day, K. and Devlin, R.A. 94
Deakin, N. 16, 37, 54, 156, 249–50, 268, 285
'decentring' policies (Wolch) 37
see also devolution policies; Wolch, J.R.
deinstitutionalisation, New Zealand 118
Demerath, N.J, et al 174
Department of the Environment, Transport and the Regions (DETR) 40, 60, 141, 153
Department of Health (DH) 141
Department for Social Development (DSD) 183
Department of Social Welfare 156
devolution policies 36–7
impact of new funding pathways 18–22, 41–3, 44
New Zealand 76–7, 115–16, 118–22
Dewar, Donald 39
'disentitlementarianism' *24*, 25
Doherty, P. and Poole, M.A. 182
domestic violence initiatives 41
Donley, J. and Hinton, B. 119
Dorman, A. 94
Dow, D. 74
Drake, R. 120, 129
Driver, S. and Martell, L. *24*, 25, 34
Drumchapel (Scotland) 38
Dunn, K. 223
duplication of services 124

Durkheim, E. 215

E

EAC NSW (Ethnic Affairs Commission New South Wales) 213, 214
Easterhouse (Scotland) 38, 41
Ebaugh, H.R. et al 154
Edwards, B. and Woods, M. 56–7, 60, 62
Edwards, B. et al 56, 58, 64
Ernst and Young 77
Esping-Andersen, G. 23, 287
ethnic communal places
Australia 210–11, 215–25
development types 217–18, *217*
ethnicity and voluntarism 275, *276*
experiences in Australia 214–15, 215–25
see also immigration issues and voluntarism
Etzioni, A. 1, 16, 25
European Structural Funds 18
European Union, funding pathways 18, 21
Evans, B.M. and Shield, J. 98
Evans, R. and Harding, A. 18

F

Fairclough, N. 54
faith communities
Christian social service organisations (New Zealand) 153–68
Jewish voluntary sector (UK) 135–48
see also faith-based welfare provisions
Faith Communities Capacity Building Fund 178–9
Faith Communities Unit (FCU) 173, 178–80
Faith and Community (LGA) 178
faith-based welfare provision 153–4
key themes 143–4
New Zealand 153–68
North America 174–8
typologies 177
Northern Ireland 181–4
UK 135–48
government policies 153, 178–80, 185
Faithworks Movement 185
Farnell, R. et al 153, 154, 185
Fear, H. and Barnett, P. 81, 83
Fenwick, P. 121
Field, F. 34
Finlayson, A. 16
Fisk, M. 136, 138
'floor targets' 19, 20
formal volunteering, defined 3
Foucault, M. 137
funding pathways
bidding processes 22, 38, 41–3, 198–9
winners and losers 42–3, 126–7
for ethnic communal meeting places 222–4
for faith-based welfare 176–7, 178–9
for local project development 21–2, 41–3, 44
in rural communities 54, 55, 57–63

in Canada 194, 195–6, 197–9
in New Zealand 75–6, 120–2, 125–7, 156
impact on governance 18, 20–2, 54, 55–6
and state dependency 120–1, 126, 128
and voluntary sector change 288–9
'futurebuilders' investment funds 34
Fyfe, N. 5, 231, 233
Fyfe, N. and Milligan, C. 5, 57, 61, 74, 85, 92,
166, 192, 252, 259, 268

G

Galbally, F. 215
Gamm, G. and Putnam, R. 268
GARA (Glasgow Anti-Racist Alliance) 39, 48
Gardner, R. 83
Gaskin, K. and Davis Smith, J. 85
Gatrell, A. 270
Gauld, R. 118
Gay, P. 243
Geiger, R.K. and Wolch, J. 61
gender and voluntarism 6, 275, *276*
treatment of women workers 200–1
General Household Survey (GHS) 270
on volunteering in the UK 4, 269, 270–9
Geoforum 138–9
geographical research of voluntarism 286–92
background history 3–7
cross-cultural and national studies 4–5,
268–80
future directions 291–2
individual versus area effects 269–70,
270–80, *272*, *276*
key research findings 6–7, 279–80
geographical variation in voluntary sector
provision
of immigration service fund-raising 198, 201
of institutional care 137–40
of retail charity work 236–43
of rural sector engagement 60–2
of urban regeneration initiatives 38–49
of voluntary sector care homes 142–8
of voluntary sector counselling 255–9, *257–9*
see also spatial targeting
geographically targeted initiatives *see* spatial
targeting
Gibbens, A. and Associates and Martin
Spigelman Research Associates 195
Giddens, A. 1, 16, 33
Giner, S. and Sarasa, S. 2
Glasgow, SIP developments 39–49
Glasgow Alliance 40
Gleeson, B. and Kearns, R. 117
globalisation effects 23–4
Goddard, E. 4, 268
Goffman, E. 137, 290
Goldstein, H. et al 272
Goodall, R. 233, 235
Goodwin, M. 49
Goodwin, M. and Painter, J. 92
Gorsky, M. and Mohan, J. 5–6

Gorsky, M. et al 5
Goss, K.A. 85
Gough, I. 23
governance, definitions 53, 58
governance arrangements 17–22
emerging influence of voluntary sector 53–7
background history 53–4
through partnership working 57–61
in Canada 92, *95*, 97–8, 106–7
in New Zealand 82, 84–5
in rural settings 61–6
and funding pathways 18, 20–2, 54, 55
background history 62–3
legislation 62
local level–EU level relationships *18*
'governing by culture' 126
Government policy directions for voluntarism
(UK)
background 15–28, 232–3
key initiatives 16–17, 232–3
contextual features 23–8, *24*
economic constraints 26–8
and faith-based voluntarism 153, 178–80,
185
Government Regional Offices *18*
governmentality, defined 117–18
Gracie, D. and Vincent, J. 145
grassroots organisations 37, 44, 47–8
see also rural communities
Greater Easterhouse (Scotland) 41
Greater Pollock Partnership (Scotland) 41
Greengross, Baroness 148
Gregson, N. et al 233, 235, 240
Grubesic, T. 279
Gunby, J. 167

H

Hage, G. 212
Hale, S. 25
Hale, S. et al 16
Halfpenny, P. and Reid, M. 74, 117
Hall, M.H. and Banting, K.G. 92, 94, 192
Hall, M.H. and Macpherson, L.G. 94
Hall, M.H. and Reed, P.B. 94
Hall, M.H. et al 94, 100
Hall, P.A. 268
Hall, P.D. 174–5
Hamilton, N. 184
Hamnett, C. and Mullings, B. 139, 141
Hand, D. 84
Hanlon, N.T. 94
Hanlon, N.T. and Rosenberg, M.W. 94
Harper, S. and Laws, G. 139
Harris, M. 136, 154, 173, 179–80, 184
Harris, M. et al 153
Harrison, J. 184
Harrop, A. and Grundy, E. 139
Hasson, S. and Ley, D. 4–5, 192
Hay, C. 16, 24–5
Hay, I. 74, 119

Health Canada 97
health care and voluntarism
  Canada 91–108
  New Zealand 73–86, 118–30
Health and Disability Sector NGO Working
  Group (New Zealand) 76, 81
Health Services Research Centre 73, 80
Hechter, M. et al 211
Hedley, R. and Smith, J.D. 2
Heginbotham, C. 117
Henwood, M. 140, 141, *142*
Heron, E. 25
HM Treasury 34, 55
HOCS (Home Office Citizenship Survey)
  269, 271
Hodgson, L. 34, 43
Hollander, M.J. 97
home care services
  Canada
    levels of 'need' *99, 103, 104*
    and voluntarism trends 98–105, *101*
  see also Jewish voluntary sector care homes
Home Office 16–17, 40, 178, 182, 231, 233,
  271, 285
Home Office Citizenship Survey (HOCS)
  269, 271
Horne, S. 233–4, 243
Horne, S. and Broadbridge, A. 239
Horne, S. and Maddrell, A. 233
Human Resources Development Canada
  (HRDC) 195, 199
Hunt, T. 53

I

immigration issues and voluntarism
  ethnic communal places in Australia 210–11,
    215–25
  Scotland's anti-racist and BME initiatives 39,
    47–8
  settlement services in Canada 193–204
Imrie, R. and Raco, M. 15, 26, 55
informal volunteering, defined 3
Inner Cities Religious Council (ICRC) 178
Insalaco, F. 270
Institute for Jewish Policy Research 146–7
institutional care 137–40
  versus community-based provisions 140–1
Irish Inter-Church Meeting (IICM) 184
Ironmonger, D. 224
ISS (Immigrant Services Society) 194–203

J

Jackman, S. 155, 167
James, A.M. 94
Jamrozik, A. 223
Jenkins, K. 233
Jenson, J. and Phillips, S.D. 106
Jerusalem, cross-cultural comparison studies
  4–5

Jessop, B. 26–7, 58
Jewish Care 146
Jewish voluntary sector care homes 135–48
  background
    geographies of institutional care 137–40
    history of Jewish voluntarism in the UK
      135–7
    policy debates on care 140–1
  geographies of life in care 142–8
Joassart-Marcelli, P. and Wolch, J. 4
John, P. and Whitehead, A. 18
Johnson, M. 136, 138
Johnson, N. 267
Johnson, P. 147
Jones, O. and Little, J. 64
Joseph, A.E. and Kearns, R.A. 120
Joseph, A.E. and Knight, D.B. 91
Joseph, A.E. and Martin-Mathews, A. 105–6
Joseph Rowntree Foundation 56
Jupp, J. 212, 214–15

K

Kearns, A. 54, 231
Kearns, K. et al 153
Kearns, R. 120
Kearns, R.A. and Joseph, A.E. 91–2, 93, 121
Keefe, J.M. 98
Kellaher, L. 138
Kelsey, J. 80, 120, 154
Kendall, J. 2–3, 16, 35, 37, 40, 141, 287
Kendall, J. and Knapp, M. 3, 173, 268, 285
King, A. 78, 83, 85
Knight, B. 37
Kramer, R. 250, 251
Kraus, P. 209, 214

L

Labour Party publications 34
Laing, W. 141
Lalich, W. *213*, 216, *217*, 222, *223*, 224
LaPerriere, B. 94
Larner, W. and Craig, D. 154, 156
The Last Refuge (Townsend) 137–8
Laugesen, M. and Salmond, G. 74
Le Heron, R. and Pawson, E. 154
Leach, R. and Percy-Smith, J. 53, 55
Lee, J.-A. 194, 198, 200–1
legislation (UK)
  local level council donations to VCOs 62
  review of charitable law 17
legitimacy of voluntarism
  accountability 66, 68, 74, 78–81, 199–200
  competition and scale issues 56
  decentring and marginalisation 37
  emergence of 'shadow state' (Wolch)
  mainstreaming and governmentality 34–8,
    117–18, 123–5
  professionalisation concerns 24–5, 81–2, 85,
    199, 233–5, 242, 260–2, 289

versus campaigning activities 46
Lemon, M. et al 85
Lewis, F.W. 209
Lewis, J. 154, 285
Lewis, J. et al 249
Lewis, N. and Moran, W. 91, 117, 127
Liamputtong, P. and Gardner, H. 85
Ling, T. 126
Link Family and Community Centre
    (Newtownards) 184
Lister, R. 26
Little, J. 6, 256, 268
local authorities
  and partnership working 20-1
    Scotland 40-1
local community activities *see* rural
    communities; village festivals and activities
Local Government Act 2000 20
Local Government Act 1972 62
Local Government Association publications
    178
local level councils
  relationships with voluntary sector 56, 57-69
    community enterprise donations 62-3
Local Strategic Partnerships (LSPs) 18, 20-1
localism of voluntarism 5-6, 55-6
  funding issues 20-2
  in rural communities 53-69
  in Scotland 38-49
Lochner, K. et al 93
Lukka, P. and Ellis, A. 243
Lukka, P. and Locke, M. 154
Lukka, P. et al 153
Lupton, R. 287
Lynn, P. 268
Lyons, M. 224, 285

M

Macaulay, T. 184
Macdonald, R. 4, 268, 290
MacIntyre, S. et al 270
Mackintosh, M. and Wainwright, H. 268
McClure, M. 155
McDowell, L. 139
McNeil, J. 83
Maddrell, A. 233, 236
MAFF 60
mainstreaming of voluntary sector 34-5
  policy critiques 35-8
  see also professionalisation of voluntary sector
Making Belfast Work, role of churches 184
Maloney, W. et al 268
managerialism 24-5, *24*, 234-5
  New Zealand 81-2, 85
market towns, and VCO engagement 66
marketing initiatives, charity products 234
marriage counselling services 247-50
Martin Spigelman Research Associates 195
Martin, J. 212
Massey, D. 287

'matched funding arrangements' 21
Matheson, D. 81
Means, R. 140
Means, R. and Smith, R. 140
Meegan, R. 287
mental health services
  voluntary sector initiatives 41
    New Zealand 77-8, 82-3, 84-5, 119-20
Millen, J. 119
Millennium Volunteers initiative (UK) 232-3
Miller, C. 55, 93
Miller, S. 135
Miller, W. et al 268
Milligan, C. 5, 6, 36, 39, 91-2, 105, 139, 140,
    252, 268
Milligan, C. and Fyfe, N. 5, 36, 40, 49, 61, 74,
    86, 93, 122, 231, 260, 262, 289
Ministry of Social Policy 75, 156, 285
Mintel (Marketing Intelligence) 234
Mitchell, A. 249-50
Mitchell, K. 192-3
MLwiN software 272
Modernisation Agenda 20
Mohan, J. 5, 26
Mohan, J. and Mohan, G. 26
Mohan, J. et al 279
Moran, W. 91
Morison, J. 35, 57, 60, 117, 285
Morris, D. 2
Morrow, D. 181
MOSAIC (Multilingual Orientation Service
    Association for Immigrant Communities)
    194-203
Mosely, P.A. 216
motivations to volunteer 236-43
Mujumdar, D. 285
Mulroney, B. 191
Munford, R. and Nash, M. 74
Muslim Cultural Heritage centre 179

N

Nash, V. and Christie, I. 26
National Council for Voluntary Organisations
    (NCVO) 285
  Chancellor of Exchequer's address 33
  Home Secretary's address 232-3
  Prime Minister's address 16
National Multicultural Advisory Council
    (NMAC) 218
National Service Framework for Older People
    (DH) 141
National Strategy for Neighbourhood
    Renewal 55
NCVO *see* National Council for Voluntary
    Organisations
'necessitarianism' 23-4, *24*
Neighbourhood Renewal Funds (NRFs) 21
neocommunitarianism 5, 27-8, 33-5
neoliberalism 22-3, 33, 117-18, 120, 155-6,
    161, 233, 251-2

Netting, F.E. 174
Neuwelt, P. and Crampton, P. 85
New Deal initiatives 34, 55-6, 232
New Labour 23-5
  emergence of 'community turn' 15-17, 23-8,
    33-5
  key political strategies 23-8, *24*
  see also Government policy directions for
    voluntarism (UK)
New Public Management theory (New
  Zealand) 156, 167
New Zealand Council for Christian Social
  Services (NZCCSS) 120, 129, 157, 167
New Zealand and voluntarism 73-86, 115-30
  background history 74, 118-22
  faith-based welfare provision 153-67
  health restructuring and change 75-7,
    118-22
  key voluntary sector groupings in the health
    sector 77-8
  main issues
    accountability concerns 78-81
    contracting arrangements 78-81, 121-2,
      123-5
    examples of good practice 82-4
    governmentality concerns 117-18, 123-5
    maintaining voluntary ethos 85
    management and professionalism concerns
      81-2, 117-18, 118, 122-8
    organisational interactions 118, 125-7,
      127-8
    state–NGO relationship changes 84-5,
      115-16, 121-2
Newberry, S. and Barnett, P. 77, 79-80, 82-3,
  124
Newman, J. 25
NGO Finance 234
NGOs and voluntarism, New Zealand 73-86
Ng, R. 192-4
NMAC (National Multicultural Advisory
  Council) 218
Northern Ireland, faith-based voluntarism
  181-4
Northern Ireland Executive (NIE) 182
Northern Ireland Statistics and Research
  Agency (NISRA) 183
Nowland-Foreman, G. 73, 75, 115, 120, 129,
  167
NSW EAC (New South Wales Ethnic Affairs
  Commission) 213, 214
nursing homes 138-40
  see also Jewish voluntary sector care homes
nutrition advocacy (New Zealand) 81
NZCCSS (New Zealand Council for
  Christian Social Services) 120, 129, 157,
  167

O
O'Connor, J. 23

ODPM (Office of the Deputy Prime
  Minister) 179
OFBCI (Office of Faith-based and
  Community Initiatives) (US) 173
Offe, C. 23
OFMDFM (Office of the First Minister and
  Deputy Prime Minister) (NI) 183
Ogborn, M. 138
Oldman, C. and Quilgars, D. 136, 138
Olson, M. 211
OMA (Office of Multicultural Affairs) 215
ONS (Office for National Statistics) 271
OPCS (Office of Population Censuses and
  Survey) 270
Osborne, S.P. and McLaughlin, K. 55, 57
Osborne, S.P. and Ross, K. 19
Otto Schiff Housing Association 145
outcomes of voluntarism 280
Owen, S. 75, 122-3
Oxfam 234

P
Pal, L. 192
Parent-Teacher Associations 277
parish councils *18*, 20
  participation issues 63-4
  see also local level councils
Park, J.Z. and Smith, C. 239
Parr, H. and Philo, C. 93
Parry, G. et al 268
Parsons, E. 233-4
Parsons, T. and Shils, E. 210
participation in civil society 82, 85
  geographical variations in 268-80
  on rural and local level councils 63-4
  see also volunteering
Partners for Change (DSD) 183
partnership initiatives 19-21, 34-5, 58-61
  and funding pathways 20-2
    Scotland 38-41, 41-9
  historic experiences and infrastructures 43,
    62-3
  voluntary sector experiences
    in New Zealand 76-7
    in North America 175-8
    with faith communities 175-8
    with small organisations 47-8
    in rural locations 56, 57-69
Patel, N. 136
Paton, R. 260
Patrikareas, T. 214
paying volunteers 198, 234, 260-1
  see also professionalisation of voluntary sector
Peace, S. et al 138-9, 140
Pearce, J.L. 236, 242
Peck, J. *24*, 25, 153
Peck, J. and Theodore, N. 287
Peck, J. and Tickell, A. 15, 22, 155-6, 252
People's summit 203

Performance and Innovation Unit (PIU) 25, 280
PHANZ (Public Health Association of New Zealand) 81
Phillips, S. 191-2
Phillips, S. and Graham, K. 192
Phillips, S. and Levasseur, K. 285
Philo, C. 138, 287
Philo, C. and Parr, H. 137, 139
Pierson, C. 23
Pierson, P. 23
Piliavin, J. and Callero, P. 279
Pinch, S. 91-2, 120, 124
PIU *see* Performance and Innovation Unit
Plowden, W. 33
Plunket Society 119
policy failures, and localisation 19
PONPO (Program on Non-Profit Organizations) project 174
Portes, A. 215
poverty and advocacy work 203
poverty and voluntarism
  geographies of 269-80, 287
    socioeconomic factors 275-8, *276*
  see also regeneration initiatives; spatial targeting
Poverty Street (Lupton) 287
Powell, D. 224
Powell, M. 33, 288
Presbyterian Church in Ireland (PCI) 184
Price, C. 211
Price, C. and Pyne, P. 212
primary care services, voluntary sector initiatives, New Zealand 77-8, 83-4
Prime, D. et al 269
Prince, R. et al 120, 127
Priority Partnership Areas (PPAs) 39
'priority wards' 18
product branding 234
professionalisation of voluntary sector 81-2, 85, 199, 233-5, 242, 260-2
  as driver for change 89
  and 'managerialism' 24-5, *24*, 81-2, 85
  and standards of practice development 253-5
  see also mainstreaming of voluntary sector
The Promised Woman (Patrikareas) 214
public health agencies, voluntary sector initiatives, New Zealand 78, 81, 83
Pulkingham, J. 195
Putnam, R.D. 16, 35, 83, 117, 179, 215, 280

Q
Queen II, E.L. 175

R
Raco, M. and Flint, J. 55
Raco, M. and Imrie, R. 117
Reed, P.B. and Selbee, K.L. 94-5, 106

regeneration initiatives 15-16, 17, 25, 34-5, 54
  see also 'community turn'; Government policy directions for voluntarism (UK)
Regional Assemblies *18*
Regional Development Agencies *18*, 19
regulation of voluntary sector
  accountability issues 66, 68, 74, 78-81, 199-200
  counselling services 260-3
  see also governance arrangements
Rekart, J. 94, 192-3
relationship counselling 249-63
religion and voluntarism *see* faith-based voluntarism
residential care homes 138-40
  faith-based provisions 135-48
retail charity work 236-43
'rights and responsibilities' 25-6
  and partnership initiatives 19
Rivers Buchan Associates 79
Rogers, A. and Glasby, J. 120
Rogers, Carl 249
'roll-out neoliberalism' 156
Romanow, R.J. 97, 106
Rose, N. 57, 118, 251
Rose, N. and Miller, P. 57
Rosenberg, M.W. and James, A.M. 94
Rowles, G. 139
Rowles, G. et al 139
Royal Commission on Long Term Care 141
Royal New Zealand Foundation for the Blind 119
rural communities
  background to community support initiatives 62-3
  councillor involvement 63-4
  emergence of voluntarism governance 55-6, 57-69
  Wales and Borders partnerships 58-61, *59*
Russell, L. and Scott, D. 83, 85
Russell, L. et al 22
Rutland, S. 214

S
St Peter's Hospice 235-41
Salamon, L.M. 36, 193, 268
Salamon, L.M. and Anheier, H. 291
Salamon, L.M. and Teitelbaum, F. 174
Salamon, L.M. et al 1, 117, 267
Sant, M. and Waitt, G. 214
Sargeant, A. and Lee, S. 285
Saville-Smith, K. and Bray, M. 83
Sayer, M. and Nowra, L. 214
Schlesinger, E. 146
Schmool, M. and Cohen, F. 135
school voluntary activities 277
'Schumpeterian Workfare Postnatal Regimes' (SWPRs) 26-7, *27*
Scotland and voluntarism
  counselling service provisions 247-63

crime prevention initiatives 44–7
  spatial targeting initiatives 38–49
    funding regimes 38–41, 42–3, 44, 48
Scottish Executive 49
Scottish Office 39
Seibel, W. 28
Seibel, W. and Anheier, H. 117
Selbee, K.L. and Reed, P.B. 94
settlement services and voluntarism, Canada
  193–204
'shadow state' (Wolch) 4–5, 8, 35–8, 49, 55–7,
  61, 63–4, 67–8, 93, 166, 192–4, 199, 201,
  288–9
Shaftesbury Society 153
Shannon, A. 174
*A Shared Future: Improving Relations in Northern
  Ireland* 183
Shawler, C. et al 139
Sheard, J. 238
Sherman, A.L. 173
Sibley, D. 160
Single Regeneration Budget 55
SIPs *see* Social Inclusion Partnerships
Skinner, M.W. and Rosenberg, M.W. 98
Skocpol, T. 268
Smith, C. 139
Smith, G. 154, 180, 186
Smith, G. and Ford, R. 139
Smith, J.D. et al 249
Smith, M.P. and Guarnizo, L.E. 219
Smith, S. 85
Smith, S.R. and Sosin, M.R. 175, 177
Snijders, T. and Bosker, R. 279
'social capital' 16, 35
Social Inclusion Partnerships (SIPs) 39–49
socioeconomic status and voluntarism 275–8,
  276
Soteri, A. 6
spatial targeting 35
  New Zealand 122
  regeneration initiatives 18–21, 290
  in Scotland 38–49
  versus thematic targeting 41–3
Spearritt, P. 212, 214
Speight, P. 184
Staeheli, L.A. and Brown, M. 105
*Statement of Government Intent for an Improved
  Community-Government Relationship*
  (Ministry of Social Policy - New Zealand)
  156
Statistics Canada 98–105, *99, 101, 103, 104,*
  193
Stephens, R. et al 155
Stephenson, M. and Sawyer, E. 97
Stoker, G. 53
'structural adjustment policies' 23
Stuckey, J. 145
subregional partnerships *18*, 55–69
SUCCESS (United Chinese Community
  Enrichment Services Society) 194–203
Suggate, D. 75

Sumner, K. 136, 138
Szreter, S. 179

T

target setting strategies 18–21, 29, 35, 38–43,
  122, 290
  and 'managerialism' 24–5, *24*
  see also spatial targeting; thematic targeting
Task Forces, defined *18*
Taylor, M. 3, 15, 21, 22, 26, 38, 56
Taylor, M. and Bassi, A. 57
Taylor, M. et al 55
Teather, E. 6
Tennant, M. 74, 119, 121, 155
terminology of voluntarism 2–3
Thane, P. 140
Thatcher, Margaret 54
thematic targeting 41–3
'Third sector' 16
  see also voluntary sector
'third way' approaches 1–2, 16, 33–5
Thomas, M. 214
Thomson, D. 74
town councils *18*, 20
  see also local level councils
Townsend, P. 136, 137–40
Treasury 'cross-cutting' 2002 review 55
Tukuitonga, C. 84
Turner, B.S. 35, 231
Turok, I. 49
Turok, I. and Hopkins, N. 42
Twigg, J. 139

U

unemployment and voluntary work 232
Unikoski, R. 215
United Kingdom voluntarism
  early geographical studies 4–7
  faith-based provisions 153, 178–80, 185
  governance structures *18*
  government civic renewal initiatives 16–17
  see also Government policy directions for
    voluntarism
United Nations, on volunteering 1–2
United States and voluntarism
  early geographical studies 3–5
  faith-based provisions 174–8
  evolving trends 184–5
  welfare debates 25
Uphoff, N. 180
Upton, S. 78
Urban Programme (Glasgow) 38–41

V

Vaillancourt, Y. et al 106
Valentine, G. and Longstaff, B. 138
Valins, O. 135
van Deth, J. 117

Vancouver
 cross-cultural comparison studies 4–5, 37
 settlement services 194–204
VCOs (voluntary and community
  organisations) 55, 56–7
 see also voluntary sector
Verba, S. et al 268
village festivals and activities 63
voluntarism
 background 1–2
 definitions 2–3, 56–7
 development contexts 15–28
 governance arrangements 17– 22, 53–69
 legitimacy concerns
  accountability 66, 68, 74, 78–81, 199–200
  competition and scale issues 56
  decentring and marginalisation 37
  mainstreaming and governmentality 35–8,
   117–18, 123–5
  professionalisation concerns 24–5, 81–2, 85,
   199, 233–5, 242, 260–2, 289
  'shadow state' concerns 4–5, 8, 35–8, 49,
   55–7, 61, 63–4, 67–8, 93, 166, 192–4, 199,
   201, 288–9
  versus campaigning activities 46, 80–1,
   201–3
 targeting strategies 18–21, 29, 35, 38–43, 122,
  290
 see also 'community turn'; geographical
  research on voluntarism; volunteering
Voluntary Action (Beveridge) 232
voluntary sector
 accountability issues 66, 68, 74, 78–81,
  199–200
 definitions 2–3, 38
 mainstreaming initiatives 34–5
  policy critiques 35–8
  regulation 66, 68, 74, 78–81, 199–200, 260–3
 targeting strategies 18–21, 29, 35, 38–43, 122,
  290
 unpopular client groups 41–2
 see also geographical research on voluntarism;
  geographical variation in voluntary sector
  provision; volunteering
voluntary sector 'compacts' 34, 57–8, 233
 New Zealand 76–7
voluntary sector counselling *see* counselling
 services
volunteering 82, 85
 as citizenship 231–3
 definitions 2–3
 geographical variations in participation
  268–80
 motivations and goals 231–2, 241–3
 personal experiences 235–41
 professionalisation of roles 81–2, 85, 199,
  233–5
 unpaid work demands/pressures 198
 see also participation in civil society

W
Wales, partnership and governance
  arrangements 58–62, *59*
Walker, A. 270
Wallis, J.H. 249
Walmisley, G. 80, 82, 84
Wardell, F. et al 270
Warnes, A. 139
Wat Phrayortkeo (Australia) 221
Watson, M. and Hay, C. 23–4, *24*
Weil, S. 210
Weisbrod, B. 116
Welsh Assembly Government 56
Welsh Office 54, 285
WGP (Working Group on Poverty) 203
Whale, A. 154
Whelan, R. 267
White, D. 106
Whitehead, M. 55–6
Whithear, R. 236
Wiles, J. 91, 106
Wiles, J. and Rosenberg, M.W. 93
Williams, A.M. 93, 106
Williams, C. 269, 279–80
Williams, M. 54
Williams, R. 185
Willis, E. 119
Wilson, A. and Charlton, K. 19
Wilson, C. et al 79, 85, 121
Wilson, K. and Rosenberg, M.W. 96
Wineburg, R.J. 173, 175–7
Wistow, G. 92
Wolch, J.R. 4–5, 35–8, 55, 61, 86, 92–3, 156,
  192–3, 256, 267–8, 288–9
Wolch, J.R. and Geiger, R. 4, 93, 268
Wolfenden, L. 182, 269, 280
Wolpert, J. 4
Wolpert, J. and Reiner, T. 4, 93
women's voluntary organisations 6
Woods, M. and Edwards, W.J. 56
Woods, M. et al 56, 62
Working Group on Poverty (WGP) 203
Wrigglesworth, R. and Kendall, J. 33
Wright, S. 286

Y
Yantzi, N. and Rosenberg, M.W. 102
Yee, L. and Mussenden, B. 141
Young, M. 167
youth groups, rural communities 63

Z
Zimmeck, M. 242
Zukin, S. 210
Zwart, R. and Perez, E. 85